The Blackwell Guide to Descartes' *Meditations*

Blackwell Guides to Great Works

A proper understanding of philosophy requires engagement with the foundational texts that have shaped the development of the discipline and which have an abiding relevance to contemporary discussions. Each volume in this series provides guidance to those coming to the great works of the philosophical canon, whether for the first time or to gain new insight. Comprising specially commissioned contributions from the finest scholars, each book offers a clear and authoritative account of the context, arguments, and impact of the work at hand. Where possible, the original text is reproduced alongside the essays.

Published

Forthcoming

THE BLACKWELL GUIDE TO

Descartes' *Meditations*

EDITED BY STEPHEN GAUKROGER

Blackwell
Publishing

© 2006 by Blackwell Publishing Ltd

BLACKWELL PUBLISHING
350 Main Street, Malden, MA 02148-5020, USA
9600 Garsington Road, Oxford OX4 2DQ, UK
550 Swanston Street, Carlton, Victoria 3053, Australia

First published 2006 by Blackwell Publishing Ltd

1   2006

Library of Congress Cataloging-in-Publication Data

The Blackwell guide to Descartes' meditations / edited by Stephen Gaukroger.
p. cm.—(Blackwell guides to great works)
Includes bibliographical references and index.
ISBN-13: 978-1-4051-1875-0 (hardcover : alk. paper)
ISBN-10: 1-4051-1875-X (hardcover : alk. paper)
ISBN-13: 978-1-4051-1874-3 (pbk. : alk. paper)
ISBN-10: 1-4051-1874-1 (pbk. : alk. paper)
1. Descartes, René, 1596–1650. Meditationes de prima philosophia.   2. First philosophy.   I. Gaukroger, Stephen.   II. Series.

B1854.B55 2005
194—dc22
2005009842

A catalogue record for this title is available from the British Library.

Set in 10 on 13 pt Galliard
by SNP Best-set Typesetter Ltd, Hong Kong
Printed and bound in the UK
by TJ International, Padstow, Cornwall

The publisher's policy is to use permanent paper from mills that operate a sustainable forestry policy, and which has been manufactured from pulp processed using acid-free and elementary chlorine-free practices. Furthermore, the publisher ensures that the text paper and cover board used have met acceptable environmental accreditation standards.

For further information on
Blackwell Publishing, visit our website:
www.blackwellpublishing.com

Contents

Notes on Contributors

Roger Ariew is Professor of Philosophy at the University of South Florida, Tampa. He is author of *Descartes and the Last Scholastics* (1999), and co-author of *Historical Dictionary of Descartes and Cartesian Philosophy* (2003). He has published translations of Montaigne, Descartes, and Leibniz, and edited the works of Dupleix.

Desmond M. Clarke is Professor of Philosophy at University College Cork. He is author of *Descartes' Philosophy of Science* (1982), *Occult Powers and Hypotheses* (1989), and *Descartes' Philosophy of Mind* (2003). He is translator of the Penguin editions of Descartes' writings.

John Cottingham is Professor of Philosophy at Reading University. He is author of *Rationalism* (1984), *Descartes* (1986), *The Rationalists* (1988), *A Descartes Dictionary* (1993), *Descartes' Philosophy of Mind* (1997), *Philosophy and the Good Life* (1998), and *The Meaning of Life* (2002). Among his many translations of Descartes, he is co-translator of the three-volume Cambridge edition of Descartes' writings and letters.

Edwin Curley is Professor of Philosophy at the University of Michigan. He is author of *Spinoza's Metaphysics* (1969) and *Descartes against the Skeptics* (1978). He has published translations of Hobbes and Spinoza.

Michael Della Rocca is Professor of Philosophy at Yale University. He is author of *Representation and the Mind–Body Problem* (1996).

Stephen Gaukroger is Professor of History of Philosophy and History of Science at the University of Sydney, and presently holds an Australian Research Council Professorial Fellowship. His works include *Descartes: An Intellectual Biography* (1995), *Francis Bacon and the Transformation of Early-modern Philosophy* (2001), and *Descartes' System of Natural Philosophy* (2002).

Gary Hatfield is Professor of Philosophy at the University of Pennsylvania. He is author of *The Natural and the Normative* (1991), *Descartes and the Meditations* (2002), and *Philosophy of Psychology* (2005). He has published translations of Kant.

Charles Larmore is Chester D. Tripp Professor in the Humanities, Professor of Philosophy and of Political Science at the University of Chicago. He is author of *Patterns of Moral Complexity* (1987), *Modernité et morale* (1993), *The Morals of Modernity* (1996), *The Romantic Legacy* (1996), *Les Pratiques du moi* (2004), and (with Alain Renaut) *Débat sur l'éthique: Idéalisme ou réalisme*.

Steven Nadler is Professor of Philosophy at the University of Wisconsin. He is author of *Arnauld and the Cartesian Philosophy of Ideas* (1989), *Malebranche and Ideas* (1992), *Spinoza: A Life* (1999), and *Spinoza's Heresy* (2002).

Alan Nelson is Professor of Philosophy at the University of California, Irvine. He has published papers in early modern philosophy and the philosophy of science.

Lawrence Nolan is Associate Professor of Philosophy at California State University, Long Beach. He has published papers in early modern philosophy and the philosophy of religion.

Marleen Rozemond is Associate Professor of Philosophy at the University of Toronto. She is author of *Descartes' Dualism* (1998).

Tad M. Schmaltz is Professor of Philosophy at Duke University. He is author of *Malebranche's Theory of the Soul* (1996) and *Radical Cartesianism* (2002).

Jorge Secada is Associate Professor of Philosophy at the University of Virginia. He is author of *Cartesian Metaphysics* (2000).

References to Descartes' Works

All references to Descartes' works are to the standard original-language edition: *Oeuvres de Descartes*, ed. Charles Adam and Paul Tannery, 11 vols (Paris: Vrin, 1974–89). This is abbreviated throughout to AT, followed by the volume number, and then the page numbers, e.g. AT iv, 345–6.

The standard English selection of Descartes' works is *The Philosophical Writings of Descartes*, trans. John Cottingham, Robert Stoothoff, Dugald Murdoch, and Anthony Kenny, 3 vols (Cambridge: Cambridge University Press, 1984–91). There are marginal references to the volume and page number in AT in this translation, and the original text and the translation can be correlated easily.

For ease of reference, the following volumes in AT correspond to the relevant works and volumes of the Cottingham et al. (CSM) translation:

AT i–v	Correspondence	CSM vol. 3
AT vi	Discourse on Method, Essays	CSM vol. 1
AT vii	Meditations with Objections and Replies (Latin)	CSM vol. 2
AT viiiA	Principles of Philosophy (Latin)	CSM vol. 1
AT viiiB	Notes on a Programme, &c.	CSM vol. 1
AT ixA	Meditations with Objections and Replies (French)	CSM vol. 2
AT ixB	Principles of Philosophy (French)	CSM vol. 1
AT x	Rules, Search for Truth, &c.	CSM vol. 1
AT xi	The World, Passions of the Soul, &c.	CSM vol. 1

Introduction

Stephen Gaukroger

In Descartes' *Meditations* (1641) epistemology takes center stage in philosophy for the first time, and it does so in an especially dramatic form, offering a mental purging of a kind previously only encountered in religious literature. It puts the knowing subject on the spot, demanding that any knowledge claim, even the seemingly most trivial or obvious, be justified, and this demand for justification is presented as if one's life depended on it: for Descartes wants to show us that our cognitive life does indeed depend on it. The *Meditations* aim to make one responsible for one's cognitive life in a way that the devotional texts of the Reformation and Counter-Reformation – where a range of exacting moral standards, accompanied by demands for self-vigilance which had been the preserve of monastic culture throughout the Middle Ages, were transferred wholesale to the general populace – made one responsible for the minute details of one's everyday life. Philosophy becomes personal with Descartes. It is no longer the preserve of, or exclusively of concern to, the cleric. Indeed, Descartes' view is that the person best fitted to be a philosopher is someone whose mind has not been corrupted by scholastic learning (AT x, 496). The nature of philosophy is transformed, although it does in some ways return to the notion of the philosopher as portrayed by Socrates in Plato's early dialogues, someone who has had no special training but takes nothing on trust, subjecting everything to intense examination and questioning (see Risse 1963).

In the light of this, it is not surprising that courses in the Western philosophical tradition in colleges and universities worldwide include a dialogue of Plato and Descartes' *Meditations* as introductions to philosophy. This is not because they are elementary, providing a means of acclimatizing oneself to philosophical argument before moving on to something more substantial, for they remain both the subject of serious scholarship and permanent sources of philosophical inspiration. Rather, their attraction derives from a combination of readability and depth. This combination is sometimes liable to mislead readers because it means that there is a great deal more beneath the surface than there seems.

Despite the *sui generis* impression given by the *Meditations*, there are a number of interpretative problems surrounding the text. The core arguments are given in differing versions, earlier in an autobiographical form in the *Discourse on Method* (1637), and later in a textbook form in Part I of the *Principles of Philosophy* (1644). In the latter case, they appear as a prelude to the construction of an elaborate system of natural philosophy, rather than something that stands in its own right. Yet the presentation in the *Meditations* itself suggests something self-contained. Moreover, the *Meditations*, which are very compact, appeared with a set of commissioned objections from various philosophers and theologians, and with Descartes' replies to these, and the expansions and clarifications offered in the replies are crucial to our understanding of the arguments set out in the *Meditations*, as Roger Ariew indicates in chapter 1. It should be noted that some of these arguments, above all those touching on the nature and role of ideas, are highly compressed and require a good deal of fleshing out before one can understand what is at issue properly, while others, especially the introduction of hyperbolic doubt and Descartes' response to it, are very contentious, questioning not just traditional doctrines but also challenging how one goes about doing philosophy in the first place.

One of the main ambitions of the *Meditations* was to overthrow a particular philosophical system, that of Aristotle, especially in its sixteenth- and early seventeenth-century scholastic versions. But the way in which it does this is unusual. It does not address issues in Aristotelianism directly, but rather begins by opening up the question of what our confidence in knowledge claims derives from. Descartes begins the *Meditations* by subjecting sense perception, the starting-point for knowledge in Aristotelian philosophy, to intense skeptical doubt, removing it as the source of knowledge. It has sometimes been thought that Descartes himself is advocating skepticism here, but, as Charles Larmore points out (chapter 2), this is not the case. Unlike ancient skepticism, which is associated with a way of life in which nothing is taken for granted, Descartes' skepticism is too radical to have a practical dimension. Indeed, its very radicalness indicates its role. No one could practically doubt whether they had a body or whether the physical world really existed. The fact that there is a form of doubt that undermines the grounds on which we believe such things exist shows us not that these things may not in fact exist, but that the justification that philosophers have offered for knowledge claims do not carry conviction even in cases where we are certain that the doubts are misguided. And if they do not work in cases of implausible and ridiculous doubts, we can hardly expect to use them to provide reliable adjudication in contentious cases.

Descartes' programme in the *Meditations* is, in essence, threefold: to subject all knowledge claims to radical doubt so that the need for a new epistemological foundation becomes evident; to provide this new foundation; and to reconstruct the world on the basis of this new foundation. The three are inevitably connected and shape one another. At one level, this is obvious from a reading of the

Meditations alone: it is the success of radical doubt that generates the need for foundations, and it is the foundational nature of the enterprise that constrains the kind of knowledge claims about the world that Descartes is prepared to offer at the end of the *Meditations*. But there are also connections that work in the opposite direction, which become clear only when Descartes' project is placed in the context of projects that precede and succeed it. The "clear and distinct" image of a mechanized, geometricized world that emerges in Meditation VI is very different from the common-sense world of Meditation I, and it is an image of the world not only to be found in *The World* (1631) but also in the three Books that follow the reworked and condensed version of the *Meditations* in the *Principles of Philosophy*. The *Meditations* can be read as a project in pure epistemology (for example, Williams 1978; Wilson 1978), but it can also be read as part of a larger natural philosophy project (for example, Garber 1992; Gaukroger 1995, 2002).

Whichever way it is read, however, there is a core of intractable issues that any interpretation has to come to terms with. The issue of the foundations of knowledge, the subject of Edwin Curley's discussion in chapter 3, raises the problem of the regress of justification and whether there are any truly basic beliefs that are indubitable and which could stop this regress; and, a separate question, whether, if there are any such basic beliefs, they can act as a foundation for knowledge. Our inability to doubt our own existence plays a key role and has often been taken to show that, for Descartes, we each have a privileged type of knowledge of our own mental states, but as Marleen Rozemond shows in chapter 4, in fact Descartes' conception of the mind results from a redrawing of the boundaries between the mental and the physical in view of his commitment to a mechanistic natural philosophy, rather than a commitment to the transparency of the mind.

Three central topics in the *Meditations* engage questions that had been of concern to scholastic philosophers – substance, the nature of ideas, and proofs of the existence of God – which means that some background has to be provided before the novelty of Descartes' approach can be appreciated. This is nowhere more true than in Descartes' treatment of substance, which has a fundamental role to play in Descartes' metaphysics and which, as Jorge Secada (chapter 5) shows, must be read in large part as a response to the scholastic philosopher Francisco Suárez. But if the scholastic antecedents of Descartes' concern with substance are reasonably clear cut, this is not the case with the doctrine of ideas, which was the predominant concern of later Cartesians such as Malebranche and Arnauld, but also of the British empiricist tradition, especially Locke and Berkeley. Nevertheless, the vocabulary in which Descartes couches his discussion, focusing as it does on the distinction between the formal and objective reality of ideas, directly engages a scholastic dispute over what we grasp in perception. One issue that loomed large for subsequent Cartesians was whether, on Descartes' account, what we grasp in perception is visual representations of the world, or whether we grasp the world by means of visual representations. Both are possible interpretations, but the former suggests a representational theory of perception, whereas the latter suggests a realist one. Nevertheless, as Steven Nadler points out (chapter 6), whichever reading we take there remains a deep problem about the extent to which knowledge of the world is possible; in particular, how we distinguish illusory from veridical ideas.

Proofs for the existence of God were a core question in scholastic philosophy, but they were as much about the nature of God as his existence. No one doubted the latter, but the former was very contentious: the traditional problem was not atheism but heresy. Descartes rehabilitates an argument that had been abandoned by Aquinas and his followers, namely the ontological argument, which is purely conceptual, turning on the concept of God, as well as employing more traditional forms of argument in which his existence and his nature are demonstrated from his effects. In chapter 7, Lawrence Nolan and Alan Nelson look at Descartes' two demonstrations of the existence and nature of God: the causal argument of Meditation III and the ontological argument of Meditation V. Closely connected with these is the problem of the "Cartesian circle," which is the subject of chapter 8. Descartes relies on the existence of God to guarantee the truth of clear and distinct perceptions, but his proofs about God are accepted as true simply because they are clearly and distinctly perceived. Each of these would seem to depend on the other, resulting in a charge of circular reasoning. But, as Gary Hatfield argues, a good deal depends on what exactly one thinks Descartes is trying to achieve in these arguments.

An underlying source of problems with Descartes' account of making cognitive judgments, whether about the existence of God or about the world, is that, on his account of the intellect, it is a purely passive faculty by which the mind receives and considers ideas or representations. The will, by contrast, is the active faculty within the mind that assents to, denies, or suspends judgment on the representational content of the ideas that come before the mind. In chapter 9, Michael Della Rocca explores the consequences of taking the will into account in making cognitive judgments. In particular, acts of will are not necessarily constrained by truth, which suggests some other basis for assent by acts of will. Yet there is a deep problem about how we can assent to the representational content of ideas on the basis of a criterion that is independent of truth.

One of the most common misunderstandings of the *Meditations* is the view that Descartes' project is to start with a common-sense picture of the world and show how we are not entitled to this picture because our beliefs about it lack the requisite justification, and then to show how, once we have been through the foundationalist reconstruction of knowledge, which enables us to overcome any skeptical doubts, we can return to our initial conception, perhaps with some minor revisions, confident that our basis for adhering to this picture is now secure. In fact, the reconstructed world of Meditation VI is completely different from the one we start off from in Meditation I. In chapter 10, Desmond Clarke examines just what this picture of the world is and what it derives from. In particular, he looks at the definition of matter as spatial extension, and the implications that this has for the relation between mind and body. This mind–body question is taken up in detail by John Cottingham in chapter 11. Descartes rejects the notion that the mind is simply attached to the body, as the view that they are two wholly distinct substances would lead us to believe, and he describes the relation between them in terms of an "intimate union." The mind directly experiences bodily sensations and feelings, and in considering both cognitive and affective states, it is to this mind–body union that we must turn, not to a mind connected only contingently to a body. Indeed, it is here that we can glimpse Descartes' moral vision for the conduct of life, as Cottingham shows.

The reception of Descartes' philosophy has a long and checkered history – during the eighteenth century, for example, he was often treated as a materialist who thought of animals and human beings as machines – and in the half-century after his death Cartesianism was taken up in different ways, particularly in The Netherlands, which was its stronghold, but also in France, in the German states, England, and the Italian states. In chapter 12, Tad Schmaltz explores some of the more important issues that motivated responses to the *Meditations* in the seventeenth century.

Finally, the Appendix reproduces William Molyneux's 1680 English translation of the *Meditations*, the only early-modern English translation. Molyneux (1656–98) is perhaps best known as a correspondent of Locke, who posed to Locke the famous problem of whether someone who had been blind and subsequently gained his sight would be able to identify visually those shapes he had, whilst blind, been able to discriminate only by touch. Anglophone readers read Descartes in a modern English translation, but read his English contemporaries, such as Hobbes, in the English of the time, which has the misleading effect of making Descartes look comparatively modern. Molyneux's translation, into the lively and vigorous English of the seventeenth century, gives the flavor that the work must have had at the time.

1

The *Meditations* and the *Objections* and *Replies*

Roger Ariew

There is a line of interpretation for Descartes' *Meditations* that treats the work as an attempt to construct a self-consistent unity, a geometrical whole whose structures can be revealed or whose elements can be shown as interconnected, a totality, however, that cannot fruitfully be analyzed by psychological or historical methods. The *Meditations*, it is asserted, resembles Euclid's geometry and to understand a given geometrical system it is necessary to grasp its demonstrations and its sequences. According to Martial Gueroult, interpreters who "see in Descartes only a biographical succession, and not a rational linkage . . . merely observe the simple chronological sequence of topics . . . This is evidently a way of doing things that is repugnant to the spirit and letter of Descartes' doctrine" (Gueroult 1984: vol. 1, xx.). As evidence for the order of topics being contrary to Descartes' intention, Gueroult cites a letter to Mersenne in which Descartes asserts "to proceed by topics is only good for those whose reasons are all unconnected . . . it is impossible to construct good proofs in this way" (AT iii, 266–7). Gueroult is probably the most noted interpreter who held such an internal, non-developmental reading of the *Meditations*, though many commentators in the Anglo-American tradition might appropriately be thought to accept this kind of approach. Gueroult treats Descartes' doctrine as "a single bloc of certainty, without any cracks, in which everything is arranged such that no truth can be taken away without the whole collapsing" (Gueroult 1984: vol. 1, 5). To support this interpretation, he cites various passages from Descartes' corpus. One is from a 1642 letter to Marin Mersenne: "I see that it is easy to make mistakes about the things I have written, for truth being indivisible, the least thing that is taken away from it or added to it, falsifies it" (AT iii, 544); another is from the *Seventh Set of Objections and Replies*: "for truth consists in what is indivisible" (AT vii, 548); and a third is from an earlier letter to the Jesuit Vatier: "All my opinions are joined together in such a way and so strongly dependent on one another that one could not appropriate any for oneself without knowing all of them" (AT i, 562). For Gueroult, Descartes is "a thinker of granite," a "powerful, solid, and geometrical monument, like a Vauban fortress" (Gueroult 1984: vol. 1, xx).

Gueroult's view does have substantial textual support; it is an integral part of Cartesian rhetoric. In fact, there is yet one more passage in which Descartes asserts that his views are so interdependent that they cannot be separated or changed. Early on, when he was finishing his treatise *Le Monde*, he found out that the censors of Rome had condemned Galileo because of his defense of the motion of the earth, an opinion deemed false and inconsistent with the sacred Scriptures. Descartes says to Mersenne in a 1634 letter: "Now I shall tell you that all the things I explained in my treatise, which included that opinion about the motion of the earth, were so completely dependent on one another, that the knowledge that one of them is false is sufficient for the recognition that all the arguments I made use of are worthless" (AT i, 285). This presents Descartes with a dilemma: he cannot give up the motion of the earth without abandoning his whole system, but the motion of the earth, which he thinks has been supported by "very certain and very evident demonstrations," has been prohibited by the Church. He hesitates: "I know very well that it could be said that everything the Inquisitors of Rome have decided is not for all that automatically an article of faith, and that it is first necessary for the Council to pass on it." But he decides: "I am not so much in love with my own opinions as to want to make use of such exceptions, in order to have the means of maintaining them . . . I would not for anything in the world maintain them against the authority of the church" (AT i, 285). So he stops the publication of *Le Monde*. (For more on *Le Monde* and its historical context, see Gaukroger 1995: ch. 7.) But this does not prevent him, later on, from publishing the *Principles of Philosophy* – *Le Monde* having been taught to speak Latin, as he says (To Huygens, 31 January 1642, AT iii, 782) – which contains a discussion of the heretical proposition. In fact, Descartes has no problem ultimately keeping most of his system together with the *negation* of the condemned proposition, deciding that "strictly speaking the earth does not move, any more than the planets" (*Principles* III, art. 28) and "no motion should be attributed to the earth even if motion is taken in the loose sense, in accordance with ordinary usage" (art. 29).

So, although Descartes does at times claim the complete dependence of his principles on each other, such that none of them can be changed without the whole set collapsing, it is also obvious that he did make such changes (even to principles he claimed could not be changed). In fact, it is even clear that Descartes at times understood that he was making changes to his doctrine and at times wanted others to know that he was doing so. Descartes' project itself seems to belie the treatment of the system as a single bloc of certainty: Descartes did not just publish the *Meditations*; he published *Meditations* with *Objections* from others together with his *Replies* (in two different Latin editions, plus a French translation, during his lifetime). Why bother with other people's objections if they had no real possibility of altering the doctrine objected to? Were the objections not going to be taken seriously by him?

Descartes was keenly aware of the problem. After receiving Antoine Arnauld's objections to the *Meditations*, he wrote to Mersenne on March 18, 1641:

> I am sending you at last my reply to Arnauld's objections, and I ask you to change the following things in my metaphysics, thus letting it be known in this way that I have deferred to his judgment, and so that others, seeing how ready I am to follow his advice, may tell me more frankly what reasons they have for disagreeing with me, if they have any, and may be less stubborn in wanting to oppose me without reason. (AT iii, 334)

Descartes then proceeded to list six separate corrections, which he insisted should be put between brackets "so that it can be seen that they have been added" (AT iii, 335). One reason for his openly generous behavior was that he was pleased with Arnauld's objections, which he found "the best of all" because, as he said, Arnauld "had grasped the sense of what he had written better than anyone" (AT iii, 331). Descartes' requested corrections were indeed accomplished, though, despite his request, they were not inserted within brackets.

The intended bracketed changes by Descartes were minor, but were in effect *corrections* to the *Meditations* and intended to be displayed as such. Other changes were not so minor; some of them were acknowledged as changes and others not. One does not have to delve too deeply into the *Meditations*, *Objections*, and *Replies* to understand that some central Cartesian doctrines, such as God as "positive" cause of himself (*causa sui*) and God's free creation of the eternal truths, do not occur explicitly in the *Meditations*, but are to be found in the *Objections and Replies*. Jean-Marie Beyssade (1994) enumerates many additions, corrections, and changes to the doctrine of the *Meditations* brought about by the *Replies* to the *Objections*. As additions, Beyssade lists fragments of theology, such as the pages on the Eucharist in the *Fourth Replies*, and fragments of philosophy, such as the developments concerning God's freedom and the creation of the eternal truths in the *Sixth Replies*. He also mentions the doctrine of God as self-cause in the *First Replies* to Caterus (Johannes de Kater) and quotes a passage about it in which Descartes himself announces that he is adding something new: "In fact, I will also add here something I have not put in writing before, namely, that it is not even a secondary cause at which one arrives, but certainly that cause in which there is enough power to conserve something existing outside it and that *a fortiori* conserves itself by its power, and thus which is derived from itself" (AT vii, 111, quoted in Beyssade 1994: 33–4).

While additions are frequent, corrections are more rare. Other than those from the letter of March 18, 1641, referred to above, Beyssade cites an interesting case of successive corrections, within the *Objections and Replies*, concerning the doctrine of God as self-cause (Beyssade 1994: 34–6). In the *Fourth Set of Objections*, Arnauld apparently criticized some formulations of the *First Set of Replies*, which Descartes had appended to the *Meditations* with Caterus' *Objections* before having

Mersenne distribute the set to others for further objections. To start the ball rolling, Descartes had asked his friends Jan Albert Bannius and Augustinus Alstenius Bloemaert to write some objections; they, in turn, asked the Dutch priest Caterus to do so. Caterus' *First Set of Objections*, together with Descartes' *Replies* and the manuscript of the *Meditations* were then sent to France to be printed, but Descartes left it to Mersenne to organize the rest, telling him that he would be "glad if people make as many objections as possible and the strongest they can find" (AT iii, 297). Mersenne himself collected the *Second Set of Objections*, which he said were written by "various theologians" (AT iii, 265). They cover a wide range of issues, such as the immortality of the soul (AT vii, 127–8) and what we call the "Cartesian circle" (AT vii, 125), and contain a request (possibly inspired by the astrologer Jean-Baptiste Morin) to reformulate the contents of the *Meditations* in a geometrical fashion (AT vii, 28).

A letter of March 4, 1641 to Mersenne shows Descartes asking Mersenne to correct a text of the *First Set of Replies*, which he indicates was already corrected on the initial copy: "I must also ask you to correct these words, which come in my reply to the penultimate objection made by the theologian [Caterus]" (AT iii, 329); he then tells Mersenne which text to suppress and which to substitute. And he adds:

> but please correct it in all the copies in such a way that none will be able to read or decipher the words . . . For many people are more curious to read and examine words that have been erased than any others, so as to see how the author thinks he has gone wrong, and to discover there some grounds for objections, attacking him in the place which he himself judged to be the weakest. (AT iii, 330)

Descartes speculates that the obvious erasure is why Arnauld paid so much attention to the question of God as self-cause:

> I remember that my first draft of this passage was too crude; but in the later version I amended and refined it to such an extent that, had he merely read the corrections, without stopping to read the words that were crossed through, he would perhaps have found nothing at all to say. For I do believe that everything is in fact quite in order. You yourself, when you read the passage the first time, wrote to me saying that you found it crudely expressed, but at the other end of the letter you remarked that after reading a second time you found nothing to object to. I attribute this to your having paid attention, on your first reading, to the words that are only lightly crossed through there, whereas on the second reading you took note only of the corrected version. (AT iii, 330–31)

Thus Mersenne dutifully corrected for a second time a passage Descartes corrected once before, but this time in such a way that the act of correction would not be so obvious. (For more on the development of the concept of self-cause, see Marion 1995.)

Beyssade (1994: 36) relates a couple of other interesting items in the broader category of changes. He refers to the partial synthetic exposition of the *Meditations* in the *Second Replies* as a substantial change from its canonical analytic exposition. But he also mentions the ontological argument Descartes provides for Caterus in the *First Replies*. The question can be raised whether this ontological argument is the same as the one given in Meditation V. Descartes understands that he introduced a change but explains the matter thus: "All of these points are readily apparent to one who pays careful attention, and they differ from what I have previously written only in the manner of their explanation, which I have deliberately altered so that I might suit a wide variety of minds" (AT vii, 120).

We could continue and delve more deeply into other changes that Descartes made but did not acknowledge, some of which perhaps he might not have been aware of, such as the apparent transformation of his definition of material falsity from the *Meditations* through the *Objections and Replies* to its abandonment in the *Principles*. Descartes had introduced the possibility, in Meditation III, that his idea of cold may be materially false insofar as it "represents what is not a thing as a thing" (AT vii, 43–4). He might have had in mind there the possibility that cold is merely the privation of the quality of heat, and thus it is not the thing or quality that the idea represents it to be. This sort of falsity would be called material since it derives from the idea itself rather than, as in the case of formal falsity, from a judgment concerning the idea. Arnauld objected that an idea cannot be materially false since an idea cannot fail to represent what it does in fact represent (AT vii, 207). In response, Descartes explained the material falsity of an idea by emphasizing not so much the fact that that idea represents a privation as a quality, but more the fact that the idea is obscure and confused (AT vii, 234–5). The exchange may have prompted Descartes to drop the notion of material falsity, which is not present in his later writings. (There is a considerable secondary literature on this subject, much of it precipitated by Wilson 1978, where it is argued that Descartes' reply to Arnauld is inconsistent with his doctrine in Meditation III.) But we need not to go that far: there are a number of obvious deliberate alterations that should be mentioned, setting aside the question of whether these also entail changes in Descartes' doctrine.

As we have said, during Descartes' lifetime there were two Latin editions (Paris, 1641 and Amsterdam, 1642) and a French translation (Paris, 1647) of the *Meditations, Objections and Replies* (there is also an early version of the *Meditations* in Part IV of the *Discourse on Method*, the synthetic presentation of a portion of the *Meditations* in the Appendix to the *Second Set of Replies*, and a reworking of the *Meditations* in Part I of the *Principles of Philosophy*, as well as an undated and unfinished dialogue on the same themes, called *Search for Truth*). Descartes revised the subtitle of his work between the two Latin editions: originally entitled *Meditationes de Prima Philosophia* (*Meditations on First Philosophy*), it was subtitled "*in qua Dei existentia et animae immortalitatis demonstatur* [in which the existence of God and the immortality of the soul are demonstrated]" in the first edition and "*in quibus Dei existentia, et animae humanae a corpore distinctio, demonstratur* [in which the existence of God and the distinction between the human soul and body are demonstrated]" in the second. A number of hypotheses has been advanced for the change of subtitle. Adrien Baillet, in the abridgment to his biography of Descartes, asserts that *immortalitas* in the first subtitle was a misprint for *immaterialitas*: "*Mais il faut remarquer que ce fut contre l'intention de l'auteur qu'on laissa glisser le mot d'immortalité au lieu de celui d'immatérialité*" (Baillet 1692: 171). Others argue that the subtitle was Mersenne's responsibility and his mistake. Neither hypothesis seems likely. It is true that Descartes says to Mersenne on November 11, 1640: "I am finally sending you my work on metaphysics, which I have not yet put a title to, in order to make you its godfather and leave you the power to baptize it" (AT iii, 238–9; see also AT iii, 235), but Descartes does suggest titles and subtitles to Mersenne (AT iii, 235, 238, and 297). I find convincing the following passage from a Descartes letter to Mersenne of December 24, 1640: "As for what you say, that I have not said a word about the immortality of the soul, you should not be surprised. For I could not prove that God cannot annihilate it, but only that it is of a nature entirely distinct from that of the body, and consequently it is not bound by nature to die with it" (AT iii, 265–6; see also AT iii, 272). It is Mersenne who seems to have queried Descartes about the appropriateness of the subtitle with respect to the contents of the *Meditations* and Descartes who appears to be defending it. The changes in subtitles more likely reflect a development in Descartes' thinking.

Taking Mersenne's advice, Descartes did not publish the last seven paragraphs of his *Replies* to Arnauld, concerning the Eucharist, in the first Latin edition; as he says, he censored himself at Mersenne's urging, so that he would not have any difficulty in getting the approbation of the Sorbonne theologians for his work. He writes to Mersenne: "I very much approve your having pruned what I put at the end of my Reply to Arnauld, especially if this can help us to get formal approval for the book" (AT iii, 341). Descartes explained the matter more fully in a letter to Constantijn Huygens: "Father Mersenne has pruned 2 or 3 pages from the end of my replies to the *Fourth Objections*, concerning the Eucharist, because he feared that the Doctors would be offended in that I proved there that their opinion concerning that point did not agree as well as mine with the Scriptures and the Councils" (AT iii, 772). None of this prevented him from restoring the paragraphs in the second Latin edition, when there was no need for the approbation of the Doctors of the Sorbonne. The approbation, together with the right to publish, can be seen on the title page of the 1641 edition of the *Meditations* – "*Cum Privilegio, et Approbatione Doctorum*" – but it is missing from the title page of the other editions. Whether or not Descartes actually received the approbation of the Sorbonne is a disputed issue (for the positive case, see Armogathe 1994).

Initially, the *Meditations* were published with six sets of *Objections and Replies*, but Descartes deplored the fact that there were no Jesuits among the contributors, feeling that their approval would carry much weight:

Since he [Pierre Bourdin] is a member of a society which is very famous for its learning and piety, and whose members are all in such close union with each other that
it is rare that anything is done by one of them which is not approved by all, I confess
that I did not only "beg" but also "insistently demand" that some members of the
society should examine what I had written and be kind enough to point out to me
anything which departed from the truth. (AT vii, 452)

In the 1640s the Jesuit order controlled a significant portion of French collegiate
education and Descartes thought that the Jesuits, his old teachers, were so well
regulated by their Order that they usually acted as a corporate body: "since I
understand the communication and union that exists among those of that order,
the testimony of one of them alone is enough to allow me to hope that I will have
them all on my side" (AT ii, 50). Eventually a Jesuit, Pierre Bourdin, whom
Descartes disliked for his criticism of Descartes' theories of subtle matter, reflection, and refraction, sent him a voluminous packet of objections. Descartes received
them in January 1642, when his Dutch publisher, Lodewijk Elzevier, was already
printing the second edition of the *Meditations*. So Descartes had them printed in
the second edition, with his replies interspersed within the objections, as a kind
of appendix. Since the printer was slow to complete the volume, Descartes also
added a long letter to the provincial of the Jesuits in the Île de France, Father
Jacques Dinet, in which he complained of Bourdin's methods and suggested that
the Jesuit Order should dissociate itself from him. (For more on Bourdin, the
Jesuits, and Descartes, see Ariew 1995; the various articles in Ariew and Grene
1995 are useful in providing background on the other objectors and their objections: Jean-Robert Armogathe and Theo Verbeek on Caterus, and Vincent Carraud
on Arnauld, for example.)

The *Seventh Set of Objections and Replies* and *Letter to Dinet* were not published
in the 1647 French edition of the *Meditations*. Claude Clerselier, who translated
the other *Objections and Replies*, also translated these two works and first published
them in the French edition of 1661. (Clerselier also translated the *Meditations*
into French, but Descartes preferred the translation made by the Duc de Lynes,
flattered no doubt by the attention of this high courtier.) On the other hand,
the 1647 edition did contain the other changes effectuated by the second Latin
edition: Clerselier translated the end of the *Fourth Set of Replies* for the 1647
edition, and the subtitle was changed, as in the 1642 edition – though not without
some variations, both in the title and in the subtitle of the work, each containing
an extra significant adjective not found in the Latin versions. The 1647 edition
reads *Les Meditations Metaphysiques de René Descartes touchant la première
philosophie, dans lesquelles l'existence de Dieu, et la distinction réelle entre l'âme et
le corps de l'homme, sont demonstrées*. The approbation of the Sorbonne is missing
from the 1647 title page, but one can find the indication "*Avec Privilege du
Roy*" there.

Another difference from the Latin editions in the 1647 edition was the addition
of a letter by Descartes to stand in for the *Fifth Objections and Replies*. The debate

between Descartes and Pierre Gassendi, author of the *Fifth Set*, was long and contentious. Descartes apparently was angry with Gassendi for having published *Disquisitio Metaphysica*, a separate edition with rejoinders (Gassendi 1644). Of course, it did not help that Gassendi's objections resembled those of the *Third Set of Objections* by Thomas Hobbes. Hobbes and Gassendi both rejected Descartes' method and dualism, insisting instead on the empirical basis of all our ideas and the dependence of the mind on the body. They had little sympathy with Cartesian doubt, which they found exaggerated and at best a reheated version of old skeptical arguments. Descartes had little patience with these objections; the tone of his replies was sometimes sharp and personal. So, Descartes requested that some of his friends boil down Gassendi's objections from the *Disquisitio Metaphysica* to a manageable few. Descartes then answered those in the letter he published with the 1647 edition:

> The *Fifth* [*Set of Objections*] that were sent to me did not seem to me to be the most important, and they were extremely long; but nonetheless I agreed to have them published in their appropriate place out of courtesy to their author. I even allowed him to see the proofs, to prevent anything being printed as his, of which he did not approve. But since that time he has produced a large volume containing his original objections together with several new counter-objections or answers to my replies. In this book he complains of my publishing his objections, as if I had done so against his will, and says that he sent them to me only for my private instruction. Because of this, I am quite happy to oblige him now by removing his objections from the present volume, and this is why, when I learned that Clerselier was taking the trouble to translate the other sets of objections, I asked him to omit the fifth set. (AT ixA, 198–9)

In fact, Clerselier did not abide by Descartes' request. He printed the letter in the place of the *Fifth Set of Objections and Replies*, but then included them anyway, as an appendix at the end of the volume, after the *Sixth Set of Objections and Replies* (compiled by Mersenne as he did the *Second Set of Objections*, though also adding an appendix containing the argument of "a group of philosophers and geometers").

My favorite case of a suspected change in Descartes' doctrine operates subtly through the *Meditations, Objections,* and *Replies*, but Descartes, in *Principles of Philosophy*, ultimately acknowledges it to be a genuine change. As the subtitle to the 1642 edition of the *Meditations* indicates, a major result of the work is the distinction between the human soul and body. Presumably, Descartes thinks that he has proved the distinction to be a real distinction, as the subtitle of Meditation VI (added by Descartes after January 28, 1641; AT vii, 297) and the subtitle to the 1647 French translation indicate, not merely a modal distinction or a distinction of reason. One would assume that Descartes would have worked up accounts of real distinction, modal distinction, and distinction of reason to support this important result. But when Caterus queried him, in the *First*

Objections, about his proof of a real distinction, he responded in a muddled fashion. Caterus stated:

> He [Descartes] seems to prove the distinction (if that is what it is) between the soul and the body by the fact that they can be conceived distinctly and separately. Here I leave the very learned gentleman with Duns Scotus, who declares that, for one thing to be conceived distinctly and separately from one another, it suffices that there be a distinction which he calls "formal and objective", which he claims to be midway between a real distinction and a distinction of reason. (AT vii, 100)

Descartes answered:

> As far as the formal distinction is concerned, which the very learned theologian draws from Duns Scotus, I declare briefly that a formal distinction does not differ from a modal distinction, and that it applies only to incomplete beings, which I have carefully distinguished from complete beings. Moreover, it surely suffices for a formal distinction that one thing be conceived distinctly and separately from another by an act of abstraction on the part of the intellect inadequately conceiving the thing, yet not so distinctly and separately that we understand each one as something existing in its own right and different from every other thing. (AT vii, 120)

Descartes proceeded to illustrate his thought with the distinction between the motion and the shape of the same body, ultimately dealing with the distinction between justice and mercy, which Caterus had brought up as an example. Sometime later, prodded by the use Arnauld made of his distinctions, it must have dawned on Descartes that he was confusing formal, modal, and distinction of reason. (For Arnauld's criticism, see AT vii, 200: "For our distinguished author admits in his reply to the theologian . . ." and AT vii, 218: "Further he recognizes no distinction between the states of a substance and the substance itself except for a formal one . . .".) When he finally set out formally his theory of distinctions in the *Principles of Philosophy*, Descartes stated in the article on distinction of reason: "I recollect having elsewhere conflated this sort of distinction with modal distinction (near the end of the *Reply to the First Set of Objections* to the *Meditations on First Philosophy*), but then it was not necessary to treat accurately of these distinctions, and it was sufficient for my purpose at the time simply to distinguish them both from the real" (*Principles* I, art. 62). That may be right, but still this episode imparts the distinct impression that the Cartesian doctrine was in the process of formation. All in all, Descartes' bloc of certainty looks more like a sedimentary rock; that is, a geological stratum with cracks and fissures, able to be read in historical terms.

Thus, instead of thinking of the *Meditations* as a single bloc of certainty, it may be more fruitful to treat the work as a dialogue, both internal, within Descartes himself, and external, between Descartes and his audience. The *Meditations* points the way; its first sentence sends the reader back to another time, outside the frame of the work: "Several years have now passed since I first realized how numerous were the false opinions that in my youth I had taken to be true, and thus how doubtful were all those I had subsequently built on them." The first series of thoughts from Meditation I is set in an historical, autobiographical past, Descartes having realized that he had to "raze everything to the ground and begin again from the original foundations" if he wanted to establish anything firm and lasting in the sciences. As Descartes says, he waited until he reached a point in his life that was so timely that no more suitable time for undertaking these plans of action would come to pass (AT vii, 17).

A passage from the "Preface to the Reader" can illuminate the setting for the *Meditations.* Descartes refers to the two issues of God and the human soul from the title of the *Meditations,* which he discusses, in the "Letter of Dedication to the Doctors of the Sorbonne," as "two issues that are chief among those that are to be demonstrated with the aid of philosophy rather than theology" (AT vii, 1). He says:

> I have already touched briefly on the issues of God and the human mind in my *Discourse on Method* . . . The intent there was not to provide a precise treatment of them, but only to offer a sample and to learn from the opinion of readers how these issues should be treated in the future. For they seemed to me to be so important that I judged they ought to be dealt with more than once. (AT vii, 7)

Descartes then refers to his offer, at the end of Discourse VI, to respond to criticisms. He asserts that there were only two objections worth noting and replies briefly to them "before undertaking a more precise examination of them" (AT vii, 7). Thus the *Discourse* does not just provide an early version of the *Meditations;* it constitutes the setting for the work and it provokes two preliminary objections that must be answered initially and then more fully in the *Meditations.* As Jean-Luc Marion (1995: 10–11) asserts, "contrary to a widespread legend, Descartes is neither here nor elsewhere anything like a solitary, or even autistic, thinker, soliloquizing, in the manner perhaps of a Spinoza." Marion details the steps taken by Descartes (between 1637 and 1640) to answer the two objections made by Pierre Petit to the metaphysical portion of the *Discourse,* objections the *Meditations* attempts to answer more fully. Marion concludes that "not only would it be illegitimate to read the *Meditations* in abstraction from the *Objections and Replies,* with which they intentionally form an organic whole, but it would also be wholly illegitimate to read them otherwise than as replies to the objections evoked by the *Discourse*" (Marion 1995: 20).

Marion is right to insist that we should think of Part IV of the *Discourse* and the *Meditations* as forming a "responsorial schema" of objections and replies, but the *Discourse* also does not seem self-contained; like the *Meditations,* it sends us outside itself. The first sentence of the metaphysical portion of the *Discourse* states: "I do not know whether I ought to tell you about the first meditations I engaged in there; for they are so metaphysical and so out of the ordinary that perhaps they will not be to everyone's liking" (AT vi, 31). The "there" referred to by Descartes is The Netherlands, to which Descartes moved in 1628 or 1629; so, in 1637, Descartes tells us: "it is exactly eight years ago that this desire" – that is, the desire to begin to reject totally the opinions that had once been able to slip into his head and to seek the true method for arriving at the knowledge of everything of which his mind would be capable (AT vi, 17) – made him resolve to "take my leave of all those places where I might have acquaintances, and to retire here", to The Netherlands (AT vi, 30–31). But Descartes places the origin of that desire further back, about nine years, to the famous stove-heated room in 1619, in Germany, near Ulm: "Nevertheless, those nine years slipped by before I had as yet taken any stand regarding the difficulties commonly debated among learned men, or had begun to seek the foundations of any philosophy that was more certain than the commonly accepted one" (AT vi, 30).

Thus the project of the *Meditations* began with a resolve to examine all the truths for the knowledge of which human reason suffices, which, according to Descartes, he carried out nine years later, circa 1629, having spent the first nine months of his stay in The Netherlands working on metaphysics. There is an early echo of this resolve in Rule 8 of the *Rules*, in what is called "the most noble example of all," a task that should be undertaken at least once in his life by anyone who is in all seriousness eager to attain excellence of mind (AT x, 395).

We know little about Descartes' early metaphysics, his lost "small metaphysical treatise," other than that it was left unfinished and that it concerned the existence of God and that of our souls: "Perhaps I may one day complete a little *Treatise on Metaphysics*, which I began when in Friesland, in which I set out principally to prove *the existence of God and of our souls* when they are separate from the body, from which their immortality follows" (AT i, 182). However, it looks as though the lost treatise might have been more elaborate than the metaphysical part of the *Discourse* (AT i, 350). Descartes at the time was working simultaneously on his physics (*Le Monde*) and optics (*Dioptrique*). All of this changed after the condemnation of Galileo. Although Descartes thought of including some of the older material in a new Latin edition of the *Discourse* (AT i, 350), he seems to have started seriously to think of a new presentation of his metaphysics only in 1639 (To Mersenne, November 13, 1639, AT ii, 622; see also To Mersenne, March 11, 1640, AT iii, 35–6, July 1640, 102–3, and To Huygens, July 30, 1640, AT iii, 126.) Thus began the *Meditations*, together with new rounds of *Objections* and *Replies*.

2

Descartes and Skepticism

Charles Larmore

On several occasions, Descartes rightly remarked that the skeptical doubts rehearsed in Meditation I were not particularly novel (AT vii, 130, 171; viiiB, 367). Most of them had figured in the writings of the ancient skeptics and, with the publication of a Latin translation of Sextus Empiricus' *Outlines of Pyrrhonism* in 1562, had inspired a host of neo-Pyrrhonian thinkers in France, beginning with Montaigne's *L'Apologie de Raymond Sebond* (1580) and continuing with Charron's *De la sagesse* (1601) and La Mothe Le Vayer's *Dialogues faits à l'imitation des anciens* (1630–1). Meditation I raises worries, for example, about the general reliability of our perceptual beliefs, given the ease with which we make mistakes in this area. It also argues that, some dreams being as vivid and detailed as any waking experience, we are unable to determine at any given moment whether we find ourselves in the one state or the other. All these tropes, as Descartes conceded in the *Second Replies* (AT vii, 130), were like a lot of "warmed over cabbage."

There are two important exceptions to the commonplace character of the doubts Descartes invoked. The first is that even the existence of an external reality is put into question: on what basis can we truly claim to know that a world exists apart from our own minds and ideas of things? This challenge did not form part of the ancient repertoire. Not by accident, Greek skepticism stopped short of putting into doubt the existence of the world, since it aimed to constitute a way of life (Burnyeat 1982). Viewing skeptical argument as simply an epistemological tool, Descartes was able to extend its scope to the very notion of a mind-independent reality.

The other exception is a kind of doubt that Descartes did claim to be unprecedented, at least if we can regard as reliable the transcript which Frans Burman made of their conversations in 1648 (AT v, 147). It is the possibility that an omnipotent God may have given us a nature such that we fall into error even in those matters which we have every reason to regard as certain. On this point, Descartes was not, however, so innovative as he supposed. For though unknown to the ancients, this doubt had already been explored by various medieval thinkers (Gregory 1974), as well as by Montaigne (1999 ii, 512–13, 527). The doubts presented in Meditation I are not therefore particularly remarkable for their content; that is, for the possibilities of error which they raise in order to call into question various claims to knowledge. Their originality has to do instead with the manner in which they are deployed and, even more, with the purpose they are meant to serve.

Though no skeptic himself, Descartes showed a rare appreciation of the shape that skeptical argumentation ought to take. In general, the philosophical skeptic sets out to challenge, not this or that particular belief, but the very possibility of human knowledge. Thus, the only coherent approach must be to bring to light the contradictions within the standpoint of those who claim to know various things about the world. It would be illegitimate to appeal to any notions of one's own about, say, the unreliability of perception or of reasoning (since the skeptic supposedly lacks all knowledge), and it would be ineffectual to invoke any assumptions alien to the position under scrutiny. One must instead discredit claims to knowledge by showing how they conflict with other views and principles that their advocates already accept or would have to admit. Skeptical arguments ought properly to proceed by *internal demolition*. Neither in the seventeenth century nor in our own time has this requirement always been well understood, though the ancient skeptics (both Pyrrhonist and Academic) usually hewed to it closely (Annas and Barnes 1985: 14, 45, 53). Unlike many modern thinkers, Descartes grasped the point as well, if we may judge by the structure of Meditation I.

In the third paragraph, he introduced a broadly "empiricist" conception of knowledge in the form of the principle that "everything which up until now I have taken as most true I have learned either from the senses or through the senses" (AT vii, 18). This principle, by no means one he would endorse himself, is then subjected to a series of skeptical doubts, whose common feature is that they each undermine from within a different and increasingly beleaguered version of the idea that knowledge derives from the senses. They do not lean on premises belonging to his own philosophy, but solely on views that an empiricist wedded to such a principle would have to acknowledge. (The distinction between "from" and "through" the senses, so Descartes explained to Burman [AT v, 146], is one between what we have seen ourselves and what we have heard from others.)

In fact, Descartes realized so well that skeptical argument needs to operate by internal demolition that in the next Meditation he turned the tables on the skeptic by means of the very same strategy. The truth of our own existence as thinking beings is one that the skeptic cannot deny, except on pain of contradiction. "*Cogito, ergo sum*" provides, moreover, the cornerstone of an alternative conception of knowledge that the *Meditations* have as their mission to develop. In this respect, Descartes' use of skepticism broke altogether with precedent. Having an acute understanding of the pattern of argument used by the ancient skeptics, he went on to exploit it as a tool for the construction of his new "first philosophy."

The empiricist principle that is first demolished and then replaced is, in fact, nothing other than the very basis of Aristotelian philosophy. In Aristotle's *De anima* (432a7), for example, we find the statement that "since no one can ever learn anything without the use of perception, it is necessary even in speculative thought to have some mental image to contemplate." By showing that empiricism cannot withstand the skeptic's doubts, and by then drawing out a body of truths which those doubts are themselves powerless to impugn, Descartes hoped to convince the reader to move beyond the two warring camps of the day, Aristotelian scholasticism and skepticism, and in the direction of his own position, which rested on a non-empiricist theory of knowledge. Meditation I, as he observed in the Synopsis (AT vii, 12), aims to detach the mind from its dependence on the senses (*ad mentem a sensibus abducendam*). The first benefit of this intellectual reorientation would be to establish the metaphysical truths listed in the subtitle of the *Meditations* – the existence of God and the real distinction between mind and body. But the latter result, he believed, would serve in turn to validate another anti-Aristotelian component of his thought, namely his mechanistic physics which no longer attributed to bodies quasi-mental powers or "substantial forms." Nowhere in the *Meditations* did Descartes name Aristotelianism as the principal philosophical target of the skeptical arguments with which he begins his investigation. But a letter to Mersenne of January 28, 1641 spells out his intentions explicitly:

> These six Meditations contain all the foundations of my physics. But please do not tell people for that might make it harder for supporters of Aristotle to approve them. I hope that readers will gradually get used to my principles, and recognize their truth, before they notice that they destroy the principles of Aristotle. (AT iii, 298)

The overall structure of Meditation I comes most clearly into view if we regard it as a *dialogue* which Descartes has staged between the empiricist and the skeptic, in order to prepare the way for the introduction of his own doctrines (Larmore 1998, 2000). In this light, its key moves are less likely to be misconstrued. We will not suppose, for example, that the premises on which either party relies are ones that Descartes would want to endorse. At the same time, however, we can more easily spot the decisive way that his views do intrude themselves. The dialogue is orchestrated in accord with a rule brought in from the outside. The Aristotelian succumbs to the skeptic's doubts in virtue of a supposed dictate of reason (*ratio*): "the least grounds for doubt that I find will suffice to make me reject all [my opinions]" (AT vii, 18). Descartes' rationale for imposing this principle of indubitability will occupy us later on. Let us first look in more detail at the back-and-forth between empiricist and skeptic which makes up the heart of Meditation I.

The Skeptical Demolition of Empiricism

The meditating "I," we must be careful to remember, is not necessarily to be identified with Descartes himself. In Meditation I, it generally represents a point of view to which he suspects his reader harbors some allegiance, but whose allure he intends to dispel. Each of us, says the "I," should pause and reflect at least once in our lives on the worth of all our existing beliefs, examining their credentials, not one by one, but with regard to the foundations (*fundamenta*) on which we suppose they rest. With this demand Descartes agreed, of course. But when the meditator goes on to declare that "everything which up until now I have taken as most true I have learned either from the senses or through the senses," we meet that Aristotelian principle which scarcely inspired Descartes' own thinking. In his early notebooks of 1619–22, known today as *Cogitationes privatae*, Descartes does seem to have adhered to a sense-based epistemology (AT x, 218–19), but he had certainly abandoned it by 1628, when writing his *Rules for the Direction of the Mind* (see AT x, 395f). Aristotelian empiricism had become his chief philosophical adversary. In the *Discourse on Method* (AT vi, 37), he noted disparagingly that a constant refrain of scholastic philosophy was that "there is nothing in the intellect which has not previously been in the senses."

I have already pointed out one reason that the *Meditations* keep silent about the philosophical pedigree of the empiricism they attack: Descartes did not want to give his Aristotelian-minded readers an excuse to dismiss his book straight away. But there was also another reason. Embodied creatures that we are and impelled from infancy to view the world in terms of the body's needs, we have a natural inclination, he believed, to suppose that knowledge must derive from the senses. Aristotle and his followers simply put this common sentiment into systematic form (see AT vii, 441–3). Consequently, the skeptical arguments of Meditation I are aimed at more than just one doctrinal school. Their object is a way of thinking to which every reader must feel some attraction. As Descartes remarked to Burman in discussing the matter, everyone trusts in the senses at a pre-philosophical level (AT v, 146). Indeed, this deep-seated tendency continued to drive other mechanists of the time, such as Gassendi and Hobbes, despite their similar opposition to Aristotelian physics, to look to sense experience as the source of all knowledge. The empiricism under investigation no doubt included these contemporary variants as well.

In recent years, the complaint has often been voiced that the *Meditations* presuppose without argument a "foundationalist" model of knowledge (Williams 1986). After all, the need to build up our beliefs on secure foundations (*fundamenta*) is cited twice in the first two paragraphs (AT vii, 17, 18). This objection fails, however, to do justice to the dialectical situation in which Descartes found himself. The notion that all knowledge rests upon an ultimate, authoritative source of belief was already well ensconced. It shaped the various kinds of empiricist epistemology that pervaded the thinking of his time, most notably the scholastic establishment. Once we recognize the philosophical adversaries against whom Descartes was battling, we will see that he did not so much inject his own foundationalism as seek to replace the reigning form with another. The key respect in which Meditation I is slanted in favor of Cartesian preconceptions consists instead, as I have noted, in the demand that our beliefs be immune to "the least grounds for doubt," and I shall return to what lay behind this requirement below (in the section 'Cartesian Certainty').

One apparent obstacle to regarding empiricist notions of knowledge as the target of Meditation I is that Descartes brings up for discussion the validity of mathematical beliefs. Unconcerned about whether their objects exist in the physical world (*in rerum natura*: AT vii, 20), such beliefs survive the doubt about whether, for all we can tell, we may be dreaming, and succumb only to the later doubt about whether an omnipotent God may be a deceiver. Many have supposed that mathematics is understood here as having a basis other than the senses, their reliability having been discredited by the former doubt, and that Descartes must have in mind his own view of mathematics, since the latter doubt reappears in Meditation III to challenge the reliability of his new criterion of knowledge, clear and distinct perception, with particular reference once again to mathematical beliefs (AT vii, 35–6).

But this interpretation goes wrong for a number of reasons. According to the Synopsis, the aim of Meditation I is to detach the mind from the senses. Nowhere in this Meditation does Descartes mention any other theory of knowledge than the one formulated at the beginning, which holds that *everything* (*Nempe quidquid*) accepted as true rests upon sense experience. The "perspicuous truths" of mathematics are described as containing "something certain and indubitable" (AT vii, 20) and as being such that we think we know them perfectly (21), but never as being clearly and distinctly perceived. Moreover, it is not difficult to understand how an empiricist could maintain the validity of pure mathematics even after the doubt about dreaming had undermined all sense-based beliefs about the natural world. One had only to follow Aristotle in holding that mathematical concepts, once abstracted from experience, can be reasoned about independently of their corresponding to anything in nature. Though the supreme doubt involving an omnipotent God can be made to apply, not just to this abstractionist account of mathematics, but also to the view that mathematical concepts are innate and mathematical truths clearly and distinctly perceived, it does not assume so broad a scope until (in Meditation III) this new non-empiricist conception of knowledge has been introduced. The status of mathematical beliefs in Meditation I offers a perfect example of the way that Descartes has organized the text around two standpoints, neither of them his own – the empiricist's and the skeptic's.

So let me now outline the course of the Meditation (AT vii, 18–22) as a dialogue between these two positions. Not only the main steps, but also the reason why one follows upon another, will then stand out clearly. The empiricist (paradigmatically, the Aristotelian) amends his fundamental principle again and again, in response to each new charge by the skeptic that he is caught in an internal contradiction, until at last, reduced to silence, he must admit defeat:

Empiricist: Knowledge is possible on the basis of sense experience.
Skeptic: But perception of small and distant objects is fallible.
Empiricist: Nonetheless, perception of close, medium-sized objects is veridical.
Skeptic: What of the possibility that you are mad?
Empiricist: I would be mad even to consider that possibility.
Skeptic: Still, you must acknowledge that in the past you have mistaken dreams, which turned out false, for veridical perceptions. As a matter of fact, there are no sure signs by means of which dream perceptions can be distinguished from waking ones. How can you rule out the possibility that any perception of some close, medium-sized object is really a dream?
Empiricist: Even so, the sensible elements of any perception, whether I am awake or dreaming, resemble things in reality.
Skeptic: For all you know, these sensible elements could be purely imaginary.
Empiricist: Maybe, but the simplest elements in these perceptions – mathematical notions of extension, quantity, and magnitude – express truths even if they do not refer to anything in nature. Pure mathematics remains certain.
Skeptic: Still, there is the possibility of an omnipotent God, who created you and could have given you a mind such that even what you think you know most perfectly is actually false. Or if you believe your origin must have been some natural and more imperfect course of events, you will have all the more reason to wonder whether your mind does not mislead you here.
Empiricist: [silence].

Reconstructing the arguments in this fashion helps to guard against two frequent sources of misinterpretation. First, it will not be wrongly assumed that either the empiricist's assumptions or the skeptic's doubts express Descartes' own views (although it was certainly his view that the empiricist cannot successfully answer the skeptic). Consider the doubt about dreaming, for example. Descartes did not hold that we cannot reliably distinguish dreaming from waking, since later in Meditation VI (AT vii, 89–90) he explained how, given his principles, we can do so. He was persuaded that the empiricist has no dependable basis for making the distinction, and this failing is what he used the skeptic's doubt to point out. Thus, the dreaming doubt takes for granted that if we do have a waking perception of a close, medium-sized object, then the perception is veridical (the challenge being whether we can determine that we are, in fact, awake). Such an assumption is scarcely one that Descartes himself would endorse, as the mechanistic theory of vision laid out in the *Dioptrics* makes plain. There he argued that though our sensory organs respond systematically to the world, the images they give us under the best of circumstances need not resemble the way things are (AT vi, 112–13). The assumption reflects instead the Aristotelian idea that perception under normal conditions is not subject to error (Feyerabend 1978), and that is why the skeptic is portrayed as turning it against the empiricist. Some have thought that the doubt concerns whether waking experience is veridical (Wilson 1978: 20–4). But Descartes described it from beginning to end as concerned with the difference between waking and dreaming (AT vii, 19, 89), and its eventual resolution consists in showing how to determine that we are awake: we check whether our perception coheres with the rest of our experience (AT vii, 90). This doubt, like the others, proceeds by drawing out an internal contradiction within the position of the Aristotelian empiricist.

Secondly, it becomes evident why one doubt in particular, the idea that we might be mad, is not taken seriously. "I would seem no less mad," exclaims the meditator, "if I were to apply the madman's case to my own" (cf. AT vii, 19). Some have claimed that Descartes dismissed this kind of doubt because questioning whether we are even sane would wreck the very enterprise of reasoning about the proper basis of belief (Frankfurt 1970: 38) – that he refused, unlike sixteenth-century writers such as Erasmus and Montaigne, to acknowledge folly as an abiding possibility, since his goal was to establish the sovereignty of reason and to make us "masters and possessors of nature" (Foucault 1972: 56–8). Strictly speaking, however, the one who rejects the doubt about madness is not Descartes himself but rather the empiricist, whose reliance on the senses provides the object of investigation. (This is made explicit in the undated dialogue entitled *The Search for Truth* [AT x, 511].) The chance that we may be mad forms no part of the Aristotelian's perspective, or indeed of anyone's who follows the natural inclination to trust in the senses. Moreover, Descartes has the skeptic go on to raise another possibility, that we may be dreaming, which the empiricist cannot similarly exclude, and this challenge succeeds in undermining from within the same conviction against which the previous doubt was aimed: the reliability of perception under apparently normal conditions. Meditation I does not hold back on doubts that might imperil Descartes' own views. It focuses on those which the empiricist cannot disarm, since its aim consists in showing that empiricism offers no match for the traditional weapons of the skeptic.

The Skeptic's Undoing

The skeptic emerges victorious at the end of Meditation I, only to have his own strategy of internal demolition turned against him in the next. The proposition *sum* ("I am"), the meditator realizes, is one that the skeptic cannot coherently doubt. Plainly, *sum* is supposed to prove undeniable in virtue of a premise, *cogito* ("I think"), but the precise way in which the skeptic is thereby defeated has long been the subject of controversy. If *cogito, ergo sum* is understood as an argument in which Descartes himself advances a premise and draws a conclusion (see, for example, Kenny 1968: 51–5), no skeptic need feel discomfited. Such an argument seems hopelessly circular, since any reasons for not yet assenting to a conclusion as elementary as *sum* would entail doubts about the premise as well. Besides, ever since antiquity, skeptics had pointed out a basic difficulty in regarding proof as a vehicle of knowledge: the premises themselves stand in need of justification, yet seeking to prove them too must lead to an infinite regress.

Some have therefore denied that the refutation of the skeptic hinges on an inference from "I think" to "I am" (Hintikka 1962). But what can *ergo* signify, if not an inferential connection? Though the famous phrase itself – *cogito, ergo sum* – does not appear in the *Meditations*, but only in the *Replies* (AT vii, 140), as well as earlier in French in the *Discourse on Method*, Meditation II clearly presents *sum* as a conclusion following from a premise to the effect that one is thinking. For instance, the meditator first formulates the point by saying: "If I convinced myself of something, then I certainly existed" (AT vii, 25).

The solution lies in recognizing that the inference does not, at least initially, constitute an argument advanced by Descartes himself. Instead, it is the skeptic who provides the premise. (The pioneers of this approach were Frankfurt [1970: 111] and Curley [1978: 84–8], though neither sees that Descartes is thereby deploying against the skeptic the skeptic's own strategy of internal demolition.) The sentences leading up to the one just quoted reproduce the skeptic's point of view: 'I have convinced myself that there is absolutely nothing in the world, no sky, no earth, no minds, no bodies. Does it now follow that I too do not exist? No, if I convinced myself. . . .' So too in the next two formulations of the indubitability of *sum*, which follow in rapid succession (AT vii, 25): the premise to the effect that he is thinking comes from the skeptic, when he states his doubt involving an omnipotent deceiver. *Cogito, ergo sum* enters the scene, not as an argument that Descartes himself puts forward, but as an inference whose import the skeptic cannot elude. It points out a truth about existence (*sum*), to which the skeptic cannot help but commit himself by the very act of exercising his skepticism. As a result, he contradicts himself when claiming to suspend judgment about the truth or falsity of all propositions. The *cogito* serves to undermine from within the skeptic's position, just as the skeptic demolished the position of the empiricist.

Of course, if even the skeptic must acknowledge the certainty of *sum,* then so must everyone. *Cogito, ergo sum* thus becomes an argument which we all can endorse in our own voice. Accordingly, the meditator promptly switches from demolishing from within the skeptic's position to announcing a truth which everyone – Descartes included – will now take as established, no matter what else they may believe: "*I am, I exist,* is necessarily true whenever it is put forward by me or conceived in my mind" (AT vii, 25).

Two points of detail call for discussion. First, the skeptic is portrayed in Meditation II as asserting that there is no world or that there is an omnipotent deceiver, such assertions embodying the fatal premise to the effect that he is thinking. Yet obviously no real skeptic would ever make such statements, as Gassendi complained in the *Fifth Objections* (AT vii, 257–8). The business of skepticism is not to deny prevailing views, but to raise possibilities of error. Descartes knew this very well. He had the skeptic speak in the assertoric mode because, as he explained at the end of the previous Meditation (AT vii, 22; also 59, 461), it is easier to withhold assent from beliefs of the sort in question – subject to doubt, yet still more likely to be true than false – if they are imagined to be false. Moreover, formulating the doubts in the properly hypothetical mode will not avert the evil day. Insofar as the skeptic claims that he doubts that anything can be known to exist, he falls into self-contradiction, since that very claim entails that he is thinking and thus that he exists. In fact, the *Principles of Philosophy* (I, art. 7) and *The Search for Truth* (AT x, 515) present the self-refutation of the skeptic in just this fashion.

It is worth noting, however, that this strategy may fail to work against the skeptic who does not assert that he doubts, but expresses his point of view interrogatively, as Montaigne (1999 ii, 527) did with his "*Que sais-je?*," and did so precisely in order to avoid the similar charge of self-refutation which Augustine (*De civitate Dei* XI. 26) had lodged against the skeptic (Larmore 1998: 1149–50, 1170; 2004). Oddly, Descartes never took up the challenge represented by Montaigne's formula.

A second point has to do with the structure of the inference itself. Does not *sum* follow from *cogito* only in conjunction with another, general premise stating that whatever thinks, exists? Different passages in Descartes' writings suggest contrary answers to this question. In the *Second Replies* (AT vii, 140–1), he denied that *cogito, ergo sum* works as a syllogism, which would certainly require appeal to a major premise of that sort. In the *Principles of Philosophy* (I, art. 10), however, he appeared to concede that the inference assumes that "it is impossible that that which thinks should not exist." Asked by Burman about the seeming inconsistency, Descartes explained (AT v, 147) that though the general premise is presupposed by the inference, it does not in Meditation II figure explicitly before the mind; it is not yet an item of knowledge. At that stage, he said, "I am attending only to what I experience within myself," and I recognize the inference, in the words of the *Second Replies*, as "something self-evident by a simple intuition [*intuitus*] of the mind."

It well behooved Descartes to reply in these terms. If the general truth, "whatever thinks, exists," had to be known in order for us to see that *sum* follows from *cogito*, then the inference could not serve to undermine from within the position of the skeptic, who certainly lays no claim to such knowledge. But the reply also involves a broader aspect of Cartesian thought, which he went on to spell out to Burman. In cases like the one at hand, "we do not separate out these general propositions from the particular instances; rather, it is in the particular instances that we think of them." Some inferences we intuit as compelling without having to grasp explicitly the principles that make them valid; in fact, only by analyzing such inferences do we come to recognize the truth of those principles. In other words, "whatever thinks, exists" may be logically prior to our apprehension of the truth of *sum*, but it comes afterwards in the development of our thinking, or, as Descartes would say, in the "order of reasons" (AT iii, 266–7).

Such views about inference belong to what has been called Descartes' "intuitionism" (Belaval 1960: 23–83), and they appear once again in Meditation III, where he begins to set out his own conception of knowledge. We must be able, he believed, to intuit some propositions as true without appealing to a criterion of truth, for only so can we learn what the correct criterion is – and only so, it might be added, can the ancient skeptical problem of the criterion (how is the choice of a criterion to be justified if not by invoking the criterion itself?) be disarmed. Accordingly, the meditator turns to the one basic truth in his possession, namely, *cogito, ergo sum*, and extracts from it a standard of truth, clarity, and distinctness of perception, to replace the discredited idea of relying on the senses:

> I am certain that I am a thinking thing. Do I not therefore also know what is required for my being certain about anything? In this first item of knowledge there is simply a clear and distinct perception of what I am asserting . . . So I now seem able to lay it down as a general rule that whatever I perceive very clearly and distinctly is true. (AT vii, 35)

In this way, then, the self-refutation of the skeptic delivers the very basis of a new, non-empiricist conception of human knowledge. What exactly Descartes meant by a "clear and distinct" perception, besides simply its indubitability, has always been difficult to nail down, of course. But that for him the basic truths we thus arrive at stem from focusing on our own thought independently of the senses is perfectly plain. Such is the way we grasp our own existence. And as we attend more closely to our nature as thinking beings, we also see, for example, that our idea of material body, as essentially an extended substance enduring through a series of changes, comes not from the senses or the imagination, but from the mind alone. That is one of the lessons of the wax example given in Meditation II (AT vii, 31). Ideas of this sort count as "innate," deriving from the "power of thinking within us" (AT viiiB, 358), and they make up the *a priori* framework within which alone, according to Descartes, we can go on to acquire knowledge from experience.

Cartesian Certainty

Let us now return to the demand for indubitability which Meditation I lays down at the outset as regulating the dialogue between the empiricist and the skeptic:

Since reason [*ratio*] now leads me to think that I should hold back my assent from opinions which are not completely certain and indubitable just as carefully as I do from those which are patently false, it will be enough to reject them all if I find in them the least grounds for doubt [*aliquam rationem dubitandi*]. (AT vii, 18)

Descartes is often accused of having simply assumed that knowledge aims at certainty. But the problematic element is not so much his quest for certainty (it sounds strange to say "I know it's raining but I'm not certain") as the particular meaning that he attached to that notion, which comes to the fore in this passage. No belief will count as certain if we cannot eliminate even the slightest, most improbable way in which it might turn out to be false. Showing an otherwise exemplary understanding of the properly internal strategy of the skeptic, why should Descartes have apparently decided in this case to impose from without a principle of his own, having it shape the skeptic's doubts?

For consider: though indubitability is presented as a dictate of reason, it is not a principle that an empiricist would necessarily be inclined to endorse. On the contrary, I have already noted that for Aristotle sense perception serves as the basis of knowledge because of its reliability, not under all possible, but under normal conditions: ordinarily, the Aristotelian would say, we may feel certain of the truth of what we see, even if the occasional dream may trip us up. Indeed, empiricists or not, we generally consider a belief to be certain if we have disposed of the sorts of error that we have some positive reason to fear or that we have some evidence to think may be at work. We do not feel the need to remove every conceivable doubt, however improbable. Descartes surely knew this well. Why, then, is the skeptic allowed to insist that knowledge must be indubitable?

The answer lies in the sentences that immediately precede the announcement of this demand. There it is said that the evaluation of claims to knowledge (on the part of the empiricist, as it turns out) will take place under rather extraordinary conditions: "I have freed my mind of all cares [*curis*] and have arranged for myself a solid stretch of free time [*otium*]" (AT vii, 17–18). When time is short and resources limited, when practical concerns are in play and we must act, we cannot afford the luxury of rejecting every belief for which we can imagine the slightest grounds of doubt. We must go with the view for which there is deemed to be sufficient evidence. But, Descartes supposed, pursuing knowledge for its own sake is a different affair. If we look only to reasons for belief that have to do with the truth and falsity of opinions (as opposed to the utility of adopting them), if our business is not action, but solely knowledge (AT vii, 22), then indubitability becomes an appropriate objective. As he put the point in the *Discourse on Method*: "Since I now wished to devote myself solely to the search for truth, I thought it necessary to . . . reject as if absolutely false everything in which I could imagine the least doubt, in order to see if I was left believing anything that was entirely indubitable" (AT vi, 31).

The situation in which the meditator finds himself is one which Bernard Williams aptly called "pure enquiry" (1978: ch. 2). In this setting, Descartes supposed, reason requires that we seek beliefs that are immune to every conceivable doubt. Given that he showed so fine an appreciation of the skeptic's proper form of argument, he presumably held as well that if people having an empiricist conception of knowledge do not see themselves bound by this dictate of reason, that is only because they are letting the demands of action interfere with the exclusive search for truth. Were they to pursue knowledge alone, they too would endorse the rule of indubitability, and thus the skeptic is entitled under the present circumstances to hold them accountable to it.

The question remains why Descartes should have thought that the object of pure enquiry must consist in the indubitable. Unfortunately, he never explained his reasons, proceeding as though the point were obvious. But that is not so at all. On his telling, suspending all practical concerns would leave us with but a single purpose, "the search for truth." In reality, we would be confronted with at least two distinct goals: acquiring truths, but also avoiding falsehoods. The two aims are not the same, since if we were interested only in the former, we would believe everything, not worrying about how many false beliefs we took on in the process; whereas if we cared only about the latter, we would believe nothing, for that would mean immediate success. Each of these options is irrational, to be sure. We need to pursue the two goals in tandem. Yet plainly there are in principle many ways to do so. Since the two goals can come into conflict with one another (methods of acquiring truths often give us falsehoods too, avoiding sources of error can mean missing certain truths as well), we have to determine which should take precedence in various sorts of circumstances. Thus, different kinds of rankings, different cognitive policies, are possible.

The ranking that Descartes in effect adopted, the particular weighting of the two goals of pure enquiry that lies behind his phrase "the search for truth," is not difficult to make out. If the slightest, unlikeliest grounds for doubt suffice to preclude assent to a proposition, then avoiding error is being considered as always coming ahead of acquiring truths. We are never to set about satisfying the latter goal unless we have assured ourselves of having fully complied with the former. "The search for truth" is therefore a rather misleading formulation of what Descartes had in mind, since steering clear of error was a more important concern.

It seems equally clear, however, that other ways exist of ordering these two goals under the conditions of pure enquiry. Instead of making the avoidance of error always paramount, for instance, we might decide to give it greater weight only when the errors in question are of the sort that occur in the normal course of events and that there is thus some reason to expect. As for the possibility that we may have made an unusual kind of mistake (because, say, we were dreaming), we would then accord it less importance than the chance of discovering some truth by eliminating simply the ways of going wrong that we have good grounds to fear. The sciences operate in more or less this fashion, and they do not appear to count as any less "pure" for doing so. Yet many today who do not think of themselves as followers of Descartes still suppose that practical concerns alone lead us to settle for less than indubitability, claiming as they do that, because Cartesian certainty is unattainable, the very idea of "pure theory" must also be abandoned.

One example was Bernard Williams himself. He claimed that if time were not short and resources not limited, we would want as many of our beliefs to be true as possible, and, as he noted, the best way thus to maximize the "truth-ratio" among our beliefs would be to reject all those containing the least possibility of error (Williams 1978: 46–9). Because we would thereby end up believing almost nothing, Williams concluded that the ideal of "pure enquiry" has to be discarded (1978: 210). The mistake in this reasoning should now be apparent. Truth acquisition and error avoidance, even when pursued for their own sake, admit of many different combinations.

If Descartes had any basis for holding that reason requires indubitability, once all practical concerns are suspended, it must be that he thought more was involved than just the pursuit of those two goals. And that was indeed the case. Consider again the (un-Cartesian) principle that we need only dispose of the normal possibilities of error in order to accept a proposition as true. This principle is useless without a prior conception of what constitutes the ordinary course of experience. It must already be clear what sorts of error we have good grounds to worry about. A policy of this sort makes sense therefore only if we can place from the start the prospects of human knowledge within a comprehensive view of the world. If, as I pointed out earlier, Aristotle saw in sense experience a reliable source of knowledge whenever standard forms of error have been eliminated, it is therefore no accident that he also thought we determine the nature of perception itself by seeing how it fits into the natural order. To understand the mind's powers, he wrote (*De anima* II. 4), we must look at its distinctive activities, and to understand the latter, we have to ascertain the sorts of objects on which they are typically exercised.

Descartes, by contrast, rejected the notion that knowledge is to be defined by reference to a general picture of the mind's place in the world. That would be to put the cart before the horse. We cannot rightly claim to know what the world is like, unless we first settle what it is to know. The proper starting-point, as he announced in the *Rules for the Direction of the Mind*, is to take the mind by itself, to consider the knowledge (mathematics) it can acquire independently of the world, and then to draw from this case a general method of enquiry, relying on "order and measure," which will determine what may count as knowledge of any subject whatsoever (AT x, 377–8). It was two of Descartes' core convictions – the primacy of epistemology and the priority of method over subject-matter – that ruled out accepting anything as true just because we have no ordinary reason to doubt it. Reason, he supposed, requires that we take care of every possible sort of error because only so can reason map out by its own lights the basic architecture of the world. Herein lies the real basis of the skeptic's assumption in Meditation I that only indubitable beliefs will do.

3

The *Cogito* and the Foundations of Knowledge

Edwin Curley

Descartes was clearly, in some sense, a foundationalist. He thought that among our beliefs, some are based on other beliefs we have, whereas others are not. The ones not based on others we can call *basic beliefs*. The ones based on others we can call *derivative beliefs*. Our basic beliefs provide the foundations for our system of beliefs; our derivative beliefs are the superstructure. This metaphor of our system of beliefs as a building, which has foundations and a superstructure, and might collapse if the foundations were not solid, is prominent both in Descartes' *Discourse on Method* and in his *Meditations*. It is there, for example, in the opening lines of the *Meditations*:

> Some years ago now I noticed how many falsehoods I had accepted as true in my earliest years, and how doubtful the things were which I had subsequently built on them. I realized that it was necessary, once in my life, to overturn all my beliefs, from the bottom up, and start again, from the first foundations, if I ever wanted to establish anything firm and lasting in the sciences. (AT vii, 17)

There is a more elaborate version of the foundationalist metaphor in the *Discourse* (AT vi, 13–14).

When I say here that one belief is *based on* another, and ultimately on one or more basic beliefs, I mean that the basic beliefs are the beliefs we might ultimately offer as reasons for our derivative beliefs if we were asked to give as full a justification for them as we could. If we take one belief as a reason for another, then we think that the second belief can be inferred from the first by some legitimate means of inference. And we also think that we are somehow entitled to hold the first belief.

As so far described, foundationalism may seem innocuous. It may even seem inevitable, obviously true. But the account so far raises important questions which it does not answer. What are the 'legitimate means of inference' we use to justify our beliefs? How can we justify the claim that they are legitimate? And what entitles us to hold the belief we use as a reason for the belief we are trying to justify?

These questions are troubling because it looks as if there might be infinite regresses in the offing. Suppose we justify belief *p* by appealing to another belief, *q*. Our belief in *q* cannot, it seems, provide much justification for *p* unless our belief in *q* is itself justified. So what justifies us in believing *q*? That we have inferred it by legitimate means from some other belief, *r*, which we are also entitled to believe? Perhaps, but this will, of course, prompt the same question about *r*. On the plausible assumption that we cannot break off the threatened regress by going back to *p* and using it to justify *r* (or *s*, or *t*, or whatever belief it is we are trying to justify in this apparently circular way), and that we cannot go on indefinitely justifying one belief in terms of another which itself requires justification, it looks as though the only way we can have justified beliefs is to find some beliefs we are entitled to hold without our inferring them from other beliefs we are entitled to hold, some beliefs which are, as some would now say, *properly basic*.

There is, of course, a similar problem about justifying the principles of inference we use in this argument. Suppose *r* is an inferential principle we use to move from our justified belief in *p* to a justified belief in *q*. If *r* is not itself properly basic, then we must try to justify it by appealing to an argument, which will have at least one premise and at least one inferential principle. And the same questions will arise about the premise(s) and inferential principle(s) of that argument. So a crucial problem for foundationalism is that of explaining how our premises and inferential principles can be properly basic.

On a popular interpretation of Descartes, his answer to this question was that beliefs are properly basic when they are either *self-evident* or *incorrigible reports of the contents of our consciousness*, and not otherwise. If this is correct, then Descartes will say that all of our justified derivative beliefs can be traced back, via finite, legitimate inferential paths, to justified basic beliefs of one or the other of these two kinds. Outside of mathematics, the basic beliefs which provide our foundation will normally include both kinds of properly basic belief. Within mathematics, the only basic beliefs required are those which are self-evident.

I think that common interpretation of Descartes is wrong – or at least, wrong about the *mature* Descartes, the Descartes of works like the *Discourse* and the *Meditations*, works he liked well enough to publish. It is not, in my view, wrong about Descartes' earliest substantial attempt to formulate a theory of knowledge, the *Rules for the Direction of the Mind* (for short, the *Regulae*). But I think Descartes came to see that the version of foundationalism he advocated in the *Regulae* was not a position he wanted to defend. That is why he left it unfinished and never published it. And I think he came up with a more interesting version of foundationalism in the works he did publish.

In Rules I–III of the *Regulae* Descartes lays out a program for reducing all the separate sciences to one science, modeled on mathematics, which would start with assumptions known by intuition, and derive the rest of knowledge from those initial assumptions by deduction. Descartes conceives intuition as a faculty of intellectual perception – the conception of a clear and attentive mind – which enables us to know the simplest truths with absolute certainty. He conceives deduction as a process in which we infer something 'as following necessarily from some other propositions which are known with certainty' (AT x, 369). As Descartes conceives it, deduction itself depends on intuition, since it is ultimately intuition which provides us, not only with our properly basic beliefs, but also with the principles of inference we use in getting to the derivative beliefs. The legitimacy of those inferences is not a matter of their formal validity. Descartes has little use for formal logic. He thinks syllogistic reasoning, for example, is doomed to sterility because it is inevitably question-begging (AT x, 406).

In the *Regulae*, Descartes holds that we should reject all merely probable knowledge, and take as our starting-points truths we know perfectly, truths which cannot legitimately be doubted. We know these indubitable truths by intuition. Among the truths so known he cites (AT x, 368–9) such propositions as:

1   I exist
2   I think
3   A triangle is bounded by just three lines
4   2 plus 2 equals 4
5   3 plus 1 equals 4

and

6   that it follows from (4) and (5) that 2 plus 2 equals 3 plus 1.

Notice that this last example is not as simple as the first five, but concerns the logical relationship between two propositions and a third proposition. It can be regarded as a substitution instance of the general proposition "Things equal to the same thing are equal to each other." But, as we will see later, there is a reason why Descartes gives us the substitution instance, not the more general proposition.

Descartes' mature work, I claim, is not content to simply regard such propositions as the self-evident products of an infallible faculty of intellectual perception. It seeks to justify those basic beliefs – though not, of course, by deducing them from other justified beliefs. Why did the mature Descartes reject the version of foundationalism he had originally embraced?

In Curley (1978), I conjectured (under the influence of Richard Popkin: see Popkin 1964) that sometime in the late 1620s Descartes came to feel the impact of Montaigne's skepticism, which did, in the *Apology for Raymond Sebond*, extend even to basic principles of logic, mathematics, and metaphysics. I would not suggest that Descartes first discovered Montaigne in the late 1620s. Montaigne's work was so widely read that it is hard to imagine that Descartes did not have some familiarity with it before then. But I do think that by the winter of 1628–9, when he retreated to The Netherlands to begin writing the treatise on metaphysics which was to become the *Meditations*, he had come to take Montaigne seriously and had abandoned the *Regulae*, realizing that the theory of knowledge faced deeper problems than those he had up to that point identified in scholastic philosophy.

Montaigne had questioned even basic principles of logic, using the liar paradox, for example, to cast doubt on principles as evident as *if p, then p*:

> Let us take the sentence that logic itself offers us as the clearest. If you say "It is fine weather," and if you are speaking the truth, then it is fine weather. Isn't that a sure way of speaking? Still it will deceive us. To show this, let us continue the example. If you say "I lie," and if you are speaking the truth, then you lie. (Montaigne 1965: 392)

He also used the incomprehensibility of God's power to cast doubt on such simple propositions of arithmetic as $2 \times 10 = 20$:

> In the disputes we have at present in our religion, if you press your adversaries too hard, they will tell you quite shamelessly that it is not in God's power to make his body be in paradise and on earth, and in several places at the same time. And that ancient scoffer [Pliny the Elder], how he takes advantage of it! At least, he says, it is no slight consolation to man to see that God cannot do everything: for he cannot kill himself even if he wished, which is the greatest privilege we have in our condition; he cannot make mortals immortal, or the dead live again, nor can he arrange that the man who has lived shall not have lived, or that the man who has had honors shall not have had them; he has no other power over the past than that of oblivion. And to bind this association of man to God further by comical examples, he cannot make two times ten not be twenty. That is what he says, and what a Christian should avoid having pass out of his mouth. (Montaigne 1965: 393)

It is irreverent for a Christian to say anything of the form "God cannot do *X*," no matter what *X* is, and no matter how incomprehensible it may be to us that God should do that. Montaigne applies this pious dictum, not only to simple mathematical truths, but also to metaphysical principles like the fixity of the past: it is no less irreverent to say that God cannot arrange that a man who has lived shall not have lived than to say that he cannot make two times ten not be twenty.

That Descartes had come, by early 1630, to have considerable sympathy with Montaigne's view will be evident from his correspondence with Mersenne in April and May of that year (AT i, 144–53). I suggest that he came to think he could not simply claim that our knowledge is based (in substantial part at least) on our possession of an infallible faculty of knowledge, which enables us to identify propositions so evident in themselves that they require no argument. If each claim-ant to knowledge were permitted to pick his own ultimate principles, on no better grounds than that the propositions in question were just obvious (i.e., obvious to him), the theory of knowledge would be an anarchic mess. If there are no standards for a properly basic belief other than strength of conviction, then any belief whatever might be claimed to be properly basic, no matter how controversial. But declaring your favorite controversial principle to be properly basic is much too quick a way of dealing with non-believers. And Descartes wants to deal with non-believers (AT vii, 1–2).

The term "self-evident," of course, appears frequently in English translations of Descartes' mature works (for example, at AT vii, 69, 111, 112, 115, 138, 140; AT viiiA, 6, 8, 19, 70). But that seems to me an unhappy tradition among the translators. The Latin in these cases is always *per se notum* or some variant thereof (*per se manifestum, per se patet*). If the work was written in French, the French is normally *évident* (for example, at AT vi, 7). But these phrases do not, for Descartes, have the connotations that the English term "self-evident" has had since the days of Locke; that is, producing "universal and ready assent on hearing and understanding the terms" (*Essay Concerning Human Understanding*, I, ii, 18). Descartes will apply the phrase *per se notum* and its equivalents to propositions which he knows full well do not generate universal and ready assent as soon as the terms are understood, such as the proposition that God exists (AT vii, 69, 163–4, 167), or the basic laws of motion (AT viiiA, 70). Things which some people can see clearly without argument, others cannot see until they are freed of prejudice.

Nevertheless, if Descartes left every proposition liable to a demand for extrinsic justification, he faced the threat of an infinite regress, as Montaigne had not failed to point out (Montaigne 1965: 454). What to do? As I read Descartes, he came up with an ingenious strategy for shifting the burden of proof. He would concede to the skeptic that any proposition whatever was in principle subject to reasonable doubt, even those which a more conventional foundationalist might have claimed to be self-evident. But he would insist that the skeptic provide a reasonable ground for doubting it. To qualify as reasonable, a prospective ground of doubt would not have to satisfy any stringent evidential requirements. In particular, it would not have to be *known* to be true, or *probable* on the evidence. It would not even have to be something the inquirer *believed* to be true. The only evidentiary requirement a ground of doubt would have to satisfy is that it *not* be *known to be false*. If a proposition survives attempts to cast reasonable doubt on it, when the evidential requirements for a reasonable ground of doubt are set *that* low, then the skeptic cannot dismiss its acceptance as arbitrary and dogmatic.

We see this dialectic at work in Meditation I. Early in the Meditation, Descartes proclaims his intention to reject any of his past beliefs which he can find *some* reason for doubting. It need not be what we would ordinarily consider to be a *strong* reason. So he rejects sense-based beliefs, even when they are about ordinary-sized objects in his immediate vicinity, because he recalls having been deceived in the past by dream experiences which were as distinct as his most vivid waking experiences. He makes no claim to *know* that his recollection of these deceptive dreams is accurate; it is sufficient that this is how he remembers them. That recollection provides him with *some* reason for doubting his previous sense-based beliefs because it opens up some possibility that they may be mistaken.

Then he rejects beliefs not based on the evidence of the senses, even when they are about simple mathematical matters, because he believes he has been created by an omnipotent being, who *might* have made him in such a way that he would be deceived even about things like the sum of two plus three. This doubt is based partly on beliefs he holds (that he has been created by an omnipotent being) and partly on beliefs he does not hold, but does not know to be false (that the omnipotent being who created him might be deceiving him). He of course believes God to be supremely good; but when he reflects on how often he makes mistakes, he recognizes that he does not *know* that God is not a deceiver. If he was created by an omnipotent, supremely good being, it must be consistent with that being's goodness to permit him to be deceived. And that is sufficient, it seems, to generate a reasonable doubt about *all* his former beliefs.

Descartes stresses three points about the doubt toward the end of Meditation I (AT vii, 21–2):

1   that none of his former beliefs is indubitable (i.e., not such that no doubt can properly be raised about it);
2   that his doubt concerning the things which have formerly seemed most evident to him is not frivolous, but based on powerful and well-thought out reasons (*validas & meditatas rationes, raisons très fortes et mûrement considérées*); and
3   that the beliefs he doubts are nevertheless (in some cases at least) highly probable; in spite of the "powerful" grounds he has to doubt them, it is much more reasonable to believe them than to deny them.

Eventually Descartes will reformulate the hypothesis of a deceptive creator as the supposition that he was created by an omnipotent being who is evil, not good, a malicious demon. He does not *believe* that such a being exists, or think it likely. It is enough that he *does not know* that such a being does *not* exist. This is sufficient to justify the doubt even about those things which formerly seemed to him most evident.

Since the evidential requirements for reasonable doubt are set so low, the question naturally arises whether they are not so low that Descartes will never be able to escape from universal doubt. Is he doomed to the position that he can assert nothing, since anything he might be tempted to assert is subject to reasonable doubt? That is the danger which threatens him at the end of Meditation I. He escapes that danger, or so it seems, in Meditation II, when he decides that, in spite of what he had said in Meditation I, his own existence is an exception to the generalization about his former beliefs: it is not subject to reasonable doubt.

The reason he escapes, on my reading of the *Meditations*, is that the very weak evidential requirements for reasonable doubt are not the only requirements reasonable doubts must satisfy. There is also an explanatory requirement. A reasonable ground of doubt must explain, at least conjecturally, how error is possible. The grounds of doubt considered in Meditation I all met this requirement. The dream doubt explained how sense experience might deceive us by reminding us of deceptive experiences most of us have had which cannot be distinguished with any certainty from the experiences we take to be non-deceptive. The deceiving God hypothesis explained how we might be mistaken in all our other beliefs because we do not know the origin of our belief-forming mechanisms, and have no reason to assume them to be reliable. This is true even of the atheistic hypothesis Descartes flirts with briefly after he first introduces the hypothesis of a deceiving God. If the cause of my beliefs is an infinite series of impersonal causes, which had no prevision of the effects they were producing, how could I expect my cognitive faculties not to be very imperfect?

A skeptical hypothesis which offers even a conjectural explanation of the possibility of error must presume that there is thinking going on, which it alleges to be subject to error. So it must entail that I think. This explanatory requirement is what is doing the work in the *cogito* argument of Meditation II. Suppose

> there is I-know-not-what deceiver, supremely powerful, and supremely cunning, who deliberately and constantly deceives me. Then I too undoubtedly exist, if he is deceiving me. And let him deceive me as much as he can, he will never bring it about that I am nothing, so long as I think that I am something. (AT vii, 25)

The hypothesis that a demon is deceiving me about my own existence is self-defeating, and therefore not a valid ground of doubt, because it entails the very proposition which, in this case, it is intended to cast doubt on.

This way of thinking about the *cogito* sheds light, I claim, on the perennial puzzle about the nature of Descartes' argument in Meditation II. In the *Discourse on Method* (AT vi, 32) Descartes had used the inferential formula which will be forever associated with his name: "I think; therefore, I exist." This way of putting his argument makes it look as though Descartes is deducing his existence from his thought. And on standard foundationalist assumptions, it raises the question: how do you know that you think? Indeed, the author of the Second Objections (Mersenne?) raised precisely that question about the argument of the *Meditations*, reinforcing it with the reminder that Descartes claims he cannot be certain of anything until he has a clear and certain knowledge of the existence of God, a result he cannot claim to have achieved by the beginning of Meditation II (AT vii, 124–5).

But in Meditation II, notoriously, Descartes does not use the formula he had used in the *Discourse*. He does not say "I think; therefore, I exist." In the *Meditations* the "*cogito*" passage concludes by saying: "So, having weighed all these matters very carefully, I must in the end maintain that this proposition, *I am, I exist*, must be true whenever I mention it or conceive it in my mind."

This has suggested to many readers that in the *Meditations* Descartes is claiming intuitive certainty for his own existence, as he had in the *Regulae*. So people ask: is Descartes' knowledge of his existence intuitive or inferential? It seems to be inferential in the *Discourse on Method*. It is clearly intuitive in the *Regulae*. And it seems to be intuitive again in the *Meditations*. And, of course, there are various other passages which can be used to support one or other of these alternatives.

I claim that the solution to this puzzle is that the *cogito* is, in a sense, both inference and intuition, though I hasten to add that Descartes tends to avoid talk of intuition in the works he wrote after the *Regulae*. I think the reason for this is that he does not want to appear to be resting anything substantive on his possession of a supposedly infallible cognitive faculty. So I prefer to say that the proposition "I exist" is *both* a first principle, insofar as it is a proposition which Descartes takes himself to be justified in accepting without its being the conclusion of an argument whose premise Descartes need claim to know, *and* the conclusion of an inference, whose premise is part of whatever *hypothesis* might be proposed as grounds for doubting it. I emphasize the word "hypothesis" here to make it clear that the "I think" is not a premise which Descartes is responsible for justifying.

When Descartes is writing in a popular vein, as he is in the *Discourse*, he is content to write "I think; therefore, I exist," though this is apt to prompt the skeptical query: "And how do you know that you think?" When he is writing more systematically, as he is in the *Meditations*, he is careful to keep the hypothetical status of his thinking clear: "*If* a demon is deceiving me, then I am thinking, and must exist. The same conclusion follows from any other skeptical hypothesis I might consider in an effort to cast reasonable doubt on my existence. Therefore, I am entitled to affirm, with certainty, but without further argument, that I exist."

I add that Descartes might offer exactly the same rationale for taking the proposition "I think" as a first principle. That too is entailed by any skeptical hypothesis we might entertain in an attempt to doubt it, if that hypothesis meets the explanatory requirement mentioned above. So Descartes *could* present the *cogito* as a demonstration of his existence from his thought. But there would be no advantage in doing so. If this way of justifying first principles is acceptable – that is, if you may take a proposition as a first principle whenever it is entailed by any reasonable ground you might consider in an attempt to doubt it (where the evidentiary requirements for a reasonable ground of doubt are set very low) – then the existence of the self is acceptable as a first principle, without needing to be presented as the conclusion of an inference from the proposition, "I think," which is neither more, nor less, justified than the proposition "I exist."

At some point even those who are sympathetic with this line of interpretation may object: "All right, I understand how Descartes might think he was entitled to assume the truth of the proposition 'I think' as a premise in the inference to his existence. But what about the conditional proposition 'If I think, then I exist.' Isn't that a further assumption which is necessary for the validity of the inference of existence from thought, and which he must justify before he can make the inference? We needn't think of this as a suppressed premise; we can think of it as a principle licensing his inference, a principle allowing the legitimacy of that inference. But even if we think of it as an inference license, it's still a principle which foundationalism will require Descartes to justify. And he couldn't justify it in the way he justified his assumption that he thinks, could he? The conditional proposition connecting thought and existence does not seem to be entailed by any skeptical hypothesis which might be offered to cast doubt on his existence."

In the end, I think Descartes would agree that this is a reasonable objection and would have a procedure for dealing with it. But his acceptance of this requirement is obscured by his resistance to the idea that inferences must be formally valid if they are valid at all. He resists representing the *cogito* as a syllogism, having the form:

Whatever thinks exists.
I think.
Therefore, I exist.

He explicitly rejects that representation of the argument in the *Second Replies* (AT vii, 140), when he replies to the objection from Mersenne described above. There is a fallacy of relevance here, since Mersenne had *not* claimed that the *cogito* was a syllogism with a suppressed major premise. His question had concerned the minor premise. But it is interesting that Descartes sidesteps the question Mersenne actually asked to answer a question he did not ask.

One thing at work in this odd exchange is Descartes' antipathy to formal logic. He thinks that there are valid inferences whose validity is not a matter of form, and that those scholastic philosophers who insisted on making them formally valid were being unduly fussy. The inference "I think; therefore, I exist" is one of those inferences which are valid without being formally valid. So nothing but obscurity is gained by treating it as a syllogism. But part of Descartes' resistance to putting the *cogito* into syllogistic form comes from his sense that the universal premise the inference would have in that form does not make a substantive claim about the world. (This will perhaps be more clearly true, if we represent the argument not as a syllogism, but as an instance of *modus ponens*, with the suppressed conditional premise *If I think, then I must exist*.) It is rather a purely conceptual claim about the relation between thought and existence. So it is an assumption of an entirely different kind from the premise "I think."

In the end, though, Descartes acknowledges that his argument does, in some sense, assume a general connection between thought and existence. He admits this when he presents his philosophy in synthetic form in the *Principles of Philosophy*:

When I said that the proposition *I think, therefore I exist* is the first and most certain
of all those which occur to anyone who philosophizes in an orderly way, I did not
thereby deny that one must first know what thought is, what existence is, and what
certainty is, and that it cannot happen that what thinks does not exist. But because
these are very simple notions, and ones which on their own provide us with no
knowledge of anything which exists, I did not think they needed to be listed.
(*Principles* I, art. 10, AT viiiA, 8)

When Burman questioned him about the apparent inconsistency between this
passage and his rejection of the syllogistic representation of the *cogito* in the *Second
Replies*, he reaffirmed the doctrine of the *Principles*, adding that the meditator
who infers his existence from his thinking presupposes the general principle implicitly, but does not need to be explicitly aware of it. In fact, he discovers that general
connection between thought and existence when he finds himself unavoidably
making the inference from *his* thinking to *his* existence. Knowledge of particular
cases must precede knowledge of general truths (AT v, 147).

I do not think this acknowledgment of the need for a general assumption about
the relation between thought and existence represents a shift of doctrine between
the *Meditations* and the *Principles*. Descartes indicates this in a remarkable passage
in Meditation III. He had begun this Meditation by making what he evidently
regarded as a false start. He enumerated a number of truths which he believed he
could claim to be certain of: that he was a thinking thing; that he had thoughts
of various kinds; that he affirmed some things, denied others, understood a few
things, and was ignorant of many others; that he imagined some things; and even
that he had sensations, provided he understood the word "sensation" as designat-
ing only a certain mode of thought, without implying the existence of any bodies
whose alterations might be causally responsible for the sensations. He then asked
himself what conclusion he might draw from these initial certainties. And since he
thought that what made him certain of these truths was simply the fact that he
perceived them clearly and distinctly, he was tempted to conclude that anything
he perceived so clearly and distinctly must be true.

"Tempted to conclude," but not, in the *Meditations*, really ready to conclude.
In the *Discourse on Method*, he had drawn this conclusion at this stage of his argument (AT vi, 33) and never looked back. But in the *Meditations* he permits himself
a series of reflections which requires him to dig a little deeper. He recalls that there
have been many things which he *thought* he perceived clearly and distinctly, but
which he had nevertheless come to doubt. These included even the simplest truths
of arithmetic and geometry, though they also included metaphysical principles,
such as the principle of the fixity of the past. When he thinks concretely about
these propositions, thinks about particular examples of mathematical or even
metaphysical truth, he finds that he cannot doubt them:

Whenever I turn my attention to the things themselves which I think I perceive with
utmost clarity, I am so completely persuaded by them that I spontaneously break out

in these words: let whoever can deceive me, he will still never bring it about that I am nothing, so long as I think that I am something; or that it should at some time be true that I have never existed, even though it is true now that I exist; or that two plus three should m ake more or less than five; or any other things in which I recognize a manifest contradiction. (AT vii, 36)

But when he thinks about these "evident" propositions in general terms, simply under the rubric "things I perceive as clearly as possible," and thinks at the same time about the supreme power of God, he cannot help but confess that it would be easy for God to cause him to err even about these things.

So even after the apparent establishment of a number of certainties in Meditation II, he is in a quandary. He concludes the overture to Meditation III with the reflection that, until he has examined whether God exists and can be a deceiver, and resolved these issues, he cannot *ever* be certain of *anything*. This is the stunning conclusion of the fourth paragraph of Meditation III:

To remove that [metaphysical reason for doubting], I ought, as soon as the opportunity presents itself, to examine whether there is a God, and if there is, whether he can be a deceiver. For so long as I do not know the answer to these questions, I do not seem to be able, ever, to be certain of any other thing. (AT vii, 36)

Notice that Descartes does *not* say: until I know whether God exists and can be a deceiver I cannot be certain of *anything except the existence of the self and its thoughts*. He says he cannot be certain of *anything*. When I first read this passage as a graduate student, I was astonished by it. Surely, I thought, he is not taking back the results of Meditation II. He is not telling us that he cannot be certain of *anything at all, including his own existence*. But by the time I published Curley (1978), I had decided, partly as a result of reading the work of Alan Gewirth (see Gewirth 1941), that Descartes means precisely what he says.

One persuasive consideration Gewirth adduced was the fact that when Descartes was enumerating those propositions he found he could not help but believe when he attended to them, but could doubt when he considered them under the general heading of "things I perceive with the utmost clarity," he included a principle equivalent to the inferential principle of the *cogito*: "let whoever can deceive me, he will still never bring it about that I am nothing, so long as I think that I am something." That is, if I think I am something, I must be something. I take it that Descartes is recognizing here that, without a proof of the existence and veracity of God, he cannot be certain even of the existence of the self, because he cannot be certain of the validity of the inferential principle he used to derive his existence from the hypotheses a skeptic might propose in order to cast doubt on his existence.

This is not a happy conclusion. Many critics of Descartes have argued that in the first two Meditations he dug himself into a hole he could not climb out of. He might have good grounds for regarding his own existence as certain, they conceded. But if he requires a proof of the existence and veracity of God before he can be certain of anything else, he cannot get past his own existence, cannot justify any ontological claim more meaty than solipsism. For how is he to construct his proof of the existence and veracity of God? Only, it seems, by making such metaphysical assumptions as: there must be at least as much reality in the cause as there is in the effect; or the cause of my ideas must possess at least as much formal reality as the ideas possess objective reality.

Those are assumptions which it seems Descartes in fact makes in his arguments in Meditation III. Let us set aside the question whether they are plausible. Suppose they are. Nevertheless, Descartes' argument for the existence of God will be a *proof* only if the assumptions it makes are ones he can be certain of. And by his own admission, he cannot be certain of those assumptions unless he has a satisfactory proof of the existence of God. And this will be a problem no matter what the details of the argument he makes are. Any argument for God's existence must make *some* assumptions. And even if he comes up with an argument which is more attractive than the arguments of Meditation III are, the same question will arise: how can he claim certainty about the assumptions of that argument consistently with the position he takes at the end of the fourth paragraph of Meditation III?

Consistently with his own requirements, he can never provide the proof of God's existence and veracity which he needs in order to be certain of his clear and distinct ideas. This is the famous problem of the Cartesian circle. But on my reading of Descartes (and Gewirth), it looks like an even more serious problem than it is usually thought to be. For if what we have claimed is correct, he will not even be entitled to claim certainty about his own existence. To draw the conclusion he wants to from the skeptical hypotheses, and justify his taking his own existence as a first principle, he must assume that there is a necessary connection between thought and existence, a connection he will not be entitled to assume in the absence of a proof of God's existence.

I think this is a bullet we must bite. I think Descartes does have a plausible solution to the problem of the circle. The key, I think, lies in a certain feature of clear and distinct ideas which I have already alluded to: whenever we attend to a particular clear and distinct idea, we cannot help but assent to it. Descartes mentioned this in that passage from Meditation III which I quoted earlier, and he comes back to it again in Meditation IV, where he writes that "When I was examining recently the question whether something exists in the world, I noticed that, *from the very fact that I considered that, it followed evidently that I existed*, I really could not help but judge that what I understood so clearly was true" (AT vii, 58, emphasis added). Notice that Descartes does not claim here that what he understood clearly, and could not help but judge true, was the proposition that he exists. Rather, it is the logical connection between his thinking, his considering the issue of his existence, and his existence. It is that inferential principle, and others like it, which he needs his proof of God's existence and veracity to justify.

But how does it help that our clear and distinct ideas are assent-compelling, that when we attend to them, we cannot help but judge them to be true? Let me introduce here the idea of an assent-compelling argument. By an assent-compelling argument, I mean one whose premises are assent-compelling, and whose inferential moves are assent-compelling. Suppose we have an assent-compelling argument from a premise, p, to a conclusion, r, via an intermediate conclusion, q; p must be assent-compelling in its own right, and q will become assent-compelling when we recognize that p is assent-compelling, and that the connection between p and q is also assent-compelling; similarly, r will become assent-compelling once we have recognized that q is assent-compelling, and that the connection between q and r is assent-compelling. I claim that what Descartes is trying to do in the *Meditations* is to construct an assent-compelling argument to the conclusion that God exists and cannot be a deceiver.

What good will that do? Cannot the skeptic just point out that the assent-compelling character of the premises and inferential moves does not justify us in being certain of the conclusion? After all, he might say, could not an omnipotent being cause us to be compelled to assent to false propositions? Do these assumptions possess anything more than psychological certainty? And have we not long ago rejected psychological certainty as a sufficient reason for accepting a proposition?

Now I think Descartes' response to this would be to say that once he has an assent-compelling argument to the conclusion that all our clear and distinct ideas (i.e., all our assent-compelling ideas) are true, it is no longer enough to claim, without supporting argument, that a demon might be deceiving us when we assent to these ideas. He is shifting the burden of proof again. In Meditation I, the unsupported claim that an omnipotent being might deceive us, even about those matters which seemed most evident to us, constituted a reasonable ground of doubt because we had no compelling argument to set against it. We may have had particular clear and distinct ideas, which we could not doubt when we focused our attention on them. But we did not find the general proposition that all our clear and distinct ideas are true assent-compelling. So we were vulnerable to skeptical suggestions that they may not be true, that a sufficiently powerful being might deceive us even about such matters as the simplest truths of mathematics.

By the end of Meditation IV we are supposed to have an assent-compelling argument against that skeptical hypothesis. So it no longer constitutes a reasonable ground of doubt. The validity of a ground of doubt is situational, in the sense that what constitutes a valid ground of doubt at one stage of the argument, when we have no assent-compelling argument against it, will no longer be valid when we do have such an argument. Descartes makes this clear in his reply to the *Seventh Objections*. Father Bourdin, the author of those objections, had fastened on Descartes' somewhat surprising rejection, midway through the third paragraph of Meditation II, of the existence of minds. That rejection is surprising, partly because Descartes will affirm the certainty of his own existence (presumably as a thinking thing) by the end of that very paragraph, but partly also because minds had not been mentioned in the preceding Meditation. Bourdin, Descartes complains, seems to think that once Descartes has doubted something, he can never reverse himself.

But this involves a fundamental misunderstanding of the method of doubt, as Descartes, with some exasperation, points out:

> At the outset, when I was supposing that I had not yet sufficiently perceived the nature of the mind, I numbered it among the doubtful things; but later on, noticing that a thing which thinks cannot not exist, and using the term "mind" to refer to this thinking thing, I said that the mind existed. My critic proceeds as if I had forgotten that previously I had denied this very thing (when I was taking the mind to be something unknown to me); he talks as if the things I was denying earlier (because I found them doubtful), I must have thought were always to be denied, as if it was impossible that such beliefs could be rendered certain and evident to me. It should be noted that throughout he treats doubt and certainty not as relations of our thought to objects, but as properties of the objects which inhere in them permanently. This means that if we have once realized that something is doubtful, it can never be rendered certain. (AT vii, 473)

Bourdin's objections to the *Meditations* are prolix, and tiresome, and do not show a good or sympathetic grasp of Descartes' philosophy. As a translator, I can sympathize with that translator of Descartes who said that Descartes must have had a very strong desire to stand well with the Jesuits, to take Bourdin as seriously as he did. It is understandable that they should not have received very much attention from Descartes' commentators. (Alan Gewirth was an honorable exception to this generalization.)

Unfortunately, when we neglect Bourdin's objections, we also neglect Descartes' replies. In doing so, I believe, we miss an important clue to understanding the procedure of the *Meditations*. The preceding quotation from the *Seventh Replies* illustrates the point that the validity of a ground of doubt is situational, that it varies depending on the epistemic situation. But it does not say much about how a ground of doubt which is valid at one stage can become invalid at a later stage. The next passage helps to explain that:

> There are reasons which are strong enough [*satis validae*] to compel us to doubt, even though these reasons are themselves doubtful, and hence are not to be retained later on . . . The reasons are strong so long as we have no others which produce certainty by removing the doubt. Now since I found no such countervailing reasons in the First Meditation, despite meditating and searching for them, I therefore said that the reasons for doubt which I had found were "powerful and well thought-out" [*validas & meditatas*]. But this is beyond the grasp of our critic, for he goes on to say "When you promised me powerful reasons, I expected certain ones, ones of the kind demanded by this little pamphlet of yours" – as if the imaginary pamphlet he has put together can be related to what I said in the First Meditation. (AT vii, 473–4)

Bourdin was not the last person to think that "powerful" grounds of doubt must be certain ones. Some critics of the dream argument make the same assumption when they ask Descartes: "How do you know you've had experiences just as vivid as your most vivid waking experiences, which you subsequently decided were illusory, because they occurred when you were asleep and dreaming?"

But the crucial point in this passage is the part where Descartes says: "The reasons [for doubt] are strong so long as we have no others which produce certainty by removing the doubt." My claim is that Descartes will have produced these reasons strong enough to remove the skeptical doubts when he produces an assent-compelling argument that God exists and is not a deceiver. It is sufficient that the premises of the argument and the inferential moves be psychologically compelling. It is not necessary for them to be indubitable in the strong sense which implies that they cannot properly be doubted.

In Curley (1978) I endeavored to justify this procedure as a kind of circumstantial *argumentum ad hominem* against the kind of Pyrrhonian skepticism you find in Montaigne. The Pyrrhonian advocates what he calls the principle of equipollence, according to which for every argument in favor of a proposition an equally strong argument against it can be found. As Montaigne puts it: "[The Pyrrhonians'] expressions are: 'I establish nothing; it is no more thus than thus, or than neither way . . . the appearances are equal on all sides; it is equally legitimate to speak for and against'" (Montaigne 1965: 373–4). The criterion of the strength of an argument here is its degree of psychological persuasiveness. The principle of equipollence is what is supposed to justify the characteristic Pyrrhonian resolution to suspend judgment about everything, and not, like the academic skeptics, to deny that we can have certain knowledge, but concede that some propositions may be highly probable.

When someone who holds the principle of equipollence is confronted with an assent-compelling argument in favor of the truth of our clear and distinct ideas, he can no longer cast doubt on that conclusion by simply postulating the possibility of deception by an omnipotent being. He must produce an equally strong argument, i.e., an assent-compelling argument, in favor of the opposite conclusion. In the absence of such an argument, Descartes is entitled to his conclusion.

So far my discussion has focused on two kinds of basic belief: necessary truths, like the inferential principle underlying the *cogito*, and two contingent truths, the propositions that I think and that I exist. But Cartesian foundationalism holds that there are other contingent truths which are also properly basic. On the popular interpretation of Descartes' foundationalism, which I mentioned at the beginning of this chapter, all my beliefs about my own mental states and activities are properly basic because they are incorrigible in the following sense: if I believe that I am in a particular mental state, or engaged in a particular mental activity, then necessarily I am in that state or engaged in that activity.

This is a view often ascribed to Descartes, along with the companion view that our mental states and activities are transparent, in the sense that if I am in a particular mental state, or engaged in a particular mental activity, then I know that I am in that state or engaged in that activity, by a continuous, direct, non-inferential awareness. Let us call the combination of these doctrines of transparency and incorrigibility the doctrine of our privileged access to our own mental life.

I do not believe that Descartes consistently held to a fully general doctrine of our privileged access to our own mental life. In Curley (1978), I argued that the textual evidence is very mixed, but that sometimes Descartes explicitly rejects the doctrine of privileged access. A striking example occurs in the *Discourse on Method* when Descartes writes that to discover the opinions that people really hold we should attend to their actions rather than to their words, because "few people are willing to say everything they believe, and . . . many people do not know what they believe, since believing something and knowing that one believes it are different acts of thinking, and the one often occurs without the other" (AT vi, 23). Elsewhere, Descartes makes similar points about the difficulties we face in knowing our own passions. In Curley (1978), I argued that in passages like this Descartes showed himself to be part of a long tradition, counting among its members such philosophers and theologians as Plato, Augustine, Luther, and Calvin, who all regarded self-knowledge as a difficult achievement rather than something which was inescapable.

Nevertheless, I do think that Descartes held a weak version of the doctrine of privileged access. There are some of our mental states or activities which he thinks we can know with a certainty that it would not make sense to question. A prime example would be our own sensations, when sensation is construed properly, as a state which does not presuppose any physical occurrences, but involves only my being in a state in which it seems to me, sensorily, that something is the case. This is the argument of the second movement of Meditation II (AT vii, 25–9). I see a light (or so I think). If I think of this sensation as an awareness of an object external to me, mediated by the organs of my body, I may be mistaken about my seeing a light. It may be that there is no light there which is causing me to have the sensations I am having. It may be that I have no body. But I cannot be mistaken if I limit my claim to reporting the current state of my consciousness, that it seems to me that I see a light.

Why can I not be mistaken about this? Or, better, why does it not make sense to suppose that I am mistaken about this? My answer would be that if I try to cast doubt on my sensations, so understood, I must have a reason for doing so, and the skeptical hypotheses I might entertain in order to do that must meet the same explanatory requirement we discussed earlier, in connection with my knowledge that I think and that I exist. I say I see a light and the skeptic tells me I may be mistaken. "Perhaps," he says, "you only seem to see a light. Perhaps the visual experiences you're having now are a consequence of a blow to the head, or a pressure exerted on your eyeballs, or a chemical substance which someone put in your drink." But whatever the skeptic says, in attempting to explain how I might be mistaken, will imply that I'm having certain experiences which mislead me.

When I insist that "at least *it seems to me* that I see a light, that much is certain," he cannot go on to say: "Well, no, perhaps *it only seems to you that it seems to you* that you see a light; but that's consistent with the claim that it doesn't actually seem to you that you see a light." To attempt to iterate the "it seems to me" operator in that way is to talk nonsense, quite literally. It is to say things we simply cannot understand. But if the skeptic must concede my propositions about how things seem to me, I'm entitled to take those propositions as properly basic beliefs.

I do not think it follows from this line of reasoning that I am entitled to claim all beliefs about my present mental states as properly basic. In particular, propositions about what I believe do not seem to be apt for this line of defense. In many (if not all) judgments, I think, Descartes will want to say that part of what is going on is my being in a state in which something seems to me to be the case. For example, when I affirm that there is music playing now in my study, my ground for that belief is that it seems to me that I hear music playing. But the belief involves more than my just being in that state. As the analysis of judgment in Meditation IV implies, there is also an act of will involved, an act by which I assent to my sense impression. I could withhold that act of assent, in which case, though it would still *seem to me* that I hear music playing, I would not *judge* that I hear music playing. This extra element which is involved in belief, but not in mere sensation, does not seem to be something which would be open to being defended by the maneuvers I have used to defend our certainty about our sensations. So I think Descartes would have a principled reason for not treating all his beliefs about his own mental states as properly basic. This seems to me as it should be.

My account of Cartesian foundationalism, and of the role the *cogito* argument plays in that project, is now essentially complete. But there is one objection which someone might make to it which I would like to deal with, briefly. Some readers may find this defense of Descartes disappointing. They may say: "This works, if it works at all, only against a certain kind of skeptical opponent. You've presented Descartes' defense as a kind of *argumentum ad hominem* against Pyrrhonian skepticism, and attempted to capitalize on the Pyrrhonian's acceptance of the principle of equipollence. But this is an exceptionally radical form of skepticism, which will have little appeal to readers who have not been seduced by the charms of Montaigne. The argument won't, and can't, work against more moderate and credible forms of skepticism, which don't embrace the principle of equipollence."

No one to whom I have presented my interpretation of Descartes has ever said this to me. But it surprises me that they have not, since it seems to me a natural objection, much of which I agree with. My reply would be that, although Descartes' argument does seem to me to be designed for use against that particular form of skepticism, and limited in its effectiveness to that form of skepticism, this is not such a serious limitation. First, I would be quite happy to get from a critic the concession that Descartes' argument is, in fact, effective against that form of skepticism. Descartes' argument is so often dismissed as hopeless that getting such a concession would seem to me no small accomplishment. Second, if Descartes does achieve a victory over Pyrrhonian skepticism, we might regard that as the first battle in a campaign which would then go on to attack the more moderate and credible forms of skepticism which the critic imagines to be more dangerous. In that campaign, we might find Montaigne useful, since his defense of Pyrrhonism involves a sharp critique of academic skepticism.

But I am not, in fact, prepared to say that Descartes' defense of knowledge achieves a victory even over the Pyrrhonian skeptic. All I have attempted to do is to show that Descartes has a defense against the charge of circularity, *if* he can produce an assent-compelling argument that God exists and is not a deceiver. I do not think he has produced that kind of argument for those conclusions. So the fact that he has a defense against the charge of circularity, while nice, does not vindicate his overall defense of knowledge.

4

The Nature of the Mind

Marleen Rozemond

Descartes is commonly regarded as the origin of mind–body dualism and the modern mind–body problem. A little historical reflection reveals that this picture cannot be entirely accurate: some form of dualism is at least as old as Plato. Furthermore, long before Descartes, a central component of the Christian tradition had been the idea that the human soul is immortal and this idea was often (although not always) supported by arguments to the effect that it is incorporeal. So the incorporeality of the human soul or mind was not a novel idea. But there is reason to say that Descartes made a significant contribution in a different way: he redrew the boundary between mind or soul and body and between the corporeal and the incorporeal. In brief, before Descartes, the incorporeal mind was generally identified with the intellect. But Descartes formulated our modern conception of the mental as including far more: sense perception, imagination, feeling, emotion. The mind, in his words, is a thing that thinks, *res cogitans*, and he defined thought in terms of consciousness: "I understand by the term 'thought' everything that is in us in such a way that we are immediately conscious of it. Thus all operations of the will, intellect, imagination and the senses are thoughts" (AT vii, 160). So Descartes initiated the modern mind–body problem in the sense that he formulated the modern view of what belongs to the category of the mental, the category which we investigate in its relation to the physical.

This is not a novel picture of Descartes' contribution, but it is rarely taken into account in scholarly interpretations of his writings. And whether or not this broad picture of Descartes' contribution is entirely accurate, it does capture an important aspect of his own view of the matter. Descartes aimed to supplant Aristotelianism, as he indicated to his friend Mersenne:

> [T]hese six Meditations contain all the foundations of my physics. But please don't say so, for those who favor Aristotle would perhaps have more difficulty approving of them. And I hope that those who read them will gradually get used to my principles

and recognize their truth before realizing that they destroy the principles of Aristotle. (AT iii, 298)

Descartes speaks of his physics here, but crucial to his physics, as we will see, is the way in which he drew the boundary between the mental and the physical. And while Descartes spoke of Aristotle, he was more specifically concerned with Aristotelianism as it existed in his day, scholastic Aristotelianism.

I will relate Descartes' treatment of the mind in Meditation II to Aristotelian scholasticism. This approach helps us to understand the structure of his argumentation: it helps us to see what he thought needed a lot of argument, and what he thought would be readily accepted. I will focus on St Thomas Aquinas and on Francisco Suárez, an influential Jesuit who closely preceded Descartes. Next, I will turn to an idea that has often been central to the conception of Descartes' view of the mind in contemporary (certainly analytical) philosophy: the idea that each of us has a special, privileged type of knowledge of her own mental states; the doctrine of transparency of the mental. I will argue that there is good reason to believe that Descartes did not accept this doctrine. His conception of the mind results from a redrawing of the boundaries between the mental and the physical in view of his commitment to mechanistic science rather than a commitment to transparency.

Descartes' Novel Conception of the Mind

The Aristotelian scholastics did not agree on all matters concerning the nature of the soul, but for our purposes some generalizations apply. For the Aristotelians, the soul is the form of the body; this is true for any living thing. The soul, *anima*, is what makes something a living thing, and for a particular living being, say a cow, its soul makes it the particular kind of living thing that it is. The soul is the principle of life, and life is manifested in a range of activities: nutrition and growth in plants; in animals, also motion and sense perception; in humans, intellectual activity and will. The presence of these functions is explained by the soul. So for an Aristotelian, the term "soul" is a broad term that does not have religious connotations. For the Christian Aristotelians, only the human, intellectual soul can exist after the death of the body. And there was a strong tradition among the scholastics of arguing for this claim on the basis of the nature of the intellect. Medieval Aristotelians attributed the idea that intellection is not an operation of the body to Aristotle (Aristotle 1968: III. 4, 429a 18–28, 5, 430a 10–25). Then Aquinas, for instance, argued:

> The intellectual principle which is called the mind or intellect has an operation through itself [*per se*] in which the body does not participate. Nothing, however, can operate through itself unless it subsists through itself; for activity only belongs to a

being in act, and hence something operates in the same way in which it is. For this reason we do not say that heat heats, but that something hot heats. Consequently, the human soul, which is called intellect or mind, is something incorporeal and subsisting. (Aquinas 1964: I. 75. 2; see also Suárez 1856: I. IX.)

So intellectual activity is an operation of the human soul alone, and that requires that this soul is a subsistent entity, an entity that exists in its own right, and that can exist without the body. Much of what I will say about the intellect is also true of the will – which the scholastics saw as intellectual appetite (Aquinas 1964: I. 80. 2) – but the discussions both in scholasticism and in Descartes focus on the intellect.

The scholastics had a different view of sense perception, and other activities we now regard as mental. Aquinas draws the contrast as follows:

> Certain powers are related to the soul alone as their subject, such as the intellect and the will. And such powers necessarily remain in the soul when the body is destroyed. But other powers inhere in the composite [*conjuncto*] as their subject, such as all the powers of the sensitive and nutritive parts. (Aquinas 1964: I. 77. 8)

So for Aquinas, sense perception pertains to the soul–body composite, rather than the soul alone. And we can see now a striking difference between Aquinas's conception of the soul and modern worries about the mind–body problem: Aquinas focuses on human *intellectual* activity in defending the soul's incorporeity, whereas in contemporary philosophy the question of whether the mind can be understood in physical terms focuses on experiences like pain, color sensations, experiences that belong to the realm of the sensory, which, for Aquinas, pertain to the body–soul composite rather than the soul alone. This difference finds its origin in Descartes' reconceptualization of the mental, although I will argue that the transition is not complete in his thought.

Let us now turn to Descartes. Meditation II begins where Meditation I leaves off: he has brought out the full skeptical machinery, and now the question is whether any firm footing can be found in the middle of the resulting skeptical morass. The first item he retrieves is his knowledge that he himself exists. But another question arises immediately: *what* is he? He considers several answers: a man – an answer he dismisses quickly. Then he turns to ideas that used to occur to him "spontaneously and naturally": first, the idea that he is a body, and then the following list of activities, which shows him reflecting on the Aristotelian conception of the soul as principle of life: "It occurred to me that I was nourished, that I walked, sensed, and thought: which actions I referred to the soul" (AT vii, 26). The question Descartes raises now is this: assuming that there is a very powerful deceiver what can I still claim I am? He dismisses the idea that he is a body without argument, no doubt because he is at this point skeptical about the existence of body. He then uses the doubt about body to sort through the Aristotelian list of activities pertaining to the soul:

Nutrition or movement? But I do not now have a body, these things are nothing but imaginings. Sensation? This also does not happen without a body, and I seem to sense many things in dreams that later I notice I did not really sense. Thinking? I have found it: it is thinking; this alone cannot be taken away from me. I am, I exist, that is certain. But for how long? For as long as I think, for certainly it could happen that if I cease to think entirely, I thereby entirely cease to be. I now do not admit anything unless it is necessarily true; I am then strictly speaking [*praecise tantum*] only a thinking thing, that is, a mind, spirit, intellect or reason, words whose meaning was previously unknown to me. I am a real thing, and really exist, but what kind of thing? I have said it, a thinking thing. (AT vii, 27)

It is tempting to interpret Descartes' claim that he is a thinking thing in light of the broad list of mental states that includes sense perception and imagination. But, in fact, he has really only identified himself as an intellectual being: he says he is a "mind, spirit, intellect or reason [*mens, sive animus, sive intellectus, sive ratio*]," and these terms only refer to the intellectual aspect of the scholastic soul.

This result – Descartes accepts intellectual thought but not sense perception in the face of the doubts about body – makes perfect sense given the Aristotelian background, where sense perception, but not intellectual activity requires the existence of body for its subject of inherence. And so the skeptical doubts about body stand in the way of attributing sense perception to oneself in a way that they do not for intellectual activity. But later in Meditation II he takes a different stance, and writes: "I am a thing that thinks. What is that? Something that doubts, understands, affirms, denies, wills, is unwilling, and also imagines and senses" (AT vii, 28). This is the characterization of a thinking thing that corresponds to his definition of thought in terms of consciousness (although it is worth noting that in the *Meditations* Descartes never uses the notion of consciousness to characterize thought or a thinking thing). Descartes is now deliberately developing a conception of the mind as including not just intellectual and volitional activity, as the Aristotelians would have it, but also imagination and sense perception, which for them reside in the body–soul composite. (Imagination was counted among the internal senses; see Aquinas 1964: I. 78. 4.) One can see the significance of the Aristotelian background in the way in which Descartes presents the expanded list. He thinks there is no need or possibility to explain that he has the traditional functions of the mind: "For the fact that I am the one who doubts, understands, wills, is so manifest that nothing occurs by which it can be explained more evidently." He expects his readers to accept this much quite readily. But he does see a need to offer an argument for his sensing and imagining:

But I am also the same who imagines; for although perhaps, as I have supposed, no imagined things are at all real, the very power of imagination does, however, really exist and is part of my thinking. And again I am the same who senses, or who notices corporeal things as if through the senses; for instance, I see light, I hear noise, I feel heat. These things are false, for I am asleep. But certainly I seem to see, hear, become warm. This cannot be false, and this is properly what is called sensing in me, and this strictly speaking is nothing other than thinking. (AT vii, 29)

In fact, Descartes departs from his scholastic predecessors in his conception of the soul and mind in two ways. What we just saw is that he expands the conception of the mind. But, on the other hand, he narrows the role of the soul by making it the principle of thought and removing from it various traditional functions: nutrition, growth, motion. Thus he explains in response to Gassendi:

> the first men did not perhaps distinguish between, on one hand, that principle in us by which we are nourished, grow, and perform without any thought all the other functions we have in common with the brutes, and on the other hand, that principle by which we think. They applied to both the single term "soul." Then, noticing that thought is different from nutrition, they called that which thinks "mind," and believed that it is the principal part of the soul. I, however, noticing that the principle by which we are nourished is entirely different from the principle by which we think, have said that the term "soul" is ambiguous when it is used for both. And in order to understand it as the first act or principal form of man, it must only be understood as the principle by which we think. To this I have as much as possible applied the term "mind," in order to avoid ambiguity. For I do not regard the mind as a part of the soul, but as the whole soul, which thinks. (AT vii, 356)

What happened to the other traditional roles of the Aristotelian soul? Descartes relegated those to the realm of mechanistic explanation. This is not explicit in the *Meditations*, but it is central to his famous discussion of humans, animals, and machines in the *Discourse*. There Descartes argues that the human body is "a machine, which, having being made by God, is incomparably better ordered, and contains within itself more admirable motions than any of those that can be invented by men" (AT vi, 56). Human beings also have a soul, which accounts for thought and thus for behavior that manifests thought. But animals are just machines; all of their behavior can be explained mechanistically.

Two other aspects of the contrast with the Aristotelian scholastic view are especially worth noting. Philosophers today tend to question Descartes' dualistic view that the mental cannot be explained scientifically and that it must be immaterial. But from the perspective of his contemporaries, Descartes went rather far in his claims about what is within the scope of materialistic scientific explanation and in thinking that quite so little required a soul. Thus his friend Arnauld wrote:

> As far as the souls of the brute animals are concerned, M. Descartes elsewhere suggests clearly enough that they have none. All they have is a body with a certain configuration, made up of various organs in such a way that all the operations that we observe can be produced in it and by means of it. But I think that in order for this conviction to find faith in the minds of men, it must be proved by very valid reasons. For it seems incredible at first sight that it can happen without the help of any soul

that the light reflected from the body of a wolf into the eyes of a sheep moves the
very thin optical nerves, and that upon that motion reaching the brain, animal spirits
are diffused through the nerves in such a way as is necessary to make the sheep flee.
(AT vii, 205)

So Arnauld thought Descartes went awfully far in thinking that mechanistic explanation could account for all animal behavior.

Finally, Descartes had a striking view of how his position fits into the relationship between religion and science. Historically, expanding the scope of scientific
explanation has often created tensions with religion, and, of course, most relevant
to Descartes is Christianity. Thus the idea that scientific explanation can account
for the mental generates tension with the idea of an immortal soul. But Descartes
thought that his own expansion of the scope of scientific explanation *strengthened*
the defense of the immortality of the soul. Seeing that our souls are radically different from those of animals means, he thinks, that "one has a much better understanding of the reasons that prove that our soul is of a nature entirely independent
of the body, and that, consequently, it is not subject to dying with it" (AT vi,
59–60).

Why does Descartes think that his view helps support immortality for human
souls? One reason is that on his view, as Arnauld pointed out, only humans have
souls, not animals. One difficulty for his contemporaries had been to explain why
only our souls, and not those of animals, should be immortal, as Christianity would
have it. Indeed, one purpose of the discussion in the *Discourse* is to respond to
philosophers like Montaigne who had argued that the difference between animals
and humans simply is not that radical (for discussion, see Gilson 1976: 425–9 and
435–6). But on Descartes' view there clearly is a radical difference. Another reason
is that scholastics like Aquinas argued for the incorporeity of the human soul on
the basis of intellectual activity. And Descartes restricted the soul to its intellectual
part, the mind, so he restricted it precisely to those functions that support its
immortality, as opposed to other functions that can only be carried out by an
ensouled body.

Indeed, although full discussion of this issue would lead us too far afield, it is
worth noting the following. Descartes' principal argument for dualism is generally
regarded as based on a conception of thought in his broad sense, but in fact it should
be understood as focused only on intellectual activity. This is strongly suggested by
his remarking, right *after* the conclusion of the argument in Meditation VI:

Moreover, I find in me faculties for certain special modes of thinking, namely the
faculties of imagining and sensing. I can clearly and distinctly understand myself as
a whole without them; but not *vice versa* them without me, that is, without an intelligent substance in which they are. For they include some intellection in their formal
concept: hence I perceive that they are distinguished from me as modes from a thing.
(AT vii, 78)

Sensation and imagination are modes of the mind, but the argument for dualism had been based on a conception of its essence which Descartes presents as intellectual. And, indeed, he repeatedly suggests that focus on sensation brings out the union of mind and body rather than their distinction (AT vii, 81, 228–9). So in this regard, Descartes' argument for dualism is akin to Aquinas's argument for the status of the soul as a subsistent incorporeal entity. And both differ sharply from the modern mind–body problem with its focus on sensory states.

The Intellect and the Senses

Descartes modifies the Aristotelian conception of the mind significantly, then, in assigning sense perception to the mind rather than to the soul–body composite, and similarly for imagination and emotions. Or to be more precise, he assigns an aspect or stage of sense perception to the mind. In Meditation II, after claiming that he senses, he qualifies this claim on the ground that the skeptical worries about the existence of body imply that he might not really be sensing. But, he continues, he certainly seems to sense, and "this is properly what is called sensing in me, and this strictly speaking is nothing other than thinking" (AT vii, 29). What does this "seeming to sense" mean exactly? What aspect of sense perception is Descartes trying to assign to the mind?

The phrase "seeming to sense" could mean different things, but in the *Sixth Replies* Descartes offers a clear view of what aspect of sense perception is supposed to pertain to the mind. He explains that sense perception consists in three stages, or "grades": the mechanical process in the body, and then two stages that occur in the mind:

> The second [grade] contains everything that results immediately in the mind due to the fact that it is united to the corporeal organ so affected, and such are the perceptions of pain, pleasure, thirst, hunger, colors, sound, flavor, smell, heat, cold, and the like, which result from the union and, as it were, intermingling of mind and body, as I said in Meditation VI. The third grade comprises all those judgments about external objects which we have been used to making since our earliest childhood on the occasion of the motions of the corporeal organ. (AT vii, 437)

So now we can see what components of sense perception pertain to the mind: the immediate affects in the mind and the subsequent judgments. Given Descartes' definition of thought in terms of consciousness elsewhere, the immediate affects are no doubt conscious sensations of the types mentioned.

On the other hand, this passage hints at a complication in Descartes' view that emerges more clearly in other contexts: sense perception and intellection do not belong to the mind in the same way. The second grade of sensation, he writes here, results from "the union and, as it were, intermingling of mind and body."

In Meditation VI, Descartes had written that sensations arise from the "union and, as it were, intermingling of mind and body" and that this shows that the mind is not united to the body merely as a sailor to a ship, or else the mind would instead have purely intellectual perceptions of what goes on in the physical world (AT vii, 81). Descartes sees a metaphysical contrast between sensation and imagination, on the one hand, and intellectual activity, on the other hand. Consider the following statements about the nature of intellectual activity:

> [W]hen the mind understands, it turns in some way towards itself and inspects one of the ideas which are in itself; but when it imagines, it turns towards the body and looks at something in the body which conforms to an idea understood by the mind or perceived by the senses. (Meditation VI, AT vii, 73)

> I have also often distinctly shown that the mind can operate independently of the brain; for certainly the brain can be of no use to pure intellection, but only to imagination or sensation. (*Fifth Replies*, AT vii, 358; see also AT vii, 385, and AT ii, 598)

But in what sense does sense perception require the union? Does it simply require the body to be united to the mind so that it can act on the mind and provide the efficient causes of sense perception? (Chappell 1994b: 404–6; Kenny 1999; Margaret Wilson sees evidence of interactionism as well as a different view in Descartes: Wilson 1978: 205–20). But some of his analyses suggest something stronger. Consider *Principles* I, art. 48:

> I do not, however, recognize more than two highest types of things: first, intellectual or thinking things, that is, those pertaining to the mind or thinking substance; second, material things, or those which pertain to extended substance, that is, body. Perception, volition, and all the modes of perceiving and willing are referred to thinking substance; magnitude, or its extension in length, width and depth, shape, motion, place, the divisibility of parts and the like are referred to extended substance.

This much suggests a straightforward dualistic picture. Immediately afterwards, however, Descartes adds:

> But we also experience certain other things in us, which must be referred [*referri*] neither to the mind alone, nor to the body alone, and which, as will be shown below in its proper place, arise from [*proficiscuntur*] the close and intimate union of our mind with the body; namely the appetites of hunger and thirst etc.; similarly, the emotions or passions of the soul, which do not consist in thought alone, such as the emotion of anger, joy, sadness, love, etc.; and furthermore all sensations, such as the sensations of pain, pleasure, light and colors, sounds, smells, flavors, heat, hardness and the other tactile qualities.

So Descartes claims that there are only *two* highest types of things, ones referred to body and ones referred to mind, but at the same time acknowledges ones that "arise from [*proficiscuntur*] the close and intimate union of our mind with the body." How should we understand this view? Some interpreters have argued that Descartes in fact acknowledges a distinct, third type of mode (Cottingham 1986: 127–32; Schmaltz 1992). But I wish to propose a different view. In letters to Regius and Gibieuf, he suggests that sense perception is not *pure* thought, or an act of the *pure* mind:

> we perceive that sensations of pain and all other sensations are not pure thoughts of the mind distinct from the body, but confused perceptions of the mind really united [to the body]; for if an angel would be in a human body, it would not sense like us, but only perceive the motions that would be caused by external objects and in this way he would be distinguished from a real human being. (AT iii, 493)

> I do not see any difficulty in understanding that the faculties of imagination and sensation belong to the soul, because they are species of thought; nevertheless *they only belong to the soul insofar as it is joined to the body*, because they are sorts of thoughts without which one can conceive the soul entirely pure [*toute pure*]. (AT iii, 479, emphasis added)

Intellectual activity, Descartes claims, is an activity of just the mind by itself, the pure mind. But sensations are impure thoughts and belong to the mind as united to the body.

The first of these passages is similar to the discussion in Meditation VI, where Descartes contrasts the mind–body union with the union of a pilot and a ship. This passage suggests that sensation does not merely require that the body acts on the mind in order to produce sensory states as an external efficient cause. That idea is compatible with the body causing perceptions of motions and other primary qualities like an angel would have if united to a human body, according to Descartes. He seems to think that the nature of the union of mind and body in a human being explains not just the occurrence of mental states on the occasion of states of the body, but it explains the qualitative nature of sensory states: it explains that we see colors, hear sounds, sense smells rather than merely perceive configurations of primary qualities, as an angel would, in accord with his mechanistic picture of the physical world. The sensory affects in the mind are the result of the mind's close, special union with the body; it is, as it were, intermingled with the body, for Descartes.

Now it is not clear what that means; the talk of mixture is an analogy – the mind is *as it were* [*quasi*] intermingled with the body. Since the mind is incorporeal, indivisible, for Descartes, it cannot be literally mixed in with the body. But the letters to Gibieuf and Regius do suggest a specific view about the ontology of sensations. They are modes of the mind, but modes of the mind insofar as it is united to the body. The mind is not in the right metaphysical state to be the subject of sensory states when separated from the body. Sensations are not a third type of mode in addition to intellectual thoughts, but they are a peculiar kind of sub-species of thought.

In a sense, then, there is after all a similarity with the scholastics: as we saw for Aquinas, for him too a separated soul cannot have sensations, but only intellectual states. For him too something is missing in the metaphysical subject of inherence when the soul is separated from the body. Descartes differs from Aquinas (and others) when he moves a stage of sense perception into the mind; sense perception is not a mode of the body, even the ensouled body, or of the mind–body composite. But he is similar in thinking that sense perception requires that the mind be united to the body to constitute the appropriate metaphysical subject. In its union with the body in the human being, the mind is in a special state that makes it capable of having a certain type of mode, sense perception.

There is a further element of continuity. Descartes defined the mind as a thinking thing and thinking in terms of consciousness so that it includes more than just intellectual activity. This may suggest a broad conception of the essence of the mind. But, as we saw at the end of the previous section, in his principal argument for dualism in Meditation VI, Descartes presents the essence of the mind as intellectual: the argument relies on claims about the essence of the mind, and afterwards he contends that it can be conceived as a whole without sensation and imagination which belong to the mind because they include intellection in their formal concept. So the definition of thought in terms of consciousness is perhaps best seen as a definition that picks out what pertains to the mind without revealing its essence: in Lockean terms, it is a nominal rather than a real definition. So, for Descartes, the mind's essence is intellectual, as was the case for the scholastics.

Transparency

Descartes' definition of thought in terms of consciousness makes clear that he held that we are conscious of all our thoughts. He is also commonly thought to accept transparency of the mental, a strong view of our knowledge of our own minds; our knowledge of what goes on in our own minds is characterized by certainty and immunity to error. But there is good reason to believe that Descartes was not committed to transparency, although this is not a simple matter (see Curley 1978: 170–93; Wilson 1978: 150–65). I will not attempt a full treatment of this issue, but confine myself in this issue to Descartes' treatment of the mental in the context of the use of the skeptical arguments in Meditation II. The issue of transparency raises the question of Descartes' primary purposes, in particular, in the *Meditations*. Interpreters (at least in the English-language literature) have primarily offered two different views on this issue. One view makes the purpose of defeating the skeptic primary (for example, Frankfurt 1970: 174; Curley 1978: 44). On the other view, which has been more prominent in recent decades, Descartes was in the first place concerned with a set of purposes having to do with his dualism and his mechanical conception of the physical world, and the role of the senses; the skeptical argument served a subsidiary role (see Wilson 1978: esp. 1–11; and, for a more recent source, Hatfield 2003: ch. 1).

When we focus on Descartes' attempt to defeat the skeptic, it may seem natural to read him as committing himself to a type of transparency in Meditation II: self-ascriptions of particular thoughts escape the strong skeptical arguments, and so (or because) they are infallible, or incorrigible, or indubitable. I will argue, however, that the escape from skepticism neither relies on nor generates a commitment to transparency. When one focuses on the metaphysics, it is less obviously tempting to attribute such a commitment to Descartes. It is true that sometimes his dualism has been seen as intimately connected to transparency on the ground that what for Descartes distinguishes the mental from the physical is its special epistemic status (Ryle 1960: 13–15; Rorty 1980: 54–9; McDowell 1986). But his principal argument for dualism, which relies on the treatment of the mind in Meditation II, does not appeal to anything like transparency and the extensive literature on the argument reflects this fact (Wilson 1978: 185–201; Shoemaker 1983; Rozemond 1998: ch. 1).

The idea of transparency of the mental comprehends various forms of knowledge, not all of which will be at issue here. I will focus on the possibility of error about occurrent mental states. When we consider the issue of latent mental items, it is easy to see that it is quite implausible that Descartes would be committed to full-fledged transparency: he was an innatist, and clearly thought that we all have various innate ideas of which we are not aware, or whose content we do not know. We all have innate ideas of God, the mind, the nature of body, mathematics. And he thinks that we can be confused about the contents of these ideas. Indeed, part of his undertaking in the *Meditations* is to render these ideas clear and distinct, and this can take a lot of work.

It is useful to distinguish between two types of special knowledge about occurrent mental states that have been attributed to Descartes, although they are not the only ones: (a) when I think I am in a particular mental state, I am in that state. Such judgments are certain. Scholars have used subtly different epistemic notions – infallibility, incorrigibility, indubitability. I will speak of indubitability. (b) The other claim is roughly the converse: when I am in a particular mental state, I cannot fail to know this: I am, one might say, omniscient about my mental states. Descartes' definition of thought in terms of consciousness has been thought to imply this thesis (for criticism of this idea, see Radner 1988: 447, 449). The discussion of the mental in Meditation II raises the question of whether, for Descartes, our self-ascriptions of mental states have special status of type (a), and I will focus on this question.

In Meditation II, Descartes uses the method of doubt to develop his notion of the self, in effect, the mind, in three stages: (1) he knows that he exists, the result of the *cogito*, although not all interpreters think that Descartes relies on the *cogito* here (Broughton 2002: 109–19); (2) he is a thinking thing; (3) thinking includes a wide range of activities that belong to him. And as we saw, at this last stage he focuses on an aspect of sensing about which he thinks this is true.

We can see relatively quickly that the first and second stages of self-exploration do not commit Descartes to transparency. He does sometimes write as if the *cogito* relies on full-blown self-reports, reports that specify the contents of thoughts – I think I am seeing, I think I am walking – (*Principles* I, art. 9, *Fifth Replies*, AT vii, 352). This would seem to imply that we are certain that such specific self-reports must be certain, indubitable, or else they could not serve as the foundation for the certainty of one's own existence. But philosophically speaking all one needs is the generic claim "I think," and on one occasion Descartes himself suggests as much. He rejects the idea that one could infer one's own existence from the observation that one is breathing. One must start with the premise that one thinks that one is breathing:

> For the thought of breathing is present to our mind before the thought of our exist-ing, and we cannot doubt that we have it while we have it. To say: "I am breathing therefore I exist" in this sense, is simply to say "I think, therefore I exist." *If you pay attention, you will find that all the other propositions from which we can thus prove our existence, reduce to this same one* [*reviennent à cela même*] . . . (To Reneri for Pollot, April or May 1638, AT ii, 37–8, emphasis added)

At the next stage in Meditation II, Descartes turns to the question of what he is, and he throws out everything from his old conception of himself to retain only thinking: "I am therefore precisely only [*praecise tantum*] a thinking thing, that is, a mind, intelligence, intellect or reason, words whose significance was previously unknown to me. I am a thing that is real and that really exists; what kind of thing? I have said it: a thinking thing" (AT vii, 27). At this stage, again, little or no transparency could be at stake, since here too Descartes makes a generic claim, the claim that he is certain that he thinks: he is not claiming that he knows what particular mental state(s) he is in.

Up to this point, then, Descartes' argumentation does not rely on or imply transparency. But matters are more complicated at the third stage of self-exploration, the stage where he defends his fuller list of what counts as thought, which includes imagination and sense perception. One might think that, in par-ticular, his discussion of sense perception here commits Descartes to the general indubitability of specific self-reports. I will question this interpretation from four different angles.

(1)   On various occasions in his writings Descartes allows for errors about one's own mental states:

> For experience shows that those who are the most strongly agitated by their passions are not those who know them best, and that the passions are to be numbered among the perceptions which the close alliance of mind and body renders confused and obscure. (*Passions* I. 28)

I thought too that in order to discover what opinions [the most sensible among us] really held I had to attend to what they did rather than what they said. For as a result of our declining morals, few people are willing to say everything that they believe; and besides, many people do not know themselves what they believe, since believing something and knowing that one believes it are different acts of thinking, and the one often occurs without the other. (*Discourse on Method*, AT vi, 23)

What is this wax, which is perceived only by the mind? It is of course the same wax which I see, which I touch, which I imagine, finally it is the same wax which I thought it to be from the start. And yet, and this is what must be pointed out, *the perception I have of it* is a case not of vision or touch or imagination – nor has it ever been, although it seemed to be so before. It is an inspection of the mind alone, which can be imperfect and confused as it was before, or clear and distinct, as it is now, depending on how carefully I attend to what it consists in. (*Meditations*, AT vii, 31, emphasis added)

And when the body was affected by nothing very beneficial or harmful, [the mind] had various sensations corresponding to the diversity of the parts in which and to the ways in which it was affected, namely what we call the sensations of flavors, odors, sounds, heat, cold, light, colors and the like, which do not represent anything posited outside our thought. And at the same time it perceived also sizes, shapes, motions, and such. These were exhibited to it not as sensations, but as certain things, or modes of things existing outside our thought, or as at least capable of so existing, even if it did not yet notice this difference between them. And next, when the mechanism of the body which is so constructed by nature that it can move in various ways by its own power, twisting around heedlessly seeking what is beneficial or fleeing what is harmful, the mind attached to it began to notice that what it thus sought or fled is outside it. And it attributed to it not only sizes, shapes, motions and the like, which it perceived as things or modes of things, but also flavors, odors and such, of which it noticed that sensation was produced in itself by that very thing [*ab ipso*]. (*Principles* I, art. 71)

The first two quotes contain commonsensical comments about our capacity for errors about our passions and beliefs. In a more theoretical vein, in the third quote Descartes argues that we all make mistakes starting in childhood about whether what we now call primary and secondary qualities are presented to us in our minds in the same way. But perhaps particularly relevant is the wax passage, which occurs in Meditation II itself.

Descartes gradually reveals a clear and distinct perception of the wax. He takes a piece of wax and brings it closer to the fire. Initially, he describes it in terms of the qualities we attribute to it on the basis of sense perception, such as its (current) scent, color, shape, size. Then he brings it closer to the fire, and notes that these qualities change: "it loses its residual flavor, its smell disappears, its color changes, its shape is lost, its size increases, it becomes liquid, warm, it can hardly be touched, and when you strike it, it no longer emits any sound" (AT vii, 30). Yet he thinks it is still the same piece of wax. Some perception of it other than the sensory one must underlie that judgment. After eliminating the possibility that it was the imagination that provided this perception, Descartes concludes that it is an intellectual perception of the wax as extended, flexible, and changeable that made us judge that it was numerically the same through its change in appearance. And this is not a case of revealing an idea that was merely latent until it has been clarified. From the beginning, we had a certain conception of the wax *that we relied on* to identify it as the same through its changes in appearance, even though we were initially confused about its content and about what faculty was its source.

Descartes' more theoretical remarks in the *Principles* and in the wax passage strike me as the more relevant ones. For, whether or not sometimes Descartes may look like he believes in transparency, the more interesting question is whether his philosophical system and argumentation involve real dependence on and commitment to transparency. Given his denial of transparency elsewhere in his writings, we may now ask ourselves whether his treatment of sense perception in the third stage of self-exploration in Meditation II commits him to indubitability of our self-reports.

(2)   Let us first turn to the metaphysical purposes Descartes has in mind. In this third stage of self-exploration he is preparing the way for his mind–body dualism, but he is focused on what exactly is included in the mental rather than on the claim that the mind is distinct from the body. And he is developing a conception of the mind different from the Aristotelian scholastic one, by including sense perception, or rather, an aspect of sense perception: full-blown sense perception also contains a bodily component. So he is trying to isolate that aspect of sense perception. Now does doing so require or imply transparency? I do not think so.

To begin with, the doubts in Meditation II that Descartes reiterates are doubts about body. Already at the end of Meditation I, that is his focus (AT vii, 22–5). And to assign sense perception proper to the mind, it is enough if doubts about body do not generate doubts about sensing proper. That much is sufficient to generate the conceptual distinction and independence between the mental and the physical. This conceptual separation is important for Descartes' principal argument for dualism (although how he uses the distinction is a complex matter): in Meditation VI he arrives at dualism on the ground that he has a clear and distinct idea of himself as a thinking, unextended thing, and of body as an extended thing that does not think (AT vii, 78). And it underlies Descartes' view that sense perceptions are modes of the mind and not of the body. In the technical terminology of the *Principles*, a mode presupposes – ontologically and epistemologically – the attribute of the substance it pertains to (*Principles* I. arts 53, 61), and so this part of Meditation II supports the idea that (an aspect of) sense perception belongs to the mind, rather than the body. It is enough for these purposes if I am certain that I have some sort of sensation while doubting the existence of body. I may be unclear or mistaken about what exactly it is I am sensing, but what matters is that I seem to sense something. This leaves open the possibility that I can doubt whether what I seem to feel is an itch or a pain. There is a sense in which there is no appearance–reality distinction: when I have a particular sensation, I am directly conscious of it. But I may have trouble analyzing, labeling, making a judgment about my mental state. If I think you are putting a knife to my throat, I may mistake a sensation of cold for the pain caused by a cut.

This point may help address the following objection. In the argument under discussion, Descartes claims that he is certain that he seems to sense something, but in the wax passage he suggests that we can be mistaken about what faculty is responsible for a particular perception. This point raises the whole question of just what sorts of errors Descartes does and does not envision we can make about our thoughts. I cannot offer a full treatment of that question here; my current focus is on the question of what emerges from the use of the doubt in Meditation II. When Descartes carves out the mental aspect of sensation he is only focused on arguing that doubts about body do not generate doubts about my seeming to sense. The discussion in the wax passage, on the other hand, implies a possibility of error about our mental states that has nothing to do with doubts about body.

This approach may well leave one with the following worry: if Descartes only applies the doubts to the existence of body, is he not limiting the force of his own skeptical arguments in an illegitimate fashion? Perhaps so, but it does not follow that we should understand his line of reasoning as implying transparency after all. This objection amounts to a philosophical criticism of Descartes' use of the skeptical arguments, but it leaves standing the claim that his use of these arguments here does not imply transparency.

(3)   Before further addressing this last point, it is important to consider the examples of sense perception Descartes uses: seeing light, hearing sound, feeling heat. These examples correspond to what in the Aristotelian tradition were known as proper sensibles. A proper sensible is an object of sense that is perceived by only one sensory faculty: light or color by sight, sound by hearing, heat by touch. Aristotle had claimed that the senses do not err about their proper sensibles but they do err about so-called accidental sensibles. In the Latin translation of Moerbeke, which Aquinas used (see Aquinas 1948), the relevant passage reads: "[E]ach sense judges about its proper sensibles, and is not deceived; sight is not deceived that there is color, hearing that there is a sound. But they can be deceived about what is colored or where it is, or what makes the sound (Aristotle, *De anima*, II. 6 15–17). This view can also be found among the Aristotelian scholastics. In his commentary on Aristotle's *De anima*, Aquinas writes that each of the external senses "judges about its proper sensibles and is not deceived about them; thus sight is not deceived that there is such a color [*quod sit talis color*], nor is hearing deceived about sound" (Aquinas 1948: n. 384). In the *Summa*, he offers more detail and introduces a caveat. He writes that the senses are never deceived about the proper sensibles except "*per accidens*": "from the impediment of an organ as when the taste of a person with a fever judges that sweet things are bitter because the tongue is full of bad humors" (Aquinas 1964: I. 85. 6).

In his *De anima*, Francisco Suárez acknowledges the possibility of mistakes in specific judgments about proper sensibles: thus we can be mistaken in thinking we see a particular color. But he is optimistic about generic claims: "A sensory power cannot be mistaken about its own proper adequate sensible [*circa sensibile proprium adaequatum*]; so sight cannot be mistaken when it judges that something is colored, nor hearing when it judges that there is a sound" (Suárez 1856: III. X. 2; see also Aquinas 1964: I. 85. 6). So sight cannot be mistaken about sensing color, but it can be mistaken about what particular color is present. In addition, Suárez readily agrees with Aristotle that the senses can make mistakes about so-called accidental sensibles: the things that have colors, make sound.

Now it is hard to imagine that Descartes did not choose his examples – seeing light, hearing sound, feeling heat – deliberately, given that they are instances of proper sensibles. The examples vary in how specific they are: sensing heat is more specific than hearing noise [*strepitum*], although perhaps Descartes had in mind sensing temperature. And he speaks of seeing light, whereas the Aristotelians tended to focus on color in their discussion of sense perceptions that cannot be mistaken. But this difference may be explained as follows. Another relevant notion in this context was the notion of the adequate object of a sensory power, the object that the sensory power is suitable to know. And the Aristotelians asked themselves what is the adequate object of sight: light or color (Suárez 1856: III. XVI. 1)? Suárez opts for light, offering a complex discussion about the nature of the relationship between light and color (Suárez 1856: III. XVI. 6). And in favor of the certainty of sensory judgments about proper sensibles, he cites the argument that a sensory power cannot be wrong about its *adequate* object. So in light of this consideration (certain kinds of) judgments about either color or light would seem to be immune to error.

So it seems significant that Descartes does not suggest that you can be certain that, say, you seem to see a red garment or seem to hear the sound of the crackling fire. I imagine what he had in mind was this: you might think that you cannot be mistaken in thinking that you see light etc., the most certain type of sensory judgments as an Aristotelian would have it. But what if you are dreaming or some very powerful being makes you believe in a physical world that does not exist? This suggests instead that all you might be incapable of making a mistake about is that you *seem* to be seeing light, hearing noise, and feeling heat.

This approach offers a very different perspective on what Descartes is up to from the usual kind of perspective. The usual perspective holds that he is striking for holding a strong *positive* view about the level of certainty of a particular type of knowledge, our knowledge about our own mental states. But we can now see that Descartes' retreat from certainty that "I see light, hear noise, feel heat" to "I seem to see, hear, become warm" means that in relation to the Aristotelian background he is *limiting* the range of certainty. Furthermore, we cannot assume that Descartes would be willing to generalize from the certainty of our judgments about perceptions of proper sensibles, which from the point of view of the

Aristotelian tradition were privileged, to certainty for all claims about what we seem to sense (or otherwise think or experience). Indeed, his allowance for error about our mental states in other contexts suggests not.

(4) Finally, how should we understand Descartes' discussion of self-reports in Meditation II in light of his aim to respond to skepticism? This question requires us to consider why for him the self-reports escape the doubt. On one possible view, defended recently by Janet Broughton (2002: 131–43), Descartes concludes that our self-reports are indubitable on the ground that they are conditions for the possibility of doubt. So reflection on the doubt reveals that using it presupposes that we can ascribe various thoughts to ourselves: the very skeptical scenarios, the dream scenario, the deceiver hypothesis require this.

Now it seems true that in order to make sense of the doubts of Meditation I, I must assume self-reports. The coherence of the skeptical scenarios – the possibility that I am dreaming or that a demon deceives me – requires that I seem to have sensory experiences. But does it now follow that the details of such self-reports, the details of what exactly we seem to sense, cannot be subject to error or doubt? I do not see why this should be so. And so, on this approach, only quite a narrow range of self-reports emerges as indubitable, and a rather weak version of transparency emerges, a version so weak that it seems to me that not enough is left to warrant the label "transparency."

On another approach, the certainty of one's self-reports emerges in a different way: Descartes simply finds that it is impossible to make mistakes about them and that is why they escape the skeptical doubt (Wilson 1978: 152; Rorty 1980: 54–9). But his claims elsewhere to the effect that we do make mistakes about our thoughts suggest otherwise: the possibility of such mistakes suggests that our self-reports are dubitable (especially since in Meditation I he had suggested that we doubt our mathematical judgments on the ground that we make mistakes in them). What should we make of all this?

At this point, I propose that we ask ourselves the following question: we may be inclined to approach Descartes either assuming that he was committed to some version of transparency about the mental or asking the question of whether he was. But was this question on Descartes' mind? Furthermore, one way to take his treatment of self-reports in Meditation II is that he applies the skeptical doubts to them and thinks they are immune to the doubts. But another way to look at the matter is that Descartes simply does not give "the Deceiver Hypothesis the full force that seems, logically, to be implicit in it" (Wilson 1978: 152). And I think this approach makes it easier to make sense of his various comments on errors about the mental. As we saw before, in Meditation II Descartes' focus is on the doubts about body, and I suggest that he did not really apply the doubts to self-reports; he did not seriously consider the possibility of deception about them by the deceiver. We may see this as a philosophical shortcoming. But here it is relevant again that from an Aristotelian point of view he has already enlarged the realm of doubt quite far by narrowing the scope of certainty with respect to sensory judgments from judgments that we perceive proper sensibles to judgments to the effect that we seem to perceive them.

This suggestion brings us back to the question of what Descartes' focus was: a preoccupation with skepticism and certainty or with other metaphysical and epistemological purposes, such as his campaign against the senses, a defense of his dualism and his conception of the physical world? The latter perspective fits more comfortably with the suggestion that he failed to give the skeptical arguments their full force. This failure is more understandable if he engages with skepticism primarily not for its own sake, but in view of other purposes. His discussion of the range of operations that he wishes to include under the category of thought in Meditation II is surely aimed at developing his dualism and from the perspective I am proposing this is his primary aim rather than the refutation of skepticism.

Let us take stock of the results of our discussion. There are several reasons for doubting that Descartes is committing himself to indubitability for our judgments about our mental states in the third stage of self-exploration in Meditation II. First, elsewhere he allows for mistakes in such judgments. Furthermore, Descartes is focused on the idea that such claims are unaffected by the doubts about body, which point is important for his dualism. But this does not mean that they are utterly certain and indubitable. In addition, he limits his claims of certainty here to a narrow range of examples. Finally, even his concerns with skepticism do not clearly commit him to transparency, and I have suggested that in fact he did not really apply the skeptical arguments to self-reports.

So what was his view about one's knowledge of one's own mind? I cannot fully address this question here. But if it is true that he did not really apply the skeptical arguments to self-reports, we should examine this question outside of a discussion of his treatment of skepticism.

Conclusion

There is ample reason to think that Descartes did not see transparency as the mark of the mental; he did not develop his novel conception of the mind by assigning to it all those types of human functions to which transparency applies. We might then ask why Descartes offered his particular conception of the mental. In order to answer this question we need to turn to his well-known preoccupation with mechanistic science. Doing so does not yield an explicit argument from Descartes for his particular conception of the mental, but it does explain from within his system why he adopted this conception.

Descartes developed a conception of the physical world as purely mechanical in nature, thus making it safe for his view that all physical phenomena can be explained mechanistically. He eliminated other types of entities from the physical world, arguing that they involve a projection of the mental onto the physical. Thus he eliminated Aristotelian substantial forms (claiming that the human soul is the only one: AT iii, 503, 505) and real qualities from the physical world, and cleared out secondary qualities, which he called sensible qualities. The latter category is particularly relevant for our purposes: qualities like color, flavor, smell, sound, hot, cold. The true story about these, for Descartes, is that configurations of mechanical qualities in bodies produce the sensations as of these qualities in our minds. The common-sense view, which the Aristotelians shared, that these qualities as we perceive them really exist in the physical world is the result of the projection of sensations onto the physical world. As we saw him saying above at *Principles* I, art. 71, we wrongly assimilate our sensation of such qualities to our perceptions of mechanical qualities, and thus erroneously think they pertain to physical objects. In the *Meditations* he cures the problem as follows. When he argues in Meditation VI that the physical world does exist, he only concludes that it exists insofar as it has mechanical qualities, types of qualities we perceive clearly and distinctly. Sensible qualities we only perceive obscurely and confusedly, he argues in Meditation III (AT vii, 43–4), and he refuses to attribute them to bodies (AT vii, 80–3). They are left with the status of sensations.

But now it is important that sensations pertain to the mind, rather than the body. For consider, for contrast, the Aristotelian view: on that view, in sensation so-called species, likenesses, of sensible qualities occur in the ensouled body. When I see a red vase, its redness transmits to the sensing subject a likeness of itself, which is a special form of existence of redness. Such species come to exist in the sense organs, and they are non-mechanical. Descartes' mechanistic conception of the human body leaves no room for such entities. But we do have the experience as of something red, or the smell of roses, or the taste of wine. And we have what Descartes calls internal sensations, sensations of what occurs in our own body: pains and tickles, hunger and thirst. They all wind up in the mind without, in his words, resembling what occurs in the physical world (Meditation VI, AT vii, 83, and *The World* ch.1). In this way, his conception of the mind as including sensations (as well as other non-intellectual states) contributes to the purely mechanical conception of the physical world, including the human body.

In sum, Descartes' peculiar brand of dualism, his peculiar way of drawing the boundary between the mental and the physical, which underlies the modern conception of the mind, derives from a commitment to mechanical philosophy rather than from an interest in transparency.

5

The Doctrine of Substance

Jorge Secada

The notion of substance lies at the core of Descartes' metaphysics. Substances, ultimate bearers of properties, are the most basic constituents of Cartesian reality. If we were to have asked Descartes "What is there, ultimately and most fundamentally?," he would have answered: "Substances and their properties." In this, he belonged to a tradition which went back to Aristotle and which had been richly developed by Descartes' immediate predecessors and most significant philosophical influences, the sixteenth-century Jesuit late scholastics who themselves took off from Aquinas as he had been expounded and built upon since the thirteenth century. Descartes, however, was to rework the notion, driven by his radical and proclaimed intellectualist essentialism.

All the same, the term "substance" does not figure prominently in the text of the *Meditations*. It makes its first appearance in the earlier half of Meditation III (AT vii, 43), followed a few pages later by a terse and obscure account of the notion and of the meditator's knowledge of it. It reappears toward the middle of the last Meditation (AT vii, 78), but not enough is added then to provide a clear understanding of its meaning. Still, its importance is apparent from the fact that the notion is discussed in the *Replies* to the *Objections* which Descartes wished to publish together with the *Meditations*, and also briefly in the short Synopsis preceding it.

Substance is first mentioned in the *Meditations* in the course of a discussion of the claim that some ideas "have more . . . reality in them" than others: ideas of substances "amount to something more" than those of modes or accidents, and an idea of an infinite being to more than those of finite substances (AT vii, 40). The next appearance of the notion is particularly perplexing. Substance is listed as one of the few things the meditator perceives "clearly and distinctly" in his ideas of corporeal things (AT vii, 43). Given the only previous use of the term, one wonders what justifies this claim. There is a complex story to tell here, which is relevant to our purposes and indispensable when trying to understand the *Meditations*, but which can only be sketched in this chapter.

When making the claim, the meditator is already in possession of the essential tool for philosophical understanding: a clear and distinct intellectual gaze, unclouded by sensory perception. This has been attained in the previous two Meditations. After the skeptical crisis at the end of Meditation I, designed to shake the complacent, sensorially possessed mind into the state of intense epistemic anguish and self-reflection from which Meditation II begins, the meditator is led to focus on her intellect and its contents, her intellectual powers are honed, and she overcomes her natural trust in the senses, which, though an epistemic obstacle, has been reinforced through schooling. This indeed is the point of Meditation II, which should not be read as a reply to the skeptical doubts of Meditation I. That comes only in Meditation III (see AT vii, 36). Meditation II is instead designed to provide the meditator with the necessary intellectual tools so that she can establish solid metaphysical foundations. Failure to grasp this point can support misunderstanding of Descartes' thoughts on substance (as in Markie 1994: 80 and 81 n.21).

In this process the meditator will intellectually perceive her own existing essence, a substance, and within it she will discover a world of essences or possible substances. So, by Meditation III, the meditator has come across a substance, her own self, and she has perceived it clearly and distinctly with the pure intellect, as is necessary for firm understanding and knowledge. Furthermore, the reflection on the piece of wax in Meditation II is overtly introduced as one more step in securing intellectual powers and curbing sensation, even when dealing with individual bodies around us; but, as has been pointed out, this epistemic and heuristic reflection has metaphysical import: it reveals not just how we know material things, it also tells us something about how things are in reality (see, for example, Williams 1978: 221–2). At the end of the reflection on the wax, the meditator has a clear and distinct perception of a possible body or corporeal substance.

This is one strand of the story behind the listing of "substance" amongst the notions the meditator perceives clearly and distinctly in Meditation III. The other strand has to do with the baggage the meditator brings with her to the meditational exercise. As we mentioned, the notion of substance was a central piece of the Aristotelian philosophy the meditator would have learnt at the schools of the time. Indeed, in order to understand Descartes' thinking on substance, we will need to acquire some knowledge of the scholastic doctrine. When the meditator claims to perceive substance clearly and distinctly, he is alluding to a notion acquired during his (scholastic) philosophical and metaphysical schooling, and then re-examined, transformed, and reformulated with the use of his intellectual powers, in particular, in Meditation II when perceiving his own nature and existence, and when examining the origin of his knowledge of material things.

What is this notion? Let us start by becoming clearer about what it is that we are looking for. What must a doctrine of substance do? First, of course, it must tell us what it is to be a substance. Substances are said to be bearers of properties, so we are seeking an account of what it is to be a property, and be "had" by a substance, and what it is to be a subject of properties or substance, and to "have" properties. Second, since substances are said to be ultimate bearers of properties, a doctrine of substance must provide an account of this ultimacy. Further, on the basis of these accounts of inherence and ultimacy, it should tell us in what sense substances are the basic constituents of reality, independent one from the other. Third, a doctrine of substance must tell us what constitutes the individuality of substance, what makes something numerically one substance; and also what constitutes the identity of a substance in time, what it is for the same substance to change and what for a substance to be destroyed and to be generated. Finally, we must be offered an account of what it is to be this or that kind of substance. That is, we seek an account of the *what it is* of a substance, some account of its nature or essence, of the unity which substance brings to all its properties, of the scope of its possible change and development.

Clearly, these various requirements are not unrelated, and their satisfaction should form a coherent and interdependent whole. We will find that for Descartes the independence of one substance from another is related to the simplicity of substantial natures, which is at the core of his understanding of substance as subject of properties, and of its intrinsic oneness and sameness. These are general requirements for any theory of substance. There are also special requirements that a Cartesian theory of substance must satisfy, which originate in Descartes' own philosophical outlook, and to which we will attend shortly.

Let us now turn to what we are told about substance in the *Meditations*. Substance is placed with extension, shape, position, motion, duration, and number, as what is perceived clearly and distinctly in the ideas of material things. It is contrasted with properly sensorial qualities or materially false ideas. The contrast hinges on the claim that the latter are obscure and confused so that whether they are ideas of real things or not, and what their true causes are, remain unknown. What initially marks substance in this passage is that it is known intellectually and independently of the senses. The meditator then reflects on the fact that she "could have borrowed [the clear and distinct perception of substance] from [her] idea of [herself]" (AT vii, 44). She offers an example: though she conceives a stone as extended and unthinking and herself as thinking and unextended, "so that the two conceptions differ enormously," both a stone and she herself fall under the term "substance." In the course of this example, the meditator offers a general characterization: substance is "a thing capable of existing by itself [*per se, de soi*]" (AT vii, 44; ixA, 35). Shortly after, she introduces the phrase "modes of a substance," and applies it to corporeal properties like "extension, shape, position, and movement" (AT vii, 45: the phrase "modes of thought [*cogitandi modos*]" is used in AT vii, 34). In the French translation these modes are compared to "garments under which the corporeal substance appears to us" (AT ixA, 35: also see AT vii, 30 and compare with AT ixA, 24 where *ces formes* translates *modis istis*). These corporeal modes, the meditator reflects, "are not contained in [her] formally, since

[she] is nothing but a thinking thing" (AT vii, 45; "formally" means "actually" or "literally").

A substance, then, is something which can exist on its own or by itself; it can be thinking or extended, like myself or the meditator, or a stone or a piece of wax; and it has modes in it, properties which are related conceptually to the kind of substance it is. An unextended, thinking substance cannot formally or actually have size or motion, properties which can belong to a corporeal or extended substance.

One last important claim made in these pages is that God is an infinite or absolutely perfect substance. The text does not make clear whether this infinite substance is a substance in the same sense in which a stone or you are substances: "though the idea of substance is in me since indeed I am a substance myself, I would not however have the idea of an infinite substance, I who am a finite thing, if it had not been placed in me by some substance which was truly infinite" (AT vii, 45). The passage leaves undecided whether what the meditator would lack is merely the idea of infinity, or whether, in lacking that idea, she would also be deprived of the idea of a *substance* which is infinite.

The features used to describe God, "infinite, independent, supremely intelligent, supremely powerful" and creator of all else that exists, are not said to be "modes." Instead, the meditator refers to these as "perfections" (for example, AT vii, 46, 50). Of course, since the term "substance" is applied to God and to the meditator and a stone, there must be some pertinent relation between all of these, though the similarities and differences between a stone and myself, on the one hand, and God, on the other, might not be the same as those between myself and a stone, all taken strictly as substances. As we shall see, Descartes addresses this very issue in *Principles of Philosophy*, the textbook which he hoped would replace those of the Aristotelians.

Some of these ideas reappear in Meditation VI. There the meditator uses the claim "that I have a clear and distinct idea of myself, in so far as I am only a thinking, non-extended thing; and . . . I have a distinct idea of body, in so far as this is only an extended, non-thinking thing" to draw the conclusion that "I am really distinct from my body, and can exist without it" (AT vii, 78). Earlier in the paragraph he had explained that, in general, "that I can clearly and distinctly understand one thing apart from another is enough to make me certain that the two things are distinct." The suggestion is that two different substances, things which exist by themselves and apart from each other, can be conceived clearly and distinctly entirely independently one from the other; and vice versa.

In the course of this paragraph, the meditator appears to move from a clear and distinct understanding of herself as just a thinking, non-extended thing or substance to the claim that "absolutely nothing else belongs to [her] nature or essence except that [she] is a thinking thing." In the next paragraph, the term "inhere [*inesse*]" is used to refer to the relation between, on the one hand, modes and faculties, and, on the other, the thing or "substance" of which they are modes or faculties (AT vii, 78–9; ixA, 62; the French text uses the term "*attachées*" for the Latin "*insint*," making a perhaps unconscious reference to the scholastic treatment of this matter; see below). The meditator identifies the thinking thing which she is with an "intellectual substance" (AT vii, 78). And she states that the "distinction between the modes of a thing and the thing itself" corresponds to the distinction between what cannot be understood without a thing in which to be, and what can be understood whole (*totum*; *tout entier*) on its own (AT vii, 78; ixA, 62). While one can understand an intellectual substance or mind, actual thought, as a whole existing on its own without supposing it has faculties of sensation or imagination (or, one might add, any one particular act or any faculties beyond intellect or thought), the "formal concept" or essential definition of sensation or imagination (or of any mental act or faculty) includes reference to intellection, and so to an intellectual substance. This point is intended generally and it is immediately applied to the "faculties . . . of changing places, taking various shapes, and the like" in relation to the "corporeal or extended substance" in which they must "inhere," since "extension is contained in their clear and distinct conception" (AT vii, 78–9).

As we mentioned, there are special requirements which a Cartesian theory of substance must satisfy, which originate in Descartes' own philosophical outlook, and which we can appreciate at work in these passages from the *Meditations*. The meditator is enjoined to abandon the senses, feign that all they deliver is false and unreal, and trust only in the intellect and its clear and distinct perception. This, of course, imposes significant constraints on a doctrine of substance. For instance, it eliminates from the start the account of some modern empiricists, who take substance to be a congeries of properly sensorial qualities (see Secada 2000a, b). Also, Descartes must provide an account of how it is that one grasps individuals purely intellectually. This is not a problem for Aristotle's scholastic followers, nor for modern empiricists, but it is a problem for Descartes. As we have seen, the meditator claims to perceive particular substances and to establish the distinction between two numerically different substances with the use of the intellect alone. And it is an upshot of the reflection on the wax that we can perceive things like a piece of wax or the paper on which this is printed exclusively with the intellect.

In the course of clarifying the *Meditations* to his contemporaries, Descartes adopted an essentialist doctrine: he wrote that if one knows that a substance exists, one must also know its essence or nature. Furthermore, in Meditations V and VI he made clear that, at least in some cases, one may know the essence or nature of a substance without knowing whether it exists (see AT vii, 63 and 71; on knowledge of the essence and existence of God, AT iii, 273; on knowledge of one's own essence and existence, AT vii, 359; and generally on knowledge of the essence and existence of any entity, AT vii, 107–8). The roots of essentialism can be traced back to claims made in Plato's *Meno* which Aristotle criticized in his *Posterior Analytics* (see *Meno* 80d–81e in Plato 1997: 879–80; *Posterior Analytics* I, 1 in

Aristotle 1984: vol. 1, 114–15). Descartes is reformulating the Platonic doctrine in opposition to the existentialism of the scholastic Aristotelians. Essentialism stands in opposition to existentialism. Essentialism (existentialism) is the doctrine, first, that one cannot know the existence (essence) of any substance without knowing its essence (existence), and, second, that one can know the essence (existence) of some substance without knowing its existence (essence). The order in question is logical. The essentialist affirms what the existentialist denies, that knowledge of existence entails knowledge of essence; and he denies what the existentialist affirms, that knowledge of essence entails knowledge of existence (see Secada 2000c: 1–26).

There can be no doubt that Descartes espoused universal essentialism, and that he considered it an important doctrine. It is also clear that the doctrine is of considerable historical and metaphysical significance, and that it imposes further requirements on the doctrine of substance, which must cohere with it. It is most important to attend to these Cartesian requirements, particularly given certain contemporary tendencies toward the elimination of real essences and their substitution by nominal definitions, and toward subjective metaphysical doctrines and foundations, tendencies which Descartes did contribute to bring about, but which he himself did not fully embody. Indeed, there is here a most fertile ground for historical and philosophical work. So, what are we to make of the texts from the *Meditations* in light of these Cartesian peculiarities and of the general requirements that any doctrine of substance must satisfy?

First, we should note the striking similarities and differences between some of these passages and claims found in the works of Descartes' scholastic predecessors. Before we can proceed, then, we will need to discharge our earlier promise and review the scholastic doctrine of substance. There were many variations, of minor and major detail, in the accounts of these matters offered by nominalist, Scotist, Thomist, and diversely eclectic Aristotelian scholastics, but fortunately it will suffice for our purposes to sketch a general common outline, designed to serve as background to what we find in the *Meditations*. Our source will be Francisco Suárez, the great Aristotelian thinker whom Descartes used to confirm standard philosophical usage (see AT vii, 235). We will find that by using Suárez much light is shed on the Cartesian texts.

Coming after a long tradition of development and discussion of the Aristotelian notion, Suárez wrote that substance in its proper and general sense is that which exists "in itself and by itself [*in se ac per se*]" (Suárez 1960–6: XXXIII, 1, 1). He made clear that "by itself [*per se*]" is opposed to "in another [*in alio*]" (ibid., XXXI, 5, 9), and used that phrase (instead of just *in se*) to underscore the difference between substance as what is in and by itself, and substance as subject of accidents or properties. He maintained that though God and creatures are both in and by themselves, God is not a subject of accidents as some creatures are (ibid., XXXIII, 1, 2). Suárez distinguished being "*per se*" (by itself), which he bundled together with being "*in se*" (in itself), from being "*a se*" (by its own agency).

Before exploring the notion of substance, he provided an account of the division of being into "*a se*" and "*ab alio*" (or "*ex se*" and "*ex alio*"), which he took to be equivalent to "infinite" and "finite," "uncreated" and "created," "necessary" and "contingent," "pure act" and "potential," and "essential" and "by participation" (ibid., XXVIII, 1, 3–17). He separated this conceptual mapping, which articulates the distinction between God and creatures, from that which divides being into "*per se ac in se*" and "*in alio*" and which properly does not distinguish God from creatures but rather substances, whether divine or created, from created accidents. According to Suárez, the term "substance" is said analogically of God and of creatures (ibid., XXXII, 1, 9). But the "analogy" in question appears to amount to univocity. A term properly applied to creatures is then applied to God, when both creatures and God are so intrinsically. So there is a common meaning of the term as it applies to both. The difference between God and creatures is that since there is no composition in God, he is substance absolutely and essentially, while they are substances merely "aptitudinally" (*aptitudine*; ibid., XXXII, 1, 7; see also, XXXIV, 4, 27). What does this mean?

Suárez explained that being in or by itself and being in another are "modes" that determine the existence of an entity (ibid., XXXIV, 4, 23–7). Existence, considered strictly as such, "is indifferent to the mode of existing sustained by another and to the mode of existing by itself without depending on another as sustainer" (ibid., XXXIV, 4, 23). So if a created entity which is a substance were considered without such mode, it would be considered merely as an existing entity capable of being a substance and existing in and by itself without actually being so. But God cannot be considered except as being in and by himself; he necessarily must exist in that way. Creatures depend on God for the composition of their existence and its determining mode, so they can be considered independently of such mode, and then they are seen as merely having the aptitude or inclination to be completed by it (ibid., XXX, 4, 3–7; XXXIV, 4, 1–41) Nonetheless, since creatures can be substances intrinsically, they can be defined as such without reference to God (ibid., XXVIII, 3, 15). Indeed, the notion of substance, and any other notion with which we can know God, originates in our knowledge of creatures.

Created substances, unlike divine substance, are subjects of accidents. Like other Aristotelians, Suárez espoused hylomorphism (ibid., XXXVI, 1, 1). He analyzed created, non-spiritual substances into matter, substantial form, accidents, and modes. These variously dependent entities all come together into the congeries which is an individual material thing. All creatures have a capacity for change and not-being: they are a mixture of potency and act. Only God is pure act, necessary and eternal, not in potency to be anything other than what he is. Prime or pure matter is the first subject of change, and a principle of created potency. Though in itself it is only potency, merely a capacity to be something or other, it possesses a certain real entity, so as to be able to receive a substantial form and to be the underlying subject of the generation and corruption of substances (see ibid., XIII, §§1, 4–9). But, Suárez explains, since this "substantial change is hidden and cannot be sensed by itself," we humans know prime matter only by "analogy" with subjects of other mutations (ibid., XIII, 6, 3). And our concept of prime matter "is . . . not entirely distinct and as it is in itself, but partly negative and partly obscure" (ibid., XIII, 6, 4).

Substantial form actualizes matter into a substance, whose existence as substance is, for Suárez, determined by a further entity, the mode of being in and by itself (ibid., XV, §§1, 4–7, 9). Substantial form accounts for the essence or nature, the *what it is*, of a substance. It constitutes a unity with its matter, and when that unity is broken, the substance is destroyed and the substantial form perishes. The exception is the human soul, which, though it is the substantial form of the living human body and is incomplete without it, can exist separated from it. In this sense, the human substantial form or soul is a quasi-substance (see ibid., XXXIV, 5, 5–52). An accident is a dependent entity with an "aptitude or propensity for inhering" or existing in a subject, and actually inhering in one when its existence is determined by the mode of being in another (ibid., XXXIV, 4, 24; see also XXXVII, 2, 8–9). Modes, however, do "essentially include not just the aptitude but also the actual affection of or conjunction with the thing of which they are modes" (ibid., XXXVII, 2, 10).

There are further distinctions that can be drawn here as the analysis of created material substance is completed, but we need not be concerned with these details. The main picture on which I want to focus is already drawn. Material substances are congeries of diverse entities, some of which are, in certain ways, separable from each other. Knowledge of these diverse entities and of their peculiar interdependence relies on the senses, though in some cases an appeal to revealed, theological fact may be necessary in order to make certain conceptual points and distinctions perspicuous (see, for example, ibid., XXXIV, 1, 1 and 8; 2, 5–7, 9–15; 3, 3–4; 4, 22 and 23).

Some Aristotelians adopted universal hylomorphism, asserting that all creatures are material, and that this accounts for their capacity for change and their contingency (see ibid., XIII, 15, *passim*). They argued that matter grounded the individuality of creatures and, more importantly, that if they lacked matter, creatures would be pure acts and therefore not creatures. Others, however, held that there are spiritual substances which, though not material, are not pure acts nor necessary, unchanging beings (see ibid., XXXV, 1–3). Their potency arises from their contingent nature, and their individuality is accounted for either, as in Aquinas, through specific differences, so no two spiritual substances could be of the same species, or, as in Suárez, through individual differences. Again, the details here are not important for our purposes. Individual substances are known empirically. Substances contain an element of pure potency, prime matter, which cannot be grasped distinctly by the human intellect and which is knowable only sensorially. Their kinds and natures are discovered empirically, as is, insofar as it is, the range of accidents they may have. Even our concept of God's substantiality originates in sensation.

Let us return to the passages from the *Meditations*. Descartes' characterization of substance as "what is capable of existing by itself [*rem quae per se apta est exist-ere*]" is reminiscent of Suárez's own definition (AT vii, 44). The difference, however, is significant. To qualify the existence of substances, Descartes uses exclusively the Latin phrase "*per se*," without adding "*in se*." And he does not offer any explication of how this phrase is to be understood. This is unfortunate. The Latin "*per se*" suffers from a similar ambiguity as the English "by itself," pointing at least in two different directions relevant to our present interests: by itself in the sense of being on its own, and by itself in the sense of by its own agency. The French "*de soi*" is also equivocal (see Dubois et al. 1992). Reference to the dependence of creatures on God suggests the second sense, while contrasting substance with inhering modes suggests the first. In the *Meditations*, the conceptual relation between being the subject of properties and being uncaused is not examined.

One feature of Descartes' treatment of substance in these passages of the *Meditations* on which we have already remarked is his requirement that we turn away from the senses when seeking clear and distinct understanding. Indeed, Descartes' approach to substance is permeated by his intellectualist essentialism, and this constitutes another major divergence from his Aristotelian predecessors, who all espoused forms of empiricist existentialism. He maintains that the essence of a substance is known purely intellectually, and that one can know possible substances, and know them in their individuality, purely intellectually. He holds that the non-sensorial conception of a possible and separately existing whole, an independent entity, is the conception of a possible substance, and that from such conception one can obtain knowledge of the essence or nature of such substance.

Also notable is Descartes' use of "mode" to refer to the inhering properties or accidents of a substance. Even if we set aside the differences between various scholastic authors, it is obvious that here Descartes is departing from scholastic doctrine, while borrowing its concepts. Whenever this is so, we can be sure he knew what he was doing and was, in fact, relying on how the terms would be understood by his scholastic readers. In these cases, the job of commentators is to make clear what is being preserved and what discarded from the scholastic baggage. By using "mode" to refer to the accidents of a substance, Descartes seems to indicate that all accidents are determinations or ways of being of the subjects in which they inhere. The implication is that substance itself is intrinsically determinable, and not just an underlying substratum of added accidental entities. Descartes dispenses with Suarecian accidents whose proper concept need not involve reference to their subject and instead makes all real accidental properties of a substance modes which essentially include such reference.

There is a conceptual connection, graspable purely intellectually, between a Cartesian substance, its essence, and any of its inhering properties or modes. A mode implies a certain essence and an essence implies a unique range of possible modes. Following Suárez, Descartes states that inhering modes cannot be understood apart from their substance on account of the fact that they contain the notion of their subject in their "formal concept" or essential definition (AT vii, 78). We know he did not disregard standard scholastic terminology, and he was certainly cognizant of Suárez's treatment of these matters in the *Metaphysical Disputations*. In fact, the oddity of the claim that all accidents are modes, when placed on the side of scholastic doctrine, is evident: for the Aristotelians, the concept of an accident need not contain the notion of its subject. For them, the properties of being four cubic feet large or of having two legs or of being fast can inhere in substances with different essences or natures, say a human being, a monkey, or an ostrich; not so for Descartes, who would hold that all these properties can only inhere in the same substance, namely, the material universe. This reinforces the suggestion that Cartesian properties stand in a relation of determination to their subject.

A relation which fits the Cartesian treatment of substance, essence, mode, and inherence is the relation between determinates and their determinables. Highest-order determinables (for example, color) and their determinates (for example, red, green, gold, and the various other colors) form independent, tightly structured logical wholes. Highest-order determinables are conceptually independent of any other such determinables, as is the case, for example, between color and taste. Determinables imply the range of their determinates and determinates imply their determinables. If B is a determinable and C_1, C_2, C_3 . . . C_n are its possible determinates, then "A is C_1, or C_2, or C_3 . . . or C_n" follows from "A is B." For example, "A is a triangle, or a square, or a circle, or an ellipse, etc." follows from "A is a plane closed figure." And "A is C_x" (where x ranges over 1, 2, 3 . . . n) entails that "A is B," as "A is a figure" follows from "A is a triangle."

Color, of course, is not a good candidate for Cartesian substantiality, since it is a properly sensorial object which can be clearly and distinctly understood "only as a sensation or thought" and not as a thing "existing outside our mind" (AT viiiA, 33). But there are non-sensorial determinables. Indeed, Descartes suggests that there are two kinds of highest-order determinables which can be grasped purely intellectually, can be clearly and distinctly conceived to exist outside any mind, and which exhaust the whole of the reality which we can know: extension (i.e., size, shape, and movement) and thought (i.e., perception and will). This points in the direction of an ontological reductionist program: all real properties can be analyzed into extension, thought, and their determinates. And an argument to support taking substantial inherence as determination is thereby suggested, for if the program is successful, then it can be claimed that this provides the best metaphysical account of what there is.

Still, these texts in the Third and Sixth Meditations are merely suggestive. To acquire a fuller understanding of Descartes' notion of substance, we have to turn to other of his writings, where we find more extensive discussions. Descartes deals with the notion in the *Replies* to the *Objections* to the *Meditations*, in the *Principles of Philosophy*, and in his letters. To these texts we now turn.

We shall start with the well-known paragraphs on substance in *Principles of Philosophy*, I, §§51–4. Descartes first offers a general characterization of substance as "a thing which exists so that it needs no other thing for its existence." He then provides an explication of his meaning: "we can understand only one substance which needs absolutely no other thing, namely God. Indeed, we perceive that all others cannot exist without the aid of God's concurrence." In order to exist, creatures need to be created by God. Furthermore, they must be conserved by him at all times, so that any activity or state of a creature supposes the concurrence of God. God, of course, exists necessarily without being created or conserved.

Substantial independence is here made out to be a kind of causal autonomy. A gradation in substantiality could be imagined, allowing some creatures to be substances in a secondary sense, insofar as they are causes which depend only on God's causal support. A problem with this suggestion is that it is unclear that, for Descartes, any creature possesses the kind of causal power that God displays in creation and conservation. And it is in any case fairly clear that for him bodies do not possess it, while, as we have seen, he is willing to talk of "extended substance." Moreover, the text itself undermines it.

Descartes continues: "as they say in the Schools, the term 'substance' does not apply to God and [creatures] *univocally*; that is, there is no meaning of the term common to God and creatures which can be distinctly understood." (See the French translation, AT ixB, 47, where the scholastic view is commended: "they are right to say in the School. . . .") He does not, here or anywhere else, indicate that the term is applied analogically. He must, then, be read as stating that it is applied equivocally to God and creatures. Descartes is explicitly invoking scholastic doctrine, that "substance" is not used univocally of God and creatures, but then holding that it is applied equivocally. The informed reader must find this passage to be directly, even if covertly, at odds with Suárez's account. (One interesting consequence of this Cartesian doctrine is that, if we know God at all, we know him directly; see AT vii, 52; see also Marion 1981: 140–59; 1986; and, most importantly, Devillairs 2004).

Descartes' initial explication of the independence of substances in *Principles* is unpromising. The French translation adds two sentences, probably from Descartes' own hand: "but since amongst created things some are of such nature that they cannot exist without some others, we distinguish them from those which do not need anything but the ordinary concourse of God, calling them substances, and those others the qualities or attributes of substances" (AT ixB, 47). The reference to a distinction between substances and attributes or qualities points in the direction of a non-causal dependence. In order to make sense of the demand that there be no common meaning of the term applying to God and creatures, we must take Descartes' substantial independence to be covering two different relations when applied first to God and then to creatures. God is creator and conserver and no creatures are such, while some creatures are subjects of properties in a way God is not. A more implausible reading might insist that the only dependence relation here is causal and that substances and their properties stand as causes to their effects.

Some questions arise at this point. Why did Descartes think it appropriate to use "substance" both of God and of creatures? And why would he, or for that matter anybody, think that causal autonomy grounds the ontological independence of substance (can one not conceive an uncaused but ontologically dependent property?), or even just that causal dependence is incompatible with ontological independence? An answer to the first question is that this was, in fact, how the term was used in the School. And given both Descartes' rejection of metaphysical analogy and the Suarecian account of substance, this answer may help explain the rather forced account Descartes offers, and provide an answer to our second question: substance is what is independent (or exists *per se*); God is absolutely independent, and in particular, as creator and conserver *ex nihilo*, he is independent in a way no creature is, to any degree; as highest-order determinables, creatures are independent in a different way, one which does not apply to God, not of course because he is dependent in this way but because he bears no modes or determinations. Descartes rejects the scholastic doctrine of substance, and with it Suárez's doctrine of the determining modes of creaturely existence. But he does agree with the scholastics that God is not a subject of accidents. So he must find another way of still applying the term "substance" to him. Since, unlike Suárez, Descartes can find no sense of being by itself common to God and creatures, he takes the notion of independence or being by itself in its most general sense, focuses on the causal dependence of creatures on God, and ends up with an account of how the term "substance" applies to both of them only equivocally.

The passage continues unhelpfully repeating the characterization of created substances as "things which need only God's concurrence in order to exist" (AT viiiA, 25; see also AT iii, 429). What we want is an explication of the dependence of properties on their substances, and hence the start of an account of the substantial independence of created substances. Descartes appeals to "the common notion that no attributes, that is to say, no properties or qualities are of nothing." But this does little more than restate that properties "inhere" in substances; it is of no use when seeking to clarify what "inherence" amounts to. Again, an earlier claim that we do not know substances merely on account of their existence, taken by itself, is unhelpful in this context. These pages give the impression that Descartes had certain readers in mind, readers trained in the scholastic philosophy, and that he took for granted that the use of the terminology of the School would make his text comprehensible to them.

The next paragraph adds two significant doctrines regarding the essence of a substance and its relation to its properties. There is only one property that constitutes the essence of a substance, and all "modes" of a substance "are referred" to it (AT viiiA, 25). Shortly after, Descartes explains that the essence of a substance and the substance itself are merely conceptually distinct; that is, they do not designate two different entities, but rather the same one entity considered in two different ways (AT viiiA, 30–1). In this case, the distinction holds between a substance considered as an independent subject of properties, and a substance considered as an intelligible nature which necessarily remains unchanged while its diverse modes or determinations may change.

All these texts, then, appear to point in the direction of the view that Cartesian substances are highest-order determinable natures. This interpretation gets further confirmation from Descartes' reply to Arnauld's objections regarding the criterion for a real distinction between two substances (AT vii, 198–204 and 219–29). Some commentators have found Descartes' reply unsatisfactory, at best obscure (for a recent example, see Almog 2002: 23–4 and 25; and for a corrective, see Secada 2003: 441–5; instructive reconstructions are found in Curley 1978: 193–206 and Wilson 1978: 177–200). But when it is read from the perspective of the doctrine of substance that we have seen emerging from the text of the *Meditations* and the *Principles*, it presents a cogent and definitive reply.

As we have seen, Descartes maintained that a distinction between two substances may be established from the purely intellectual, clear, and distinct conception of each. In the *Meditations*, the distinction between the meditator's mind and body is established from the fact that she can conceive each separately from the other. In Meditation VI, the meditator stresses that substances can be conceived "whole" and by themselves (AT vii, 78). Toward the end of the *First Replies*, Descartes writes that

> I understand completely what a body is when I take it to be only something extended . . . and deny of it anything which belongs to the nature of a mind. Conversely, I understand a mind to be a complete thing . . . even though I deny that it has in it any thing which is contained in the idea of a body. This would be quite impossible if there were not a real distinction between the mind and the body. (AT vii, 121)

These texts invite an obvious objection. In his comments on the *Meditations*, Arnauld forcibly presents it: "how does it follow, from the fact that he is aware of nothing else belonging to his essence, that nothing else does in fact belong to it?" (AT vii, 199). For the argument to proceed, the meditator would have to have an "adequate" concept of the thing in question, one which included all of its properties, but that is impossible (AT vii, 200). Consider a right-angled triangle (AT vii, 201–2). Is it not possible to have a clear and distinct conception of a triangle which has one right angle, while denying that its sides are such that the square of the longest is equal to the sum of the squares of the other two sides?

Nonetheless, the seamless move from "understand completely [*complete intelligo*]" to "understand to be a complete thing [*intelligo esse rem completam*]" indicates that Descartes did not implausibly require that in order to establish a real distinction one's notion of a thing must contain all its real properties, or even just all its necessary real properties. In his replies to Arnauld, Descartes makes exactly this point: he was using "understand completely and understand to be a complete thing with one and the same meaning" (AT vii, 221.) So the crux of Descartes' reply is found in this notion, "to be a complete thing," a thing "endowed with the forms or attributes which suffice to recognize it is a substance" or "an entity in its own right which is different from everything else" (AT vii, 85, 221, 222). Descartes first explains that substances are "things subsisting by themselves [*per se*]." Shortly after, he writes that "it is of the nature of substances that they should mutually exclude each other" (AT vii, 227). So the real distinction hinges on having two separate conceptions, each of which is the conception of a substance, a thing which may exist by itself. Conceptions are separate if whatever is in one can be clearly and distinctly denied of the other.

Descartes' answer to the right-angled triangle example makes exactly these points. First, even if we take a right-angled triangle to be complete thing or substance existing by itself, "it is certain that the property of having the square of the base equal to the squares of the sides is not a substance" (AT vii, 224). But further, one cannot clearly and distinctly conceive each of these terms while denying the other of it. One may clearly and distinctly conceive a right-angled triangle without considering the relations between its sides, but one cannot then deny that a certain relation holds between its sides, which, in fact, does necessarily hold between them, and still maintain that one has a clear and distinct conception of the triangle. On the other hand, while "it is not possible to have a concept of a triangle such that no ratio is understood to hold between [its sides] . . . nothing at all which belongs to the mind is included in the concept of body, nothing at all which belongs to the body is included in the concept of mind" (AT vii, 225).

All the objects we know to exist in reality are either substances or modes of substances, "things, or the affections of things" (AT viiiA, 22). Different substances are separate one from the other and their concepts are mutually exclusive: nothing in the concept of one is contained in the concept of another. Again, the reply to Arnauld suggests that substance is an essence which can be conceived purely intellectually to exist in reality and which has the completeness and independence belonging to highest-order determinables.

Definitive confirmation of the view that Cartesian inherence should be understood as determination is found in an exchange between Descartes and Hobbes in 1641 (see Secada 2000c: 190–3). Responding to earlier assertions by Descartes, Hobbes had asked:

> How does he understand that the determination is in the movement? As in a subject? It is absurd; for movement is an accident. It is just as absurd to say that white is in the color . . . But as absurd as it is to say that the determination is in the movement as an accident is in a subject, still Mr Descartes does not refrain . . . (AT iii, 343; the determination in question is the direction of the movement)

Descartes did not refrain because he saw nothing wrong with treating determinates as properties of the determinable natures which they determine. So he curtly dismissed Hobbes' point:

The Englishman . . . uses a frivolous subtlety when he inquires whether the determination is in the movement as in a subject; as if it were here a matter of knowing
if the movement is a substance or an accident. For there is no problem or absurdity
in saying that an accident is the subject of another accident . . . (AT iii, 354–5)

Descartes did not take Hobbes's "frivolous subtlety" very seriously. So he did not
spell out how he understood substance and the relation between existing subjects
and their real properties. But he defended his claim that "the determination is in
the movement as in a subject" by arguing that "an accident can be the subject of
another accident," and that one commonly predicates one accident of another. It
is clear that whatever the oddity of "the determination is in what is determined"
(or of particular cases like "the circle is in the shape," or "the [direction] is in the
movement" in AT iii, 324), Descartes took "B determines A," when both A and
B exist in reality, to imply that B is in A as a property is in a subject. In addition,
he took "accident B inheres in substance A" to itself imply "B determines A." For
him the direction determines, or inheres in, the movement, as the movement
determines, or inheres in, the body.

Descartes rejected the Aristotelian hylomorphic account of substance. He maintained that substance is an essence subsisting in reality, an entity defined through
an intellectual principle of unity and identity. By conceiving inherence as determination, he was able to understand the relation between a substance and its properties
purely intellectually. The distinct and complete conception of a substance, which
is just the conception of its essence, contains its possible modes or properties. And
the distinct conception of any accident or mode involves the conception of its
substance's nature. Cartesian substantial essences (and also determinable modes)
are both individual and determinable. In his exchange with Hobbes, Descartes
was referring to "concrete things" (AT iii, 355–6). The "concrete" movement to
which he was referring is an individual mode or determination of the determinable
extended substance (see Leibniz's discussion of extension and substantiality in
Conversation of Philarete and Ariste in Leibniz 1976: 619–27; and in Leibniz
1989: 257–68).

In the *Principles*, Descartes wrote that "we can . . . easily come to know a
substance by one of its attributes"; and that "if we perceive the presence of some
attribute, we can infer that there must also be present an existing thing or substance to which it may be attributed" (AT viiiA, 25). These statements should not
be read as in any way suggesting the notion of substance as a property-less substratum. Descartes' substance is not a support of properties with a character not
captured by any of its attributes, the result of a Lockean "supposition of he knows
not what support of . . . qualities" (Locke 1985: 295).

A Cartesian substance is not this obscure and unmentionable something. If
accidents or determinations inhere in what they determine, an ultimate subject is
not a property-barren substratum but an essence that determines no higher determinable. In his conversation with Frans Burman, Descartes clearly rejected the
idea of substance as a bare substratum when he said that "all the attributes taken

together are identical with the substance" (AT v, 155). Substance is nothing beyond its real properties, but amongst real properties some are ultimate and independent subjects and others, modes of these natures. This is how one should take Descartes' claim to Burman that "in addition to the attribute which specifies the substance, one must think of the substance itself which is the substrate of that attribute" (AT v, 156).

The character of substances as basic ontological units arises from their intelligible independence and unity as highest-order determinable natures: it is in this sense that they are the ultimate, simple, and fundamental things that there are. The identity of a substance through change is the identity of a determinable as its determinates change. And the numerical individuality of a substance is the individuality of the determinable nature which it is. The conception of two distinct substances is the conception of two intelligibly separate wholes having nothing in common: Cartesian essences are individual, and they make the substances which they are one, rather than being made one by their substances.

One remarkable consequence of the Cartesian doctrine of substance is that not just substantial essences, but all the real properties or modes of a substance are individual in the sense that no other substance can have modes or properties of the exact same type. If some substance is F, where "F" designates a mode or real property of the substance, then anything which is F is the same substance. We can call this the Cartesian principle of the identity of similars, a stronger principle than Leibniz's identity of indiscernibles. While the Leibnizian principle dictates substantial identity on the basis of the identity of all real properties, the Cartesian principle dictates substantial identity merely from the identity of one mode.

Descartes distinguishes between the universal "thought" and the "particular nature which takes on [modes of thinking]" (AT v, 221). Each mind is an individual consciousness. That a mental act is necessarily an "*I* think" makes thought individual. For Descartes, the first-personal character of consciousness is not to be seen as a peculiar take the mind has upon itself, but rather as manifesting its essential individuality: "I" is the name of a unique consciousness, a thinking whose individuality is part of its very nature (see Anscombe 1981). Unfortunately, Descartes does not offer a discursive account, however brief, of this unique, but intellectually apprehensible, individual character of thought. If we want to grasp it, his recipe is to introspect: "there are things which we obscure by trying to define them, for they are most simple and clear . . . [T]hought . . . can be included amongst these things . . . [T]he only way we can learn of [it] is by . . . that awareness or internal testimony which everyone experiences within himself" (AT x, 523–4). Though with his articulation of the self as thinking substance Descartes presented modern philosophy up to our day with one of its central problems, his own account of the individuality and identity of the self, even when sympathetically reconstructed, faces insurmountable difficulties (see Williams 1978: 95–101 and 278–303; see also the discussion and references in Secada 2000c: 247–63).

The Cartesian account of substance does not face analogous problems when dealing with the individuality of material things: there is strictly only one body which is "this world or the whole of corporeal substance" (AT viiiA, 52). Nonetheless, Descartes recognized that "this word 'body' is extremely equivocal" (AT iv, 166). Apart from the sense just indicated, where "body" is "taken generally," that is, to mean all the parts of the single corporeal substance, he acknowledged two other senses (AT vii, 14). The first refers to all proper parts of matter. These are individuated by their size and shape and their relative location, and they are such that "if any particle of [their] matter were changed, [they would be judged] no longer numerically the same" (AT iv, 166). The second refers to an aggregate of diverse parts of matter which are extrinsically defined as one. For instance, one human body is just "the whole of matter which is united to [some one] soul," and it remains "numerically the same" in spite of changes in its size and shape, or whether it losses or acquires matter (see AT iv, 165 where a similar point is made about a river).

Neither of these two latter senses is ontologically fundamental, a fact which Descartes is careful to indicate by making reference to the dependence on thought of any determination of individual parts of the one material substance (see AT viiiA, 28–9; AT vii, 222; also AT vii, 13–14 where Descartes states that "absolutely all substances" cannot perish unless annihilated by God, a doctrine reiterated at AT vii, 153–4, and incompatible with the claim that the many bodies or parts of the material substance are all strictly substances; for an opposing account, see Slowik 2002: ch. 4). Here one might distinguish between, on the one hand, the division of the one material substance, or "the quantity" which composes "the whole visible universe" (AT iv, 166 and viiiA, 315), into proper parts at any given time, a division which, given the infinite divisibility of matter, must depend partly on some external determination by the considering mind, and, on the other, its division into proper parts through a certain duration, a division which adds the preservation of shape and size through movement.

Descartes' talk of many bodies or material substances is motivated by his desire not to unnecessarily antagonize the School nor make patent the opposition between his and their natural philosophy. When this is the case, here and elsewhere, he also provides the elements so that readers can discern his considered thoughts on the matter, as we have just seen.

Apart from God, the one material universe, and the many created souls or minds, there are no more substances. Though Descartes writes of a substantial union of the human soul or mind with a human body, and some commentators have taken this to indicate a reference to a third substance, the human person or embodied mind, there is no textual need to go down this path, which is generally acknowledged to be difficult to make compatible with the rest of Descartes' metaphysics. The Cartesian union of mind and body in humans can be rendered in terms of causal interaction and the peculiar phenomenology of sensations, feelings, passions, and emotions, which make us aware of our body as if possessed by it.

Descartes presents us with a conception of substance and reality which leaves no room for the claim that, for instance, thought might be discovered to be a property of certain material organisms. Mental acts could not "emerge" from bodies, whatever their structure, nor could they in any way be properties of bodies. There is a unity to substance, a tight conceptual interconnection between all its possible properties, which precludes that possibility. To say that there is only one thing here, where we have corporeal and mental properties, demands an account of the individuality asserted, and Descartes' account makes such a statement incoherent.

But is this not science by fiat? Not quite. Descartes' ontology, his account of substance and its properties, is offered as comprehensive, and as having the virtue of intellectual transparency. It is proposed as a clear and distinct account, free not only from incoherence but from obscurity. Furthermore, and this is a crucial point, Descartes claims that the whole of human knowledge, all that the sciences can tell us, and all that we know firmly in any sphere of human activity, will fit into this ontological picture. All known true predications can be analyzed so that in the end no reference need be made to anything but these orders of determination, extended, corporeal substance, and thinking substances or minds.

Descartes must not only explain true predications which appear to refer to properties other than thought and extension and its determinates, he must also analyze away apparent common predications, and of course explain the apparent plurality of substances of the same nature. He devoted most of his time to pursuing this project by developing a natural science which could be cast exclusively in terms of size, shape, and motion, and by articulating a corresponding science of the mind in terms only of perception and will, the two highest-order modes of thought. The impressive results of his efforts are found in *The World*, *Treatise on Man*, *Discourse on Method*, *Principles of Philosophy*, *The Passions of the Soul*, and some of his other writings.

Yet Descartes himself did not finish his project; and there are serious conceptual difficulties with the picture he painted, some of which we have already mentioned. Though Descartes' account of properly sensorial qualities as objects in the mind has survived to our day in the doctrine of secondary qualities, and his nominalist account of universals, of Suarecian inspiration, is not easy to dismiss, his reductionist project was hardly successful even within his own time. It was not long before Cartesian mechanistic physics was discarded in favor of a science that is incompatible with Descartes' conception of corporeal substance as mere extension. (On Descartes' natural science, see Gaukroger 2002: 93–179.) And even more decisively, Leibniz brought out the vacuity of this conception (see his *Critical Thoughts on the General Part of the Principles of Philosophy* in Leibniz 1976: 383–412, esp. 390 and 392).

Further, Descartes offered no clear account of the relation between causation and inherence. In fact, literally taken, the passages on substance in *Principles* bring the two together obscurely. As we pointed out, Descartes could be read, perhaps uncharitably, as holding that created substances are to be understood as causally dependent only on God, as opposed to their modes which stand to them as effects stand to their causes. Things are compounded by a late letter where Descartes indicates that the notion of substance, strictly taken, entails infinity or absolute perfection:

> By "infinite substance" I understand a substance having true and real, actually infinite and immense, perfections. This is not an accident added to the notion of substance, but the very essence of substance taken absolutely and qualified by no defects; for in relation to substance these defects are accidents while infinity or infinitude is not. (AT v, 355–6)

Descartes' insistence that God is properly substance, while creatures are so only imperfectly and qualifiedly, seems to be at odds with his claim that there is no meaning of "substance" which applies univocally to God and to creatures. Furthermore, it opens up the issue of the relation between causation and inherence.

Shortly after Descartes' death, Spinoza was to provide an articulation of the relation between these two relations which is deeply troubling for the Cartesian doctrine of substance. Consider the following argument: substances are highest-order determinable natures; cause and effect are like each other; things which are like each other share a real property or determinate mode; things which share a real property or determinate mode are the same determinable nature or substance; therefore, nothing can cause something other than itself. Given that everything has a cause, it follows that all existing substances are self-caused. This, abbreviated and simplified, is the argument with which Spinoza begins Part I of his *Ethics* (see *Ethics*, I, props. 1–16 in Spinoza 1985: 408–25). Starting from a Cartesian understanding of substance, and using causal intuitions which Descartes himself used, Spinoza arrived at the claim that there is only one substance, infinite and self-caused.

Renford Bambrough once said that most of what Spinoza wrote in the *Ethics* was false, but that this fact, if it was a fact, did not in any way diminish his interest or his stature as a great philosopher. To be sure, philosophers are not studied because they will tell us what is true. They generate interest in their work because they help us to understand ourselves and the things amongst which we live. And this they can do even when they do not attain truth. Furthermore, the interest in them is renewed with each generation as knowledge, aims, and perspectives change, and the past acquires a new voice. Descartes' *Meditations* and its doctrine of substance can help us reformulate many of our deeper assumptions, by seeing ourselves in our modern origins. The rejection of hylomorphism is a decisive feature of the early modern metaphysical revolution. Revisiting Descartes' seminal intellectualist and essentialist version of that rejection can be a source of considerable philosophical enlightenment.

6

The Doctrine of Ideas

Steven Nadler

By the beginning of Meditation III, Descartes has been able to retreat somewhat from the epistemological abyss that confronted him at the end of Meditation I. No longer facing a complete skepticism about all knowledge, he can now be sure of at least two things: that he exists (*ego sum, ego existo*) and that he is a thinking thing (*sum res cogitans*). Even if the meditator's being, and consequently his faculties, are the result of the designs of an evil genius who is bent on seeing him systematically deceived, these most simple and basic truths about himself remain indubitable.

However, Descartes' ambitions go beyond the limited security of solipsistic beliefs. He is not content simply to have in his possession certain knowledge about himself as a mind or spirit. His goal in the *Meditations* is to provide epistemological and metaphysical foundations for the sciences, especially the new mathematical science of nature for which he, along with Galileo, Mersenne, and others, is a leading early-modern proponent. He is seeking knowledge of independent and objective eternal verities and of the most universal principles of the world around him. Somehow, therefore, he is going to have to find a way to move beyond the certainty that he, at the beginning of Meditation III, has about his own being and nature toward certainty about the existence and nature of that world. He needs, in other words, a bridge from his own mind to external things.

This is where the doctrine of ideas comes in. Descartes will rely on these immediately accessible and absolutely certain contents of his own mind to demonstrate, first, the existence of an all-powerful, all-perfect, benevolent, non-deceiving God who created him. Having established this, he will be able to conclude that, as long as he uses his God-given, hence inherently reliable, rational faculties properly and only gives his assent to what he clearly and distinctly perceives, he can be confident in the truth of his certain beliefs about things in the world.

Descartes' doctrine of ideas thus plays a crucial role in the overall argument of the *Meditations*. It serves as the fulcrum that will allow him to move outside of himself and toward the metaphysical truths about God and, eventually, nature that provide secure foundations for the sciences. It is also, however, one of the more difficult and, to our twenty-first-century minds, puzzling aspects of the argument of the work. In this chapter, I shall address some of the important elements of the doctrine and explain the role that they play in the meditator's project.

What are Ideas?

Descartes is well aware of the ambiguities of the word "idea." In fact, his own use of the word is equivocal and inconsistent. He usually uses it to refer to immaterial images in the mind, and this is the understanding of the word which dominates the *Meditations* and with which we will be concerned below. Sometimes, however, it is used also to refer to volitional acts by the mind; and at other times it is used to refer even to material images in the brain (see, for example, AT vii, 181 and AT xi, 174).

For the most part, we can distinguish two senses of "idea" for Descartes: a broad sense and a strict sense. In the broad meaning of "idea" – "idea" as genus – the word refers to any mental item, any state of the mind, whether it be an image, an affect, or a volitional act. Ideas in this general sense are states of consciousness, and these come in a great variety: perceptions, imaginings, thoughts, desires, feelings, willings, doubtings, and so on. In the narrow sense – "idea" as species – the word refers only to those mental items that are "as it were images of things [*tanquam rerum imagines*]" or representational states. These include sense perceptions of physical things, pure intellectual thoughts (e.g., of mathematical figures), imaginings (e.g., of unicorns), dreams, and sensations and feelings (pain, pleasure). Both the sensory appearance of the sun as a small, yellow, warm disc and the conceptual understanding of the sun as an enormous body of gas are equally ideas in the narrow sense.

Descartes vividly draws this distinction between the narrow and broad meanings of "idea" in this passage from Meditation III:

> Some of my thoughts are as it were the images of things, and it is only in these cases that the term "idea" is strictly appropriate – for example, when I think of a man, or a chimera, or the sky, or an angel, or God. Other thoughts have various additional forms: thus, when I will, or am afraid, or affirm, or deny, there is always a particular thing which I take as the object of my thought, but my thought includes something more than the likeness of that thing. Some thoughts in this category are called volitions or emotions, while others are called judgements. (AT vii, 37)

At the core of every idea in the broad sense is an idea in the strict sense, giving it a specific content or referent. When I desire an ice cream cone, there is, in addition to the affirming state of mind that constitutes the desiring, an idea or image of an ice cream cone that makes it the particular desire that it is.

In sum, then, we can say that ideas generally speaking are the states of consciousness of which the mind is immediately aware. This, in fact, is precisely how Descartes defines "thought" in the *Principles of Philosophy*: "By the term 'thought', I understand everything which we are aware of as happening within us, in so far as we have awareness of it" (I, art. 9). An "idea," correlatively, is what is apprehended by the mind when one is conscious of the thought: "Idea: I understand this term to mean the form of any given thought, immediate perception of which makes me aware of the thought" (*Second Replies*, AT vii, 160). Strictly speaking, however, ideas (in the narrow sense) are those states of consciousness that are image-like appearances. Ideas (in the narrow sense) are all those visions, thoughts, feelings and other *imagines* that stand before the mind's eye in consciousness and that are the objects of the mind's active attitudes (affirming, denying, willing, desiring, and so on). An idea is what is immediately "there" to the mind, regardless of what may or may not be the case outside of the mind.

For this reason, ideas have a special epistemic status in Descartes' system. Our apprehension of them is absolutely certain, even if everything else has been placed in doubt. There may not be an external world of bodies at all. For all I know – and this is the meditator's situation as Meditation III begins – there is only myself as a thinking thing. Nonetheless, the contents that stand immediately before me as a thinking thing – my ideas, my thoughts – are indubitably there, and there can be no doubt whatsoever about this. I may be wrong in my judgment as to whether or not there is a table in front of me, but I cannot possibly be wrong in my judgment that I have an idea or thought (or the appearance) of a table in front of me.

> I am a thing that thinks: that is, a thing that doubts, affirms, denies, understands a few things, is ignorant of many things, is willing, is unwilling, and also which imagines and has sensory perceptions; for as I have noted before, even though the objects of my sensory experience and imagination may have no existence outside me, nonetheless the modes of thinking which I refer to as cases of sensory perception and imagination, in so far as they are simply modes of thinking, do exist within me: of that I am certain. (*Meditations* III, AT vii, 34–5)

This is a point he will later make again in the *Principles of Philosophy*:

> If I say "I am seeing, or I am walking, therefore I exist," and take this as applying to vision or walking as bodily activities, then the conclusion is not absolutely certain. This is because, as often happens during sleep, it is possible for me to think I am seeing or walking, though my eyes are closed and I am not moving about; such thoughts might even be possible if I had no body at all. But if I take "seeing" or "walking" to apply to the actual sense or awareness of seeing or walking, then the conclusion is quite certain, since it relates to the mind, which alone has the sensation or thought that it is seeing or walking. (I, art. 9)

I may be able to doubt that *x* truly exists outside the mind, but I cannot possibly doubt whether or not I have an idea of *x*. Philosophers often put this point by saying that my beliefs about my ideas are *incorrigible*: if I believe that I have an idea of or am thinking of *x*, then I do have an idea of or am thinking of *x*.

Formal vs Objective Reality

Most first-time readers of the *Meditations* are particularly confused by some technical vocabulary that Descartes uses in Meditation III to distinguish between two different aspects of ideas. The distinction is actually first introduced in the work's Preface. Descartes early on alerts the reader to yet another ambiguity in the word "idea," although in this case the ambiguity is restricted to ideas taken in the strict sense, as *imagines* appearing before the mind: "There is an ambiguity here in the word 'idea.' 'Idea' can be taken materially, as an operation of the intellect, in which case it cannot be said to be more perfect than me. Alternatively, it can be taken objectively, as the thing represented by that operation' (AT vii, 8). In Meditation III, this distinction between the material reality of an idea and its objective reality reappears as the distinction between the idea's formal reality and its objective reality.

Now what is usually confusing to the modern reader is that the word "objective" is ordinarily understood to refer to something that is out there in the real world, external to the mind and regardless of whether anyone is perceiving it. The contrast is with what is "subjective," which is what is in the mind. To refer to something's "objectivity" is taken to refer to its real, extra-mental being. In a sense, as we shall see, Descartes completely reverses this meaning and uses "objective being" to refer to something's being in the mind by way of being thought about. When he speaks of something existing "objectively," he will in a certain respect mean what we mean when we speak of something existing "subjectively."

Let us begin, however, with the "formal reality" or "material reality" of ideas. By these terms, Descartes is referring to the true ontological reality or being of a thing. In particular, to ask about the formal reality of something is to ask in the most general and metaphysical way what kind of thing it is and what its status is in reality. For Descartes, there are only two kinds of things – substances and modes (or modifications) of substances. Substances have the highest ontological status. They are true beings, and exist independently of other things. Strictly speaking, only God is a true substance, since God alone requires nothing else for its existence. Still, finite things, such as human souls, have a sufficient degree of ontological independence to qualify as substances in a secondary sense, since they depend on nothing other than God for their being. A mode or attribute or property, however, can exist only as the mode or attribute or property of something. Modes are not free agents, but necessarily belong to substances. Modes are simply the ways in which substances exist or manifest themselves.

The modes of material or extended substances are shape, size, divisibility, and mobility. The shape of the table is one of its modes. The modes of thinking substances, on the other hand, are thoughts. The formal reality of ideas, then, which are nothing but a species of thought, is that they are modifications of thinking substance. Insofar as it is considered simply as a mental event, an idea is nothing but a property of the mind. In terms of their formal reality, all ideas are identical. They are all equally mental items dependent on the minds to which they belong, and there is in this regard no difference whatsoever between them. "In so far as the ideas are [considered] simply [as] modes of thought, there is no recognizable inequality among them: they all appear to come from within me in the same fashion" (Meditation III, AT vii, 40).

But what *kind* of mental property is an idea? There has been a great deal of debate, both among Descartes' seventeenth-century followers (such as Antoine Arnauld and Nicolas Malebranche) and in recent scholarship, over whether ideas for Descartes are modes of the mind in the sense of mental things perceived by the mind or in the sense of the mind's perceptions. Are Cartesian ideas, in other words, *mental objects* or *mental acts*? Descartes speaks in ways that seem to lend support to both readings. On the one hand, he speaks of ideas as what are immediately perceived by the mind. For example, in Meditation III he says that an idea is "what appears before my mind," and appears to treat it as the object of the mind's attention. On the other hand, in the Preface to the *Meditations*, an idea is defined not as some inert object perceived by the mind, but rather as an active "operation of the intellect [*operatio intellectus*]." This makes it seem as though an idea is not what is perceived but is the perceiving itself through which we apprehend external things.

The debate has been fueled by a worry that if ideas are mental objects, then Descartes seems to have surrounded the mind with what has been derisively called "a veil of ideas." Ideas, on this account, would be the direct and immediate objects of perception and stand between the perceiving mind and the external world, with the latter only indirectly perceived. A person would apprehend ideas as a kind of picture show, beyond which lies the reality which is the ultimate object of knowledge. But then how could we ever know anything for certain about that external world? The epistemological problem that Descartes has set himself in the *Meditations* would have to be framed in terms of how to determine whether things in the world outside the mind are at all like the mental images or pictures in the mind that we apprehend. But since all we ever directly and immediately perceive are ideas, there would be no direct evidence for how things "really" are – we certainly could not step outside the "veil of ideas" and compare those things with the ideas – and thus (especially given the problems that notoriously plague Descartes' demonstrations of God's existence and veracity) no satisfying resolution to the skeptical puzzles with which the work begins.

But it seems to me that the question of whether Descartes' ideas are objects of the mind or acts of the mind is, epistemologically speaking, irrelevant. No matter what ideas are ontologically, Descartes must clearly confront the main skeptical question that he has set himself in the *Meditations*: how can he know to what degree the way things in the world (or in mathematics, or in any scientific domain whatsoever) appear to him to be is in fact the way they really are? Ideas are appearances, the way we perceive or conceive things. It does not matter whether Descartes holds a representational theory of perception (whereby the immediate objects of perception are mental objects) or a direct realist theory of perception (where ideas are the perceptions themselves by which we apprehend external objects). The direct realist, as much as the representationalist, has to concede that at least some claims to perceive or conceive how things really are, are false; after all, we commonly make sensory errors and get taken in by our dreams, and our intellectual reasonings often go astray. The direct realist certainly must admit the distinction between the way an object appears and the way it actually is. The real question is not whether ideas are objects or acts, but rather how can one know on any particular occasion that the perceptual or conceptual experience (or at least aspects of it) is not illusory? More generally, how can one have any confidence that our mind's faculties, when properly used, tell us something about reality? This problem confronts Descartes no matter what ideas are ontologically. In fact, this is *the* epistemological problem of the *Meditations*, and can be answered for Descartes only through the proof of God's existence and goodness and thus by providing a certain class of ideas or appearances with a divine guarantee. It cannot be answered simply by showing that Descartes' ideas are acts rather than objects.

So much for the question of the formal reality of ideas. Ideas as modes of the mind bear no differences among them. But, Descartes continues, "in so far as different ideas [are considered as images which] represent different things, it is clear that they differ widely." While we cannot distinguish one idea from another in terms of its formal reality or ontological status as a mental event, we certainly can distinguish one idea from another in terms of its content – that is, in terms of *what* it is an idea of. Thus, the idea of the sun differs from the idea of a human being not as an idea *per se*, but insofar as the former is the idea "of the sun" and the latter is the idea "of a human being." Similarly, two oil paintings on canvas may not differ from each other in terms of their formal or material reality, since both are nothing but oil-based pigment on canvas, but they will differ inasmuch as one is a portrait of Descartes and another is a portrait of Socrates.

This content of an idea, which allows us to discriminate one idea from another by its object, is what Descartes is referring to when he speaks of an idea's "objective reality." It is what the idea represents (or, better, presents) to the mind. The objective reality of an idea is what makes the idea "like a picture or image" and allows it to make something (e.g., the sun, in the case of the idea of the sun) immediately present to the mind. An idea's objective reality gives the idea what philosophers have called "intentionality." It makes an idea the idea *of* something.

> *Objective reality of an idea.* By this I mean the being of the thing which is represented by an idea, in so far as this exists in the idea. In the same way we can talk of

"objective perfection," "objective intricacy," and so on. For whatever we perceive as being in the objects of our ideas exists objectively in the ideas themselves. (*Second Replies*, AT vii, 161)

Descartes' terminology comes from a medieval categorization of different ways of being. According to thirteenth- and fourteenth-century thinkers such as St Thomas Aquinas, William of Ockham and Johannes Duns Scotus, a thing can have being in two ways. It can possess *esse formale*, or actual concrete being as a real thing (as a physical object or a mental entity), and it can have *esse obiectivum*, objective or conceptual being. For something to have objective being does not imply that the thing actually exists in space and/or time. Rather, it means that the thing exists in some mind insofar as it is being thought about by that mind. It is a mode of being in the understanding, not as a real property of the understanding (such as its acts or operations) but as the intentional *object* that the understanding grasps. In a word, something is in the mind "objectively" when it is thought about, understood, or perceived. When I think about the sun, the sun thereby has objective existence in my mind, in addition to the formal existence it has in the sky.

Thus, when Johannes Caterus, one of the first critics of the *Meditations* and a man educated in the scholastic tradition, asks Descartes for clarification of some points relative to the nature of ideas, Descartes responds in language that should seem familiar to him:

"Objective being in the intellect" . . . will signify the object's being in the intellect in the way in which its objects are normally there. By this I mean that the idea of the sun is the sun itself existing in the intellect – not of course formally existing, as it does in the heavens, but objectively existing, i.e., in the way in which objects are normally in the intellect. (*First Replies*, AT vii, 102)

We can say, in fact, that for Descartes objective reality is a defining feature of the mind's ideas: "Some of my thoughts are as it were images of things, and it is only in these cases that the term 'idea' is strictly appropriate." It is essential to an idea that it has a representational content that it displays to the mind. "The objective mode of being belongs to ideas by their very nature" (Meditation III, AT vi, 42). In this respect, Descartes anticipates later thinkers in the phenomenological tradition, such as Edmund Husserl, who make intentionality the hallmark of the mental.

It is a particularly vexed question as to just *how* ideas are supposed to perform their representational function, especially in the light of Descartes' commitment to a radical dualism between mind and body. What does it mean, for example, to say that an unextended mental idea represents an extended material body? On occasion, Descartes speaks as though ideas represent external things by resembling them, just as a painted portrait represents its sitter by a certain degree of resemblance. The idea of body or matter, he says, "comes to us from things located outside ourselves, which it wholly resembles [*omnino similis est*]" (*Principles* II, art. 1). However, it cannot truly be the case that ideas represent by way of resembling their objects. The idea of a table is not itself table-like in *any* respect. The Cartesian dualist must say that the idea of the table and the physical table cannot have any properties whatsoever in common. An idea, unlike a table, cannot be square, since shape is something that belongs only to bodies. In fact, I do not think that Descartes ultimately believes that resemblance or similarity is necessary for a relationship of representation between image (material or mental) and object. In his work on optics, Descartes notes that, while a painted picture that resembles its subject will serve well to represent that subject, nonetheless signs and words can also represent things without in any way resembling the things they represent (*Dioptrics* IV, AT vi, 112–14). Unlike signs and words, however, ideas do not become representations through use or stipulation. Descartes, I believe, regarded the representational feature of ideas as a *sui generis* capacity that they have by nature to make things present to the mind. It is something that cannot be defined or explained (except metaphorically) in terms of any other relationship. Not that the matter ended there. This issue generated a good deal of heated discussion in the seventeenth century among his followers and critics.

The objective reality of ideas will play a crucial role in Descartes' proof for God's existence in Meditation III. He knows that it is perfectly possible that he is the cause of all of his ideas insofar as it is their formal reality that is in question; all of his ideas, as modes of the mind, need only the mind for their "material" being. But he will now have to determine whether there are any ideas whose representational content exceeds his own causal powers. His answer will be that there is at least one such idea, namely, the idea of an infinite being, God.

Innate, Adventitious, and Fictitious Ideas

In pursuit of his ultimate goal in the *Meditations*, and particularly when, having remarked upon the certainty of his ideas and their nature both as mental states and as representational, he starts to make his move towards establishing the existence of something outside himself, Descartes must take up an important question: where do these ideas come from? Given the epistemic limitations he has set himself in the first two Meditations, this seems to be the only question he *can* ask that will lead him anywhere beyond the world of his ideas. And in investigating the sources or causal origins of his ideas, Descartes draws a threefold distinction.

> Among my ideas, some appear to be innate, some to be adventitious [foreign to me and coming from outside], and others to have been invented by me. My understanding of what a thing is, what truth is, and what thought is, seems to derive simply from my own nature. But my hearing a noise, as I do now, or seeing the sun, or feeling the fire, comes from things which are located outside me, or so I have hitherto

judged. Lastly, sirens, hippograffs and the like are my own invention. But perhaps all my ideas may be thought of as adventitious, or they may all be innate, or all made up; for as yet I have not clearly perceived their true origin. (Meditation III, AT vii, 37–8)

In the most basic reading of the distinction, innate ideas are derived from the mind's own resources; adventitious ideas (from the Latin *advenire*: to come to) come to the mind from external sources; and fictitious ideas are made up by the imagination.

But the way Descartes has framed the distinction in Meditation III is a little misleading. For there is a sense in which *all* ideas for Descartes are innate. As modes of the mind or mental events – that is, in terms of their formal reality – ideas just are ways in which the mind is; the formal reality of every idea has its origin in the mind itself, in its active power to produce its own states. But even the representational content of any idea, which is itself nothing but a feature of a mental event (a mode of a mode, so to speak), is, strictly, also the work of the mind. Nothing ever literally comes into the mind from outside it. Descartes himself explicitly says as much in a later work:

If we bear in mind the scope of our senses and what it is exactly that reaches our faculty of thinking by way of them, we must admit that in no case are the ideas of things presented to us by the senses just as we form them in our thinking. So much so that there is nothing in our ideas which is not innate to the mind or the faculty of thinking, with the sole exception of those circumstances which relate to experience. (*Comments on a Certain Broadsheet*, AT viiiB, 358)

Outside the mind there is nothing but extended bodies and their motions. And certainly neither material particles nor motion can be communicated into the mind; since the mind is immaterial, it cannot receive any of the properties that belong to bodies. Nor do material bodies have anything immaterial or spiritual that they can send into the mind. The mind–body metaphysical gap, while not necessarily causally closed, does not allow anything to cross back and forth. Thus, none of the ancient and medieval theories of perception according to which external things literally transmit tiny material or immaterial images (or "species") into the mind are, in Descartes' metaphysical schema, possible. No so-called "influx" model of causation can explain how ideas arise in the Cartesian mind. What, in fact, happens in ordinary sense experience is that external objects communicate motions through the sense organs to the brain. When the motions reach the brain and create a material image therein – and the brain image is nothing but a structuring of the pore openings in the brain's internal surface caused by the flowing of spirits through the nerves – this bodily process stimulates the mind to form a particular idea. Descartes insists that we judge that our ideas are caused by external objects "not because these things transmit the ideas to our mind through the sense organs, but because they transmit something [motions] which, at exactly that moment, gives the mind occasion to form these ideas by means of the faculty innate to it" (*Comments on a Certain Broadsheet*, AT viiiB, 359). Thus, he concludes, our sensory ideas of bodies, their motions and figures, "the ideas of pain, colors, sounds and the like," must all be innate if "on the occasion of certain corporeal motions, our mind is to be capable of representing them to itself."

If all ideas are innate, then what does Descartes mean by differentiating between innate, adventitious, and fictitious ideas? This is one of the more difficult issues in understanding Descartes' doctrine of ideas. Part of the difficulty stems from Descartes' failure consistently to distinguish causal questions about ideas from epistemic questions, and dispositions to have certain thoughts from the occurrent thoughts themselves. Here, nonetheless, is a plausible interpretation, one which I do not pretend resolves every problem raised by Descartes' account of innateness.

The distinction between innate, adventitious, and fictitious ideas should be seen as based not on the proximate and general cause of ideas – which is always the mind – but rather on the distal or remote cause that may be required to occasion or stimulate the mind to think of something or to have a particular conscious appearance. If the mind's occurrent perception or thought of some concrete and particular thing comes about only because the mind's faculty of thought is triggered by a material image caused in the brain by an external object, then the resulting idea is adventitious (and there should be some kind of correspondence between the content of the idea, the brain image, and features of the object itself). Thus, the sensory process that begins in the motions of the particles of the sun and terminates in a specific image in the brain corresponding to those motions will occasion the mind to produce a round, yellow, warm idea: an adventitious idea of the sun. In other words, with an adventitious idea, the mind's faculty of thought must be stimulated by physical sense experience. If I never look at the sun or at least at some material representation of the sun, then I can never have the (adventitious) sensory idea of the sun.

On the other hand, innate ideas in the strict sense of the term are not sensory appearances of particular things, but rather the general and objective intellectual concepts that are in the mind by its very (God-given) nature. These include mathematical ideas (e.g., the concept of the circle), metaphysical ideas (the concept of being) and, most importantly for Descartes' purposes, the idea of God. Innate ideas comprise what Descartes calls "simple natures," as well as the eternal truths, which he says "are all inborn in our minds just as a king would imprint his laws on the hearts of all his subjects if he had enough power to do so" (To Mersenne, April 15, 1630, AT i, 145). They also include notions that the mind can come to have simply by reflecting on itself and on its own mental operations (such as the ideas of thought, of substance, and of duration).

Moreover, as Descartes intends to show by his progress within the *Meditations* itself, the mind's summoning of these ideas from its inner resources does not require any external sensory stimulation; in fact, unlike adventitious ideas, their appearance in the mind is, at least in principle, completely independent of the body. Nor are innate ideas, like fictitious ideas, willfully constructed by abstraction and composition from the contents of other ideas (such as my idea of a gryphon, which combines elements from the ideas of different animals). The contents of innate ideas and their presence in the mind are independent of sense experience and of the will. Of course, one may be stimulated to think of a geometric triangle by seeing a triangular physical object, and one may come to think of God after looking at a painted representation of God (say, in Michelangelo's Sistine ceiling). But what distinguishes innate ideas is that sense experience is not a necessary condition for the having of an idea. What the summoning of innate ideas from the faculty of thinking really requires is deep reflective thought, something with which sensory ideas often interfere.

At one point in Meditation III, Descartes says that while "it is not necessary that I ever light upon any thought of God," nonetheless he can "bring forth the idea of God from the treasure house of my mind, as it were . . ." (AT vii, 67). And in a letter from the same year as the publication of the *Meditations*, Descartes says that an infant "has in itself the ideas of God, itself, and all such truths as are called self-evident, in the same way as adult humans have them when they are not attending to them; it does not acquire these ideas later on, as it grows older" (To Hyperaspistes, August 1641, AT iii, 424). From other contexts, however, it seems clear that Descartes does not think that innate ideas are actual concrete and occurrent thoughts stored up in the mind like the contents of a warehouse. Rather, certain ideas are innate in the mind insofar as the mind is so structured that it is predisposed to have certain occurrent thoughts, even if it never actually has them.

> I have never written or taken the view that the mind requires innate ideas which are something distinct from its own faculty of thinking. I did, however, observe that there were certain thoughts within me which neither came to me from external objects nor were determined by my will, but which came solely from the power of thinking within me; so I applied the term "innate" to the ideas or notions which are the forms of these thoughts in order to distinguish them from others, which I called "adventitious" or "made up." This is the same sense as that in which we say that generosity is "innate" in certain families, or that certain diseases such as gout or stones are innate in others: it is not so much that the babies of such families suffer from these diseases in their mother's womb, but simply that they are born with a certain "faculty" or tendency to contract them. (*Comments on a Certain Broadsheet*, AT viiiB, 357–8)

Innate ideas, Descartes says, "always exist within us potentially . . . in some faculty." It is only when I actually think of God that this potentiality becomes actualized in the form of an occurrent idea.

Descartes insists that, while the proximate cause of any idea is the mind, and the remote cause of an adventitious idea is the material image in the brain and the external object that has generated this image, the ultimate cause of all of our ideas is God. It is God who has placed innate ideas in the "treasure house of the mind" (that is, who has given the mind such a nature that certain distinctive dispositions or potentialities are within it); and it is God who has so created the mind and established its correspondence with the body that, on the occasion of certain motions in the brain, the mind has certain sensory ideas.

> I maintain that when God unites a rational soul to this machine [the human body] . . . he will place its principal seat in the brain, and will make its nature such that the soul will have different sensations corresponding to the different ways in which the entrances to the pores in the internal surface of the brain are opened by means of the nerves. (*Treatise on Man*, AT xi, 143)

Clarity and Distinctness

As if there were not enough distinctions already in the realm of Cartesian ideas, there is yet another to be made, one that is crucial for his project of providing a divine guarantee for human knowledge.

Through the process in Meditations I–III of trying to find some indubitable truths, some beliefs that are immune to skeptical doubt, Descartes comes upon his alleged criterion of truth. That is, he discovers just what it is that makes a particular class of ideas so subjectively certain that, as long as he is attending to them, he cannot conceive of them being false. The *cogito* itself provides him with the paradigm case for this criterion, although he soon realizes that other ideas – for example, those expressing mathematical propositions – manifest the requisite character to a very high degree as well. As he proclaims at the opening of Meditation III:

> I am certain that I am a thinking thing. Do I not therefore also know what is required for my being certain about anything? In this first item of knowledge there is simply a clear and distinct perception of what I am asserting; this would not be enough to make me certain of the truth of the matter if it could ever turn out that something which I perceived with such clarity and distinctness was false. So I now seem to be able to lay it down as a general rule that whatever I perceive very clearly and distinctly is true. (AT vii, 35)

Of course, Descartes is not quite out of the woods yet. The criterion itself – the principle that what one clearly and distinctly perceives to be true *is* in fact true, that what is subjectively certain is also objectively true – needs to be validated, something that will be accomplished only by the proof that an all-powerful and benevolent God is the source of my faculty for perceiving things clearly and distinctly. But Descartes has now identified an important feature of some of his ideas, a feature that will allow him to distinguish those perceptions or conceptions that are candidates for being veridical and reliable guides to truth from those perceptions or conceptions that are most likely illusory and misleading.

What, then, does the clarity and distinctness of ideas consist in? What makes one idea clear and distinct and another idea obscure and confused? One thing is certain, namely, that the clarity and distinctness of a clear and distinct idea are features of its representational content. However, they are not determined by the *object* represented in the idea; after all, one can have a clear and distinct idea and an obscure and confused idea of one and the same object. Rather, clarity and distinctness are found in the character or quality of the representation. Here is what Descartes says when he offers formal definitions of clarity and distinctness:

> I call a perception "clear" when it is present and accessible to the attentive mind – just as we say that we see something clearly when it is present to the eye's gaze and stimulates it with a sufficient degree of strength and accessibility. I call a perception "distinct" if, as well as being clear, it is so sharply separated from all other perceptions that it contains within itself only what is clear. (*Principles* I, art. 45)

The clarity of an idea is a matter of its vivacity. A clear idea strikes the mind with a force that compels attention. It is strong and impressive. The distinctness of an idea, on the other hand, looks, from the definition above, to be more of a relational feature of an idea – that is, a matter of whether the idea can be distinguished from other ideas. But this ability of the mind to "sharply separate" an idea from others is also a function of the idea's own intrinsic content. An idea's limits or boundaries are discerned because its content is well defined and delineated. A distinct idea is a semantically discrete idea. It provides evident information on the properties of its object and leaves no room for doubting what does and does not belong to it. There is no mistaking the idea for any other.

It is important to keep in mind that a distinct idea does not provide one with just *some* evident information about its object. Arnauld, for one, in his *Fourth Set of Objections*, is concerned that when Descartes says that he has a clear and distinct perception of himself as a thinking thing independent of his body, he is merely performing an act of abstraction or inattention and simply considering his thinking without also taking into account what else may belong to his being. Why should the fact that I can think of myself without a body imply that I as a thinking thing alone am something real and complete? "So far as I can see, the only result that follows from this is that I can obtain some knowledge of myself without knowledge of the body. But it is not yet transparently clear to me that this knowledge is complete and adequate, so as to enable me to be certain that I am not mistaken in excluding body from my essence" (AT vii, 201). Perhaps I have only abstracted my thinking from other, equally necessary aspects of my being, just as (to use the example Arnauld provides) one can think of a right-angled triangle and ignore or suspend judgment about whether the square of the hypotenuse is equal to the sum of the squares of the other two sides.

But Descartes essentially denies that Arnauld's triangle example is truly a case of perceiving something clearly and distinctly. He replies that, with the clear and distinct idea of a thing, one is able to determine with absolute certainty what does and does not belong to the thing. Thus, in the distinct idea of a right-angled triangle one can know exactly and clearly what is included in its content (e.g., having three sides, having the sum of the figure's interior angles equal to one hundred and eighty degrees, having the square of the hypotenuse equal to the sum of the squares of the other two sides) and what is not (e.g., having four angles, having its area equal to the square of its side). In other words, in a clear and distinct idea, the mind can see with a certain irresistible strength what the content of the idea necessarily contains and, just as importantly, what it excludes. "We cannot have a clear understanding of a triangle having the square on its hypotenuse equal to the squares on the other sides without at the same time being aware that it is right-angled . . . It is true that the triangle is intelligible even though we do not think of the ratio which obtains between the square on the hypotenuse and the squares on the other sides, but it is not intelligible that this ratio should be denied of the triangle" (*Fourth Replies*, AT vii, 224, 227).

As this passage indicates, not every clear and distinct idea is a *complete* idea of its object. Thus, one can have a clear and distinct idea of a thing but still not actually be aware of every single property that belongs to it. For example, I may know clearly and distinctly what a right-angled triangle is but not know that it satisfies the Pythagorean proportion. However, for every property one does in fact consider carefully, one will be able to determine through reasoning whether or not it belongs to the object. If one truly has a clear and distinct idea of a right-angled triangle and an understanding of what the Pythagorean proportion is, one would see right away that such a property could not, without contradiction, be denied of it.

An idea can be clear but not distinct. The sensation of pain or the perception of a bright color may have the requisite "strength and accessibility," but its identity and individuation may be uncertain.

> When someone feels an intense pain, the perception he has of it is indeed very clear, but is not always distinct. For people commonly confuse this perception with an obscure judgment they make concerning the nature of something which they think exists in the painful spot and which they suppose to resemble the sensation of pain. (*Principles* I, art. 46)

On the other hand, an idea cannot be distinct without being clear. That is because unless its content has the strength and accessibility demanded for clarity, it cannot be "sharply separated" from other perceptions. As Descartes says in the formal definition above, a distinct idea "contains within itself only what is clear."

Clarity and distinctness are closely bound up with another alleged feature of some ideas that has caused a great deal of confusion among Descartes scholars: material falsity. Descartes says that, strictly speaking, ideas have no truth value: they are neither true nor false. To have an idea (again, in the narrow sense of the word) is simply to entertain a thought or have an appearance before the mind. One either perceives or thinks of something or one does not. Truth and falsity belong to judgments, not ideas or perceptions. It is my assertion that my idea of the triangle accurately represents what a triangle is, or my judgment that my perception of the table as square is veridical and not illusory, that can be true or false. (This notion that ideas and judgments are distinct from each other, and that an idea can be found without any assertion or denial, was strongly criticized by Spinoza and others.) In Meditation III, Descartes notes that:

> as far as ideas are concerned, provided they are considered solely in themselves and I do not refer them to anything else, they cannot strictly speaking be false; for whether it is a goat or a chimera that I am imagining, it is just as true that I imagine the former as the latter. As for the will and the emotions, here too one need not worry about falsity; for even if the things which I may desire are wicked or even non-existent, that does not make it any less true that I desire them. Thus the only remaining thoughts where I must be on my guard against making a mistake are judgments. And the chief and most common mistake which is to be found here consists in my judging that the ideas which are in me resemble, or conform to, things located outside me. (AT vii, 37)

And yet, Descartes concedes, ideas can indeed have a kind of falsity. Just what this species of falsity is, however, is hard to determine. When he first introduces the notion of material falsity, in the *Meditations*, it seems as though it consists in an idea *misrepresenting* its object.

> Although, as I have noted before, falsity in the strict sense, or formal falsity, can occur only in judgments, there is another kind of falsity, material falsity, which occurs in ideas, when they represent non-things as things. For example, the ideas which I have of heat and cold contain so little clarity and distinctness that they do not enable me to tell whether cold is merely the absence of heat or vice versa, or whether both of them are real qualities, or neither is. And since there can be no ideas which are not as it were images of things, if it is true that cold is nothing but the absence of heat, the idea which represents it to me as something real and positive deserves to be called false; and the same goes for other ideas of this kind. (AT vii, 43–4)

It appears, on first glance, that an idea is materially false if it presents something in a way that it is not. Thus, on this understanding of the notion, an idea of x that represents x as F when x is in fact G (for example, that represents cold as something real and positive when it is, in fact, an absence of heat) would be materially false. But if this is what Descartes means by material falsity, then it is hard to see how it differs from what he calls "formal" falsity, that is, the lack of correspondence between a judgment or assertion and reality. Moreover, as Arnauld makes clear in the *Fourth Objections*, treating ideas as false in this way does not make any sense. If an idea presents x as F, then it is simply and truly the idea of Fx; it is not the false idea of Gx. What is false is my judgment that x actually is F rather than G (that is, my judgment that my idea of Fx accurately represents what x is). My idea that cold is a real thing is a positive idea that truly represents something (although what it represents may not be coldness); it is not the false idea of something else. All ideas that present something to the mind, Arnauld concludes, are true in the material sense – they all have a positive content.

> Although it can be imagined that cold, which I suppose to be represented by a posi- tive idea, is not something positive, it cannot be imagined that the positive idea does not represent anything real and positive to me. For an idea is called "positive" not in virtue of the existence it has as a mode of thinking (for in that sense all ideas would be positive), but in virtue of the objective existence which it contains and which it represents to our mind. Hence the idea in question [that represents cold as a positive thing and not merely as an absence of heat] may perhaps not be the idea of cold, but it cannot be a false idea. (AT vii, 207)

If the idea of cold represents cold as an absence of heat, then of course it is true in a number of senses. But if the idea represents its subject as a positive thing in its own right (and not merely as an absence of heat), then it is still a "materially true" idea, but just not the idea of cold (which is nothing but an absence of heat).

Arnauld's objection gave Descartes the opportunity to clarify what he means by material falsity. What makes an idea materially false, he replies, is not that it is actually false (as a judgment is, through a lack of correspondence with the way things really are) but that it provides material for and makes possible – and even encourages – false judgments. Materially false ideas are not ideas that *misrepresent* their objects. Rather, they are ideas that are so defective in their representational content that it is not at all clear *what* they are presenting and so they can easily mislead us in our judgments. In reply to Arnauld, Descartes says that

> my only reason for calling the idea [of cold] materially false is that, owing to the fact that it is obscure and confused, I am unable to judge whether or not what it displays to me is something positive which exists outside my sensation. And hence I may be led to judge that it is something positive though in fact it may merely be an absence. (*Fourth Replies*, AT vii, 234)

It is not the case that all ideas are "as it were images of things" in the same manner and to the same degree. That is, not all ideas present something to the mind in a clear and distinct manner such that there can be no mistake in the judgments that result from them. Materially false ideas are false in the sense that, unlike clear and distinct ideas, they do not successfully present something to the mind as a real and positive thing with a clearly identifiable character. Their representational content is so confused and obscure that one cannot tell whether what they are representing is something positive and real or not. This is, I believe, what Descartes originally had in mind in the *Meditations* themselves. As he says in the passage from Meditation III quoted above: "For example, the ideas which I have of heat and cold contain so little clarity and distinctness that they do not enable me to tell whether cold is merely the absence of heat or vice versa, or whether both of them are real qualities, or neither is." From my idea of cold alone, I cannot determine whether cold is an absence of heat or a real and positive thing in its own right. From an idea of pain, I cannot tell distinctly what condition of my body is being represented. In contrast with a clear and distinct idea, the evidence here is just not good enough for making an informed judgment. The representational content of the idea is, in a sense, hazy and murky, and for that reason indeterminate. Clear and distinct ideas, by contrast, display their content with such a high quality that, as Descartes says, they "give the judgment little or no scope for error," that is, for mistakes in determining what the idea is properly representing.

Sensations – colors, pains, and other *qualia* – are all materially false ideas. The senses generally provide the mind only with obscure and confused data.

> But as for . . . light and colors, sounds, smells, tastes, heat and cold and the other tactile qualities, I think of these only in a very confused and obscure way, to the extent that I do not even know whether they are true or false, that is, whether the ideas I have of them are ideas of real things or of non-things. (*Meditations* III, AT vii, 43)

The intellect, on the other hand, is the source of clear and distinct ideas: mathematical concepts, moral truths, metaphysical ideas, and the idea of God.

There remains the question of whether clarity and distinctness are characteristics *only* of items of the understanding. Do the senses provide us with any clear and distinct ideas? My ideas or perceptions of an object's color, taste, warmth, and so on are obscure and confused. But what about my sensory perception of its particular quantitative properties: its shape, size, and motion? That we do have clear and distinct ideas of these features of things through the senses is suggested by the following passage from Meditation III:

> If I scrutinize [my ideas of corporeal things] thoroughly and examine them one by one, in the way in which I examined the idea of the wax yesterday, I notice that the things which I perceive clearly and distinctly in them are very few in number. The list comprises size, or extension in length, breadth and depth; shape, which is a function of the boundaries of this extension; position, which is a relation between various items possessing shape; and motion, or change of position; to these may be added substance, duration and number. But as for all the rest, including light and colors,

sounds, smells, tastes, heat and cold and the other tactile qualities, I think of these only in a very confused and obscure way. (AT vii, 43)

The way the paragraph moves from the clear and distinct ideas of quantitative or geometric features of objects to the obscure and confused ideas of their qualitative features suggests that the former, like the latter, have their origin in sense perception. Elsewhere, Descartes insists that there is something objective about our sensory ideas of the geometric features of bodies but not our sensory ideas of their color, warmth, and so on:

When we suppose that we perceive colors in objects . . . we do not really know what it is that we are calling a color; and we cannot find any intelligible resemblance between the color which we suppose to be in objects and that which we experience in our sensation. But this is something we do not take account of; and, what is more, there are many other features, such as size, shape and number which we clearly perceive to be actually or at least possibly present in objects in a way exactly corresponding to our sensory perception or understanding. (*Principles* I, art. 70)

But does Descartes mean that we clearly and distinctly perceive through the senses the particular extension of this or that body? He does say that "we have sensory awareness of, or rather as a result of sensory stimulation we have a clear and distinct perception of, some kind of matter, which is extended in length, breadth and depth, and has various differently shaped and variously moving parts which give rise to our various sensations of color, smells, pain and so on" (*Principles* II, art. 1). Or is it his view that, when I sense perceive a body, there is also involved in the conscious experience a conceptual element of the intellect that is a clear and distinct idea and that informs the perceptual acquaintance with the particular body? Descartes' distinction between clear and distinct ideas and obscure and confused ideas is often said to be a precursor to Locke's distinction between the sensory ideas of primary qualities (which are supposed to "resemble" the features in bodies that cause them) and the sensory ideas of secondary qualities (which are only qualitative effects in the mind and bear no resemblance to their material causes). But this cannot be truly determined until we know whether or not for Descartes *any* sense perceptions qualify as clear and distinct. The failure successfully to resolve this latter problem must, despite the many other distinctions that we can draw with or on behalf of Descartes, leave a rather significant gap in our understanding of his doctrine of ideas.

Further Reading

Alanen (1994); Beyssade (1992); Chappell (1986); Cook (1975; 1987); Costa (1983); Cronin (1966); Danto (1978); Gewirth (1967); Jolley (1990); Kenny (1967); McRae (1965); Normore (1986); Wilson (1993); Yolton (1975).

7

Proofs for the Existence of God

Lawrence Nolan and Alan Nelson

The Simplicity of Descartes' Proofs and the Relation between Them

To a reader voyaging through the *Meditations* for the first time, Descartes' proofs for the existence of God can seem daunting, especially the argument of Meditation III, with its appeal to causal principles that seem arcane, and to medieval doctrines about different modes of being and degrees of reality. First-time readers are not alone in feeling bewildered. Many commentators have had the same reaction. In an attempt at charity, some of them have tried to tame the complexity of Descartes' discussion by reconstructing sophisticated arguments with numerous premises. This has had the effect of making Descartes' arguments seem not more compelling, but less so.

We deploy another strategy in this chapter, one that springs from a conviction that Descartes intended his theistic proofs to be quite simple, if indeed he regarded them as proofs at all. What matters most for Descartes is that the meditator acquire the proper clear and distinct perceptions and that she "philosophize in the proper order." He thus spends the bulk of his time trying to induce these perceptions in the meditator in an order that he thinks will best engender knowledge. This is important because one is tempted to force each of Descartes' statements into the form of a premise, when what he is usually trying to do is to motivate his "premises," which tend to be simple and few in number.

Descartes develops two main arguments for the existence of God – the causal argument of Meditation III and the ontological argument of Meditation V – raising questions about the order and relation between them. Given Descartes' views about the foundational character of our knowledge of God, theistic arguments play a central role in the epistemological project of the *Meditations*. This shapes the character of the arguments he deploys. The meditator requires arguments that will establish not merely the existence of God, but the existence of a certain kind of God, namely one who is supremely perfect and is the creator of all things. Only then can he be assured that he was created by an omni-benevolent being who would endow him with a faculty for attaining truth and who would not deceive him)

Both of Descartes' arguments are adapted from traditional proofs of their kind. The causal argument bears a striking resemblance to the traditional "cosmological argument" found at least as far back as Aristotle but also in medieval thinkers such as St Thomas Aquinas. The standard version takes as its premise the existence of something perceived by the senses, such as the universe, and then seeks the source of this entity in the existence of a First Cause. But this traditional demonstration suffers from a serious shortcoming. It tells us precious little about the nature of this First Cause, which is an embarrassment for a Christian philosopher like Aquinas who would like to identify the First Cause with the God of scripture. Descartes sees it as an attraction of his argument that it yields a stronger conclusion, one that does deliver on God's nature (AT viiiA, 13). It proceeds from the idea of God as an infinite being having all perfections. The nature of God is built into this idea.

The ontological argument picks up where the causal argument leaves off. It too has a long history, but receives its classic formulation in the eleventh-century philosopher Anselm of Canterbury, who attempts to prove God's existence from the fact that we define "God" as a being no greater than one which can be conceived. If such a being did not exist, Anselm argues, he would not be the greatest conceivable being, which is contradictory. Against Anselm, Descartes thinks little of definitions of God. (The fact that we define the term "God" in a certain way proves nothing about whether such a being exists in reality (AT vii, 115)) For Descartes, one does not need to resort to a definition, for each of us has at his or her disposal a self-validating idea of God which is given to him or her in consciousness, and which represents God as existing.

The main relation between the causal and ontological arguments, then, is that they both proceed from the idea of God – an idea that is sufficiently rich to satisfy the epistemic needs of his project and the theological requirements of religion. But there is more. As a rationalist, Descartes subscribes to a theory of innate ideas. He takes the idea of God to be the clearest and most distinct of our innate ideas. (The innateness of this idea is central to both the causal argument, which purports to show that God causes our idea of him by implanting it in us at creation) and to the ontological argument, which, as we shall see, hinges on a crucial distinction between innate ideas and those fictitious ideas that we form in our imagination.

The Causal Argument

The method of the *Meditations* requires that only what has been accepted in Meditation II can be used to develop knowledge of God in Meditation III. This means that the meditator, a thing that thinks, is restricted to resources found in his own thought. It is, therefore, ideas and in particular the idea of an infinite thing, God, that will form the basis for the meditator's knowledge of the actually and necessarily existing God. The basic strategy is simple: the meditator's actually existing idea of God must derive its being from something else, and the only thing that could serve as the source of this idea's being is God. So God exists.

But what is the idea of God, and why should it, or any other idea, require a source, or cause of its being? And for that matter, what is an idea? The term "idea," in the usage so familiar since Descartes, does not appear in the *Meditations* until Meditation III. It is introduced there to draw attention to a particular feature of the thinking thing's thought: "Some of my thoughts are as it were the images of things, and it is only in these cases that the term 'idea' is strictly appropriate" (AT vii, 37). This means that the thoughts called ideas have objects, as it were. Ideas are *of* people, chimeras, God, and so on. Descartes immediately points out that a common error in thought is to suppose that what we naturally take as the objects of ideas exist apart from thinking them, and that this error is compounded by supposing that these objects exist outside thought in a way that resembles the idea. Since the meditator of Meditation III is maintaining the stance that nothing exists apart from his thought, it is crucial to isolate this error. This is accomplished by referring to the "as it were the image of a thing" feature of an idea as its *objective being*. This is distinguished from the *formal being* the idea has as a thought of a thinking thing. Descartes uses the term "formal being" for the ordinary being of anything that happens to exist, the meditator's thought, for example. Now this transformed medieval jargon can be used to characterize the error to which the meditator is prone. It is that one prematurely judges that the objective being of an idea strongly resembles some formal being apart from or "outside" that idea.

The structure of Descartes' argument can be given more fully once we have one more piece of terminology. The meditator's idea of God is said to represent an actually infinite amount of reality in virtue of its having God as its object or objective being. In the third set of *Replies*, Descartes writes: "I have also made it quite clear how reality admits of more and less. A substance is more of a thing than a mode . . . and, finally, if there is an infinite and independent substance, it is more of a thing than a finite and dependent substance" (AT vii, 185). The meditator is already aware of himself as a thing with many thoughts. So the meditator is a finite "substance" and his particular thoughts are his "modes." Each of these modes is said to depend on the thinker for its existence; they would not exist if the thinking thing did not exist. The thinking thing is not said to depend on any particular mode for its existence because it thinks many things. Descartes thus identifies three distinct levels of reality. Infinite substance (if it exists), finite substance (the thinking thing, for example), and modes (particular thoughts of the thinking thing, for example) exemplify these degrees of reality *formally*. But a thought of infinite substance is said to have the infinite level of reality *objectively*. And, similarly, for two lower levels of objective reality corresponding to the formal reality of finite substances and modes. To summarize these stipulative definitions:

Highest Level
INFINITE FORMAL REALITY: God (if God exists)
INFINITE OBJECTIVE REALITY: An idea of God

Second Level
FINITE FORMAL REALITY: A substance
FINITE OBJECTIVE REALITY: An idea of a substance

Third Level
MODAL FORMAL REALITY: A mode of a substance
MODAL OBJECTIVE REALITY: An idea of a mode.

It is important to realize that everything to this point is to be regarded as introducing terminology to refer to items that are easily found in thought. We are, in other words, just finding names for thoughts that are fully available in a Meditation II context, so we have not yet made a substantive advance beyond the Archimedean point of the *cogito*. The first logically substantive advance is made when Descartes asserts that the meditator does, in fact, think an idea whose object is God. Even though the idea Descartes wants here, in virtue of its objective being, represents infinite reality, it would not justify the immediate conclusion that infinite formal reality exists, i.e. it could not yet be concluded that God exists outside thought. Descartes seems to take it for granted that every meditator will easily think the idea of "a supreme God, eternal, infinite, [immutable], omniscient, omnipotent, and the creator of all things that exist apart from him" (AT vii, 40), but it seems he must verify that the meditator has the right idea of God.

In fact, he does provide the material for an argument to induce in an attentive meditator the requisite idea of God. This material is introduced to block the empiricist objection that what we call the idea of God is merely an augmented or enlarged idea of ourselves or some other finite thing (AT vii, 47). The required idea of God must represent *actually* infinite reality. Actual infinity is complete and perfect in the sense that it can in no way be augmented. The meditator's knowledge is imperfect insofar as he has doubts, and desires more knowledge. This knowledge, for example, could be endlessly augmented. Since it can be augmented without end or limit, it might be termed "infinite," but this is a potential or incomplete infinity. Descartes preferred the term "indefinite" for this imperfect kind of infinity. The crucial move now comes in understanding that if something might be endlessly augmented, this is the same as understanding that its augmentation will never be completed. But to understand that it will never be completed is to understand what it is that the process of augmentation can never reach. And that unreachable end is a completed, actual infinity. The point is that insofar as our idea of an incomplete infinity can be made distinct, it is by negatively contrasting it with the prior, positive idea of a complete infinity.

Numbers provide a good analogy here. Natural numbers are endlessly augmentable insofar as any specified natural number, no matter how large, has a successor. Descartes would say that this is a kind of potential infinity – we can conceive no limit of natural numbers. But this is not an actual infinity precisely because any particular sequence of natural numbers, no matter how large, is "incomplete" and can always be augmented. What is more, it might be argued that if one understands that natural numbers have no limit, this induces the idea of the cardinality of the natural numbers. Something like this is indicated in the modern mathematical concept (which Descartes would have rejected in this context because of his philosophy of mathematics) of "omega," which is, as it were, the set of natural numbers viewed as complete. In other words, the modern mathematical idea of the cardinality of the natural numbers functions in a way similar to the idea of complete infinity (God) in Descartes' philosophy.

The case of numbers is merely analogical, but Descartes thinks we can draw this distinction non-analogically in the case of our own knowledge. And it is primarily knowledge as a kind of thought that is relevant here because the meditator is certain only that he is a thing that thinks. Applying the point about numbers to knowledge, we get the idea of actually infinite knowledge, or omniscience. We might do the same for power and omnipotence, or any other attribute of God. If we focus more generally on the finite being or reality revealed in the *cogito*, we similarly arrive at the idea of infinite being or reality. Descartes insists that the idea of infinity is prior to, and even clearer and more distinct (AT vii, 45–6), than any other. The sense of "priority" here is obviously not temporal priority. The *cogito* comes before the idea of God when philosophizing in the correct order. Instead, the meditator comes to realize the idea of anything finite is a limitation or bounding of the idea of the infinite. This set of considerations replaces the empiricist view that what we call the idea of the infinite is an augmentation or enlargement of finite ideas. We can now reconstruct the first substantive step of Descartes' argument:

STEP 1:   There exists in the meditator's thought an idea with infinite objective being that represents actually infinite reality.

The second substantive step is a very plausible, general causal principle. Descartes writes: "Now it is manifest by the natural light that there must be at least as much [reality] in the efficient and total cause as in the effect of that cause" (AT vii, 40). Descartes motivates this by noting that if an effect had more reality than its total cause, the incremental reality would have to come from nothing. But "nothing" has no properties, which means that it has no causal powers. Therefore, "nothing" cannot be the cause of anything. The Latin slogan is *ex nihilo, nihilo fit*. This suggests, incidentally, that this Causal Principle is a version of the famous philosophical doctrine, the Principle of Sufficient Reason. Nothing comes from nothing, so wherever there is something, one can inquire about its source.

Now the Causal Principle is applied to the idea of God. In particular, we are to inquire after the cause of the objective reality represented by the idea: "yet the mode of being by which a thing exists objectively [or representatively] in the intellect by way of an idea, imperfect though it may be, is certainly not nothing, and so it cannot come from nothing." What then could account for this objective reality in the idea of God? Descartes makes this point rather bluntly at one place in Meditation III: "But in order for a given idea to contain such and such objective reality, it must surely derive it from some cause which contains at least as much formal reality as there is objective reality in the idea" (AT vii, 41). This expresses the notorious principle that is sometimes called OR-FR, short for objective-reality-to-formal-reality principle. The notoriety stems from the principle's seeming to extend beyond any plausibly innocent causal principle. "Surely," Descartes' critics have argued, "an argument postulating a bizarre sort of being (i.e., actually infinite objective being) and then requiring God (i.e. actually infinite formal being) as its cause cannot be a convincing proof of God's existence." But does Descartes' argument proceed this crudely?

Let us advance more carefully. Let us first consider how OR-FR would apply to an idea of a mode. An idea of a mode is not an idea of nothing; it has the third, modal level of objective reality. It follows from OR-FR that it must have a cause with at least the formal reality of a mode because that is the least formal reality anything can have. It can thus be proved that the objective reality of an idea of a mode is caused by something with at least the formal reality of a mode without using the fully general OR-FR; we require only that the idea have some cause, that it not be nothing or come from nothing.

Consider next an idea of a substance that has the second, finite substantial level of objective reality. This case seems harder, since we seem to need some implausibly robust OR-FR. Otherwise it is not immediately clear how to rule out as a cause for the second-level objective reality something with merely the third, modal level of formal reality. It is significant, however, that even on the (false for Descartes) supposition that a mode does cause an idea of a substance, we can still infer that a substance actually exists. We can apply the relatively innocent Causal Principle, "Nothing has no properties (i.e. modes)", to the mode we are supposing to have caused the idea of a substance. That mode must depend on some substance for its being, for that is what it is to be a mode. So the appropriate existential conclusion again requires only the relatively innocent Causal Principle. This case does not require some more robust version of OR-FR. To be perfectly rigorous, it must be marked that this second case, the case of an idea with the second level of objective reality, does not require even the Causal Principle to establish second-level formal reality. It is, after all, the *meditator's* idea of a finite substance that is under consideration and the meditator already has it from the *cogito* that he is a thinking thing, a finite substance.

Descartes does avoid bringing this out for a while by using the Latin *res* or "thing" (but we do get *ego autem substantia* at AT vii, 45 and thereafter). The meditator knows early on that, as a thinking thing, he himself has sufficient formal reality to serve as the source of finite objective reality in any of his ideas. So the absolutely crucial point is, of course, the treatment of the idea of God with its actually infinite objective reality. Could the meditator himself serve as the formal cause of the highest level of objective reality? Here Descartes makes another use of the distinction between that which is subject to augmentation and potentially infinite, on the one hand, and that which is complete and actually infinite, on the other. As we have seen, the meditator has arrived at an idea of God that is clear and distinct, and that contains absolutely nothing that is potential. He also understands that he can in no way construct the idea of an *actually* infinite thing from finite means. The meditator discovers his clear and distinct idea of actual infinity while investigating the process of augmenting and compounding ideas with finite objective reality. It follows that he cannot be the cause or sufficient reason of his idea of infinite objective reality. Only formally infinite reality can serve as the cause. So we have:

STEP 2:   The infinite objective reality of the idea identified in STEP 1 depends on infinite formal reality (God).

This concludes the argument. A striking thing about this reading is that no direct appeal is made to some implausibly robust OR-FR. The argument requires only that everything have some cause or other. We do not need the offending clause, namely, that the cause has as much formal reality as the idea has objective reality. The reasoning clearly has a transcendental character: it is given that the meditator has the idea of an actually infinite thing, and it is given that he could not have put this idea together from his store of ideas of finite, merely potentially infinite things, so the meditator could not be the cause of this idea. The existence of this idea must, therefore, be caused by an actually infinite thing outside his thought.

One might object here that a more robust causal principle is needed to rule out the possibility that some external substance other than God has caused the idea of the actually infinite. But even here we can do without. Anything aside from God that the meditator supposes to exist outside his thought has no more reality than he. Angels might be more "perfect" in various ways – even animals might have "perfections" that the meditator lacks – but angels and the rest still have the finite level of reality characteristic of created substances. The meditator himself can generate ideas of only potentially infinite things from finite means. He is, therefore, entitled to conclude that no other substance can do any better in this regard. Since the only thing that is at issue is finitude, an angel could not produce an idea of an actually infinite thing in its own mind. The reasons are exactly the same as in the case of the meditator himself. Furthermore, since an angel could not produce an idea of infinite objective reality for herself, she surely could not transmit it to the meditator – that is simply the innocent Causal Principle.

After giving the proof discussed above, Descartes acknowledges that a meditator might allow himself to become confused. One might still have the uncomfortable suspicion that Descartes is trading on the bizarre construct of "objective reality." Descartes writes: "I cannot so easily remember why the idea of a more perfect being than myself must proceed from some being that really is more perfect. This makes me want to inquire further whether I myself, who have the idea, could exist, if no such being existed" (AT vii, 47–8). As Meditation III continues, the argument shifts from a focus on the objective reality of an idea to the existence of the thinking thing having that idea. In other words, we are going to proceed to consider the issue of God's existence paying attention only to considerations of formal reality. The device of objective reality completely drops out. What follows is often referred to as Descartes' "second" causal argument for God's existence. Is it really a new argument? In correspondence about the *Meditations* written after their publication Descartes wrote: "It does not make much difference whether my second proof, the one based on our existence, is regarded as different from the first proof, or merely as an explanation of it" (to [Mesland] May 2, 1644, AT iv, 112). As we shall see, the basic structure of the "second" proof is exactly the same as the "first." And since the second makes no use whatsoever of OR-FR, Descartes' providing this additional proof or explanation is further evidence that the real philosophical foci of the proofs are the power of the idea of God and the Causal Principle.

The meditator now inquires about the total and efficient cause of his formal being as a thinking thing. Could he, himself, be the source of his own being? The same considerations apply this time too. Since the meditator is aware of his own limitations (for example, his doubting some things), he is not an infinite thing. As a finite thing, his formal reality requires an external source. To see this, suppose instead that he were the source of his own being. Then he either creates himself from nothing, or else he sustains his own being from eternity. But to create himself from nothing violates the Causal Principle unless his power to create is infinite. In other words, only an omnipotent being could create being from nothing. So if the meditator were the source of his own being, he would have to sustain his own being from eternity. Descartes claims that this too is impossible on the ground that conserving or sustaining being requires the same power as creation from nothing. Existence at one time is not by itself a sufficient cause for existence at any other time, so the sufficient cause must again be something actually infinite. Here, the meditator's distinct realization that he is unable to serve as the source of his own being is tantamount to his earlier realization that actual infinity is required as the total and efficient cause, the sufficient cause, of his being.

Again, it cannot be objected that the meditator might derive his formal being from a different finite thing. For where would that other finite thing derive its existence? A very long regress of finite sources, even an indefinitely long regress, would itself require a source. It would not help to suppose that a second regress of causes was the source of the first indefinitely long regress because then the two taken together would now be a single, new, indefinitely long regress and no progress would have been made. This way of blocking an infinite regress of finite, formal causes of being is isomorphic to the way in which Descartes' blocks the empiricists' claim that the idea of God can be formed by augmenting ideas with finite objective reality. A merely potentially infinite series of causes cannot do the work of an actual, complete, infinite cause. In short, since the *cogito* gives us that *this* thinking exists, the ultimate source of that existence must be a something which itself requires no source – a formally infinite being. So, we can again state that Descartes' causal argument for the existence of God has two steps.

STEP 1′: The meditator exists as a thinking thing that thinks of an actually infinite thing.

STEP 2′: The sufficient cause for the meditator's existence must be actually infinite.

Each of these steps involves an explicit, powerful philosophical assumption. But these assumptions are not bizarre, anachronistically medieval, or particularly obscure.

The Ontological Argument

The first thing to recognize about Descartes' ontological argument is that it is not a proof. This sounds paradoxical, but the point is that what is called an "argument" is something very different from a *formal* proof. Certainly, Descartes uses the language of proof and logical inference in the context of Meditation V and, in some texts, even presents one or more syllogisms for God's existence. His considered view, however, is that the so-called ontological "argument" is a self-evident axiom, grasped by intuition or – what is the same for Descartes – clear and distinct perception. Indeed, he maintains that we ultimately obtain knowledge of God's existence by discovering that necessary existence is contained in the clear and distinct idea of a supremely perfect being.

> I ask my readers to spend a great deal of time and effort on contemplating the nature of the supremely perfect being. Above all they should reflect on the fact that the ideas of all other natures contain possible existence, whereas the idea of God contains not only possible but wholly necessary existence. This alone, without a formal argument, will make them realize that God exists; and this will eventually be just as self-evident to them as the fact that the number two is even or that three is odd . . . (AT vii, 163–4)

To say that the existence of God is ultimately known through intuition is not to say that it is *immediately* self-evident. If that were so, then there would have been no need for the causal argument. On the contrary, Descartes thinks that

God's existence is something that only *becomes* self-evident after careful meditation. A formal argument can serve as useful heuristic in attaining the relevant
intuition of God, but this is only a means to an end that is ultimately dispensable
(see Nolan 2006). Consider a key passage on this point from Meditation V:

> But whatever method of proof I use, I am always brought back to the fact that it is
> only what I clearly and distinctly perceive that completely convinces me. Some of the
> things I clearly and distinctly perceive are obvious to everyone, while others are dis-
> covered only by those who look more closely and investigate more carefully; but once
> they have been discovered, the latter are judged to be just as certain as the former.
> In the case of a right-angled triangle, for example, the fact that the square on the
> hypotenuse is equal to the square on the other two sides is not so readily apparent
> as the fact that the hypotenuse subtends the largest angle; but once one has seen it,
> one believes it just as strongly. But as regards God, if I were not overwhelmed by
> philosophical prejudices, and if the images of things perceived by the senses did not
> besiege my thought on every side, I would certainly acknowledge him sooner and
> more easily than anything else. For what is more self-evident than the fact that the
> supreme being exists, or that God, to whose essence alone existence belongs, exists?
> (AT vii, 68–9)

Here again we find Descartes asserting that it is not proofs that convince him of
God's existence ultimately, but clear and distinct perception – specifically the perception that necessary existence is included in the idea or essence of a supremely
perfect being. But he qualifies this point by noting that God's existence is not
immediately self-evident to most meditators. Initially, it is akin to a theorem in
geometry, such as the Pythagorean theorem, which takes great effort and perhaps
even a proof to discover. But once we have fully withdrawn from the senses and
relinquished our philosophical prejudices, God's existence becomes as self-evident
as an axiom or definition in geometry, such as that the hypotenuse of a right-angled
triangle subtends its greatest angle.

Descartes' reference to "philosophical prejudices" in this last passage is highly
significant because it indicates why, on his analysis, God's existence is not immediately self-evident. It also is relevant to his account of how God's existence can
become self-evident and reveals what the Fifth Meditation is primarily designed
to do – namely, to dispel our prejudices, so that God's existence can be directly
intuited. As a way of exploring these issues, let us reflect for a moment on some
of the central features of Descartes' epistemology. Descartes is a nativist, meaning
that he subscribes to a doctrine of innate ideas. He thinks that the ideas of God,
soul, and body have been implanted in us by God and constitute the "seeds of
knowledge" (AT x, 217). Attaining knowledge, according to this view, would seem
to be a simple affair. One simply turns one's attention to the ideas that are innately
within the mind and reads off their contents. In reality, things are quite a bit more
complicated. For one thing, one needs a divine guarantee that one's innate, clear,
and distinct ideas are true. Following Plato, Descartes also thinks that one's innate

ideas are often "submerged" from consciousness and need to be "awakened" in the mind. But most importantly for our purposes, he holds that one's innate ideas tend to be highly confused prior to meditating. This confusion results from various philosophical prejudices that one forms in childhood, typically as a result of relying on the senses and on traditional philosophy derived from Aristotle. To render one's innate ideas clear and distinct, and ultimately attain knowledge, one must extirpate these prejudices (AT ixB, 5; vii, 157).

By the term "prejudices," Descartes means false judgments that accompany our ordinary thoughts and perceptions. Typically, such judgments have become so habituated that we do not realize that we are making them (AT viiiA, 22). Instances of such prejudices abound, especially those stemming from the senses. Let us consider a few. Part of the Cartesian revolution in science consists in banishing so-called sensible qualities such as colors, odors, sounds, and so on from the physical world. But Descartes thinks that most of his meditators will have formed the habit of imputing such qualities to the objects around them. The ordinary person, for example, judges that greenness is in the grass and that sweetness is in the apple. Descartes maintains that such prejudices prevent us from intuiting that the whole essence of physical objects is extension. Prejudices stemming from the senses also pose an obstacle to our conception of immaterial beings. In fact, Descartes thinks that the greatest obstacle to forming clear and distinct ideas of the soul and God is our tendency to conceive everything in sensory and/or corporeal terms (AT vii, 131). In Meditation II, he speaks, for example, of his former tendency to judge that the soul is an airy material substance that permeates his body rather than a purely thinking thing (AT vii, 26). The ordinary Christian also tends to conceive God as a bearded, fatherly figure shining forth from the highest mountain top.

By Meditation V, the successful meditator has learned to withdraw from the senses and the prejudices they engender (AT vii, 53). But other prejudices remain and, as we shall discover, Meditation V targets those pertaining to God specifically. Descartes distinguishes two such prejudices, both of which must be removed if the meditator is to intuit God's existence. The first prejudice involves a habit that Descartes believes his seventeenth-century reader would have acquired from what was then part of the standard educational curriculum – viz., scholastic philosophy. This is the habit of distinguishing a thing's essence from its existence. The second prejudice derives from the habit of inventing mental fictions. The worry here is that God, conceived of as an existing being, might just be one of those fictitious entities that our mind is prone to fashion in the imagination. Although distinct, these two prejudices are closely related and reinforce one another, and consequently their dissolution is achieved in a similar manner. Before examining Descartes' strategies for dispelling them, let us begin by investigating each of them at greater length.

Descartes sometimes characterizes the so-called ontological argument as a proof from the "essence" or "nature" of God, arguing that necessary existence cannot be separated from the essence of a supremely perfect being without contradiction (AT vii, 66). In casting the argument in these terms, he is relying on a traditional medieval distinction between a thing's essence and its existence. According to this tradition, one can determine what something is (i.e., its essence) independently of knowing whether it exists. This medieval distinction serves Descartes' purposes very well, but it also poses something of a danger: one might be tempted to draw the distinction too sharply, such that existence is not included in God's essence. Among medieval thinkers, there were different ways of understanding the distinction, at least as it applies to finite, created beings. All parties agreed that, in God, essence and existence are the same. God's essence just is to exist. But in the case of finite beings, some medieval thinkers drew a very sharp distinction between essence and existence, treating them as two distinct things. According to this broadly "Thomistic" view, a finite thing's essence enjoys an attenuated form of being eternally in the divine intellect, and existence is something that is added to it in creation. This is the theory of "real distinction" between essence and existence, a term that rightly evokes Descartes' theory of the real distinction between mind and body. In both cases, the *relata* of the distinction are real entities that can have being apart from each other.

At the other end of the spectrum from the Thomistic position is the doctrine that there is merely a conceptual distinction between essence and existence in all things. Proponents of this view held that a thing's essence and its existence are identical in reality and that the distinction between them is confined to our thought. Essence and existence are not distinct things, but one thing regarded in different ways. Reason draws a theoretical distinction where there is no distinction in reality (see Nolan 1998). This view was popular among many scholastic "nominalists," who were eager to avoid multiplying entities beyond necessity. It is also the doctrine most amenable to the Cartesian system, which denies that there is anything (such as essences in the divine intellect) prior to God's will. Descartes expresses his allegiance to it as follows:

> I do not remember where I spoke of the distinction between essence and existence. However . . . because we do indeed understand the essence of a thing in one way when we consider it in abstraction from whether it exists or not, and in a different way when we consider it as existing . . . I call it a conceptual distinction. (AT iv, 349)

Although Descartes was committed to the view that essence and existence are merely conceptually distinct in all things, he worried that his readers would have likely been most influenced by the theory of real distinction between essence and existence. Indeed, he even refers to the latter as the "customary distinction" (AT v, 164). This is a problem because a meditator who has grown accustomed to drawing a real distinction between essence and existence in finite things might easily be tempted to extend this distinction to God. But to judge that, in God, essence and existence are really distinct is to suppose that existence is *not* contained in the divine essence. "Since I have been accustomed to distinguish between existence and essence in everything else, I find it easy to persuade myself that existence can also be separated from the essence of God, and hence that God can be thought of as not existing" (AT vii, 66).

The second prejudice pertaining to God is far less technical than the first. It concerns an issue that was first treated with some care in Meditation III, and thus reveals one of the most significant linkages between the causal and ontological arguments. The issue is whether our idea of God is innate or fictitious. If it were fictitious then, in the context of Meditation III, there would have been no reason to posit an infinite being as its cause. The meditator, with his finite intellect, could be the cause, just as he is the cause of many fictitious ideas that have no existence outside thought. But the meditator discovers that, as a finite mind, he cannot be the cause of the idea of an actually infinite being. Thus, his idea of God is not invented but innate – the "mark of the craftsman stamped on his work" (AT vii, 51). In a surprising move, Descartes returns to the question of the origin of the idea of God in Meditation V, insisting after lengthy discussion that it is innate (AT vii, 68). Why does he revisit this question if it had already been settled earlier?

To answer this question, it helps to consider how fictitious ideas are formed. According to Descartes, such ideas are produced by arbitrarily combining other ideas, or elements of other ideas, in one's imagination. For example, one forms the idea of the mythical creature Pegasus by combining the ideas of horse and wingedness (AT vii, 117). By its very nature or structure, a fictitious composite cannot be distinct in Descartes' definitional sense of clarity and distinctness; a distinct idea is one that is "sharply separated from all other perceptions" (AT viiiA, 22). But if an idea is not clear and distinct, then it cannot be relied upon to reveal the true nature of reality. Consider now what was discovered about the idea of God in Meditation III. Descartes gives us two lists of attributes; included among these are infinitude, omnipotence, omniscience, eternality, and so on (AT vii, 40, 45). Noticeably absent from these lists, however, is "necessary existence."

To discover the other attributes, it was sufficient for the meditator to train her mind to withdraw from the senses and to conceive God through the intellect alone. Necessary existence, however, is much more elusive. Much of the difficulty would seem to lie with the nature of the attribute to be perceived. It is one thing to perceive that the idea of God includes, say, omnipotence; quite another to determine whether necessary existence is properly included. For only in clearly and distinctly perceiving the latter are we compelled to conclude that God exists. Such a result could raise suspicions about whether we are dealing with a true idea or one of those false, invented ideas that lack existential import. So although it was established in Meditation III that the idea of God is innate, the question now is whether the idea of God *qua* necessary being is innate. The meditator may judge that he has corrupted or "fictionalized" the true idea of God discovered in

Meditation III by superadding necessary existence to it. This is where the compositional theory of invented ideas comes into play. In perceiving that my idea of God contains necessary existence have I merely unveiled one of its further contents or have I arbitrarily superadded another idea to it? (see Nolan 2006).

Now that we have a strong sense of the two prejudices themselves, let us turn to Descartes' efforts in Meditation V and elsewhere to extirpate them. In this regard, it is important to keep in mind that Descartes conceived the *Meditations* as a kind of guidebook to the truth. Each meditator has to discover the truth for herself, but Descartes thinks that he can aid her in this process by leading her through various cognitive exercises that are designed to dispel prejudice and induce clear and distinct perceptions. The famous method of universal doubt provides the most important and familiar example of such an exercise. The greatest benefit of hyperbolic doubt, we are told in the Synopsis of the *Meditations*, "lies in freeing us from all our prejudices, and providing the easiest route by which the mind may be led away from the senses" (AT vii, 12). The method of doubt is intended to be universal, but does not dispel all of our prejudices, which are difficult to overcome owing to their habitual nature. Moreover, some of our prejudices are formed, or at least become manifest, in the course of meditating. This is clearly the case in this instance, where the judgments that my idea of God is invented, or that essence and existence are really distinct in all things, arise in a context in which one is considering whether God exists. Although the method of doubt is not completely successful in eradicating our prejudices, it provides a useful model for understanding the cognitive exercises that Descartes deploys in Meditation V.

The first prejudice stems from the habit of drawing a real distinction between essence and existence in all things. From the perspective of Descartes' own theory of the relation between essence and existence, both the second prejudice and the scholastic habit that produced it are mistakes. It is just as wrong to ascribe a real distinction between essence and existence to created beings as it is to attribute such a distinction to God. In both cases, there is merely a conceptual distinction. Descartes, however, does draw a sharp distinction between different "grades" or kinds of existence: "Existence is contained in the idea or concept of every single thing, since we cannot conceive of anything except as existing. Possible or contingent existence is contained in the concept of a limited thing, whereas necessary and perfect existence is contained in the concept of a supremely perfect being" (AT vii, 166). The insight that one cannot conceive anything except as existing is often mistakenly credited to Hume and Kant. Here we find Descartes expressing his own commitment to this principle, though with one important qualification: he distinguishes two different kinds of existence – possible and necessary. Necessary existence is unique to the idea or essence of God, and so it follows uniquely from our idea of God that such a being exists.

Given its source, the most powerful way of defeating the first prejudice would be to break the habit itself, which in fact is Descartes' strategy. To suppose that there is a real distinction between essence and existence abroad in all things would be to exclude existence from our clear and distinct ideas. But Descartes thinks that if we reflect on the matter carefully, we shall discover that we cannot conceive anything except as existing. Existence is contained in the clear and distinct idea of every single thing. In fact, if the meditator is having trouble intuiting that necessary existence is contained in the idea of God, it helps to turn to the clear and distinct ideas of finite things, and to observe that contingent existence is contained therein. Repeated reflection on this fact will break one of the habit of ascribing to all things a real distinction between essence and existence.

Descartes' strategy for defeating the second prejudice is a variation on this same device. Recall that the reader whose mind is confused by this prejudice falsely judges that he has "fictionalized" his innate idea of God by combining it with the idea of necessary existence. To form such a composite in the mind, however, one would have to derive the idea of necessary existence from some other source, perhaps by abstraction from the idea of some finite thing. But this is not possible. A careful survey of our clear and distinct ideas reveals that necessary existence is unique to our idea of God. Possible or contingent existence is contained in the clear and distinct ideas of all finite things, while necessary existence is peculiar to the idea of a supremely perfect being. We could not have derived the idea of necessary existence from any other source. One can now appreciate the force of the passage with which we began this section:

> I ask my readers to spend a great deal of time and effort on contemplating the nature of the supremely perfect being. Above all they should reflect on the fact that the ideas of all other natures contain possible existence, whereas the idea of God contains not only possible but wholly necessary existence. This alone, without a formal argument, will make them realize that God exists . . . (AT vii, 163–4)

At first sight, this request seemed baffling, but put in the proper context, the motivation is now clear. Observing that necessary existence is unique to the idea of God is a useful exercise for overcoming the prejudice that we have invented such an idea. Once such prejudices are removed, God's existence will be self-evident (see Nolan 2006).

So far, we have discussed the strategies for dispelling prejudice that Descartes deploys in texts designed to elucidate and expand upon Meditation V. But in Meditation V proper he deploys another set of cognitive exercises, some of which more directly link the ontological argument to the earlier causal argument. At the end of Meditation III, Descartes appeals to an important phenomenological feature of our idea of God to establish its innateness. He notes that the idea of God differs from invented ideas in that we cannot "take away anything from it or add anything to it" (AT vii, 51). In Meditation V, he develops this point, crafting it into a powerful device for eradicating our prejudices.

We learned above that invented ideas on Descartes' account are ones that the mind forms by combining two or more other ideas (or the elements of other ideas). Notice that ideas that have been composed arbitrarily in this way, more or less at will, can also be *de*composed at will. If I form the idea of a winged horse by combining the ideas of "wingedness" and "horse," then I can also conceive those elements apart from one another. Innate ideas, however, are not like that. Because they were created by God, and not by me, innate ideas impose their content on my thought. This is not to say that I am ever compelled to think about one of these ideas, but whenever I choose to summon an innate idea from what Descartes calls the "treasure-house" of my mind, I am compelled to regard it in certain prescribed ways (AT vii, 67). To put it differently, once I acquire facility with my innate ideas through meditation, I can think of them at will, but I cannot alter them at will. They are in this sense "incorruptible." Here Descartes cites various geometrical examples. To wit, I might not have noticed initially that the sum of the angles of a triangle are equal to two right angles, but once I discover this property to be contained in my innate idea of such a figure, I cannot exclude it by a clear and distinct operation of the intellect (AT vii, 64, 67–8, 117–18). The aim of Descartes' discussion, of course, is to show that the innate idea of a supremely perfect being also constrains the ways in which we are able to conceive it clearly and distinctly: "existence can no more be separated from the essence of God than the fact that its three angles equal two right angles can be separated from the essence of a triangle" (AT vii, 66).

The distinctive character of innate ideas provides Descartes with another means for defeating the two prejudices discussed above. For example, suppose one has formed the prejudice that there is a real distinction between essence and existence in God. This is tantamount to judging that existence can be excluded from the idea of a supremely perfect being by a clear and distinct intellectual operation. But to *judge* that something can be excluded from our ideas and actually *to perform the exclusion* are two very different mental operations. Like all prejudices, this one results from the failure to consult our clear and distinct ideas. Thus, Descartes invites his readers to attempt to exclude necessary existence from the clear and distinct idea of a supremely perfect being, fully expecting that their efforts will fail. Again, Descartes thinks that innate ideas have something like the character of "read-only" documents, to use an analogy with computers. Trying to exclude necessary existence from one's idea of God is akin to attempting a "search-and-replace" operation on a read-only document, in which a phrase such as "necessary existence" appears. Since the document is read-only, one cannot alter its contents, and the attempt to delete something serves only to highlight the very item that one is attempting to expunge. A more Cartesian analogy can be found in the *cogito*, where the effort to doubt one's existence is self-defeating and only confirms that one does exist as a doubter.

The ontological argument has been the target of several famous objections. Many of these were familiar to Descartes and his contemporaries from the classical debate between Anselm and a monk named Gaunilo. Descartes treats these objections in a unique way, one that squares with his view that God's existence is ultimately attained through intuition rather than by means of an argument. According to his diagnosis, all such objections are rooted in one of the two prejudices discussed above. Thus, his strategy for dealing with them is to attempt to dispel the objector's prejudices.

Gaunilo famously objected that Anselm's version of the ontological argument makes an illicit logical leap from the mental to the extra-mental. The claim is that even if we were to concede that necessary existence is inseparable from the idea of God, nothing follows from this about what does or does not exist in the actual world. Descartes considers an objection like this in Meditation V:

> [E]ven granted that I cannot think of God except as existing, just as I cannot think of a mountain without a valley, it certainly does not follow from the fact that I think of a mountain with a valley that there is any mountain in the world; and similarly, it does not seem to follow from the fact that I think of God as existing that he does exist. For my thought does not impose any necessity on things; and just as I may imagine a winged horse even though no horse has wings, so I may be able to attach existence to God even though no God exists. (AT vii, 66)

Notice that in his formulation of the objection, Descartes takes the issue to be whether he has attached the idea of necessary existence to his idea of God in the way that one combines the ideas of horse and wings to imagine a winged horse. As he sees it, Gaunilo's objection is motivated by a suspicion that our idea of God *qua* existing being is fictitious like that of the winged horse. If it were fictitious, then Descartes would agree, nothing follows from it.

Descartes replies to this objection as follows:

> But there is a sophism concealed here. From the fact that I cannot think of a mountain without a valley, it does not follow that a mountain and valley exist anywhere, but simply that a mountain and a valley, whether they exist or not, are mutually inseparable. But from the fact that I cannot think of God except as existing, it follows that existence is inseparable from God, and hence that he really exists. It is not that my thought makes it so, or imposes any necessity on any thing; on the contrary, it is the necessity of the thing itself, namely the existence of God, which determines my thinking in this respect. For I am not free to think of God without existence (that is, a supremely perfect being without a supreme perfection) as I am free to imagine a horse with or without wings. (AT vii, 66–7)

There are two main points being made here, one for each of the ideas that are presented as disanalogous to the idea of God. First, the clear and distinct idea of God differs from the idea of a mountain without a valley (or, better, the idea of an upslope without a downslope) in that it contains necessary existence. So, Descartes holds, existence follows in the first case but not in the second. Second, and this is the more important case, the idea of God differs from the idea of a winged horse in that the first is innate and the second is fictitious. I know that the idea of God is innate precisely because I am "not free" to think of him without existence, whereas I am free to imagine ideas that I have invented, such as a winged horse, in any way that I like. Again, innate ideas are incorruptible in the sense that their content is imposed on my thought. I cannot add anything to them that is not contained in them and I cannot subtract or exclude anything that is contained in them. Seeing that this is true of the idea of God is a powerful cognitive exercise for dispelling the prejudice that this idea is fictitious. Once this prejudice is removed, God's existence will be self-evident, or so Descartes maintained.

The most famous objection to the ontological argument is often stated in the form of a slogan, known by every philosophy major worth her salt: "existence is not a property (or predicate)." This objection is often attributed to Kant and Bertrand Russell, but it was previously articulated by Pierre Gassendi, one of the official objectors to the *Meditations* (AT vii, 323). The point of the objection is that existence bears a very close relation to the thing that exists. It is not a property like other properties, for how can a thing even have properties if it does not exist? If someone brags to you about the various appointments of her new sports car, you would be perplexed if one of the options she listed was existence. Existence is not one of the car's options (if it is, it's the most expensive option!), but a pre-requisite for having options in the first place. Kant puts the point in terms of concept-containment, observing that existence does not add anything to the concept of a thing. There is no intrinsic difference, for example, between imagining one hundred *real* dollars and imagining one hundred *possible* dollars. In both cases, we are imagining a set of existing dollars (which is not to say, of course, that they do exist).

It is often thought that Descartes succumbs to this objection by asserting that (necessary) existence is a property that can be listed among God's other perfections. But, in fact, he agrees with his critics about the status of existence. Indeed, in passages cited earlier, we find Descartes asserting, along with Kant, that existence is included in the idea of every single thing. We cannot clearly and distinctly conceive anything except as existing (AT vii, 116, 166). He also affirms that existence is not an extra ontological category: there is merely a conceptual distinction between a substance and its existence (AT iv, 349; also see AT viiiA, 26, 30). Descartes maintained that we can draw a distinction in our thought between a thing and its existence, but this does not entail that existence is a mode (in his terminology) or that "the thing itself can be outside our thought without its existence" (AT iv, 349). Where he differs from his critics is in drawing a distinction between two kinds of existence – contingent and necessary. Contingent existence is contained in the clear and distinct idea of every finite thing, while necessary existence is uniquely contained in the clear and distinct idea of God, which is why, according to Descartes, actual existence follows uniquely from the concept of the latter (see Nolan 2001).

8

The Cartesian Circle

Gary Hatfield

After Descartes had written his six *Meditations on First Philosophy*, he invited various philosophers and theologians to offer objections to his arguments and conclusions. One of the most famous objections came from the theologian Antoine Arnauld, in the *Fourth Objections*:

> I have one further scruple, about how the author avoids a circle when he says that we are sure that what we clearly and distinctly perceive is true only because God exists. But we can be sure that God exists only because we clearly and distinctly perceive this. Consequently, before we might be sure that God exists, we ought to be sure that whatever we clearly and evidently perceive is true. (AT vii, 214)

The problem seems to be that Descartes relies on the existence of God to guarantee the truth of clear and distinct perceptions, but his proofs about God are accepted as true simply because they are clearly and distinctly perceived. Each result – the existence of God and the truth of clear and distinct perceptions – would seem to depend on the other, resulting in a charge of circular reasoning.

Descartes responded only briefly to Arnauld. He said that there is no circle if, when we prove the existence of God, we in fact carefully attend to the arguments for this conclusion and we in fact do clearly and distinctly perceive that God exists (AT vii, 245–6). The conclusion of this proof can then be recalled if doubts arise about the truth of clear perception on an occasion when we are not entertaining such perceptions. In effect, he said that in the proofs of God's existence, clear and distinct perception can stand on its own, a claim that seems to ignore his own assertion that we know such perceptions to be true only because we know that God exists (and is no deceiver). Subsequently, some philosophers have found that Descartes' response to Arnauld "begs the question," that is, that it simply assumes the very point under dispute. Other philosophers, however, have proposed various strategies for defending Descartes against the charge of circularity (see Doney 1987).

The problem of the Cartesian circle, as it is called, has sparked continuing debate, which intersects several important themes of the *Meditations*. Discussions of the circle must address questions about the force and scope of the famous method of doubt introduced in Meditation I, and they must examine the intricate arguments for the existence of God and the avoidance of error in Meditations III–V. These discussions raise questions about the possibility of overturning skepticism, once a skeptical doubt has been introduced. More generally, the problem of the circle resonates with recent questions about the foundations of knowledge. Must we be able to validate our methods of reasoning or of knowing before using them? If we must, would we not be forever stuck at the beginning, unable to use our methods of reasoning or of knowing in their own validation? The problem of the Cartesian circle raises general questions about the validation of reason and the possibility of knowledge.

This chapter examines the Cartesian circle in the context of Descartes' central project in the *Meditations*: to secure the foundations of metaphysics. In carrying out this project, Descartes felt the need, or adopted the strategy, of examining the possibility of human knowledge more generally. Such an examination can be interpreted in various ways. Depending on the interpretation given, the roles assigned to the method of doubt and the proofs about God may differ, thereby altering how we see the problem of the circle. We therefore need first to consider Descartes' metaphysical project, along with the methods and strategies he adopted in carrying it out. Subsequently, I will explain and evaluate several main approaches to the problem of the circle. The chapter concludes with some reflections on the relation of Descartes' metaphysics of knowledge to other prominent positions in the history of philosophy.

Descartes' Project in the *Meditations*

Descartes offered his *Meditations* as a presentation of the "elements of First Philosophy in its entirety" (AT vii, 9). He used the term "first philosophy" synonymously with "metaphysics" (AT vii, 156–7; also, AT iii, 183). Hence, as in the title of the French translation of the work (1647), the *Meditations* should be viewed as "metaphysical meditations" (AT ixA, xi).

Metaphysics, in Descartes' view, was the most basic area of science (that is, of systematic knowledge). As he suggested in Meditation I, the aim of his metaphysical meditations was to establish "something firm and lasting in the sciences" (AT vii, 17). Metaphysics would provide the basic concepts and principles for other areas of knowledge, as in Descartes' famous image of a tree of knowledge, with metaphysics as the roots, physics as the trunk, and medicine, mechanics, and morals as the branches (AT ixB, 14). Descartes specifically intended his *Meditations* to provide the foundations for his physics or natural philosophy; that is, for his general account of the natural world. In letters to his friend Marin Mersenne from late 1640 and early 1641, he confided that "these six Meditations contain all the foundations of my Physics" (AT iii, 298; also iii, 233). These "foundations," or basic concepts and principles, included the ontology of mind and matter (that the essence of mind is thought, and the essence of matter is extension), the laws of motion, and the explanation of human sensation through mind–body union and interaction.

These foundations showed some similarity with ancient atomism (the view that matter consists of indivisible particles), but with this difference: Descartes viewed matter as infinitely divisible, and denied the possibility of a vacuum. By contrast with other corpuscular philosophers of his day (such as Galileo, Gassendi, and Hobbes), who used only empirically based arguments to support their atomism, Descartes claimed to arrive at his conception of the essence of matter by attending to innate ideas perceived by the intellect alone. This turn to innate ideas has similarity with the Platonic conception of knowledge as "reminiscence" of a direct acquaintance with eternal Forms, though Descartes' position differed from Plato's in ways that will become clear.

Although various philosophical positions, including Stoic, atomistic, and Platonic positions, were known to Descartes and his contemporaries, the dominant philosophy of the time was scholastic Aristotelianism. Aristotle's philosophy, as variously interpreted within differing schools of thought in both Catholic and Protestant universities across Europe, was ubiquitous in Descartes' world. Descartes had been educated in this philosophy, and he was highly sensitive to its dominant position (AT i, 522; iii, 432). His conception of the mind–body relation and of the basic properties of matter contrasted sharply with the core positions of mainstream Aristotelianism. He was determined to overturn this philosophy; that is, to foment a revolution in thought. The *Meditations* was to accomplish the destruction of Aristotelian philosophical principles (as he further confided to Mersenne [AT iii, 298]).

According to Aristotelian philosophy, corporeal or material substances contain a form or "active principle" that directs their motion and change. In human beings, the rational soul is the principal form. It is not something separate from the body, but is an intrinsic power in the human body that renders the human being alive. The rational soul has vegetative powers (that govern nutrition, growth, and reproduction), sensitive powers, and rational powers of thought. Non-living things also contain active principles; thus, earthy matter moves toward the center of the earth itself because its inner active principle directs its motion toward that location. Descartes denied the existence of such forms, holding that matter itself is passive (AT v, 403–5; Hatfield 1979); he restricted activity to human minds and God (and, perhaps, angels). The Aristotelians also held that sense perception occurs when representatives of the forms of things, such as the "form of color," are transmitted to the eye. Descartes rejected the need for such "real qualities" in things; that is, for forms in things that (in his words) "resemble" the color we experience (AT vi, 112; vii, 75; iii, 420, 492). Finally, the Aristotelians held that all knowledge relies on the senses, and that the intellectual power of the rational soul merely "abstracts" what is in common among various things presented through the senses, thereby discerning their essences (what makes them be the kind of thing they are). By contrast, Descartes held that the human intellect, operating independently of sensory experience, has direct knowledge of the essences of things, including mind, matter, geometrical objects, and the essence of God.

If Descartes wanted to convince a primarily Aristotelian audience to accept his metaphysics, he would have an uphill battle. He would need to convince them that they should accept principles radically opposed to Aristotelian physics and metaphysics. Further, he hoped to do so by appealing to a source of knowledge that they did not recognize: clear and distinct perceptions of the pure intellect, operating independently of the senses.

In order to achieve his aims, Descartes adopted the strategy of writing his *Meditations* as meditations. In other words, he modeled his book in metaphysics and the theory of knowledge (or "epistemology") on a form of religious writing, that of "meditations" or "spiritual exercises" (Hatfield 1986; Sepper 2002). In spiritual exercises, which were common in Jesuit schools such as the one Descartes attended (La Flèche), readers learn to abandon the world of the senses and sensuality and to focus on God. In spiritual exercises of an Augustinian (hence Neoplatonic) flavor, this involved completely abandoning the senses to search for the idea of God within (as Augustine had done in his *Confessions*). Descartes adapted this literary form in a way that might be conducive to wooing his readers, including the Aristotelians among them, away from the senses and toward purely intellectual knowledge. Because the *Meditations* is constructed in the hope that each reader will take on the identity of the "I" of the narrative, the presumed reader of the text is called "the meditator." Descartes hoped to provide each meditator with immediate evidence of purely intellectual knowledge, by eliciting examples of it in each meditator's own consciousness.

This strategy is suggested by what Descartes said in the Preface to the *Meditations*. He informed his readers that he had "set out the very thoughts which have enabled me, in my view, to arrive at a certain and evident cognition of the truth, so that I can find out whether the same arguments that have persuaded me will enable me to persuade others" (AT vii, 10). He asked readers to "meditate seriously" with him, and to "withdraw their minds from the senses and, at the same time, from all preconceived opinions" (AT vii, 9). He encouraged them to attend to the order and sequence of his arguments (also an important feature of spiritual exercises). He did not expect everyone to be persuaded or convinced right away. In order to become convinced, he advised readers to spend "several months, or at least weeks," just on Meditation I (AT vii, 130), and also to study the *Objections* and his *Replies* to them. He wanted readers to consider the arguments for themselves, and to entertain the possibility of changing their current opinions.

The Introduction of the Doubt

In considering the charge of circularity, it will be important to keep in mind Descartes' aims for the *Meditations*, and also his strategy of leading readers away from their previous beliefs and toward the (in his view) one, true metaphysics. In line with the meditative strategy of purging former beliefs and turning away from the senses, Meditation I introduces a radical doubt. This doubt is directed first at the senses, whose trustworthiness is undermined through charges of inaccuracy, through the "dream argument" (which challenges whether waking reality can be distinguished from vivid dreams), and by evoking the "long-standing opinion that there is an omnipotent God who made me the kind of creature that I am" (AT vii, 21).

The hypothesis of an omnipotent God provides the most pervasive ground for doubt about the sensory world. Descartes has the meditator reason that it would be possible for such a God to ensure that "things appear to me to exist just as they do now," even though material objects do not exist (AT vii, 21). That is, this God presumably could create sensory experiences in our minds which give the appearance of the world as we think we know it, even though no such world exists.

This hypothesis of a deceiving God permits a second target of doubt: the "transparent truths" of mathematics, such as that two and three make five. Even about cases in which we consider ourselves to possess "the most perfect knowledge," the meditator asks: "how do I know that God has not brought it about that I similarly go wrong every time I add two and three, or count the sides of a square, or in some even simpler matter, if that is imaginable?" (AT vii, 21). There are really two grounds for entertaining the possibility of error here. The first is the *intervention hypothesis*, according to which the deceiving God interferes (or might be interfering) with our thoughts every time we add two numbers or engage in simple reasoning. On this view, there would be nothing inherently wrong with our reasoning ability, but we might be unable to rely on the results if we believed a deceiving God (or a "malicious demon" [AT vii, 22]) were interfering with our thoughts in ways we could not notice. In that case, this God (or this demon) might make us believe with firm conviction that two and three do not make five.

The second ground for doubting the "transparent truths" of mathematics pertains to our reasoning ability itself. I call this the *defective design hypothesis*. The "long-standing" opinion that Descartes has the meditator recall is of "an omnipotent God who made me." What if this God made our reasoning faculty inherently defective, so that it regularly produces defective results that we nonetheless believe with great certitude? In this case, we would go wrong in simple addition or in counting, not because of interference on each occasion but because our reasoning faculty is itself flawed. We would be like a calculator with a defective computer chip.

This second ground is quite radical, as Descartes was aware. He augmented its force by introducing a further consideration pertaining to defective design. If the meditator prefers not to allow the existence of a powerful God, then he or she will need to posit an alternative causal chain for his or her origin. Descartes offers the meditator three alternative hypotheses: "fate or chance or a continuous chain of events" (AT vii, 21). The first would suppose a force in the universe, fate, which has arranged for each human being to exist; the second would suppose that processes of chance have led to our existence; the third would hold that a deterministic chain of causes, extending back infinitely, has led to each human being's existence. Descartes suggests that because these causes are less powerful than an omnipotent God, they are more likely to produce an imperfect being. According to this ground for doubt, we might suppose our reasoning faculty to be inherently defective because of its less than omnipotent originating cause. Indeed, Descartes has the meditator reason, "the less powerful . . . my original cause, the more likely it is that I am so imperfect as to be deceived all the time" (AT vii, 21).

Descartes has raised these radical doubts as part of his meditative strategy. As he explained to Hobbes, he raised such doubts (a) "to prepare my readers' minds for the study of the things that are related to the intellect," that is, purely intellectual truths known independently of the senses; (b) to show that his philosophy could reply to such doubts; and (c) to show "the certainty of the truths" that he propounded later on (AT vii, 171–2). However, once these radical doubts have been raised, it is natural to wonder how they can be met. If we might "be deceived all the time," how could we ever be sure of anything?

Initial Results and the Truth Rule

Famously, Descartes arrives at some certain truths in Meditation II, through the famous *cogito* reasoning. Despite his state of doubt, he recognizes that so long as he doubts, or is deceived, or thinks anything at all, he must exist. He therefore concludes that "this proposition, *I am, I exist*, is necessarily true whenever it is put forward by me or conceived in my mind" (AT vii, 25). So here is something that Descartes proposes the meditator should accept as certain: that he or she exists, or rather, exists as a thinking thing (AT vii, 27–8; see chapter 3 of this volume).

At the beginning of Meditation III, Descartes seeks to build on this result. He sums up the result with the phrase "I am a thing that thinks" (AT vii, 34). Importantly, this result stands as an instance of *knowledge*. It is something the meditator, despite the effects of the doubt, has accepted as certain. But perhaps this bit of knowledge can serve as the basis for further knowledge. How so? By serving as an example of how to know:

> I am certain that I am a thinking thing. Do I not therefore also know what is required for my being certain of anything? In this first item of knowledge there is simply a clear and distinct perception of what I am asserting; this would not be enough to make me certain of the truth of the matter if it could ever turn out that something which I perceived with such clarity and distinctness was false. So I now seem to be able to lay it down as a general rule that whatever I perceive very clearly and distinctly is true. (AT vii, 35)

Descartes asks the meditator to generalize the method by which the *cogito* result has been obtained into a general method for knowing (or for achieving certain truth). In this argument, the result "I am a thinking thing" is not used to derive further results about myself or about thinking things simply *qua* thinking things. Rather, it is used as an instance of unshakable knowledge, and the meditator is directed to ask what must be the case if this one thing is known.

The quoted passage contains what may be called *the extraction argument*, by which a general rule of truth is justified: the rule that "whatever I perceive very clearly and distinctly is true." The argument, which is valid, runs as follows:

1 I know with certainty that I am a thinking thing.
2 This knowledge is based solely on a clear and distinct perception of its truth.
3 Clear and distinct perception would not be sufficient to yield such knowledge if it were in any way fallible.
4 Therefore, clear and distinct perception provides a sufficient ground for knowledge; whatever I so perceive is true.

Premise (1) is the previously accepted result. Premise (2) describes how it is known; that is, it makes a claim about the method by which (1) is known. Premise (3) makes the plausible claim that a fallible method could not yield the absolute certainty that is claimed for premise (1). Hence, to attack the argument, one would need to challenge (1) or (2). Both have been challenged at one time or another. However, our aim here is not to evaluate the extraction argument, but to consider further challenges to its conclusion, (4).

In the subsequent paragraphs, Descartes sets up a dialectic of doubt: a conflict between, on the one hand, the apparent certainty of clear and distinct perception, and, on the other, the radical doubt engendered in Meditation I. The dialectic arises between individual instances of clear and distinct perceptions, such as that two and three make five, or the *cogito* result, and the preconceived opinion that there is a God who can do anything and who might be deceiving him. When the meditator entertains the "preconceived belief in the supreme power of God," he or she should "admit that it would be easy for him, if he so desired, to bring it about that I go wrong even in those matters which I think I see utterly clearly with my mind's eye" (AT vii, 36). That is, a doubt can arise about the entire class of clear and distinct perceptions, and so the conclusion (4) is called into question. At the same time, the meditator should find that when he or she attends to individual clear and distinct perceptions, these cannot be doubted:

> when I turn to the things themselves which I think I perceive very clearly, I am so persuaded by them that I spontaneously declare: let whoever can do so deceive me, he will never bring it about that I am nothing, so long as I continue to think I am something; or make it true at some further time that I have never existed, since it is now true that I exist; or bring it about that two and three added together are more or less than five, or anything of this kind in which I see a manifest contradiction. (AT vii, 36)

The *cogito* result and the simple truths of mathematics, and anything else found to be as evidently true as these, cannot but be affirmed when the meditator entertains them.

How might one resolve this conflict? One might try to entertain individual clear and distinct perceptions only, in which case the doubt could not arise. That effort would be futile, since no one can fix their attention that steadfastly over a long period of time (AT vii, 69). More importantly, this strategy could not succeed unless the grounds for doubt themselves were not clear and distinct perceptions. But so far as the meditator knows, the possibility of a deceiving God might or might not be among the clear and distinct perceptions. Indeed, at the present time, the grounds for doubting clear and distinct perceptions rest on the "preconceived belief" in a God who is capable of anything, including deception. Although this ground for doubt was judged to be "powerful and well thought-out" in Meditation I (AT vii, 22), it is now described as "slight" and "metaphysical" (AT vii, 36). Why the change? In Meditation I this ground was considered adequate to cast doubt on simple mathematical truths. Perhaps it now appears weaker because it is being contrasted with the criterion of clear and distinct perception as extracted from the more immediately convincing *cogito* result and then made general (in the extraction argument).

In any case, the meditator is now directed to examine "whether there is a God, and, if there is, whether he can be a deceiver" (AT vii, 36). This investigation would seem to be needed if the meditator is to hold on to any knowledge: "if I do not know this, it seems that I can never be quite certain about anything else" (AT vii, 36) – presumably because the deceiving God hypothesis, or the defective design argument, would persist as a ground for doubt.

The rest of Meditation III is devoted to investigating the existence of God. The meditator begins by investigating ideas as bearers of truth and falsity. This investigation depends upon "the natural light," which appears to be a reintroduction of clear and distinct perception (paired with the *cogito* result as an example of its use). The meditator is directed to trust the natural light as something beyond doubt. The reason it cannot be doubted is that "there cannot be another faculty both as trustworthy as the natural light and also capable of showing me that such things are not true" (AT vii, 38). Various metaphysical premises are then secured by the natural light and used to prove that God exists. In the course of this proof, it is revealed that God is a perfect being. From this it follows "that he cannot be a deceiver, since it is manifest by the natural light that all fraud and deception depend on some defect" (AT vii, 52).

Meditation IV then argues that since our faculties of judgment are derived from God, we must be able to avoid error if we use them correctly. But, clear and distinct perceptions compel our assent. Since we cannot help but assent to them, and since God has set us up this way, he would bear responsibility for our error, and hence would be guilty of causing us to be deceived, if they could ever be wrong. Hence, clear and distinct perceptions must be true. Finally, in Meditation V, Descartes brings the meditator to the conclusion that all knowledge depends on the knowledge of God's existence and perfection. Although, as in the dialectic of doubt, no one can help but affirm as true whatever they clearly and distinctly perceive, when they are not having those perceptions a doubt can arise. But this doubt arises only if they "are unaware of God" (AT vii, 69). Once they know that God exists and is no deceiver, they know that their origin is such that their clear and distinct perceptions must be true (by the reasoning of Meditation IV).

Circularity and Begging the Question

At various places, Descartes writes that the meditator cannot be certain of, or know, anything unless he or she first knows that God exists. But the proof for God's existence relies on various premises that the meditator claims to know by "the natural light," or through clear and distinct perception. ("The natural light" has been interpreted either as equivalent to clear and distinct perceptions or as involving only a subset of clear and distinct perceptions; for example, pertaining to causal reasoning and degrees of reality, as in Meditation III.) So Descartes claims to know some things, the very premises used in proving that God exists, before having shown that anything can be known. Taking Descartes at his word, that "nothing can ever be perfectly known" (AT vii, 69) prior to proving God's existence, his arguments are, at the very least, guilty of begging the question: of taking something to be known, when the very matter in question is whether anything can be known.

Arnauld, however, did not accuse Descartes merely of begging the question. Rather, he accused him of circular reasoning: of relying on one thing, let us call it A, to prove another, let us call it B, and also of using B to prove A, thus closing the circle. In this regard, A would be "that God exists and is no deceiver," and B would be "that clear and distinct perceptions are true." The charge of circularity arises because Descartes claimed to prove B by appeal to A, and to prove A by appeal to B.

Descartes' argument would constitute a formal circle only if he actually appealed to the general principle (GP) "that all my clear and distinct perceptions are true" *as a premise* in his argument for the existence of God, and then used the existence of God to prove that same general principle. That would constitute a logical circle because the claim about GP would occur among the premises for the existence of God, and that conclusion (the existence of God) would appear among the premises for GP.

It is not clear that Descartes did include GP among the premises for his argument for the existence of God. Truly, he asserts GP on the basis of the extraction argument, early in Meditation III (or, he says that he "seems" to be able to accept it). Moreover, when he argued for the existence of God, he claimed to know various premises by "the natural light." He also claimed that what was evident to the natural light "could not be doubted" and hence should be accepted as true (AT vii, 38). But it is open to question whether he actually intended GP, or a similar principle about the natural light, to be a premise in his arguments about God. He might instead have intended his remarks about the natural light merely to be methodological. In that case, he would simply be recommending that the natural light be trusted in deciding various matters. (A similar distinction can be made in discussions of formal systems between accepting inference rules, such as *modus ponens*, as a method of inference, and formally introducing inference rules as premises.)

Even if appeal to the natural light is merely methodological, Descartes could be charged with a kind of circularity: that of using a particular method to establish the reliability of that very method. This sort of methodological circularity is observed in inductive arguments in favor of induction. Induction is the method of arguing from what has been previously observed to conclusions about other cases, as yet unobserved. It does not have the status of logical proof: what has happened in the first hundred cases of observation (say, the observation of a hundred swans that are white) does not prove that all cases will be the same (that all swans are white, which they are not). What justifies inductive argument, if such argument is not a species of formal proof? One might argue that induction has always worked before. But that would be to appeal to the method of induction in order to justify the conclusion that that very method is reliable. While not a formal circle (the statement "induction is reliable" does not appear as a premise), it is methodologically circular, in that it uses a certain method to justify itself. Similarly, Descartes might be accused, in Meditation III, of using the method of clear and distinct perception in order to prove (via the proof of God's existence and perfection) that that very method yields certain truth.

The decision on whether Descartes should be charged with a formal circle, a methodological circle, or simply with begging the question depends on how his various arguments in Meditations III–V are construed. The question of whether he is guilty of such charges also depends on how his conclusions are construed, including what conclusion about clear and distinct perception he intends to establish in those Meditations. So let us now turn to the question of whether Descartes is guilty as accused. It will be convenient to address this question by evaluating the success, or the conditions for success, of various strategies for avoiding the circle, in relation to various construals of Descartes' more general aims in the *Meditations*.

Descartes' Aims and the Circle

There are two main strategies for interpreting Descartes' arguments so as to avoid the circle. One type of strategy reduces the ambition of Descartes' conclusion: he was not seeking to establish the absolute truth of clear and distinct perception, but something weaker. The weakest version of this *limit-the-aim* strategy is to suppose that Descartes was aiming merely to establish the unshakable persuasiveness of clear and distinct perceptions from a human point of view.

The other main strategy is to limit what Descartes needs in order to vindicate clear and distinct perception. Perhaps he need not know that all clear and distinct perceptions are true before he uses some of them to prove God's existence and perfection. Or perhaps he need not prove that God really does guarantee clear and distinct perceptions; perhaps it is enough to show that the hypothesis of a deceiving God is inconsistent with the idea of God, and so undermines itself. We can call this general strategy the *limit-the-grounds* approach because it seeks to limit the grounds needed for concluding that clear and distinct perception can be trusted. Some versions of limiting the grounds needed for vindicating clear and distinct perception operate by limiting the grounds for doubting such perceptions in the first place, or limiting the scope of the original doubt.

These two approaches might be combined: one might seek to show both that the aims are less ambitious and the grounds less stringent than has sometimes been supposed. By combining different versions of each strategy, numerous possible strategies for avoiding the circle might be generated. In the remainder of this chapter, I will consider five construals of Descartes' arguments and aims in relation to the circle. These are:

1   *Certainty, not truth*. The aim of the arguments in Meditations III–V is to show that clear and distinct perceptions yield an unshakable conviction that is not subject to any lasting grounds for doubt; achieving such conviction is to be distinguished from the more ambitious claim that clear and distinct perceptions are true.

2   *Limit the doubt*. The doubt does not properly extend to individual clear and distinct perceptions, but only to GP. Hence, Descartes can legitimately use

clear and distinct perceptions (or some subset of them, known by the natural light) to prove the existence and perfection of God, who then guarantees GP. By distinguishing GP from individual clear and distinct perceptions, the grounds needed to remove the doubt and vindicate GP are made narrower than GP itself.

3   *Remove the doubt.* In order to be left with the conclusion that clear and distinct perceptions are true, Descartes does not need to show that God guarantees them to be so; he only needs to show that the hypothesis of a deceiving God is not sustainable upon rational evaluation. GP is then left standing unchallenged. As a variant, the claims made for GP may themselves be limited to less than an absolute standard of truth, by invoking a notion of "human truth" or the like.

4   *Presumption in favor of the intellect.* This position assumes that Descartes is out for absolute truth in metaphysics, and that he begins from the presumption that the human intellect is capable of perceiving such truth. The burden of proof is placed on the doubter. In order to vindicate his claims to truth in metaphysics, he needs only to remove the doubt, as in (3).

5   *Strong validation.* This position assumes that Descartes wants to validate the human intellect's ability to achieve absolute truth in metaphysics without making any presumptions on the intellect's behalf. In effect, he would be trying to argue his way out of the position of radical doubt without presupposing anything.

Of these five positions, (1) and (3) limit the aims and (2) through (4) limit the grounds, while (5) does neither. Not all of the positions are equally basic. Positions (2) to (4) are variants of the strategy of limiting the doubt or the grounds needed for removing it, paired with differing conceptions of Descartes' aims and assumptions. The intent of setting out these five positions is not to provide an exhaustive taxonomy, but rather to set out a range of positions that have received discussion by philosophers or that have a reasonably strong textual basis.

All five positions are not equally plausible, textually or argumentatively. In particular, if Descartes' project is construed as in (5), there may be no way to avoid the circle. Other construals may be open to the charge that if the aim is sufficiently limited to avoid the circle, then the resultant conclusion is not adequate to establish the metaphysical truths Descartes intended to establish. Let us consider the positions in turn.

Certainty, Not Truth

On the certainty, not truth strategy, Descartes' aims in the *Meditations* are less ambitious than they would seem. He talks about uncovering the "truths" of metaphysics. Yet when faced with the challenge that what appears to be absolutely certain to a sound human mind might in fact be false, he seems to concede the point, thereby signaling that he was not seeking absolute truth after all.

The second objectors asked how we can be sure that clear and distinct perceptions are true, since God might have revealed to humans only what they need to know, reserving the "pure truth" for himself (AT vii, 125–6). God might have made it that humans do not attain the full truth, not because he was deceptive, but because mere humans could not endure a mental vision of the pure truth. Alternatively, perhaps human nature is inherently limited, as in the defective design argument. In that case, human nature might be such that all humans are always or frequently deceived even about what they think they know clearly and distinctly (AT vii, 126).

Descartes' response seems to grant the objectors' point. He promises to get them out of the doubts of Meditation I by "expounding for a second time the basis on which it seems to me that all human certainty can be founded" (AT vii, 103). This basis appears surprisingly modest:

> First of all, as soon as we think that we correctly perceive something, we are spontaneously persuaded that it is true. Now if this persuasion is so firm that it is impossible for us ever to have any reason for doubting what we are persuaded of, then there are no further questions for us to ask: we have everything we could reasonably want. What is it to us that someone may make out that the perception of whose truth we are so firmly persuaded may appear false to God or an angel, so that it is, absolutely speaking, false? Why should this alleged absolute falsity bother us, since we neither believe in it nor have even the smallest suspicion of it? For the supposition that we are making here is of a persuasion so firm that it is quite incapable of being destroyed; and such persuasion is clearly the same as the most perfect certainty. (AT vii, 144–5)

This passage, which is frequently cited in discussions of the circle, may be called the "limited aims passage" (LAP).

In this passage, Descartes seems to pull back from the aim of achieving truth in the traditional sense, and to settle for "firm persuasion" or perfect, unshakable certainty. The traditional notion of truth, held from ancient times, was that truth consists in a correspondence or conformity between thought and its object. Descartes defined truth in this manner in a letter to Mersenne in 1639: "*truth*, in the strict sense, denotes the conformity of thought with its object" (AT ii, 597). In relation to an external thing, a thought that was true would accurately portray, or would conform to, the characteristics of the thing.

If Descartes only sought firm persuasion or a kind of psychological certainty that was consistent with "absolute falsity," then he would be allowing that clear and distinct perceptions might yield certainty without guaranteeing truth (genuine conformity with objects). If so, then since he would not need to argue that God guarantees truth, he would not need to prove as absolutely true that God exists and is perfect. Rather, it would be enough if his arguments for God's existence and perfection removed any feelings of doubt, and left the meditator in a state of feeling certain. No circle would arise because no strict proofs were being offered. Rather, a state of conviction was the aim, and that might be achieved by whatever means available. (This "psychological" reading of Descartes' aims has been offered by several commentators, on which see Loeb 1992.)

What would a defender of this reading make of Descartes' ubiquitous claims to have achieved truth in his metaphysics? In LAP, Descartes equates certainty with firm persuasion. Just previously, he linked clear and distinct perception with what is "accepted as true and certain" (AT vii, 144). Perhaps Descartes is hinting that he wants the notion of truth to be redefined or reconceived in terms of certainty and firm persuasion. In that case, everywhere in the *Meditations* where Descartes speaks of truth, we should rewrite the sentences using "firm persuasion."

The weakness of this position is that it requires reinterpreting Descartes' notion of truth, against his own statement about truth to Mersenne (one year before he completed the *Meditations*). It requires us to reconceive Descartes' claims to know the essences of things as claims merely to be persuaded to think of those essences in a certain way. It renders his aim as psychological persuasion rather than genuine knowledge. Such an interpretation does not cohere well with Descartes' many claims to know the real essences and real possibilities of things. The circle is avoided, but perhaps at too great a cost.

Limit the Doubt

Perhaps Descartes did not get into the circle because he never intended to challenge individual clear and distinct perceptions. On this interpretation, the doubts raised in Meditation I are aimed only at the general principle that all clear and distinct perceptions are true (GP). They do not undermine the use of individual clear and distinct perceptions to argue for specific conclusions (Van Cleve 1979: pt 1).

The point of this interpretation is that Descartes would not need to claim to know GP in order to be justified in using individual clear and distinct perceptions. Further, he would not even need to know for himself *that a given individual clear and distinct perception is true* in order to use the individual clear and distinct perception in his proofs. It would be enough to justify his argument for the existence of God if it simply were the case that his individual clear and distinct perceptions are true. This falls in line with a present-day epistemological idea, that in order to know something, you need not know *that* your reasons for believing it are true, they merely need to be good reasons that are *in fact* true (Van Cleve 1979: pt 2).

According to this construal, Descartes does not rely on GP to found his arguments for God's existence and perfection. Initially, the role of GP is as a target for doubt: the abstract possibility that GP might be false can lead us into doubt when we are not having clear and distinct perceptions (as Descartes says in Meditation V and in reply to Arnauld [AT vii, 245–6]). Once the proof of God's existence and perfection has been secured by using clear and distinct perceptions, this ground for doubt is removed. At this point, GP has been secured by divine guarantee. Now, GP can serve to warrant all clear and distinct perceptions. But the argument that brings the meditator to this point does not rely on GP or on any more particular premise about the truth of clear and distinct perceptions; it simply relies on individual clear and distinct perceptions themselves.

This interpretation would need to explain why Descartes thinks that we could "never be quite certain about anything else" (AT vii, 36) prior to knowing about God, and that "nothing can ever be perfectly known" (AT vii, 69) prior to such knowledge. It might explain these statements by interpreting them so that they do not pertain to individual propositions while we are entertaining them. Rather, the lack of certainty, or the doubts that serve to undermine our knowledge, would arise while we are not entertaining individual clear and distinct perceptions. These doubts, in the form of the deceiving God or defective origins hypothesis, would undermine our general belief that we have knowledge. But, once we have proved God's existence and secured a benevolent origin for our cognitive powers, GP is now vindicated and stands ready to ward off skeptical doubt. We can henceforth remain sure of our knowledge, while we are not having clear and distinct perceptions, because the grounds for doubt have been removed.

This strategy may be accused of begging the question. In establishing the existence of God, it depends on the fact that clear and distinct perceptions are true, whether they are known to be true or not. Once God's existence and perfection are demonstrated, it then relies on this proof to vindicate GP. However, the soundness of this very demonstration depends on the fact that clear and distinct perceptions are true, which is the very matter in question. The fact that it merely depends on their being true, rather than needing explicitly to assert it, does not appear to help.

At the same time, we may suppose that Descartes would rather it turned out that his position was true, even though his arguments begged the question. In that case, he could still claim to have aided the meditator in finding the right way to look for the truth, through the clear and distinct perceptions of the intellect. But let us continue to look for an argument that serves Descartes' metaphysical aims and does not beg the question.

Remove the Doubt

According to the strategy of "removing the doubt," the dialectic of doubt in Meditation III leaves the meditator in a position of evaluating the original grounds for doubt. On this view, the grounds for doubt, in order to remain effective, must withstand rational scrutiny. The meditator undertakes such scrutiny in Meditation III. As it turns out, the hypothesis of a deceiving God does not pan out. When the idea of God is investigated carefully, rational reflection (using causal principles and other deliverances of the "natural light") shows that God exists, is perfect and hence no deceiver, and is the creator of the meditator's rational faculties. But then such faculties must be trustworthy, on pain of God's being a deceiver. So, the idea of God is incompatible with deception. Hence, the grounds for doubt are removed.

Why does this position not beg the question by relying on the deliverances of the natural light? One response would be to assert that no claim has been made that these causal principles are actually true, or that they really do prove God's existence. Rather, the investigation of the existence and perfection of God is undertaken merely to evaluate the rational coherence of the deceiving God hypothesis. Once that hypothesis is removed on internal grounds, no grounds for doubt are (allegedly) left standing. The best use we can make of our own rational faculties reveals that we have no grounds for doubting them.

An objection to this response is that even if it worked for the deceiving God hypothesis, it would not work for versions of the defective design hypothesis that do not invoke God as a creator. If Meditation I has raised a credible doubt based upon the possibility of defective origins, then to remove that doubt would require actually proving that God exists, is no deceiver, and guarantees our faculties (or it would require proving some other causal origin that provides a guarantee).

A second response, which also addresses this objection, would be to contend that any investigation into grounds for doubt presupposes some reasoning ability. If this minimum reasoning ability is granted, then its results should be accepted unless there are grounds for doubting them. One might suppose that the part of the natural light passage that says "there cannot be another faculty both as trustworthy as the natural light and also capable of showing me that such things are not true" (AT vii, 38) supports the notion that we have to rely on the natural light, or our rational faculties more generally, in conducting this investigation, because we have nothing else to rely on.

The responder might now also invoke the extraction argument. The extraction argument gives us initial grounds for accepting GP. If accepted, it provides a strong argument in favor of GP. The dialectic of doubt then reminds the meditator of the hypothetical grounds for doubt. Further investigation then removes those grounds. GP, as supported by extraction, is vindicated.

In reply, it may be observed that the extraction argument and further arguments all depend on the soundness of the human intellect as an instrument of truth. In the extraction argument, we accept as true the *cogito* result and the other premises (such as that this result is a product only of clear and distinct perception). But these results are accepted because they are clearly and distinctly perceived. Even if one granted the *cogito* result itself, one might question the premises that generalize it to attain GP. In any event, the question of the truth of clear and distinct perception again is begged (at least methodologically).

Barring any direct proof of the reliability of clear and distinct perception for achieving truth, the "remove the doubt" strategy simply leaves us with clear and distinct perceptions unchallenged. But the fact that they are unchallenged does not support the claim that they are capable of revealing to us the basic principles of metaphysics, which describe the way the world really is. More generally, even if we must use our rational faculties in order to evaluate any grounds for doubt, that does not give us reason to believe that those faculties can uncover the principles of metaphysics. Detecting internal contradictions in a ground for doubt is one thing. Claiming to discern the real structure of mind-independent external reality is another.

Presumption in Favor of the Intellect

Descartes sometime writes as if the burden of proof should be on the doubter from the beginning. That is, one might start from the assumption, shared with both Platonic and Aristotelian philosophers, that human rational faculties are capable of arriving at the truth, even in metaphysics. The burden of proof would then be on the doubter to provide a good ground for doubt. Some potential grounds for doubt are introduced in Meditation I, but are removed in Meditations III–V. The human intellect is left standing, but now with a presumption in its favor. Since the presumption is that it is adequate for (metaphysical) truth, then it is left standing as the arbiter, or at least as a detector, of such truth (Hatfield 2003).

Support for the view that Descartes believed the burden of proof was on the doubter might be found by re-reading the LAP passage. He there says that if our clear and distinct perceptions are such that "it is impossible for us ever to have any reason for doubting what we are persuaded of," then "we have everything we could reasonably want" (AT vii, 144). In response to the allegation that something we have no reason to doubt nonetheless might be false "absolutely speaking," Descartes asked: "Why should this alleged absolute falsity bother us, since we neither believe in it nor have even the smallest suspicion of it?" (AT vii, 145). Now, this might be read as Descartes saying he was not after absolute truth, but some lesser notion of "human truth," and we would then have a variant of the "remove the doubt" strategy, without a presumption (see Murdoch 1999). But it might also be read as dismissing the absolute falsity as *merely alleged* and without ground, which would leave absolute truth in place.

Supposing that Descartes started from the presumption in favor of the intellect, what then would be the purpose of raising the doubt? He might do so simply as a filter. Things that are found to resist the doubt presumably would be those for which the justification was strongest. We have seen that he gave this reason to Hobbes. But he also told Hobbes that he used the doubt "to prepare my readers' minds for the study of the things that are related to the intellect" (AT vii, 172). Accordingly, he would use the doubt instrumentally, as a means for acquainting the meditator with the pure intellect, or with intellectual perceptions independent of the senses.

Recall that Descartes patterned the *Meditations* after spiritual exercises. Works of religious meditation often pursued three "ways" or stages: the first stage was to mortify the body so as to turn away from the senses and sensuality; the second stage was illuminative (through the example of Christ or divine illumination); the third stage was unitive, in which one seeks to unite one's will with the divine will (Hatfield 1986: 49). In Descartes' cognitive meditations, the first stage would be to turn away from the senses; the second, to seek illumination through the pure intellect; the third, to train the will to avoid making judgments, at least concerning metaphysics, if perceptions are less than clear and distinct. Thus, the doubt would serve to discount sensory perceptions, so that the intellectual truths embodied in the *cogito* and the idea of God (a completely non-sensory idea [AT vii, 139, 181, 188]) might be found.

On this reading, Descartes' primary goal in the *Meditations* is to lead the reader to have clear and distinct perceptions. Once the meditator has them, Descartes believes that he or she will see the truth of his metaphysical arguments about God and the essences of matter and mind.

Does this interpretation avoid the circle? It does, by recasting Descartes' aim as that of leading the meditator to discover clear and distinct perceptions. There is no circularity because there is no need to prove GP; rather, the project is to discover that clear and distinct perceptions are the proper objects of the intellect, and that they can be attained independently of sensory images. The arguments of Meditations III–V serve to remove the grounds for doubt, but they do not directly validate clear and distinct perception in the sense of proving that it is reliable. From the outset, its basic reliability has been assumed unless proved otherwise.

From Descartes' point of view, this assumption would not count as begging the question because, on this reading, he has put the burden of proof on the doubter. Nonetheless, if one refused to accept Descartes' presumption, if the doubter refused to accept the burden of proof, then it would seem to the doubter that Descartes was begging the question. If one takes the defective design objection seriously, it cannot be removed by a presumption. Descartes might reply that it is not useful to hark on doubts whose grounds are weak. From his point of view, the point is to discover a system of metaphysical principles that he believes are universally available to any unclouded human intellect. In that case, the evaluative question shifts to whether we in fact do find the clear and distinct ideas of God, matter, and mind innately within our minds.

Strong Validation

The strategy of strong validation would seek to prove that the human intellect has knowledge of the world as it is in itself. It would seek to do so by starting with no presuppositions. Perhaps some minimal rational abilities for evaluating arguments would need to be allowed, but as observed above, it is not obvious that such rational abilities themselves already should be considered adequate to represent a mind-independent world as it really is (at least as regards the essences of things).

The main leverage points for such a strategy are the extraction argument and the proofs for God's existence. If the extraction argument were successful in establishing GP, then GP could be used to prove God's existence, and God's perfection could be used, as in Meditation IV, to vindicate the claim that clear and distinct perceptions reveal the world as it really is. The problem with these leverage points is that, in the face of the defective origins hypothesis, they appear to beg the question. For, as observed above, the extraction argument itself must be evaluated by clear and distinct perception.

Lessons of the Circle

If we take Descartes' aim as that of establishing the absolute truth of his principles of metaphysics, which reveal the essences of things as they really are, then it is difficult to avoid the conclusion that in the *Meditations* he fell prey to circular reasoning or else begged the question. Once the defective origins argument is in place, it is difficult to find a way out.

Assuming that Descartes wanted to prove that the human intellect discerns the real essences of things, his means for doing so were conditioned by some of his other doctrines. In particular, his doctrine that the eternal truths are the free creations of God, announced in 1630 (AT i, 145–6, 149–53) and affirmed in the *Replies* (AT vii, 380, 432, 435–6), set a framework for this problem. Previous metaphysicians, including Plato and Aristotle, had held that the human intellect directly knows the real essences of things. In Platonic philosophy, it does so by grasping mind (and God) independent Forms of things (these Forms constituting essences of things). In Aristotelian philosophy, the human mind abstracts the real essences of things from its sensory contact with them. In certain versions of scholastic Aristotelianism, real essences depend on the creative power of God, so that real possibilities can only be perceived in relation to God's essence, by understanding his creative power (Hatfield 1992). Actually existing essences can be abstracted from things present to the senses (Hatfield 1998).

By contrast, Descartes held that the real essences of things are established only when God creates the things, and that it would have been possible for him to create those essences in a manner other than he in fact did create them. According to this picture, God creates the essences and he implants innate ideas of them in the human mind. In this way, God adjusts the innate ideas of the human mind to the external reality he creates (and to the essence of the mind itself, as considered from a third-person point of view!).

This picture of harmony between mind and essence requires that Descartes rely on God as the guarantor of human metaphysical knowledge. This appeal to God is difficult to sustain in the face of the defective design hypothesis. As Kant observed in responding to a similar anti-skeptical position in the writings of C. A. Crusius, this argument falls prey to the fact that the mind must use its own (possibly defective) resources to infer God as guarantor. If we suppose that "a spirit who can neither err nor deceive" originally implanted knowledge of the world itself in our minds, we face this objection: "with the lack of sure criteria for distinguishing an authentic origin from a spurious one, the use of such a principle looks very precarious, since one can never know for sure what the spirit of truth or the father of lies may have put into us" (Kant 2004: 71). In other words, we must rely on whatever workings our mind has in order to construct the argument that a non-deceiving God has created us and has installed in our minds knowledge of the true metaphysics.

A more modest way of reading Descartes would have him seeking to provide an "all things considered best argument" for his metaphysical principles. Surely, he would like to establish their absolute truth, but he realizes that in order to claim to do so he needs to presume that the human intellect is capable of such knowledge. His most careful arguments (for the existence and perfection of God) tell him that it is so capable. But these arguments, he realizes in LAP, rely on the intellect itself. Consequently, he acknowledges that he has simply sought to do in the *Meditations* what he could: to lead his readers to see these arguments for themselves. If these arguments had in fact subsequently achieved the universal acceptance that Descartes expected, then indeed one might well ask: what more could one want? But to the extent that readers have not been led to perceive the one true metaphysics as Descartes intended, doubt is cast on his claim to have described the common deliverances of all sound human intellects.

9

Judgment and Will

Michael Della Rocca

Meditation IV is passed over quickly in any number of commentaries and courses on Descartes. This is, in a way, understandable. In comparison to the philosophical firework display in most of the other Meditations – radical skepticism, mind–body dualism, the proofs of the existence of God, and the subtext of Descartes' development of his new anti-Aristotelian conception of the extended world – Meditation IV's focus on the nature of belief and on the attempt to show that everyday errors do not impugn God's goodness can seem rather humdrum. In addition, Descartes' arguments in Meditation IV are often thought to be extremely ineffective and his conception of belief is usually seen as wildly implausible.

So why is Meditation IV so deserving of attention? First, although I agree, for reasons we will explore, that Descartes' arguments in Meditation IV are deeply problematic, I see them as also extremely elegant and resourceful. These arguments also are illuminated by and help illuminate – as we will see – his positions on the mind–body problem, on the nature of the mental, and on the notion of responsibility. Further, the argument of Meditation IV and, in particular, Descartes' notion of belief are integral to his position on the apparently more glitzy matter of radical skepticism. As I will stress presently, and also in the final section of this chapter, Descartes' response to radical skepticism is not complete or even in any way adequate without the success of his argument in Meditation IV about the nature of belief. So, in glossing over Meditation IV, one runs the risk of missing out on what is, perhaps, the critical step in his anti-skeptical strategy and of failing to gain much-needed insight into a whole range of Cartesian positions beyond merely those concerning the notions of belief and of ordinary error.

I will begin this chapter with an overview of the strategy of Meditation IV, and along the way in this section I will intersperse a few evaluative remarks. After the overview, I will delve more deeply into three important topics that Descartes takes up in Meditation IV: (a) the relation between judgment or belief and the will; (b) the nature of the freedom of the will; and (c) the bearing of Meditation IV on the Cartesian circle and on Descartes' larger epistemological aims.

The Strategy of Meditation IV

I will begin by focusing on the last point: Descartes' epistemological aims and Meditation IV. Usually, Descartes is taken to have established by the end of Meditation III that God exists and is not a deceiver. Recall that, at the outset of Meditation III, Descartes seeks to disarm the doubt about whether clear and distinct ideas are true. (For more on clarity and distinctness, see chapter 6.) To do this, he undertakes to prove that God exists and is not a deceiver. And, although he reaches the desired conclusions at the end of Meditation III, when the beginning of Meditation IV rolls along, Descartes has second thoughts about the claim that God is not a deceiver. These second thoughts are analogous to his second thoughts at the beginning of Meditation III about the truth of clear and distinct ideas. After "laying it down as a general rule" near the beginning of Meditation III, "that whatever I perceive very clearly and distinctly is true" (AT vii, 35), Descartes immediately casts this rule into doubt by raising the possibility that God is a deceiver. So, too, after finally offering an argument in Meditation III for the claim that God is not a deceiver, Descartes immediately goes on in Meditation IV to raise a doubt about this claim.

Near the beginning of Meditation IV, Descartes restates the conclusion of Meditation III: "since God does not wish to deceive me, he surely did not give me the kind of faculty which would ever enable me to go wrong while using it correctly" (AT vii, 54). He goes on to raise an important worry:

> There would be no further doubt [*dubium*] on this issue were it not that what I have just said appears to imply that I am incapable of ever going wrong. For if everything that is in me comes from God, and he did not endow me with a faculty for making mistakes, it appears that I can never go wrong. (AT vii, 54)

But obviously, as Descartes recognizes, I do sometimes make mistakes, and so the argument for the claim that God is not a deceiver and that clear and distinct ideas are true is called into doubt. Because of this doubt, Descartes will not have beaten back the skeptic about clear and distinct ideas until this issue is resolved, i.e. until he has shown how it is compatible with God's non-deceptiveness that we sometimes err. Given that Descartes wants to hold that clear and distinct ideas must be true, he is, in effect, seeking to answer the following question: how, if God is not a deceiver and thus does not allow clear and distinct ideas to be false, can God allow that I ever make mistakes, in particular with regard to ideas that are not clear and distinct? Descartes is thus seeking a relevant difference between non-clear and distinct and clear and distinct ideas which will enable him to explain the legitimacy of one kind of error but not the other.

The problem Descartes here takes up is a version of the problem of evil: how can a good God allow various kinds of evil to occur? To offer an explanation of how this is possible is to offer a theodicy: a way of justifying God's actions by showing that they are compatible with his goodness. Usually, the discussion of this problem centers around moral evil (murder, theft, and the like) and natural evil (earthquakes, illness, and the like). But, as befits the *Meditations*, a work with a heavy emphasis on belief and certainty, Descartes' version of the problem of evil concerns false belief: how can a good God allow false beliefs? And the crucial point for Descartes' overall strategy is that finding the relevant difference between clear and distinct and non-clear and distinct ideas is essential to his response to the skeptic about clear and distinct ideas. As we saw, Descartes says that some doubt still remains. (Most commentators fail to acknowledge the importance of Meditation IV in overcoming the doubt about clear and distinct ideas, but Newman 1999 is a notable exception.)

That Descartes ties Meditation IV to the resolution of doubt about clear and distinct perception is also evident from the Synopsis where Descartes says: "In Meditation IV it is proved that everything that we clearly and distinctly perceive is true" (AT vii, 15). The power of the consideration that there are errors with regard to non-clear and distinct ideas to produce doubt even about clear and distinct ideas can also be seen from the fact that, in Meditation I, Descartes makes a strictly analogous move. There he claims that the fact that we do clearly make occasional errors only serves to keep alive the doubt about whether we may be so imperfect as to be deceived in all things. Thus Descartes says:

> But perhaps God would not have allowed me to be deceived in this way [about all things], since he is said to be supremely good. But if it were inconsistent with his goodness to have created me such that I am deceived all the time, it would seem equally foreign to his goodness to allow me to be deceived even occasionally; yet this last assertion cannot be made. (AT vii, 21)

In Meditation I, as in Meditation IV, Descartes needs to find a way to show why occasional errors are compatible with God's goodness, although more sweeping errors are not.

Descartes' first stab at this problem is to invoke the inscrutability of God. Thus Descartes says: "[S]ince I now know that my own nature is very weak and limited, whereas the nature of God is immense, incomprehensible and infinite, I also know without more ado that he is capable of countless things whose causes are beyond my knowledge" (AT vii, 55). Thus, even if "I do not understand the reasons for some of God's actions" (AT vii, 55), in particular his allowing us to make some false judgments, nevertheless this should not lead me to doubt his goodness or to see him as a deceiver in some objectionable sense. I may not be able to see how to reconcile God's goodness with our occasional errors, but, Descartes is saying, I should not expect to understand how this reconciliation is possible.

Descartes' second point is that when considering our errors with regard to non-clear and distinct ideas, I need to take into account the big picture. Descartes says:

> [W]henever we are inquiring whether the works of God are perfect, we ought to look at the whole universe, not just at one created thing on its own. For what would perhaps rightly appear very imperfect if it existed on its own is quite perfect when its function as a part of the universe is considered. (AT vii, 55–6)

Thus Descartes is claiming that my errors with regard to non-clear and distinct ideas may – I know not how – contribute to greater overall perfection in the universe. If so, then God is justified in allowing me to have false non-clear and distinct judgments. This big picture strategy is essentially Leibnizian: it a central theme of Leibniz's philosophy that local imperfection may contribute to global perfection. We will see that Descartes makes this kind of move yet again at a crucial stage later in Meditation IV.

This appeal, first, to the incomprehensibility of God's purposes and, second, to our limited grasp of how errors concerning non-clear and distinct ideas may contribute to the overall perfection of the universe is, of course, problematic. The chief worry here is that each strategy, if it were legitimate, would seem to prove too much. That is, each strategy, if it showed that God's goodness may be compatible with errors with regard to non-clear and distinct ideas would also seem to show that God's goodness may be compatible with errors with regard to clear and distinct ideas. This is proving too much because Descartes obviously wants God's goodness to be *incompatible* with erroneous clear and distinct ideas. Thus consider God's incomprehensibility. If God's goodness is, in some mysterious way, compatible with errors with regard to non-clear and distinct ideas, why can it not equally and equally mysteriously be compatible with erroneous clear and distinct judgments? Similarly, if the big picture may – in a way unknown to us – justify erroneous non-clear and distinct ideas, may it not – in a way equally unknown to us – justify erroneous clear and distinct ideas? Thus, although Descartes does not express any dissatisfaction with these strategies, the problems just raised make them seem fairly unpromising. For this reason, it is encouraging that Descartes devotes the bulk of Meditation IV to a philosophically more substantial strategy for justifying God.

This more sophisticated strategy turns on Descartes' account of judgment or belief. (Following much of the literature on Descartes, I will not draw any sharp distinction between judgment and belief, but it should be noted that in this context Descartes speaks more commonly of judgment.) For Descartes, judgment requires two separate faculties of the mind: the intellect and the will. Indeed, for Descartes, these are the only two faculties of the mind. The intellect is the faculty by which the mind considers the contents of thoughts. As Descartes says, "all that the intellect does is to enable me to perceive the ideas which are subjects for possible judgments" (AT vii, 56). And, for Descartes, all ideas are representations; they are of things or at least they purport to be of things. Thus, in Meditation III, Descartes says: "some of my thoughts are as it were the images of things, and it is only in these cases that the term 'idea' is strictly appropriate" (AT vii, 37). Strictly speaking, for Descartes, the intellect does not *do* anything. It is a passive faculty by which the mind receives and considers ideas or representations.

The will, by contrast, is the active faculty within the mind (*Passions* I, art. 17). It assents to, denies, or suspends judgment on the ideas – the representational contents – that come before the mind. Such activity is manifested in "desire, aversion, assertion, denial, and doubt" which are, for Descartes, "various modes of willing" (*Principles* I, art. 32). An act of will – in particular an act of assent – is needed for there to be a belief. A mere idea by itself does not involve either false belief, i.e. error, or true belief. Error occurs only when the mind gives its assent to a representational content that is false, and true belief occurs only when assent is given to a true idea.

For Descartes, all volitions or acts of will presuppose perceiving, presuppose that the mind is considering ideas (see, for example, *Principles* I, art. 34). But the will involves something over and above mere representation; it involves mental power which is not just a matter of representation. The power in volitions is thus not itself representational, though it is brought to bear on representational states that are separate from this power.

Among the ideas presented to the mind, some are clear and distinct and some are not. This variety in our ideas occurs because our intellect is limited by nature: if our intellect were not limited, it would understand everything and we would have only clear and distinct ideas. By contrast, the will, for Descartes, is not similarly limited: it is "so perfect and so great that the possibility of a further increase in its perfection or greatness is beyond my understanding" (AT vii, 57). This is because, for Descartes:

> the will simply consists in our ability to do or not do something (that is, to affirm or deny, to pursue or avoid); or rather, it consists simply in the fact that when the intellect puts something forward for affirmation or denial or for pursuit or avoidance, our inclinations are such that we do not feel we are determined by any external force. (AT vii, 57)

And, for Descartes, it is self-evident that we do have this ability, we do have this freedom (see, for example, *Principles* I, art. 39).

Because of this freedom, we are able to assent to clear and distinct and to non-clear and distinct ideas. Error comes in precisely because the will extends beyond what we clearly and distinctly understand. When we – through our freedom – assent to non-clear and distinct ideas, we are liable to make a judgment that is false and we use our faculty of willing not as we should. "[I]f in such cases [i.e. when I have ideas that are not clear and distinct] I either affirm or deny, then I am not using my free will correctly" (AT vii, 59). Obviously, sometimes – indeed, very often – practical matters may require us to assent to ideas that are not clear and distinct, as Descartes grants: "As far as the conduct of life is concerned, I am very far from thinking that we should assent only to what is clearly perceived." But he goes on: "when we are dealing solely with the contemplation of the truth, surely no one has ever denied that we should refrain from giving assent to matters which we do not perceive with sufficient distinctness" (AT vii, 149).

Of course, when we abuse our free will by assenting to a non-clear and distinct idea, we may get lucky and hit on the truth. But, even when we are lucky, Descartes says, we are nonetheless guilty of behaving irresponsibly when it comes to forming beliefs. Even more importantly, we can say that when we get caught up in error – false belief – as a result of assenting to non-clear and distinct ideas, the fault is our own, and not God's: we can't go crying to God.

In particular, we surely cannot complain that God gave us a free will that can lead us into these errors: the will is our greatest perfection, for Descartes and "the more widely my will extends, then the greater thanks I owe to him who gave it to me" (AT vii, 60). Also, it is no ground for complaint against God that our intellect is limited – it is, after all, simply part of the nature of a created intellect to be finite. So it is not God's fault that his creatures have finite intellects. So, again, God is off the hook. In broad outline, Descartes' response to his epistemological version of the problem of evil is a classic instance of the free will defense of God: our errors are not God's fault but rather they are ours because they are due to the improper use of our free will.

But no sooner does Descartes invoke our obligations with regard to belief, than he challenges the strategy in two final and powerful ways. First, Descartes considers whether there are still grounds for complaint in the fact that God did not give me an intellect which – while still limited – nonetheless contained "a clear and distinct perception of everything about which I was ever to deliberate." Surely, Descartes says, God could have done such a thing. Equally, God could – and compatibly with my freedom – "simply have impressed it unforgettably on my memory that I should never make a judgment about anything which I did not clearly and distinctly understand" (AT vii, 61). In either of these scenarios, I would have avoided error. So is God not to be blamed after all?

In answering these charges, Descartes reverts to the Leibnizian, big-picture defense: "I cannot . . . deny that there may in some way be more perfection in the universe as a whole because some of its parts are not immune from error, while others are immune, than there would be if all the parts were exactly alike" (AT vii, 61). This is disappointing because, it seems, it would again prove too much: this line of thought would seem also to raise the possibility that false clear and distinct ideas are compatible with God's goodness.

However, Descartes seems not to be troubled by this apparent possibility, and so he concludes Meditation IV by affirming that the author of every clear and distinct perception "is God, who is supremely perfect, and who cannot be a deceiver on pain of contradiction; hence the perception is undoubtedly [*proculdu-bio*] true" (AT vii, 62). The "undoubtedly" here is important because it indicates that Descartes sees himself as now finally having removed the doubt about the truth of clear and distinct ideas.

Believing at Will

The most striking and even, perhaps, odd aspect of Descartes' attempt to get God off the hook is his claim that belief is somehow a function of the interaction between the intellect and the will. Crucial to Descartes' account is the view that assent to an idea – an assent that results in or even constitutes a belief – is a free act of our will. The flipside of this claim is, of course, that suspending judgment is also something we freely, voluntarily do. This view suggests that belief (and also suspense of belief) is under our direct control: we will to assent to a given idea, and we assent just like that, in much the same way that when we will to move our arm, typically, the arm moves just like that.

There are, of course, ways in which belief may be *indirectly* under the control of our will; for example, I may want to form a belief about whether it is raining right now in Shanghai. Lacking any evidence one way or the other, I form the intention to seek out such evidence, perhaps by tuning into the Weather Channel for their much-anticipated China report. After so tuning in, I may come to have a belief that it is raining in Shanghai. This belief came about in part because of my voluntary activity and so was in some way under my control, but it did not come about *directly* as a result of any willing to have that belief. More interesting cases of indirect control over beliefs are cases of self-deception and other kindred phenomena in which, for example, I want to believe a certain proposition, say, that I am well-liked. In order to bring about this belief, I intentionally direct my attention away from the all-too-easy-to-come-by counter-evidence and, as a result of this subterfuge on my part, I find myself with the desired belief. Here, too, the belief results from my intentional activity and, indeed, unlike the previous case, it comes about in part as a result of my willing to have that very belief. But, as in the previous case, the belief does not come about *directly* as a result of my willing to have that belief.

Such cases of indirect control are common, but, again, they do not seem to be what Descartes primarily has in mind when he subjects belief to our will. Direct control is what Descartes' talk in Meditation IV of "the freedom to assent or not to assent" most naturally suggests and, in the case of suspense, such direct control is invoked pretty explicitly in a letter to Clerselier: "in order to get rid of every kind of preconceived opinion, all we need to do is resolve not to affirm or deny anything which we have previously affirmed or denied until we have examined it afresh" (AT ixA, 204; see also AT vii, 481). No doubt, Descartes insists on this direct control as a way of maximizing our culpability for our false beliefs.

But this insistence on direct control over beliefs seems extremely implausible. To take an extreme case: let us say again that I have no evidence either way about whether it is raining in Shanghai. In that situation, can I – without engaging in the search for evidence – simply and sheerly will myself to have the belief and, without further ado, thereby come to have it? As Edwin Curley (1975: 178) says about this kind of case, "I fear that if my salvation depended on my either believing or disbelieving this particular proposition, I should be damned."

The claim that without relevant evidence we can simply will ourselves to have a belief is certainly extremely implausible. But two points in this connection: first, if we *cannot* will to believe directly and without evidence, it is not immediately clear *why* we cannot do this. Is this an impossibility stemming from the very concept of belief, or is it merely a contingent fact about human psychology, or is it something in between a conceptual truth and a merely contingent fact? Philosophers have not been able to reach any consensus on the nature of the impossibility in question (see Williams 1973; Bennett 1990). Second, it is not at all clear that Descartes endorses such direct control over belief in the absence of any evidence either way. As far as I know, Descartes never invokes such a case and, indeed, he makes it quite clear in Meditation I that the suspense of belief comes about after consideration of *reasons* for doubt and not by a simple mental fiat (see Cottingham 1988).

Thus, it is not fair to charge Descartes with the crazy view that one can believe or suspend belief just like that, independently of any evidence. Nonetheless, Descartes does seem to endorse the view that, when one considers the relevant evidence, in order for belief to occur a separate act of will is required – an assent to the idea for which one has evidence. And this account does seem still to involve the claim that belief is under the direct control of the will. Yes, perhaps the stage must be set by the relevant evidence in order for the mind – the will – to exert its direct control over belief, but in the end belief is, it seems, for Descartes, under the direct control of the will. The claim that belief is under the direct control of the will, but only when one has relevant evidence is, perhaps, less outrageous than the claim that even without any evidence one can directly will a given belief. However, the former claim is nonetheless implausible. Why, one might ask, once one has in hand the relevant evidence or the relevant reasons for doubt, is there any need for a separate act of assent – the kind of act that is needed, according to Descartes, for us to be responsible for our false beliefs? When the issue is put in these terms, I think we can see that Descartes has a good insight, but not one that goes as far as he requires for his purpose of getting God off the hook. Let me explain.

Recall that, for Descartes, there are two basic kinds of mental states: ideas and volitions. The ideas represent things, they are about things, and they are passive. Volitions are active and non-representational – or at least they involve a non-representational component, viz. the power that they have and that ideas, representations, lack. In asking why there is need for a volition in the matter of belief, one is asking in part: why is mere representation or an idea not enough for belief? In this light, the question has a clear (if not completely uncontroversial) answer: representation is not sufficient for belief because there is, it seems, all the difference in the world between having in mind the idea that – the representation that – it is raining in Shanghai and actually believing that it is raining in Shanghai. Something is needed beyond the mere representation that can "bump up" the mere representation to the level of belief. One might say, in the vein of the challenge I just articulated, that all that is needed is consideration of evidence relevant to whether the representation is true. But in order for the promotion to belief to occur, the evidence must *be taken* as evidence, i.e. it must be believed. Thus, to turn the representation that it is raining in Shanghai into a belief, it is not enough for me also to have the *representation*, the idea, that the Weather Channel just reported that it is raining in Shanghai. After all, anyone can have such a representation, even one who has not seen the report, even one who is merely entertaining thoughts about possible topics for the Weather Channel. What is needed for me to *believe* that it is raining in Shanghai is for me to *believe*, say, that the Weather Channel reported that it is raining there. So merely piling on other mere representations is not enough, it seems, to bump up my representation of precipitation in Shanghai into a belief.

One can make this point vividly in the following way: imagine two minds that are representationally exactly alike. Each contains all the same representations as the other: the representations that it is raining in Shanghai, that Michael Della Rocca is so cool, that Paris is the capital of France, and so on. Now, despite all this representational indiscernibility, it seems that we can imagine that these minds differ radically in what they believe. Thus the first mind believes that it is raining in Shanghai and that Della Rocca is cool, and so on. However, the second mind (amazingly, perhaps) denies each of these claims. The plausibility of this scenario in which there is representational indiscernibility, yet real difference with regard to believing suggests that belief is something over and above mere representation.

Thus, to the extent that in his account of belief Descartes claims that belief involves something over and above representation, he seems to have a powerful point (but it is not one that is unassailable, as we will soon see). Nonetheless, this claim falls short of the claim that this something extra beyond representation is specifically a volition – a willing to have a certain belief. Perhaps the (apparently) required non-representational feature is not volition but merely some other kind of mental power or causation, a kind that does not bring with it, as volition does, the liability to ascriptions of moral responsibility. For example, there may indeed be a distinctively rational causation in which I am guided – caused – to form beliefs by the power of reason, by the appreciation – and not mere representation – of reasons for believing. If this were the case, then perhaps appreciating the reasons for belief may be sufficient for belief without a separate act of will. Such appreciation of reasons would involve more than mere representation but would not involve volition and the responsibility that goes with volition.

So while Descartes may be right that there is a kind of mental power over and above mere representation, he has not given us good reason to think that this mental power is volitional. Since the volitional nature of the power is crucial to Descartes' pinning responsibility for error on us and not on God, it seems that, in the end, Descartes' way of getting God off the hook is not fully justified.

I have been provisionally granting that even if Descartes does not have good reason to say that belief is, in part, a matter of the will, his claim that something besides mere representation is involved in belief is a powerful one. I now want to challenge this claim. Let us assume for the sake of argument that Descartes is right that belief involves something over and above representation, and let us grant him even that this something is volition. So there would be two kinds of items in the mind: ideas – representations – and non-representational items such as those that volitions involve. The representational and the non-representational states are in the same mind and, in fact, interact with one another. As we saw, for Descartes, it is because of the non-representational volition that ideas are "bumped up" to the status of beliefs. The relation between representational and non-representational states in the same mind may seem completely unproblematic until we ask the following quite natural question: in virtue of what are these rather disparate items – say, a particular idea and a particular volition – both mental and, indeed, both states of the same mind? What *makes* these disparate states both mental? And – a related question – why, for example, is a certain bodily state not mental? Bodily states are not, of course, mental for Descartes, but why not? After all, ideas and bodily states are rather disparate in nature – the latter are extended and the former are not. But why should this difference preclude the bodily state from being mental any more than the representational disparity between volitions and ideas should preclude one or the other from being mental?

In response to this question, Descartes would certainly invoke what he sees as the defining feature of the mental: consciousness. For Descartes, volitions and ideas both count as mental simply because, despite their great disparity otherwise, they are each conscious, they are each such that one is aware of them in a charac-teristically immediate way. (See the definition of thought in the *Second Replies* [AT vii, 160], and also *Principles* I, art. 9; AT iii, 273; AT vii, 246.) For the same reason, bodily states are not mental precisely because they are not conscious.

This answer is fine as far as it goes, but it does not go very far, for we now inevitably ask: in virtue of what are the ideas and the volitions – despite their great disparity – both conscious? And in virtue of what is the bodily state not conscious? There is no natural answer to this question on Cartesian terms, and so Descartes must leave unexplained how ideas and volitions can both be mental and thus how they can both be states of the same mind. In general, on the Cartesian picture, the relation between these two items must remain inexplicable.

This worry – to the extent that it is a worry – is analogous to the mind–body problem as bequeathed to us by Descartes himself. In the mind–body case, we have two different items – the mind and the body – that stand in a certain relation, in this case a purely causal relation. Yet it is inexplicable how, given their disparity, they manage to stand in this relation (see chapter 11). Similarly, in the case at hand, two items – volitions and ideas – stand in certain relations but there is no way to explain how they do so. In effect, the will–intellect relation generates an analogue of the mind–body problem within the mind itself.

Of course, Descartes may not be worried about the inexplicability of mind–body interaction. (See, for example, AT iii, 665–6 and AT v, 222 where he blithely asserts that we are aware of mind–body interaction, but cannot explain it in terms of other things.) And so there is no reason to think that Descartes would be troubled by what we can now see as the similarly inexplicable relation between volitions and ideas. But to the extent that *we* are worried about the inexplicability of Cartesian mind–body interaction, we should also, I believe, be worried about the inexplicability of the relation between the will and the intellect on Descartes' view.

This is a real philosophical problem raised by Descartes' account of error. If we take this worry seriously, then what account of belief should we give? The way to go would be to argue that there is no duality of representational and non-representational states within the mind. Rather, all states of mind are of the same kind: they are fundamentally representational. And from their representational nature can be generated all other mental features, including belief. Thus, on this non-Cartesian view, belief would be a function of representation alone and, con-trary to what we might initially have thought, there could not be two minds that are representationally exactly alike, but that differ in terms of their beliefs. Such a non-Cartesian view was developed for roughly these reasons by Spinoza in his famous critique of Descartes' account of belief (see Della Rocca 2003). Exactly how this alternative to Descartes' view could be made to work is far from clear, but this alternative is certainly worth exploring if only in order to shed light on the opposing Cartesian view.

Freedom

As we have seen, Descartes' strategy for getting God off the hook turns on the claim that, in assenting to non-clear and distinct ideas, we assent by a free act of will to something to which we should not give our assent. In the previous section, I explored difficulties with Descartes' view that the will plays this role in belief. In the current section, I will focus on Descartes' account of freedom and, in particu-lar, what is required for us to freely give our assent to an idea. In the final section, I will investigate the basis of Descartes' claim that it is improper to use the will to assent to non-clear and distinct ideas.

A traditional distinction that may help us to understand the contours of Descartes' account of freedom is the distinction between incompatibilism and compatibilism. An incompatibilist holds that, in order for an act to be free, it must not be determined by causes other than itself. Thus, for an incompatibilist, freedom is incompatible with determinism, the thesis (roughly) that every act and every event in general is brought about by causes other than itself. Compatibilism is thus (obviously) the doctrine that freedom is compatible with determinism, that an act can be free even if it was determined by something else (see Chappell 1994a: 177).

The debate over incompatibilism is, of course, historically important, and it continues to rage in contemporary philosophy. This is completely unsurprising for at stake here is our very conception of ourselves as free agents and thus the very legitimacy of our practices of moral praise and blame. Descartes certainly agreed that freedom is central to our conception of ourselves, and he held that the will and its freedom constitute, as we saw, our greatest perfection. Nonetheless, it is surprisingly difficult to pin down Descartes' position with regard to the debate over incompatibilism (see Ragland forthcoming).

The first thing to note is that there is a clear sense in which Descartes is a thoroughgoing determinist. For Descartes everything, including our actions and thoughts, is determined by God. Thus Descartes says to Princess Elizabeth that God is "the total cause of everything; and so nothing can happen without his will" (AT iv, 314). Descartes also says that "it is certain that everything was preordained by God" and that it is "impious to suppose that we could ever do anything which was not already preordained by him" (*Principles* I, art. 40; see also *Passions*, art. 145).

Nonetheless, this determination of our actions by God does not, according to Descartes, undermine their freedom. Descartes does admit that it is difficult to reconcile our freedom with God's causal control over everything, and this puzzlement on Descartes' part indicates that he has at least some incompatibilist tendencies (see Ragland, forthcoming). After all, a dyed-in-the-wool compatibilist could say without puzzlement that God's causation of all things is compatible with our freedom. But despite this incompatibilist sentiment, and despite not being able to see precisely how to reconcile God's determination and our freedom, Descartes says quite unequivocally that we are free. Thus we find Descartes asserting: "That there is freedom in our will, and that we have power in many cases to give or withhold our assent at will, is so evident that it must be counted among the first and most common notions that are innate in us" (*Principles* I, art. 39). Thus Descartes seems to take a compatibilist line.

He goes on to suggest that, to help us reconcile our freedom with God's power, we should keep in mind that we cannot fully grasp the infinity of God's power. We can know that God "not only knew from eternity whatever is or can be, but also willed it and preordained it. But we cannot get a sufficient grasp of it [God's power] to see how it leaves the free actions of men undetermined" (*Principles* I, art. 41). This certainly does seem incomprehensible: God causes – wills – our actions and these actions are nonetheless undetermined. Indeed, this view seems to border on the self-contradictory. Descartes' view may seem somewhat less odd when we consider a subsequent letter to Elizabeth in which he says that the kind of dependence that our actions – our free actions – have on God is quite different from the kind of dependence or independence that we experience our actions to have. Descartes says: "The independence which we experience and feel in ourselves, and which suffices to make our actions praiseworthy or blameworthy, is not incompatible with a dependence of quite another kind, whereby all things are subject to God" (AT iv, 333). So, although, for Descartes, divine power over our actions is compatible with our freedom, that is only because God's power operates in ways that we cannot understand. This compatibilism differs from what may be seen as a standard compatibilism which does not invoke incomprehensible powers or different senses of determination.

A less mysterious kind of Cartesian compatibilism of freedom and determinism seems to emerge when we look specifically at Descartes' account of the determination of assent by clear and distinct perception. For Descartes, when we perceive an idea clearly and distinctly, it seems we cannot resist assenting to it. That is, it seems that clear and distinct perception determines the will. Thus to take only two relevant passages:

> [M]y nature is such that so long as I perceive something very clearly and distinctly I cannot but believe it to be true. (AT vii, 69)

> So long as we attend to a truth which we perceive very clearly, we cannot doubt it. (AT vii, 460; see also AT iii, 64, 116; AT vii, 58–9; *Principles* I, art. 44)

Descartes also holds that non-clear and distinct perceptions do not similarly determine our assent: we have, it seems, in such cases the ability not to assent. Thus in Meditation IV when Descartes speaks of cases in which "the intellect does not have sufficiently clear knowledge when the will deliberates," he says, "[A]lthough probable conjectures may pull me in one direction, the mere knowledge that they are simply conjectures, and not certain and indubitable reasons, is itself quite enough to push my assent the other way" (AT vii, 59).

Despite the apparent determination of our assent in the case of clear and distinct perception, Descartes claims that such assent is nonetheless free. Indeed, in such cases, I enjoy the greatest degree of freedom. Descartes says:

> [T]he more I incline in one direction – either because I clearly understand that reasons of truth and goodness point that way, or because of a divinely produced disposition of my inmost thoughts – the freer is my choice ... If I always saw clearly what was true and good, I should never have to deliberate about the right judgment or choice; in that case, although I should be wholly free, it would be impossible for me ever to be in a state of indifference. (AT vii, 57–8)

It seems, then, that for Descartes determination of assent by clear and distinct perception is compatible with freedom, indeed with freedom of the highest degree. This seems to be a version of compatibilism, but one that is much more straightforward than the sweeping claims of the compatibility of our free actions with incomprehensible divine determinism. Descartes makes no appeal in this case – at least no direct appeal – to mysterious divine power.

But even here, there is still room for doubt about whether Descartes' position is truly a form of compatibilism. The trouble here arises from a passage in a letter to Mesland of February 9, 1645 (for questions about the date and the recipient of this letter, see Kenny 1972: 24–6). Although, Descartes had previously said to Mesland (in the preceding May) that it is impossible not to assent to a current clear and distinct idea, in the later letter he expresses an apparently quite different view:

> [W]hen a very evident reason moves us in one direction, although morally speaking we can hardly move in the contrary direction, absolutely speaking we can. For it is always open to us to hold back from pursuing a clearly known good, or from admitting a clearly perceived truth, provided we consider it a good thing to demonstrate the freedom of our will by so doing. (AT iv, 173)

In this passage, Descartes seems to say that we can withhold assent from even a current clear and distinct perception (for a different reading, see Kenny 1972: 28–31). To the extent that Descartes comes to hold this view, he may not after all hold that clear and distinct perception strictly determines our assent. And so, Descartes' profession of the freedom of our assent to clear and distinct perception would then give no evidence that he holds a compatibilist position in this case. In the end, then, there must remain some lack of clarity as to the nature of Descartes' commitment to compatibilism.

The Mesland passage also raises a further worry, one that may seem to threaten Descartes' entire project of getting God off the hook. If, as the passage suggests, we can after all avoid assenting to a current clear and distinct perception, then why would God be objectionably deceptive if he were to allow clear and distinct ideas to be false? One might think that since we can resist the allure of clarity and distinctness, then if we fail to resist and things go badly – i.e. if the ideas turn out to be false – then we are to blame after all. Our ability to resist clear and distinct ideas makes it the case, it might be thought, that any blame for error in such a situation is to be laid at our feet and not at God's. Thus Descartes' entire strategy for showing that God would be unacceptably deceptive if clear and distinct ideas were false and for showing that clear and distinct ideas are therefore true would, one might think, be threatened. (Chappell 1994a: 182 may be expressing this kind of worry.)

The worry about this worry is that it presupposes that Descartes' strategy for exonerating God turns on the claim that we are compelled tov assent to clear and distinct ideas. But it does not: Descartes' strategy is simply to say that the falsity of clear and distinct ideas would be a black mark on God not because we are compelled to assent to clear and distinct ideas, but simply because in so assenting we are behaving as we should with regard to assent. Assenting to clear and distinct ideas is proper epistemic behavior, or at least in such a case we are not behaving as we should not. By contrast, Descartes says explicitly, the problem with assent to non-clear and distinct ideas is that in that case we are behaving as we should not; we are misusing our free will. So even if we can control our assent to clear and distinct ideas (as the Mesland letter suggests), any erroneous beliefs resulting from such assent could not be blamed on us: we were behaving precisely as we should and so, if error results, we could legitimately go crying to God. Thus, since one can never legitimately go crying to God, clear and distinct ideas must be true.

This worry stemming from the Mesland letter, though in a way easy to answer, only serves to highlight the significance of what is perhaps the most problematic aspect of Descartes' endeavor to get God off the hook: his claim that we *should not* assent to non-clear and distinct ideas. Precisely *why* is it the case that we should not assent to such ideas and, correlatively, why is it the case that in assenting to clear and distinct ideas we are behaving properly? These questions generate a worry that is, perhaps, not so easy to answer because it raises in a powerful way a new version of the problem of the Cartesian circle.

Believing as We Should and a Cartesian Circle

To begin to see how a new problem of circularity threatens to emerge, let us return briefly to Descartes' overall strategy in Meditation IV. Recall that near the outset of Meditation IV, Descartes claims that, despite the heroics of Meditation III, a doubt still remains about whether clear and distinct ideas are true. And this is because, at that point, Descartes has no answer to the question: given that God's goodness prevents him from allowing clear and distinct ideas to be false, how is God's goodness compatible with his allowing – as he surely seems to allow – that our non-clear and distinct ideas are sometimes false? Until Descartes can show that there is a relevant difference between clear and distinct and non-clear and distinct ideas, a difference that can explain why God can allow error in one case but not in the other, Descartes' doubt about the truth of clear and distinct ideas will remain.

As we saw, Descartes claims to find such a difference in the fact – as he sees it – that, although we should not assent to non-clear and distinct ideas, there is no such obligation not to assent to clear and distinct ideas. Thus, in assenting to non-clear and distinct ideas, we are behaving badly and thus God is off the hook for our assenting to non-clear and distinct ideas that are false. But if God were to allow clear and distinct ideas to be false, then, because in that case we are doing nothing improper, God would be to blame. For this reason, God cannot allow clear and distinct ideas to be false, and so Descartes has what he takes to be a guarantee of their truth. Thus we can see that, in Descartes' eyes, his claim that we should assent only to clear and distinct ideas removes the final doubt about them.

But now to return to the question from the end of the previous section: *why*, for Descartes, should we assent only to clear and distinct ideas? Without a good reason for this claim, Descartes will lack an effective way of putting to rest his doubt about clear and distinct ideas. The reason Descartes offers seems to be: we should assent to clear and distinct ideas and should not assent to non-clear and distinct because clear and distinct ideas are guaranteed to be true and non-clear and distinct are not. Before explaining how such a reason causes problems for Descartes, let me lay out some of the evidence for thinking that this is indeed Descartes' reason for saying that we should assent only to clear and distinct ideas.

Perhaps the clearest indication occurs in Meditation IV when Descartes says that, if I make a judgment with regard to a non-clear and distinct idea, "then I am not using my free will correctly." But why is this use incorrect? The answer seems to follow in the very next sentence: "If I go for the alternative which is false, then obviously I shall be in error; if I take the other side, then it is by pure chance that I arrive at the truth" (AT vii, 59–60). Descartes seems to be saying that it is because in assenting to non-clear and distinct ideas our judgment is at best accidentally true and at worst false that we should not assent to such ideas. Rather, we should restrict our assent to ideas – clear and distinct ideas – that are not true only by chance, that are guaranteed to be true. The "perception of the intellect" – and here Descartes obviously means "clear and distinct perception" – "should always precede the determination of the will" (AT vii, 60) precisely because it is only clear and distinct ideas that are guaranteed to be true.

A similar picture emerges from *Principles* I, art. 44: "When we give our assent to something which is not clearly perceived, this is always a misuse of our judgment, even if by chance we stumble on the truth." Descartes elaborates this point by saying that "if we do stumble on the truth, it is merely by accident, so that we cannot be sure that we are not in error." Again, he seems to be expressing the view that assenting to a non-clear and distinct idea is improper precisely because such an idea is not guaranteed to be true. Here Descartes presupposes that, by contrast, assenting to clear and distinct ideas is a proper use of our faculty of judgment because clear and distinct ideas are guaranteed to be true.

A somewhat earlier passage in Meditation IV than the one I have just discussed also shows that at this stage of his argument Descartes presupposes that clear and distinct ideas are guaranteed to be true. As he begins to lay out the different roles will and intellect play in judgment, Descartes says that "since my understanding comes from God, anything that I understand I undoubtedly understand correctly, and it cannot be that in this matter I am mistaken" (AT vii, 580). Although he does not yet invoke the notion of what we should do in the matter of belief, it is clear that his claim here is meant to set the stage for such a normative claim and, even more important, it is clear that at this stage Descartes is asserting that clear and distinct ideas are guaranteed to be true: "it cannot be that in this matter I am mistaken."

Finally, Descartes sometimes puts the point somewhat differently by saying that the feature which relevantly distinguishes clear and distinct from non-clear and distinct ideas is that clear and distinct ideas are capable of correcting non-clear and distinct ideas, but not vice versa (AT vii, 144; Loeb 1990 and Newman 1999 stress this way of putting Descartes' point). This claim, like the ones just quoted, asserts a connection between clarity and distinctness and truth: to say that clear and distinct ideas can correct non-clear and distinct ideas is to say that clear and distinct ideas can show non-clear and distinct ideas to be false, and that is to say that clear and distinct ideas can enable us to grasp the truth. (For a very different interpretation of the notion of correcting, see Loeb 1990.)

So Descartes' reason for saying that we should assent only to clear and distinct ideas is that such ideas are guaranteed to be true and non-clear and distinct ideas are not. As an epistemic strategy, this "take no chances" approach may have much to recommend it. But in the context of Descartes' overall aims in Meditation IV, this approach is extremely problematic. To assert or presuppose at this stage of Meditation IV – i.e. prior to the final resolution of the doubt about clear and distinct ideas – that clear and distinct ideas are guaranteed to be true is, it seems, simply to beg the question in a particularly direct way. To presuppose or assert that clear and distinct ideas are true in the course of trying to remove doubts about clear and distinct ideas is to argue in a circle. So, even if Descartes can be exonerated of the charge of circularity in connection with the Meditation III argument that God exists and is not a deceiver – and I do think that in one way or another Descartes can be exonerated of *that* charge (see Della Rocca forthcoming) – nonetheless the accusation of circularity rears up again – the criticism that would not die! – in the context of Meditation IV.

It should be noted that *this* charge of circularity is perhaps more damaging than the traditional one. The traditional charge of circularity calls attention to what might be called an external circle. In Meditation III, Descartes offers a number of premises concerning, for example, the reality of causes and effects, that lead to the claim that clear and distinct ideas are true. Although these premises do not include the claim that clear and distinct ideas are true, nonetheless the argument is circular because, it might be thought, one can be *justified* in believing these premises only if one is already justified in believing the conclusion, viz. that clear and distinct ideas are true. Or so the standard charge of circularity goes. This alleged circle is external because the conclusion is not itself one of the premises of the argument leading to that conclusion.

By contrast, in the less familiar Meditation IV circle, we find what may be called an internal circle. One of the premises needed for arguing that clear and distinct ideas are true is, as we have seen, that we should assent only to clear and distinct ideas. This claim in turn requires argument, and the argument for it seems to be based on the claim that clear and distinct ideas are guaranteed to be true. So, one of the premises of the argument for the claim that clear and distinct ideas are true is that clear and distinct ideas are guaranteed to be true. Here the conclusion – indeed, a strengthened version of the conclusion – is itself a premise in the argument. (Loeb 1990: 30, 31–2, nicely sets up the distinction between the internal and external circles.)

This problem would arise whenever the feature of clear and distinct ideas that is the basis for the claim that we should assent to them is the feature of being true, being guaranteed to be true, being able to correct (i.e. show to be false) other ideas, or even being likely to be true. To invoke any such connection to the truth in order to argue that clear and distinct ideas are true will inevitably seem question-begging, for the connection of such ideas to the truth is precisely what is in question.

Perhaps, however, the situation is not so dire. Yes, it might be granted, Descartes uses the claim that clear and distinct ideas are true in his argument for that very conclusion, and this is unacceptably circular. But perhaps a different strategy is available to Descartes: perhaps one could say that we should assent only to clear and distinct ideas not because they are guaranteed to be true or are likely to be true (or whatever), but for some other reason. But the worry now is this: why should a given feature of a clear and distinct idea other than the feature of being true (or likely to be true) generate an obligation to assent to that idea? It seems that if the feature is other than truth, then it can by itself provide no reason for claiming that we should assent to the idea in question (and should not assent to other ideas that do not have this feature). In other words, I would say that we should assent to an idea only because it has a feature that at least makes it more likely that it is true. Absent an appeal to such a connection to the truth, it is far from clear that there is an obligation to assent to the idea. But, once one does appeal to such a connection to the truth, the problem of circularity arises again, for how can one justifiably appeal to a connection between clear and distinct ideas and truth in order to argue that there is such a connection?

This latest challenge is, I believe, the most serious one facing Descartes' strategy in Meditation IV. A defender of Descartes would need to show that, contrary to what I have just suggested, there is a plausible truth-independent basis for the claim that we should assent only to such-and-such an idea. Can there be such a basis? Perhaps so, although, as I have indicated, I am dubious. Certainly, however, this issue is worth exploring further (see Loeb 1990, 1992). Here again, we see that even when Descartes' strategy in Meditation IV is under serious pressure – and precisely because his strategy is under serious pressure – it promises to shed light on and structure the debate about the nature of belief, the will, and the responsibility that goes with believing.

10

Descartes' Proof of the Existence of Matter

Desmond M. Clarke

Toward the end of 1639, when he was forty-three years old, Descartes began to write what he tentatively called a "discourse," in which he planned to develop systematically some of the thoughts about metaphysics that he had drafted ten years previously. This essay appeared two years later as the *Meditations on First Philosophy* (1641). However, this was not the first time that Descartes revealed some of his metaphysical ideas in print. The *Discourse on Method*, published in French in 1637, included a synoptic version of his arguments about God and the human soul (which is what Descartes meant by the term "metaphysics"). On further reflection in 1639, he thought it would be advisable to publish a more extended version of the same arguments in Latin, and thereby to contribute to the apologetic aims of the Catholic Church in defense of its religious dogmas. While the precise reasons for his public venture into metaphysics at this stage in his intellectual life remain unclear, it is beyond doubt that he had thought about God and the human soul during the years 1629–39 and that he was now returning to these themes to set out his ideas in a more systematic and complete manner. Besides, the choice of Latin would make his view accessible to university students throughout Europe.

It is equally beyond dispute that, up to this point, Descartes had never doubted the existence of the material world and he was not about to begin having such doubts in 1639. His attitude to skeptical arguments about the existence of the physical world is well expressed in the final paragraph of Meditation VI, where he refers to "the hyperbolic doubts of recent days [which] should be rejected as ridiculous" (AT vii, 89). Despite this clear statement, many of his first readers were so impressed by the Cartesian statement of contemporary skeptical objections in Meditation I (as are many readers since) that the impact of those objections lasted much longer than Descartes' qualified success in refuting them.

The unhappy author complained of this misunderstanding of his project, as he did of many others. For example, he had attempted as best he could to prove

God's existence and was rewarded for his efforts by being accused by Calvinist theologians of atheism. Likewise, he constructed the best arguments he could think of against the pervasive skeptical opinions of his age, and was rewarded by being described as a skeptic, by philosophers and theologians. His complaint is understandable, even if his readers' reactions are not completely unfounded either. There were signs of exasperation in his complaint to Father Dinet, when he implored him to restrain the unjustified criticism of Father Bourdin, whom he took to be a particularly unsophisticated Jesuit. He pointed out that when the most authoritative among ancient authors on medical matters, Galen, discussed the causes of disease, no one thought it reasonable to accuse him of telling people how to get sick. In exactly the same way, Descartes claims, "I did not propose any reasons for doubt with the intention of teaching them but, on the contrary, in order to refute them" (AT vii, 573–4).

Thus, Descartes was neither personally tempted by skepticism about the existence of matter, nor was he philosophically persuaded of the plausibility of arguments in favor of such skepticism. In fact, all his work during the years prior to 1639 assumed as obvious that the physical world does exist and that it can be observed, manipulated, investigated and, with appropriate guidance, explained. During these years, while he was living in the United Provinces, Descartes seems to have devoted almost all his time to writing the book that was intended as a summary of everything he had discovered to date about the universe, and which was called appropriately *The World*. However, the condemnation of Galileo in 1633, just when *The World* in draft form was ready to be shown to friends, caused an abrupt change of plan. It was withheld even from Descartes' most supportive friends, such as his dedicated correspondent in Paris, Marin Mersenne, or the Dutch politician and man of letters, Constantijn Huygens. Many sympathetic readers subsequently asked Descartes to release for publication the general theory that provided a foundation for all his physics and physiology. Their requests fell on deaf ears. He refused even to let them read *The World* unofficially. However, this act of self-censorship did not represent a change of mind on his part about the contents of *The World*. Descartes released some of its theories in the scientific essays that were published in 1637, and he used it again to write the *Principles of Philosophy* (1644), while continuing to hold to his decision not to publish *The World* in its original format. In fact, it remained unpublished throughout his life, and appeared posthumously only in 1664.

The World or, at least, that version of it that was edited by Descartes' literary executor after his death, contains his theory of matter and the first version of the three laws of nature that appeared subsequently in the *Principles* (Part II). If one wishes to know, therefore, what he was claiming about matter in the *Meditations*, or why he was arguing as he was, one has to look first to *The World*, an unfinished book that he treasured throughout the final two decades of his life and to which he frequently refers as his "physics."

Matter in *The World*

We know things by their properties. This apparently obvious fact camouflages a philosophical problem that became prominent after Galileo and remained central to philosophical discussions throughout the seventeenth century. That problem was: how do we distinguish between the apparent and the real properties of things, between how things appear to us and how they actually are in reality? We might assume, of course, that things have all the properties that they appear to have, or that there are objective features in every reality that correspond exactly to the way in which we experience them. The example used by Galileo to cast doubt on this assumption, and which was re-used by Descartes to the same effect, was the sensation we experience when we are tickled. If someone passes a feather lightly over any sensitive part of our body, we have a characteristic tickling sensation which is easy to recognize but very difficult to describe. Without trying to describe its qualitative feel, we denote it with a word that implies an appropriate external cause; if we have the sensation in the absence of a familiar external cause, we usually have reason to worry about our health.

However, no one is so naïve as to assume that there is some property, in feathers for example, that corresponds exactly to this tickling sensation. We assume, rather, that the effect of the feather lightly touching our skin somehow causes a definite, recognizable perception, which does not literally resemble anything in the feather or its motion. If we move from ticking sensations to our experience of light, colors, and so on, and if we ask what are the objective properties of light which cause us to have the sensations that we have, Descartes draws the plausible conclusion that is suggested by the tickling example. "Now I see nothing which compels us to believe that what it is in objects that gives rise to the sensation of light is any more like that sensation than the actions of a feather . . . are like a sensation of tickling . . ." (AT xi, 6).

Thus we know things by their properties, but we rarely if ever know those properties directly or immediately. We seem instead to know how things appear to us, and we have to infer, somehow, from appearances to reality. This involves an inference to the best explanation. We postulate that things have as many properties as are necessary to explain all the properties that they seem to have. In this exercise, we are expected to observe the restrictions of parsimony and not to postulate more properties than are required. Necessity is the key factor here; the fewer properties we attribute to things the better.

This is a very brief outline of the first step in Descartes' construction of a general physical theory in *The World*. He abandoned many of the properties that scholastic philosophers had assumed in matter – for example, that matter had a distinct property of heaviness – and he agreed to postulate only as many properties as seemed to him necessary to complete the project of explaining all the natural phenomena of the universe. Descartes was not renowned for his intellectual modesty. Accordingly, he failed to notice that the ambitiousness of his plan could not be realized with the extremely parsimonious conceptual restrictions within which he worked. So he accepted that matter was uniform throughout the universe, that it was divided into parts of various sizes (he thought three sizes were enough), and that its parts moved in various ways and collided with each other. That meant that he needed to add laws of motion to explain (a) why pieces of matter move as they do and (b) what happens when they collide with each other in different circumstances. With these assumptions in place, Descartes set about the task of explaining all the natural phenomena that had been observed to date, including the action of light, the colors of the rainbow, the apparent attraction or repulsion of magnetic stones, the fact that bodies fall to the earth, and so on. At a macro-level, he planned to explain how the planets in the solar system were formed, why they move in their characteristic orbits, and why we should believe that the universe extends indefinitely into what appears to be empty space.

It is not surprising, in retrospect, that Descartes failed in this extremely ambitious project or, at least, that he failed to make as much progress with it as he had originally hoped. He allowed himself far too few properties in matter to explain many of the realities to which he turned his inquiring mind. During the two decades when he was listing the properties of matter, there was no understanding of electrical or chemical properties, and there was not even a vague intimation of atomic structure or a periodic table of elements. However, the reasons for Cartesian parsimony were not simply conceptual. It was not that he could not think or imagine other properties. Nor was his reluctance to postulate properties in matter simply a function of his lack of experimental data. Rather, Descartes' niggardly attitude was inspired by a concept of explanation that was essentially correct.

Descartes did not think that we could explain any natural phenomenon by claiming that it was caused by something else that we understand even less well than what we are trying to explain. Nor could we hope to explain anything by inventing a fancy term, usually in Latin, that merely re-describes what we are trying to explain. For example, it is impossible to explain how things appear colored to us, when we look at them, by saying that they have a "capacity to appear colored," just as we cannot explain why sleeping pills work by saying – equally uninformatively – that they have a "dormitive power." Descartes thought he could understand reasonably well why moving bodies continue to move, and how they redistribute the force of their motion when they collide with other bodies. His ambition, then, was to explain all complex natural phenomena in terms of such readily intelligible, familiar realities, and to avoid the illusion of explaining things by merely re-describing them in novel, apparently technical terms.

Thus, the fundamental properties that were predicated of all pieces of matter included initially only their size, shape, their disposition in space or orientation, and the structures in which parts are related when combined into larger bodies. These properties were not unusually limited by the standards of the early seventeenth century. Even Robert Boyle, who made much more progress in developing chemistry than Descartes had dreamed of, and who published the *Origin of Forms and Qualities* sixteen years after Descartes' death, limited his description of matter to the following: "each of the primitive Fragments . . . must have two Attributes, its own Magnitude, or rather *Size*, and its own *Figure* or *Shape*" (Boyle 1999–2000: v, 307). He later adds "*Posture*" and "*Order*" (ibid., 316). Just as Boyle wrote about "these two grand and Catholick principles of bodies, Matter and Motion" (ibid., 307), Descartes also relied on matter and motion to explain all natural phenomena. One of the immediate problems that needed to be addressed, therefore, was the origin of motion and the ways in which it is distributed in the natural world.

Descartes relied on a familiar argument during the 1630s to distinguish between matter and motion. One could imagine a piece of matter that is not in motion, and therefore motion is not an intrinsic property of any particular piece of matter. It follows that it must be a distinct property, which may or may not be found in various pieces of matter. This suggested that motion is added to any given piece of matter from some external agency. If the whole of matter is considered in a similar way, motion must still be thought of as an added extra. Descartes also thought of the whole of matter together as a naturally indestructible substance. "Body, considered in general, is a substance and therefore can never perish" (AT vii, 14). Since God was assumed to have been the creator of matter, it was a simple step to attribute motion also to his creative agency. Once added to matter, motion had a similar ontological stability as matter, in the sense that it does not spontaneously self-destruct. Descartes assumed that, unless God were to annihilate matter or motion, matter would continue to exist indefinitely into the future and that the motion which was added by the creator would be constantly redistributed among its moving and non-moving parts. He clarified the latter point in a letter to Newcastle (March/April 1648): "I hold that there is a certain quantity of motion in the whole of created matter, which never increases or decreases. Thus when one body makes another body move, it loses as much of its own motion as it contributes to that of the other body" (AT v, 135). This holds even in cases where the change is imperceptible. For example, if a small stone falls to the ground and does not rebound, it must have shaken the whole earth when it lost its motion, even if the impact was not noticeable to human observers.

One could raise questions at this point about whether, in addition to being in motion or at rest, parts of matter include a distinct reality called a "force." One plausible way of reading the texts is to assume that, for Descartes, force is reducible in some way to motion or rest, or to the tendencies of bodies in motion or at rest to remain in whatever condition they are in. This is addressed in the *Principles of Philosophy* (Part II), where Descartes defines motion as the transfer of a piece of matter from the vicinity of the bodies in its immediate environment to the vicinity of other bodies. He distinguished this simple reality – a transfer of location – from "the force or action which brings about the transfer, to show that motion is always in the moving body as opposed to the body which brings about the movement" (AT viiiA, 54). He was very keen not to introduce, at this point, any mysterious entity as a possible explanation of bodily motions, such as a desire on the part of pieces of matter to move or to resist motion. He argued that traditional accounts of gravity make this mistake by attributing intentional states to pieces of matter or by imagining each piece of matter falling to the earth as if it were impelled by a soul. Once that mistake is avoided, however, he seems not to have objected to thinking of pieces of matter, either in motion or at rest, as having a property that results from the condition of motion or rest, namely, a force that could cause bodies to move or to resist motion.

The function of laws of nature, in this context, was to describe various ways in which bodies move as a result of being affected by other bodies which strike against them. The laws, therefore, describe the direction and speed of moving bodies as a result of different types of collision. Descartes offers three general principles of motion, which he describes as "laws of nature," in Part II of the *Principles*, and seven more detailed descriptions of idealized collisions between parts of matter of varying sizes and speeds, which he describes as "rules." These minimalist resources (if given in a more detailed form) exhaust the Cartesian description of matter.

Extension as a Property of Matter

The idea that matter might be understood in terms of a single defining property was probably inherited by Descartes from the scholastic tradition. Whatever its source, it appeared as a central feature of his thinking about the physical world as early as the unfinished essay that is now called the *Rules* (i.e. pre-1628), and it continued to dominate many of his discussions for the rest of his life.

There are two surprising features of Descartes' discussion of matter and extension in the *Rules*: (a) that the analysis hinges on what can be imagined; and (b) the claim that if one tries to resolve the issue by recourse to concepts, one is likely to be misled by philosophical abstraction. Descartes defines "extension" in this context as "whatever has length, breadth and depth" (AT x, 442), and then warns against imagining a completely empty, extended space. "Someone may convince himself that it is not self-contradictory for extension *per se* to exist all on its own even if everything extended in the universe were annihilated" (AT x, 443). However, that would be a mistake, "an incorrect judgment of the intellect" if it ignored the help of the imagination. Descartes goes on to argue that "extension" and "body" denote the same reality. "We do not form two distinct ideas in our imagination, one of extension, the other of body, but just the single idea of an extended body" (AT x, 444).

These provisional conclusions, although never published during Descartes' life, retained their validity for him throughout his career. They formed the basis of his argument, in the *Principles*, that space and body are one and the same reality, so that it makes no sense to try to imagine some limit to the universe. If we tried to imagine a boundary for the physical universe, then the space beyond the boundary would have the same properties of extension as the body that it bounds. The theological implications of this argument were challenged by Queen Christina of Sweden, in questions sent to Descartes two years before he assumed his official duties as her philosopher in residence. Descartes defended his position by claiming that he shared this view with Cardinal de Cusa, and he set out his argument as simply as possible.

> When I examine the nature of this matter, I find that it consists only in being extended in length, breadth and depth, so that everything that has these three dimensions is a part of this matter. There cannot therefore be a space which is completely empty, that is, which contains no matter, because we could not conceive of such a space unless we conceive these three dimensions in it and, therefore, some matter. For if one supposes that the world is finite, one imagines certain spaces beyond its boundaries which have their three dimensions and which, therefore, are not purely imaginary . . . but which contain matter. Since this matter cannot be anywhere other than in the world, it shows that the world extends beyond the boundaries that one wished to attribute to it. Since we have no reason to prove, and cannot even conceive, that the world has boundaries, I call it "indefinite." (AT v, 52)

Similar considerations persuaded Descartes to oppose Pascal's conclusions, in 1647–8, even after the famous experiment on the Puy-de-Dôme. Descartes agreed with Pascal, as did many others at the time, that a column of mercury is supported in a Torricelli tube not because nature abhors a vacuum but because the atmospheric air applies an equivalent pressure which is equal to the weight of the mercury column. However, he disagreed about how to describe the apparent vacuum at the top of the tube. Since this "vacuum" had dimensions and since it displayed other properties of a body, he argued that it must be a body of some kind rather than an absolutely empty space.

These considerations about the relationship between extension and matter constituted part of the standard Cartesian account of matter that not only predated the *Meditations* but continued to feature in all subsequent discussions of mind–body problems and discussions of the nature of space. It would have been very surprising if they disappeared suddenly from the *Meditations* and then re-appeared as suddenly in later writings, such as the *Principles*.

"Body" in the *Meditations*

In the course of developing arguments in the *Meditations* in support of the two objectives mentioned in the book's subtitle – namely, to demonstrate "God's existence and the distinction between the human soul and the body" – Descartes had occasion to talk about the essence of matter, and to offer a famous argument to support his belief in the existence of bodies. Since completing *The World* and publishing the scientific essays of 1637, he had not had second thoughts about whether the physical world actually exists. He makes that clear in the Synopsis that forms a preface to the *Meditations*. Having referred to his efforts, in Meditation VI, to present all the arguments that enable the reader to conclude that material things exist, he adds:

> The great benefit of these arguments is not, in my view, that they prove what they establish – namely, that there really is a world, and that human beings have bodies, and so on – since no sane person has every seriously doubted these things. The point is that in considering these arguments we come to realize that they are not as solid or as transparent as the arguments which lead us to knowledge of our own minds and of God. (AT vii, 15–16)

The specific objectives of this essay on metaphysics were to help readers to think coherently about the nature of the human mind and, by analogy, of God's nature and existence. These are normally very difficult topics, and readers might have assumed that we are less certain about them than about familiar realities of every-day life. Descartes wanted to turn that assumption on its head. He wanted to argue that we are more certain about some features of our own thinking, and about the nature of the human mind, than we could ever possibly be about phys-ical bodies.

If this argument were to work, however, it would not make doubtful our knowledge of the physical world or, at least, it would not make it any more doubt-ful than it was previously. The structure of the argument, in the *Meditations*, involves contrasting our knowledge of the physical world with the kind of direct, experiential knowledge of our own minds that Descartes claims to have, and then arguing that the latter is even more certain than the former. The two features of our knowledge of the physical world already mentioned above, namely, that we know the world through its properties, and we know it indirectly, are re-used here in the interests of the primary, polemical objectives of the *Meditations*.

Descartes includes "the essence of material things" as part of the title for Meditation V. His brief discussion is unsatisfactory. Part of the reason for this is that the structure of the argument in the *Meditations* prevents him, before Meditation VI, from discussing anything apart from his own ideas. Thus, rather than speculate about the properties of matter, he is confined in Meditation V to considering "the ideas of these things [i.e. bodies], in so far as they exist in my thought" (AT vii, 63). This review of ideas reveals that he can "distinctly im-agine . . . the extension of a quantified thing in length, breadth, and depth" (AT vii, 63), and that he has many other ideas of the shape, number, or motion of parts of matter. Before developing these considerations further, however, Descartes reverts to a version of the ontological argument. In his objections, Pierre Gassendi questioned whether one could assume so readily, as scholastic philosophers did, that things have immutable essences and, by implication, that matter has an essence

(AT vii, 318–19). Descartes' reply is as unhelpful as Gassendi's original objection was deemed to be unsympathetic.

However, Descartes had already given a longer version of this argument in Meditation II. Thus, despite the title, Meditation V may be primarily about the essence of shapes, such as triangles, rather than the essential property of matter in general. If it were read in that way, it would provide a natural introduction to the ontological argument. The earlier related argument, in Meditation II, depends on a review of the properties of a piece of wax. The piece of wax, which one can see, smell, feel, and so on, is introduced to counter the assumption that such things that are known through sensation are known more reliably than our own minds. The argument runs as follows. If we perceive the properties of a piece of wax, its size, shape, smell, color, or relative hardness, all these features may change (within limits) without the thing in question ceasing to be wax. It may melt when heated, it may expand in volume, it may change color, and so on. This suggests that we need a distinction between inessential features of wax – those that can change while the body in question remains a piece of wax – and its essential properties. If we imaginatively strip off, one by one, the various inessential properties of a piece of wax, and if we "take the clothes off, as it were, and consider it naked," we find that the one property that it cannot fail to have is that it is extended. In the context of Meditation II, therefore, this diversion into thinking about wax supports the interim conclusion that even things that we thought we knew well, from experiential evidence, are known reliably only when we use our intellects to discriminate between their observable properties and their essential features.

This is a strange argument, which fails to acknowledge adequately three different distinctions. (1) One distinction that is more in the background here is between what later came to be called primary and secondary qualities, i.e. those objective features of physical things that we have reason to believe exist independently of our perceptions, and those features (such as color or smell) which bodies appear to have and which are partly a function of the interaction between bodies and our perceptual faculties. This is the distinction that resulted from the discussion of tickling sensations in *The World*, and it was still very much on Descartes' mind when writing the *Meditations*. Descartes was still defending it, in 1649, when he rejected suggestions from the Cambridge Platonist, Henry More, that matter should be defined as "perceptible, tangible or impenetrable substance." Descartes argued: "It is clear that if it is defined as sensible substance, then it is defined by its relation to our senses . . . However, its nature could exist, even if there were no human beings in existence" (AT v, 268).

(2) There is another distinction between those features of bodies that distinguish them as pieces of wax from other bodies that are, for example, hard pieces of honey. Descartes had been asked a number of times, especially by his principal Dutch patron, Constantijn Huygens, to engage in research in chemistry. He declined to take up that challenge, and the failure to address such issues shows clearly in his work. In the absence of even an incipient chemistry in his natural

philosophy, the theory of matter assumed by Descartes implies that wax differs from honey simply because they are each composed of different combinations of small particles of the same matter. For example, honey might include a higher proportion of long, slippery parts (which explain its viscosity), while wax might be composed a more tightly packed small particles.

(3) Finally, Descartes wanted to establish a much more general distinction between two types of substance, between material and immaterial things, and he assumed that each type could be characterized by a single defining property. He repeats this idea in many places, including Part I of the *Principles of Philosophy*, which was written as another version of the *Meditations* in a different expository style.

> A substance may indeed be known through any attribute at all; but each substance has one principal property which constitutes its nature and essence, and to which all its other properties are referred. Thus extension in length, breadth and depth constitutes the nature of corporeal substance; and thought constitutes the nature of thinking substance. Everything else which can be attributed to body presupposes extension, and is merely a mode of an extended thing; and similarly, whatever we find in the mind is simply one of the various modes of thinking. (AT viiiA, 25)

There is no independent argument here to support the conclusion that each type of substance has one defining property, or that all substances can be classified into just two general types. The discussion of matter in this text seems to be nothing more than a restating of the type of argument already sketched in the *Rules*. If we try to imagine a body which has no extension, we fail. This suggests that, insofar as imagination is a reliable guide to knowing what matter is, being extended is a necessary condition for being material. However, that leaves unanswered so many questions that it is difficult to know how Descartes might have replied to them. For example, why should the limitations of our imagination decide the essential feature of matter? Is this a conceptual analysis that masquerades as an exercise in using the imagination? To what extent does the argument rest ultimately on what we know about physical bodies from experience, since what we can imagine depends significantly on what he have already experienced? Is the definition of matter in terms of extension partly stipulative?

The concept of body that Descartes assumes, in the *Meditations*, is evidently not one for which he provides a well-developed argument. His focus, almost exclusively, is on the two topics that he had set out to discuss, namely, the status of a human soul when separated from the body, and the nature and existence of God. He wants to show readers that we have direct knowledge of our own thinking, that it is more immediately and directly known than anything else in the universe, and that even familiar objects like a piece of wax are known less directly and less certainly than one's own mind. To persuade readers of that conclusion, he need only (he thinks) show them how unreliable and inferential is our knowledge of pieces of wax, without guaranteeing the specific account of wax that he offers.

One could possibly accept this interpretation of the *Meditations* if the Cartesian accounts of matter and mind were not interdependent, and if the arguments about the nature of mind and God did not presuppose an already agreed concept of matter. Its limitations become more evident, therefore, when Descartes has to address the apparently insoluble problem of how mind and body interact in human beings.

Body as Non-Mind

Robert Boyle famously criticized the evasion and sleight of hand involved in pretending to provide some information about something by saying what it is not (Boyle 1999–2000: xii, 474). Boyle argued that we provide very little information about what is meant by a "spirit" if we tell someone that it is not material, just as we would learn almost nothing about any of the curved lines studied in geometry (including parabolas, circles, spirals, and so on) if we were told simply that they are not straight lines. By reversing the spirit–body distinction, we would be equally uninformed about bodies if we first assumed that we understood what spirits are and if we were told only that bodies are non-spiritual. Boyle was reflecting on the effort involved, both experimental and theoretical, in discovering some of the physical and chemical properties of bodies. The claim that body is non-spiritual would seem, in comparison, close to telling us nothing at all about matter. Likewise, the claim that spirit is immaterial is equally uninformative.

This provides another perspective from which to view Descartes' parallel descriptions of matter and mind. Does he claim that the mind is known to itself, directly and experientially, and that body is known in some less reliable way – which is what the wax argument suggests? Or does he claim merely that mind and body are each known in different ways, and that the most important thing is not to confuse them or to substitute one way of knowing for the other?

A detailed discussion of the Cartesian account of how each person acquires knowledge about their own mind is beyond the scope of this chapter. Nonetheless, one way of reading the *Meditations* is to understand it as an exercise in reflecting on what is already implicitly known by each person about themselves insofar as they think. The certainty of "I think" depends on the subject's self-awareness. In a more general way, Descartes defines thought as follows:

> *Thought.* I use this term to include everything that is within us in such a way that we are immediately aware of it. Thus all the operations of the will, the intellect, the imagination and the senses are thoughts. I say "immediately" so as to exclude the consequences of thoughts; a voluntary movement, for example, originates in a thought but is not itself a thought. (AT vii, 160)

If one grants that we are aware of ourselves by an immediate consciousness of the activity of thinking, as Descartes claims, then the human mind occupies a privileged place among the realities in the world of which it has knowledge. Descartes claims that this is what is distinctive about the mind, that the activity of thinking is its characteristic or defining feature, and that it is the means by which we know anything we happen to know about the mind. There is no suggestion that each person could somehow bypass the activity of thinking and introspect directly the reality of their mind. On the contrary, we are directly and immediately aware of the activity of our own thinking, which we conceive of as an activity or property of some subject or other. Even in the case of our own mind, therefore, we know the reality in question by knowing its properties – or, in this case, its one alleged principal property.

The same principle applies in the case of physical or material things. We know them by their properties. This is clear from a number of texts in the *Meditations*. For example, Descartes replied to an objection from Hobbes: "in general no act or accident can exist without a substance for it to belong to. But we do not come to know a substance immediately, through being aware of the substance itself; we come to know it only through its being the subject of certain acts" (AT vii, 175–6). Likewise, in reply to Arnauld, he wrote: "We do not have immediate knowledge of substances, as I have noted elsewhere. We know them only by perceiving certain forms or attributes which must inhere in something if they are to exist; and we call the thing in which they inhere a 'substance'" (AT vii, 222). This principle, about the indirectness of our knowledge of substances, applies equally to mental or physical realities. The difference between the two, for Descartes, is that we are supposed to have a direct knowledge or awareness of the activity of thinking (and, through it, of the subject of which thinking is predicated), whereas we know the properties of material things only indirectly (and, therefore, there are two degrees of indirectness in our knowledge of material substances).

This is consistent with the account of knowing natural phenomena that had been sketched in the unpublished *World* and had been put to such good use in the scientific essays of 1637. We perceive the apparent properties of physical things, and we then guess what are the most likely objective features that could explain our perceptual experiences. This suggests that the Cartesian account of matter should be understood as a very general hypothesis about the stuff of the universe, which – by interacting with our senses – causes us to have the variety of perceptions that we have of it.

Basic Concepts

There is an alternative account of the limits of human knowledge in Descartes' replies to the questions raised by Princess Elizabeth, following her first query about mind–body interaction in May 1643. On that occasion she asked: "how can the human soul, which is only a thinking substance, determine the movement of the animal spirits in order to perform a voluntary action?" (AT iii, 661). This letter initiated a lengthy correspondence between Elizabeth and Descartes which continued even after her departure from The Hague in 1646. In one of those letters, Descartes tried to answer her question by introducing a radical distinction between: (a) the mind, the kind of concepts appropriate to its description, and the appropriate epistemic faculty by which knowledge of the mind can be acquired; and (b) the body, the concepts in terms of which it may be described, and the faculties by which we are most likely to know it successfully. The implication of this radical distinction was that one should never confuse these two non-overlapping areas, and nothing but confusion follows from the misapplication of basic concepts to an inappropriate subject matter.

> First of all I distinguished three kinds of primitive ideas or notions, each of which is known in its own proper manner and not by comparison with any of the others: the notions we have of the soul, of the body, and of the union between the soul and the body . . . The soul is conceived only by the pure intellect; body . . . can likewise be known by the intellect alone, but much better by the intellect aided by the imagination; and finally what belongs to the union of the soul and the body is known . . . very clearly by the senses. (AT iii, 691–2)

This does not resolve the underlying philosophical problem, and its failure to do so was noticed immediately by Descartes' royal correspondent. For, without any supporting evidence, this reply simply separates the mental world and the physical world into two non-overlapping sectors, and it assigns the "pure intellect" to one as the appropriate epistemic faculty and the intellect aided by the imagination to the other. The original question from Elizabeth asked why we should separate them so radically and, especially, how could we explain their interaction if they have no relevant properties in common.

The same division of functions is invoked in the *Principles*, which was a text that Descartes was writing at the same time as he wrote to Princess Elizabeth. On this occasion, he combines the general principles discussed above – that substances can be known only by means of their properties – with the idea that there are two general types of substance, mental and physical, and that each type has only one fundamental property.

> A substance may indeed be known through any attribute at all; but each substance has one principal property which constitutes its nature and essence, and to which all its other properties are referred. Thus extension in length, breadth and depth constitutes the nature of corporeal substance; and thought constitutes the nature of thinking substance. Everything else that can be attributed to body presupposes extension, and is merely a mode of an extended thing; and similarly, whatever we find in the mind is simply one of the various modes of thinking. (AT viiiA, 25)

By this stage, in 1644, Descartes is simply repeating the fundamental claims which had helped frame the way in which he thought about mind and body for as least fifteen years. There is an elusive intimation of an argument in the suggestion that "everything attributed to body presupposes extension." That might be translated, without confidence, as: one cannot imagine or conceive of a body which is not extended. If so, that is the argument originally used in the *Rules*. Likewise, one might assume that thought is adopted as the defining feature of the mind because the only way in which the mind is known is by reflection on its own activity of thinking (understood in as broad a sense as possible, to include everything of which we are aware). These background assumptions help explain the function and structure of the argument introduced in Meditation VI to "prove" the existence of bodies.

A Proof of the Existence of Bodies

The structure of the argument in the *Meditations* allows the skeptic to block knowledge claims about everything – apart from the ideas in the mind of the meditator and what can be deduced from those ideas – until the final Meditation. Meditation VI opens, appropriately, with the remark: "it remains for me to examine whether material things exist" (AT vii, 71). The opening paragraphs reflect the dualism of cognitive faculties already mentioned above, according to which the mind is known by the intellect whereas knowledge of physical things requires application of the imagination. This is illustrated by a well-known distinction between conceiving of a chiliagon and imagining the same figure. One can conceive of such a figure easily, without being able to imagine it clearly, because the total number of sides is such that it is almost impossible to form a stable image of a chiliagon in one's imagination and to count its sides. This suggests to Descartes that perhaps the activity of imagining is a function of the body which is so united with his mind that they both cooperate in forming an image of a chiliagon. The argument for the existence of bodies, however, comes later in the same Meditation (AT vii, 79), when Descartes argues as follows.

1   I am aware of having a passive faculty of sensory perception, that is, "a faculty for receiving and recognizing the ideas of sensible objects."
2   This passive faculty would be useless unless it were stimulated by "an active faculty," which produces those ideas.
3   The active source of my sensory ideas is either in my own mind or in some external reality.
4   It cannot be in my mind because (a) it does not presuppose any intellectual act on my part; (b) I am not able to control if and when such sensory ideas occur to me, so that some of them occur even when I would prefer otherwise.

5   Therefore, this active source of my sensory ideas is some reality distinct from my mind.

6   This independent reality is either: (a) a body; or (b) God; or (c) some other non-material entity which is distinct from God (such as an angel or another human mind).

7   God is not a deceiver.

8   If God had arranged that I receive sensory ideas from either (b) God himself or (c) some other mental reality, it would be equivalent to deception on his part that he arranged matters in this way without providing me with any way of recognizing the genuine source of such ideas. In fact, God has given me (through human nature) a strong inclination to believe that sensory ideas originate from external physical things.

9   Therefore, sensory ideas do not originate directly from God or indirectly from some mental reality which is capable of making it seem to me that I perceive things which do not actually exist in the reality in question.

10   It follows that corporeal things exist" (AT vii, 80).

For those who are tempted by skepticism about the existence of the physical world, this is a less than convincing argument, partly because it relies at a crucial stage on the contentious claim that God exists and is not a deceiver. In other words, if one accepts the validity of the skeptic's arguments and then raises high enough the threshold of certainty that a convincing refutation of these doubts must reach, it is likely that the skeptic will remain unmoved by this argument.

There is another way of reading it, however, which makes more sense. Descartes can be seen as describing, from the perspective of a thinking subject, the kinds of thought that occur to him. Some are such that he is able to control them more or less at will. For example, unless he is obsessive about something, he can choose to think about something or not to think about it. However, there are many other experiences to which he is subject and which fall within the wide extension of the term "thought." They are such that, in many cases, he cannot avoid having such thoughts no matter how much he tries to avoid them. For example, he may experience pain or hunger, he may have the sensation of hearing loud noises or of seeing bright lights. He can choose not to think about a mathematical problem, but (depending on the circumstances) he sometimes cannot avoid having a sensation of pain. Descartes can then ask: what is the most plausible explanation of the fact that I am the passive subject of those experiences which are not subject to my voluntary control? Without appealing to God's veracity, the most obvious answer is: there are realities external to my mind which cause me to have such "ideas."

Even in making this case, however, Descartes can acknowledge the qualification about the sources of our sensations on which he had relied since writing *The World*. There is no reason to believe that the ideas I experience *resemble* the objective causes – whatever they are – which explain why I have them. Thus, he adds immediately at the conclusion of the argument outlined above: "they [i.e. corporeal things] may not exist in a way that exactly corresponds with my sensory grasp of them, for in many cases the grasp of the senses is very obscure and confused" (AT vii, 80). Thus, in order to know the properties of the material objects that we assume are the sources of our sensory experiences, we are forced to speculate about what kinds of objective properties could cause us to have the subjective experiences over which we have such little control. With this kind of speculation, the project of constructing a physical account of natural phenomena is re-launched. Despite the objections of skeptics, Descartes can justifiably rejoin the project on which he had made so much progress in *The World*.

Cartesian Limitations

Many features of Descartes' account of matter in the *Meditations* are implausible and incomplete. Part of the reason for this has already been suggested, namely, that the primary focus of that essay was not the nature of matter, its properties, or how we know them, but the existence of God and the distinction between the human soul and the body. Since claims to know the latter raised serious skeptical doubts, Descartes felt the need to confront skepticism and to offer an access to metaphysical knowledge that he claimed he could defend. In that context, matter and its properties were relocated in the penumbra of his primary metaphysical concerns.

Nevertheless, this hardly explains adequately the strongly reductionist features of the Cartesian account of matter that are evident in other work where the excuse of a focus on metaphysics is not available. Why did Descartes limit knowledge of matter to such few properties, such as the size, shape, and motion of its parts, that he seemed almost inevitably doomed to failure? One possible reason is suggested by his attitude, especially in his mature years, to claims about knowledge of God.

During the final two years of his life, Descartes was asked by two philosophers about his apparently intransigent attitude to what we can know about God. The background to the queries was a discussion within Calvinism about what were traditionally called "mysteries" in the Christian tradition. One response of philosophically astute Calvinists in the seventeenth century was to argue that we cannot be asked to believe what we do not understand. Thus, even in the case of what were traditionally called mysteries, such as the Trinity, there must be some way of understanding the three-in-one formula associated with Trinitarian beliefs if one is to believe it. The role of faith, in that interpretation, is to supply for a lack of evidence about the truth of the belief, rather than to camouflage the very meaninglessness of the object of belief. An alternative interpretation was that Christians are invited to believe something which, literally, they could not hope to understand, and that the role of faith was to compensate both for the lack of understanding and for the lack of evidence.

Descartes was sufficiently close to the first strategy that he provoked similar questions from two different philosophers at about the same time, from Antoine Arnauld and from Henry More. He also offered them both the same reply, as follows. It is a mistake to assume arrogantly that the human mind can set limits to what God is or what God can do. We should assume, rather, that God transcends the limits of our intelligence so much that even our best efforts to conceptualize God are completely inadequate. However, the question to be answered is not whether the human mind sets limits to the reality of God, but whether the human mind limits what we can understand and what, consequently, we can believe. It may be true that God can do things that we regard as contradictory. However, that is irrelevant to what we can believe. Thus, the limitations that we experience in our concepts cannot legitimately be projected onto the realities to which we apply them. They merely set limits to what we can understand or what we can talk about sensibly. This principle was made famous by Wittgenstein in the *Tractatus* (5.6): "The limits of my language denote the limits of my world" (Wittgenstein, 1961: 115). In a similar vein, Descartes wrote to Arnauld (July 29, 1648):

> I do not think that we should ever say of anything that it cannot be brought about by God. For since every basis of truth and goodness depends on his omnipotence, I would not dare to say that God cannot make a mountain without a valley, or bring it about that 1 and 2 are not 3. I merely say that he has given me such a mind that I cannot conceive of a mountain without a valley, or a sum of 1 and 2 which is not 3. Such things involve a contradiction in my conception. (AT v, 224)

More raised a similar question, about whether God could do things that we regard as impossible. When he persisted with the suggestion that, although there was a contradiction in thinking that a completely evacuated container would continue to maintain its shape, it would still be possible for God to realize such a phenomenon, Descartes replied:

> For my part, I know that my intellect is finite and God's power is infinite, and so I set no limits to it. I consider only what I am capable of perceiving, and what not, and I take great pains that my judgment should accord with my perception. And so I boldly assert that God can do everything which I perceive to be possible, but I am not so bold as to assert the converse, namely that he cannot do what conflicts with my conception of things. I merely say that it involves a contradiction. (AT v, 272)

This explicit strategy, of limiting what we claim or believe to what we can understand without making any unsubstantiated claims about what we do not understand, was particularly relevant to theological questions. Descartes, however, adopted the same perspective with regard to matter.

This question was raised by Frans Burman in the conversation he had with Descartes in 1648. Burman asked about a passage in the *Fourth Replies*, in which the author denied that we ever have an adequate knowledge of anything. The reply adapted the considerations about knowledge of God, just mentioned above, to knowledge of mathematical figures, such as a triangle, and even to bodies:

> For example, let us take a triangle. This appears to be something extremely simple, of which it seems we should very easily be able to gain an adequate knowledge. However, we cannot do so. Even if we prove that it possesses all the attributes we can conceive of, nevertheless after, say, a thousand years another mathematician may detect further properties in it. It follows that we will never be certain that we have grasped everything that could have been grasped about it. The same can be said with regard to the body, and its extension, and everything else. As for the author, he has never attributed to himself an adequate knowledge of any thing whatsoever. (AT v, 151–2)

Descartes was quick to qualify this conclusion so that it did not appear to support skepticism. The argument was not that we are uncertain of everything, but that we are sufficiently certain of some things that we can confidently claim to know them without implying that there is nothing more to be known of the same realities.

This provides a new perspective of what may have locked Descartes into the apparently obstructive limitations of his concept of matter. He certainly was not in a position to say that matter had no properties apart from those that were admitted to his conceptual repertoire, and he seems to have been aware of this. The limitations within which he worked resulted, rather, from a number of independent sources, each of which may have been reasonable on its own, although their combined effect was unduly restrictive.

One limitation resulted from the Cartesian concept of explanation. By relying on an intuitive account of what we understand, Descartes argued that it is impossible to explain something that is not understood by introducing something else which is even less well understood. This was part of his objection to the substantial forms to which scholastic philosophers appealed. "Proponents of substantial forms admit that they are occult and that they do not understand them. If they say that some action results from a substantial form, that is the same as saying that it results from something that they do not understand; which explains nothing" (AT iii, 506). It remains an open question as to whether we can be said to "understand" theoretical entities which are described in terms of the properties that they must have in order to provide an explanation of the phenomena for which they were invented. However that problem is solved, Descartes adopted as a principle that it is impossible to explain some natural phenomenon by appeal to something else which is even less well understood. One of the best examples of this principle in action was the consistent opposition of corpuscularian philosophers in the seventeenth century, including Newton, to the concept of action at a distance. Since they did not "understand" how one body could affect another at a distance, the suggestion that stones fall to the ground because they are attracted to the large mass of the earth seemed like a clear example of begging the question. A change of perspective was required in order to accept action at a distance – at least temporarily – as an unexplained fact.

Another source of the limitations built into the Cartesian concept of matter was Descartes' adoption of a second principle that was generally shared by his contemporaries. It was widely assumed that nature must be ultimately simple, even if it proved extremely difficult to explain what "simple" meant. One way of applying such a principle was to limit both the number of laws and the number of theoretical entities by which natural phenomena were explained. Evidently, that kind of limitation might be applied prematurely or unwisely, so that the resources available to the natural philosopher would be manifestly inadequate to the task of explanation. Descartes may also have been unduly restricted in applying a principle of simplicity by considerations of what he could understand.

One might expect that, given his penchant for mathematical analysis, Descartes' natural philosophy and the concept of matter which informed it would be significantly influenced by what could be described in mathematical terms. This consideration was most likely to apply in the case of disciplines, such as dioptrics, which were amenable to mathematical treatment in the early seventeenth century. Apart from that, however, most of Descartes' explanations of natural phenomena were qualitative rather than quantitative, and mathematics played only a minor role in the development of his theories. In fact, the kinds of properties that Descartes was willing to predicate of matter were all borrowed from ordinary experience of familiar objects in the world around us. He explicitly appealed to the principle that the properties of microscopic bodies differ only in scale from those of macroscopic bodies. "I compare those things which, because of their small size, are not accessible to our senses with those which are, and which do not differ from the former more than a large circle differs from a small one" (AT ii, 368). When combined with what many thought was an extreme tolerance for guesswork or hypotheses, he managed to forge descriptions of how small parts of matter, with appropriate shapes and motions, could combine together to give rise to almost any natural phenomenon. The screw-shaped particles of his explanation of magnetism illustrate this tendency (*Principles* IV, arts 137–83).

The result of these restrictions was that Cartesian matter was uniform apart from the shape, size, arrangement, and motions of its parts, and that it had no other properties that exceeded our powers of understanding. What seems to have escaped notice is that what is deemed "intelligible" may vary with changes in theory, and that our collective willingness to accept new theoretical entities may be influenced by both experimental and conceptual innovations. It may also be affected significantly by realizing that the concepts used to describe the familiar macroscopic bodies of daily experience may be completely inadequate to describe those at the atomic or sub-atomic level.

11

The Mind–Body Relation

John Cottingham

The Encounter with Matter

The reader of the *Meditations* may be forgiven a wry smile when coming upon the title of the Sixth and final Meditation: "Of the existence of material things . . ." Has it really taken the author five days of intensive philosophical reflection before he is ready to establish that the material world exists? In fact, Descartes was well aware that this might seem a little strange, and he covered himself in a preface with the following comment:

> In producing all the arguments whereby the existence of material things can be inferred, my point was *not* that I thought them very useful in proving what they establish – namely that there really is a world, and that human beings have bodies and so on – *since no sane person has ever seriously doubted these things.* (AT vii, 15–16, emphasis added)

There is a directness and robust common sense here, far removed from the artificiality of our modern discipline of "epistemology" with its solemn investigations of our "knowledge of the external world." Descartes was clear that the baroque puzzles of the skeptics did not really deserve to keep anyone awake at night.

Nevertheless, the relatively late appearance within the *Meditations* of a systematic argument for the existence of matter is significant. Throughout the work, Descartes has followed the "interior" path of his unacknowledged mentor, St Augustine. *Noverim me, noverim te* ("May I know myself, may I know you") Augustine famously says in the *Soliloquies* (I, 2 and II, 4): knowledge of myself is the first step to knowledge of God. And similarly, Descartes' own inner journey has led him first to awareness of himself as a thinking thing, and then directly on to acknowledge the divine author of his being. The path, like Augustine's, has been a characteristically Platonic one – a process of *aversio* (turning away from the senses) to discover the more stable realm of truth disclosed by reason.

What does reason eventually disclose about matter? First and foremost, its mathematically describable structure. Once I know a perfect and good God to be the author of my faculty of clear and distinct perception, then (concludes Descartes in Meditation V) the mathematical intuitions of that faculty must in principle be reliable, and hence I can hope to achieve "full and certain knowledge of . . . the whole of that corporeal nature which is the subject-matter of pure mathematics" (AT vii, 71). But an understanding of the abstract definitions and theorems of pure mathematics seems to constitute knowledge of a rather austere and remote kind. If we try to imagine what it would be like to have only this kind of knowledge of matter, we might perhaps think of the kind of knowledge a disembodied spirit like an angel might have – a being who had never *grasped* matter, or bumped into it, let alone had the experience of actually *being* material, a living breathing creature of flesh and blood. So if the contents of his new edifice of knowledge are not to remain disturbingly thin and abstract, Descartes must sooner or later acknowledge our characteristically human awareness of the world: our encounter with matter – and what is more, our encounter with it not just as something "external" to us, not just as something "out there," but as the very stuff of which we humans are made.

For Descartes, brought up as a devout Catholic, it was basic (as indeed it still is for millions today) that humans are not *wholly* material. Although God forms man out of the "dust of the earth," when he proceeds to "breathe into his nostrils the breath of life"(Genesis 2: 7) the resulting creature is in part a spiritual being, made in the divine image (Genesis 1: 26; cf. John 4: 24). Descartes had echoed this teaching in Meditation III: "the fact that God created me is a very strong basis for believing that I am somehow made in his image or likeness" (AT vii, 35). In a subsequent interview, Descartes was to allow that, given the axiom that "the effect is like the cause," there is a sense in which *everything* created by God, "even stones and suchlike," must bear his image, albeit in a very "remote, minute and indistinct" way (*Conversation with Burman* [1648], AT v, 156). But the key respect in which he saw us as carrying the image of God is in virtue of our intellect and our will – faculties that Descartes (following a long tradition going back to Aquinas, and, in part, to Aristotle) held to be wholly immaterial. The "light" of the intellect, the *lux rationis*, is an incorporeal faculty directly bestowed by God – finite, to be sure, and therefore restricted in its scope, but perfect within its limits and, provided it is used correctly, incapable of error (AT vii 59, 62). This had been the burden of Meditation IV. And that same Meditation had described the human will, in its unrestricted freedom, as "so great that the idea of any greater faculty is beyond my grasp, so much so that it is above all in virtue of the will that I understand myself to bear in some way the image and likeness of God" (AT vii, 57).

It is clear from all this that the "*res cogitans*" – the understanding and willing being that I essentially am (AT vii, 28; cf. *Principles of Philosophy* (1644), Part I, art. 32) – is, according to Descartes, what we might call a "spiritual" being – not a material thing at all, but a pure incorporeal substance. In the *Discourse on Method*, published a few years before the *Meditations*, Descartes had underlined the point: "this 'I' – that is, the soul by which I am what I am – is entirely distinct from the body . . . and would not fail to be whatever it is, even if the body did not exist" (AT vi, 33). Given this radically immaterialist view of the essential self, Descartes has hardly set things up for an uncomplicated encounter with his bodily nature. On the contrary, the scene is set for something problematic and even mysterious.

In the founding narrative of the religious culture in which Descartes was brought up, one very special manifestation of the relationship between spirit and matter was, of course, already shrouded in mystery. God, the supreme, eternal and immaterial spirit, had taken bodily flesh in Jesus Christ. The Incarnation was not claimed to be something wholly transparent to reason; on the contrary, it was universally acknowledged as a *magnum mysterium*, a "great and mighty marvel." Descartes himself had reflected on this in a notebook that has survived from his formative travels in Europe as a young man of twenty-three: "The Lord has made three marvels: things out of nothing, free will, and God in Man" (AT x, 218). Here, the Incarnation, God's taking bodily form, is interestingly compared with the mystery of creation itself, whereby something material was brought into being by God *ex nihilo*, out of nothing. So the relationship of God to his material creation, and his subsequently entering that creation in bodily form, were central mysteries of the Christian faith on which the young Descartes had pondered at a crucial stage of his early adulthood. In Meditation IV, he is about to explore a far more familiar and mundane version of the spirit–matter relation: its manifestation in our ordinary experience of human situatedness in a material environment, and – even closer to hand – the relation each of us has to "the body which by some special right I call 'mine'" (AT vii, 76).

The "Strangeness" of our Embodied Experience

Descartes is often credited with the idea of the perfect "transparency" of the mind. And in one way this is accurate enough: he observes, surely correctly, that when I have a thought (for example, the thought that two plus two makes four), or make a decision (for example, decide to withhold judgment in cases where the evidence is insufficient), then something is going on in my mind that is as "clear and distinct" as could be. It is *clear* (that is to say "present and accessible to the attentive mind"), and *distinct* (that is to say, contains nothing but what is clear) (*Principles* I, art. 45). But this clarity and distinctness, it turns out, pertains to us as "thinking beings" only in the relatively narrow sense of "thinking" that comprises intellection (or understanding) and volition. When it comes to our *sensory* experience – that part of our consciousness in which bodily events are unmistakably implicated – things are rather different.

In one way, what in ordinary parlance we call a "physical sensation" is about as fundamental and straightforward a part of our human lives as one could imagine. What could be more immediate and basic than a feeling of hunger – something common to every human from the youngest to oldest, whether highly sophisticated or barely articulate? Yet early on in Meditation VI Descartes signals something strange about it: a lack of the kind of transparency that is manifest in our intellectual and volitional activities. A sensation of hunger is quite unlike being aware of the thought "2 + 2 = 4," since its content, as it were, is not rationally analyzable. What exactly are you aware of when you are hungry? If pushed to put it into words, most of us would perhaps talk about a curious, slightly uncomfortable feeling somewhere in the abdomen, though we might add that it is rather hard to describe. Descartes calls it the "I-know-not-what tugging sensation in the stomach" (*nescio quae vellicatio ventriculi*, AT vii, 76). Hunger, of course, involves a desire for food, and a desire for food seems to be something pretty transparent, more or less within the domain of "clarity and distinctness." But there does not seem to be any obvious or transparent connection between this thought, "I need to eat," and the "funny feeling" we identify as the sensation of hunger. This is how Descartes puts it:

> As for the body which by some special right I call "mine," I feel all my appetites and emotions *in*, and *on account of* this body . . . But why should that curious tugging in the stomach which I call hunger tell me that I should eat, or a dryness of the throat tell me to drink, and so on? I was not able to give any explanation of all this . . . For there is absolutely no connection (at least that I can *understand*) between the tugging sensation and the decision to take food, or between the sensation of something causing pain and the mental apprehension of distress that arises from that sensation. (AT vii, 76, emphasis added)

The curious opacity, the "I-know-not-what-ness" of our raw sensory experience (an internal feeling like hunger, an external sensation like the prick of a thorn or the pain of being scalded by hot water) has a perfectly "natural" aspect to it: as Descartes goes on to explain, such modes of awareness are perfectly normal and, indeed, essential to our continued health and survival. But what is going on nevertheless has a strange "hybrid" quality: it is not a matter of "pure" transparent thoughts (cogitations and volitions), nor, on the other hand, can it be a matter of mere physiology (for the physiological events like the contracting of the stomach would occur even if we were anesthetized, but the *feeling* of hunger would not). So what is happening in our sensory experience seems somehow to straddle the world of spirit and of matter – or perhaps we might say that it functions as a strange kind of bridge between them.

But the human being *is* precisely a bridge between the realms of mind and of matter – a kind of incarnate spirit (or at least that is the way Descartes looks at it). So the occurrence of these strange modes of awareness that are neither pure thoughts nor mere physiology turns out to be exactly what one might expect as the signature of our distinctively *human* nature. Descartes is often accused (following Gilbert Ryle) of propounding a view of the human being as a "ghost in the machine." But, in fact, he explicitly repudiated the kind of "angelism" that took us to be merely incorporeal spirits lodged in mechanical bodies. If an angel were in a human body, he told a correspondent, "it would not have sensations as we do, but would simply perceive the motions which are caused by external objects, and in this way would differ from a real human being" (To Regius, January 1642, AT iii, 493). The human being is genuinely *incarnate* – that is to say, essentially and really an embodied creature of flesh and blood – and our distinctive repertoire of feeling and sensation and emotion is the surest sign of that. As Descartes famously puts it in Meditation VI (I cite the vivid and expressive English translation of William Molyneux, reprinted in the Appendix to this volume):

> And by this *sense* of *Pain, Hunger, Thirst*, &c. My *Nature* tells me that *I* am not in my *Body*, as a *Mariner* is in his *Ship*, but that I am most *nighly conjoyn'd* thereto, and as it were *Blended therewith*; so that *I* with *It* make up *one* thing; For Otherwise, when the *Body* were hurt, *I*, who am only a *Thinking Thing*, should not therefore *feel* Pain, but should only *perceive* the Hurt with the *Eye* of my *Understanding* (as a *Mariner perceives* by his *sight* whatever is broken in his *Ship*) and when the *Body* wants either Meat or Drink, I should only *Understand* this want, but should not have the *Confused sense* of *Hunger* or *Thirst*; I call them *Confused*, for certainly the *Sense* of *Thirst, Hunger, Pain*, &c. are only *Confused Modes* or *Manners* of *Thought* arising from the *Union* and (as it were) *mixture* of the *Mind* and *Body*. (AT vii, 78)

The Union

"*Union* and (as it were) *mixture*" of mind and body. This remarkable phrase brings us to one of Descartes' most vexed and debated doctrines: that, in the human being, mind and body are, as he put it, "really"(AT iii, 494), or "substantially"(AT iv, 166) united. The appeal to the "confused" modes of sensory awareness as proof of the genuine union of mind and body is a recurring theme in Descartes. We intellectually discern the distinction between mind and body, Descartes suggested to his royal correspondent, Princess Elizabeth of Bohemia, but we *feel* the union (AT iii, 691–2). And to another correspondent, Henricus Regius, he suggested (in the passage already quoted above) that a *pure* thinking being, like an angel, would have thoughts, but would not have sensations.

But why not? Could God not implant sensations into the consciousness of an angel that inhabited a body? Presumably he could: on the occasion of bodily damage, he could give the angel an urgent and intrusive signal that threatened to disrupt the flow of its thoughts until the damage was attended to. This kind of "angelic occasionalism" might at first seem a perfectly viable model for what happens when a Cartesian *res cogitans* feels pain in the body to which it is joined. But Descartes clearly does not think of it in this way. Human pain is for him an *irreducibly psycho-physical process*. The human mind–body complex is a genuine unit, not a soul making use of a body, not even a soul endowed by its creator to have certain kinds of awareness on the occasion of damage to the body it uses. A human being is a genuine unified entity, or in scholastic terminology an *"ens per se,"* not merely a conglomeration or "accidental entity" (*ens per accidens*): mind and body are united "in a real and substantial manner" by a "true mode of union" (AT iii, 493). When *my* body is damaged (and the "my") is important, *I* feel pain. And that feeling gives us proof, the best kind of intimate proof – proof available, says Descartes, even to those who never philosophize – of the genuineness of the union (cf. AT iii, 692).

Yet the idea of the mind–body complex being a "substantial union" presents some serious difficulties. How can I, as a *res cogitans*, be a complete incorporeal substance, yet at the same time, as a human being, be really and substantially embodied? Initially, perhaps, the problem might seem not too hard to sort out. *Qua* university professor, I am essentially attached to an academic institution; but, on the other hand, *qua* person, I am not – I would still be the complete and total "me" if I retired or resigned. So why not say that my body is like my affiliation: just as *qua* professor I have my affiliation essentially, but *qua* person I do not, in the same way *qua* human being I am united to my body essentially, but *qua* thinking thing I am not?

What makes it tricky to defend Descartes along these lines is his use of the language of substance, of real and *substantial* union. For supposing I said I was *really and substantially united* to my professorship, so that my professorship and I form a genuine and essential unity. An appropriately dry rejoinder would be that not even the notoriously cushy conditions of American academic tenure could deliver this strong a union. For once it is granted that the complete me could continue to exist without my chair, it seems to follow that the link between me and my job can only be a contingent one – something that may no doubt be important to me, but which cannot be deeply implicated in the kind of substance I essentially am. And so, *mutatis mutandis*, with the body. My link with the body starts to look merely contingent – in the jargon, "accidental" rather than essential. And so Descartes' position seems to risk sliding into a kind of "angelism" or Platonism: as Descartes' critic Antoine Arnauld put it, the Cartesian doctrine "takes us back to the Platonic definition of man," reducing man's status to that of a *soul making use of a body* (*anima corpore utens*, AT vii, 203).

A serious tension in Descartes' thinking seems now to be emerging. On the one hand, we have the "dualism" for which he is so famous, asserting that there are only two ultimate kinds of substance, thinking substance or mind, and extended substance or body. But, on the other hand, he also wants to claim that the human being is a genuine entity in its own right, amounting to a "substantial union" of mind and body. Is he really entitled, given the first claim, to assert the second? And if he is, how exactly is the second claim to be understood? Is Descartes saying, in the end, that there are not two but *three* kinds of substance – the mind, the body, and the human being?

According to some commentators, this is just what Descartes did mean. But I want for a moment to put this "substantiality" issue on one side, and consider the threefold classification that is now coming into focus simply in terms of *types of property or attribute* rather than kinds of substance. The threefold or "trialistic" (Cottingham 1985, 1986) classification implies that you could have a perfectly adequate understanding of the essential properties of thinking and of extended things (and their various modes, AT viiiB, 348–9) without including sensory experiences; and, conversely, that human sensory experiences are not wholly reducible to, or fully analyzable in terms of, the properties either of thinking or of extended things. This is expressed by Descartes in terms of the claim that human sensory experience belongs to a *"third primitive notion"* – something of which he spoke eloquently to Princess Elizabeth (May 21, 1642; AT iii, 665). Note the term: "notion," *not* "substance" (but I'll return to this point later).

Now describing this third notion, of the mind–body union, as *"primitive"* may seem inconsistent with the official Cartesian position that humans owe their existence to just *two* basic substances, thinking substance and extended substance. But this problem can be obviated by construing the "primitiveness" of the union as asserting that the mind–body complex is the bearer of distinctive and irreducible *properties* in its own right; in this sense we might say that water is a "primitive" notion, meaning that it is not a mere mixture but a genuine compound, possessing attributes "in its own right" (distinctive "watery" characteristics that cannot be reduced to the properties of the hydrogen or oxygen that make it up). Or as Descartes puts it in the *Principles of Philosophy*, while he recognizes only "two ultimate classes of things," thinking things and extended things, nevertheless appetites, passions, and sensations, which arise from the close and intimate union of the two, are items which "must not be referred either to the mind alone or the body alone" (Part I, art. 48).

This kind of "trialism," then, is very different from the ontological trialism of the French Cartesian scholar Martial Gueroult, who argued that for Descartes the mind–body union is a third substance – *une substance psychophysique* (Gueroult 1968: 201ff). Descartes himself never uses such a phrase, and if he had, it would seem hard to reconcile with his view that there are only two ultimate kinds of substance. Construed attributively, by contrast – as property trialism or attributive trialism – Descartes' position is not formally inconsistent with his ontological dualism.

And yet (someone might object) if the mind–body union is said to be a genuine unit in its own right, how can the trialistic division be merely attributive? And, indeed, does not Descartes' own use of substantival language to refer to the union create problems for any such attributive interpretation? Certainly one

must admit that Descartes does use substantival language when he speaks
of the union (though he stops short of explicitly calling the mind–body unit a
substance). Why does he use such language? I think the answer takes us right back
to the original Aristotelian use of the term "substance," which manifests a certain
ambiguity – or perhaps it would be better to say that it involves certain subtle
shifts of emphasis. Aristotle sometimes employs the term "substance" in an
ontological sense, to mean a basic unit of independent existence (for example, an
individual man, or horse, or tree), but he also often uses it in a logical or gram-
matical sense, to mean simply a subject of predication (as opposed to that which
is predicated) (*Categories*, ch. 5). The reverberations of this were still present in
the philosophical culture that Descartes imbibed as a student, and this
in turn explains his way of talking when expounding his own system. In the
Cartesian system, ontologically speaking, there are only two distinct categories of
substance, mind and body (thus, each individual mind is a substance in the
Aristotelian sense of a basic unit of independent existence); but Descartes still
allows himself to talk of the human being as a substance in Aristotle's other,
weaker, sense, namely as a *subject of predication* – that subject in which attributes
inhere. It is the whole human being, the mind–body complex (and not either of
the ultimate substances that make it up) that is the subject to which certain special
kinds of attribute (namely sensations, passions, and appetites) belong, or to
which they must be referred. Once the influence of the Aristotelian usage is fully
appreciated, we have (it seems to me) a perfectly plausible explanation for Descartes'
use of substantival language to characterize the human being, the mind–body
complex – notwithstanding the fact that, from an ontological point of view, he
firmly maintained that there were only two ultimate kinds of existing thing
involved, *res cogitans* and *res extensa*.

As with so much in Descartes, it is to St Thomas Aquinas that we must look if
we want to appreciate the way in which the Aristotelian worldview was filtered
down to him. Though Aquinas believed that the intellectual part of us could
survive the death of the body, he insisted (along Aristotelian lines) that a large
number of basic human functions (in particular, sensory ones) were irreducibly
psychophysical. In the *Summa theologiae* (1266–73) he observes that "some operations that belong to the soul are carried out through bodily organs, such as seeing
(through the eye) and hearing (through the ear), and likewise for all other operations of the . . . sensitive part." And he continues in a crucial phrase that seems
to prefigure very closely Descartes' position on our sensory faculties: "Hence the
powers that are the sources of such operations *are in the compound as their subject*,
not in the soul alone" (Aquinas, 1964: Ia.77.5).

In sum: for Descartes, ontologically speaking there are only two substances,
but there are three notions because there are three distinct and irreducible types
of attribute; and since the third type of attribute, comprising sensory and passional
experience, inheres in the complete human being, as in a subject, we are justified
in talking of a "real and substantial union."

Human Nature and Cartesian Theodicy

The issues canvassed in the previous section may seem somewhat abstruse, insofar as they involve a certain amount of technical philosophical jargon – something Descartes himself aimed, not always successfully, to keep out of his work. There is, perhaps, some intrinsic interest in trying to clarify the terminology and unravel its implications. But if Descartes' theory of the "union" is to be of more than merely antiquarian interest, it is vital that we keep in view what is the *philosophical*, as opposed to merely historical, point of inquiring into his way of looking at the mind–body relation. The answer, I would suggest, is that Descartes' position reflects something of deep significance in our understanding of ourselves as human beings. The Church Fathers, following Augustine, always maintained that man has a "mixed" nature, half angel, half beast (*medium quoddam inter pecora et angelos: De civitate Dei* ix, 13), and Descartes' way of understanding human beings bears distinct traces of this outlook. In our intellect and our will, we carry the image of our divine creator, but through our immediate union with matter we are marked out as "dust of the earth," sharing the inherent limitedness and imperfection of the material universe. So humans, to use our earlier metaphor, are a bridge between the divine and material worlds.

Does this piece of religious metaphysics, lying beneath the surface of Descartes' thought, retain any relevance to our contemporary understanding of human nature? I think it does. The contemporary secularizing physicalism or naturalism that is so dominant in today's philosophical climate encounters huge problems finding a place for genuine normativity: man becomes a collection of contingent desires and dispositions, and the difficulty is to see how any of these can without arbitrariness be elevated above the others to have any genuine moral or guiding force. Those resistant to naturalism are sometimes tempted, at the other extreme, by a kind of pure Platonism (or "rampant" Platonism, as John McDowell 1994, lecture IV, has called it); this insists on the objective existence of a higher realm of value (truth, beauty, and goodness), but leaves the precise status of such a realm ultimately unexplained – the Platonic values inhabit a kind of metaphysical limbo whose relationship to the actual empirical world in which we live remains in the end unclear.

The traditional metaphysics of Christianity aims to resolve this tension by conceiving the entire natural world, for all its limitations and imperfections, as owing its very existence to a real creative power that is the source of all goodness and value. As essentially embodied creatures, we human beings are part of the natural world, and thus share its limitations; but at the same time our reason allows us access to eternal truths and values which transcend the contingent desires and inclinations that derive from our bodily nature. Descartes' views unmistakably reflect this Christian vision, his ontological dualism directing us to intellectual awareness of the self and its divine author, while his theory of the mind–body union points us toward how we must live out our daily human lives as creatures of flesh and blood. So far from being a series of abstract puzzles in that compartmentalized academic subject we now call "philosophy of mind," his account of the self is integrally linked to a cosmological vision of reality, and a moral vision for the conduct of life (cf. Cottingham 1998: ch. 3, §5).

Commentators sometimes speculate on what might have been the character of the (supposedly) never-completed moral branch of Descartes' philosophical system: the branch that he advertised as one of those emerging from the "tree of philosophy" (of which metaphysics is described as the roots and physics the trunk; AT ixB, 14). But the assumption that the moral parts of the Cartesian philosophy were no more than a promissory note is quite unwarranted. For it is clear even in Descartes' most metaphysical work, the *Meditations*, that the philosophy on which he is engaged is an organic whole; so far from being a specialized exercise in "epistemology," the task which the meditator is undertaking is a quest that is supposed to lead to an understanding of the foundations of goodness as much as of truth.

Although today's philosophical culture predisposes many scholars to turn a blind eye to the theological and moral strands running through the argument of the *Meditations*, a less-blinkered reading discloses that Descartes is committed to a strongly theistic metaphysics of value, one that construes goodness as an objective supra-personal reality, constraining the rational assent of human beings just as powerfully as do the clearly perceived truths of logic and mathematics.

At the centre of Descartes' metaphysics, resonantly expressed at the climax of the *Meditations*, lies a vision of the eternal and infinite divine source of truth and goodness: "Let me here rest for a while in the contemplation of God himself," declares Descartes at the end of Meditation III, "and gaze upon, wonder at, and adore the beauty of this immense light" (AT vii, 52). This vision, it needs to be emphasized, involves contemplation of the good as well as the true: Descartes insists, in a strongly Platonic moment, on the closest possible match between how the mind responds to truth on the one hand and to goodness on the other (AT vii, 58). The metaphysical journey from darkness and confusion to divine illumination, whether in the pursuit of truth or of goodness, involves a cooperation between intellect and will: the will must be exercised first in rejecting what is doubtful and unreliable, and then in focusing attention on the innate indubitable deliverances of the natural light that remain. Once the eye of the soul, the *acies mentis*, is turned on the relevant objects, they reveal themselves with irresistible clarity to the perceiving intellect as good or as true, and the assent of the will (to affirm, or to pursue) follows automatically: "from a great light in the intellect, there follows a great inclination in the will" (AT vii, 59).

By the time we reach this conclusion, in Meditation IV, Descartes is unmistakably embarked on a project of "theodicy," that is to say, a defence or vindication of the goodness and justice of God. If God the creator is good, runs the ancient problem, how come there is evil in the world? If our minds are illuminated with divine truth and goodness, runs Descartes' version of this problem, how come we go astray? His answer, following that of Augustine, is that our free will is to blame. While we remain focused on the light, we cannot err, but we have the power to turn away from the light. And when considering matters that fall outside the scope of what our limited intellect clearly perceives, our will can rush in and give its assent – thus allowing the possibility of error. So if only I exercise my will correctly, and "withhold judgement on any occasion when the truth of the matter is not clear," I can avoid error (AT vii, 62).

It all looks very plain sailing. But there is a snag. In matters of theoretical speculation (where the issues are "purely academic," as we say nowadays), it may be fine to suspend judgment. But when it comes to the conduct of life, we often need to act. I do not clearly and distinctly perceive that the bread in front of me is nutritious: it is fully consistent with what I am actually aware of that the loaf might unbeknownst to me contain a deadly poison. Now I am never going to be able to achieve, in everyday practical cases like this, the kind of "clarity and distinctness" that is available in pure mathematics. But if I simply avoid deciding what to do in such cases, I am going to starve.

Matters get worse. For if God is indeed our creator, then presumably he gave us not just the "pure" intellectual and volitional faculties that we possess *qua* souls or "thinking things," but also the whole apparatus of ordinary sensory responses that we possess *qua* human creatures of flesh and blood. Hunger, thirst, pleasure, pain, although they are not "clear and distinct" intellectual faculties, but on the contrary "confused" modes, are presumably given us for a purpose, and therefore surely they cannot be inherently misleading? Descartes in fact tackles this question head on, and in Meditation VI he gives a perfectly straightforward answer: "the proper purpose of the sensory perceptions given me by nature is simply to inform the mind of what is beneficial or harmful for the composite of which the mind is a part" (AT vii, 83). The strategy here is in some respects remarkably similar to what one might find nowadays from an evolutionary theorist. On the Darwinian picture, if I tread on a thorn, the resulting pain in the foot has obvious survival value in impelling me to avoid such damaging behavior in future, and hence the relevant neurological mechanisms would be selected for, since they are advantageous in the struggle for survival. In somewhat similar fashion, on the Cartesian picture, when the foot is damaged

> the best system that could be devised is that it should produce the one sensation which, of all possible sensations, is the most especially and most frequently conducive to the preservation of the healthy man. And experience shows that the sensations which nature has given us are all of this kind; and so there is absolutely nothing to be found in them that does not bear witness to the power and goodness of God. (AT vii, 87)

The argument, as Descartes develops it, is not quite as naïvely optimistic as it at first sounds: Descartes has to admit that there are many particular cases where our sensory apparatus may lead to a mistaken course of action (for example, the "dropsical man," who has a raging thirst, even though drinking in this case is not advantageous; AT vii, 89). But the system devised by God is designed to produce sensations that are *generally* beneficial for the mind–body composite; so just as a clock still operates in accordance with the laws of mechanics when its cogs are damaged and it tells the wrong time, so "notwithstanding the immense goodness of God, the nature of man as a combination of mind and body is bound to mislead him from time to time' (AT vii, 88; cf. AT v, 164). The theodicy can be patched up.

The Transition to Ethics

With the detailed knowledge provided by modern medical science of the manifold genetic and other structural and functional defects that can beset the human body, Descartes' strategy of theodicy can perhaps seem more vulnerable to us nowadays than it may have appeared to his contemporaries. But in general we may nonetheless be disposed to agree with him that our ordinary human apparatus of psychophysical sensations (hunger, thirst, and the like) for the most part serves us pretty well. Things become far more problematic, however, when we turn to the other principal type of psychophysical mode that is our birthright as human beings – the emotions or passions. We have already seen that, for Descartes, the intellectual perception of goodness compels the assent of the will: provided we focus on the light, we cannot but be inclined to pursue the good. But our passions, notoriously, are confused but nonetheless urgent and powerful human drives which may divert us from the good and sometimes incline us in quite another direction.

When he came to tackle the problem of the passions, Descartes began by following the same optimistic strategy that he had devised when discussing ordinary appetites like hunger and thirst, namely that we are dealing with a psychophysical system whose operation has a signal utility for our life and health as human beings. In the treatise on the passions that was to be his last published work, he observes that "the principal effect of all the human passions is that they move and dispose the soul to want the things for which they prepare the body – for example, the feeling of fear moves the soul to want to flee, and that of courage to want to fight, and similarly with the other passions" (*Passions of the Soul* [1649], art. 40). But the more serious pitfalls lurking behind this bland and cheerful picture are acknowledged elsewhere:

> Often passion makes us believe certain things to be much better and more desirable than they are; then, when we have taken much trouble to acquire them, and in the process lost the chance of possessing other more genuine goods, possession of them brings home to us their defects; and thence arise dissatisfaction, regret and remorse. (September 1, 1645; AT iv, 284–5)

A clear warning note is sounded here: the theme is the old battle between reason and the passions which philosophers had agonized over since the time of Plato.

Nevertheless, Descartes' aim as a moral philosopher is to reconcile the two. Since, as the argument of Meditation VI had shown, we are not pure angelic beings, but genuine human creatures of flesh and blood, the passions are in principle to be embraced, since their operation is intimately related to our human welfare. This is not to say that they are always and uncontroversially good. Because of the relatively rigid way innate physiological mechanisms and environmentally conditioned psychophysical responses operate, we may become locked into behavior that leads to distress, misery, or harm. The dropsical man feels a strong desire to drink, even when fluid is the last thing his health requires; because of early conditioning, the young Descartes (as he confessed to a correspondent) felt a strong attraction to cross-eyed women, which had nothing to do with any rational perception of their other qualities (To Chanut, June 6, 1647; AT v, 57). But the appropriate way to cope with such irrational impulses, Descartes argues, is not to retreat to an austere intellectualism, nor to suppress the passions, but rather to use the resources of science and experience to try to understand what has caused things to go awry, and then to attempt to reprogram our responses so that the direction in which we are led by the passions corresponds to what our reason perceives as the best option (cf. Cottingham 1998: ch. 3, §5).

Although we humans are strange hybrid creatures of pure mind compounded with mechanical body, we are nonetheless, at the level of our ordinary daily experience, endowed with a whole range of sensory and emotional responses which, generally speaking and in the long run, promote human fulfillment. Moreover, in addition to this, we are endowed with the divine light of reason which can afford us a clear vision of the good, provided only that we resolve to continue to focus on it. Given these positive endowments of our human nature, Descartes is ready to insist that "the pleasures of the body should not be despised, nor should one free oneself altogether from the passions" (To Elizabeth, September 1,1645; AT iv, 287). And, indeed, he immediately goes further and insists on the importance and value of the affective dimension which arises from the inescapably corporeal side to our humanity:

> The pleasures common to soul and body depend entirely on the passions, so that persons whom the passions can move most deeply are capable of enjoying the sweetest pleasures of this life. It is true that they may also experience the most bitterness when they do not know how to put these passions to good use, and when fortune works against them. But the chief use of wisdom lies in teaching us to be masters of our passions and to control them with such skill that the evils which they cause are quite bearable, and even become a source of joy. (*Passions of the Soul*, art. 212)

The message is one of reconciliation and integration. And the personal integration that is the goal of Descartes' moral teachings is paralleled by the philosophical integration that joins his moral theory to the rest of his system, as branch to stem.

By understanding our special human nature, and coming to see how its workings relate both to the operation of the bodily machine and to our rational goals as thinking beings, we can venture to hope that the traditional goal of a sound philosophical system, human happiness (cf. Eustachius a Sancto Paulo 1609: Part II, Preface), is not beyond our grasp.

If this upbeat message is the predominant outcome of Descartes' philosophy as applied to human life, he nonetheless closes his *Meditations* with a salutary warning. On the positive side, we are creatures of God, equipped with the intellect and will that provide the key to our attainment of goodness and truth. Further, we are equipped with a human nature that is designed to protect and benefit the mind–body composite. But for all that, we are *finite* – created, dependent, limited creatures. That sense of our dependency, so characteristic of the Christian worldview to which Descartes was committed, has perhaps been jettisoned by many who dissect his arguments nowadays. But it means, amongst other things, that for human beings there can never be any guarantees of success. As Descartes had underlined in Meditation IV, we humans, with our finite intellect, simply do not have a clear perception of all the matters on which we have to make decisions; and even were this defect remedied, we know we simply lack the permanent powers of attention that would allow us to keep our minds constantly fixed on the relevant goods (AT vii, 61–2). So the possibility of error and failure, and indeed of sin, can never be entirely eliminated. The implicit recognition of all this is inscribed by Descartes, like a haunting motto, in the very last sentence of Meditation VI: "we must acknowledge the weakness of our nature."

12

Seventeenth-century Responses to the *Meditations*

Tad M. Schmaltz

Introductory philosophy courses tend to include a section on the Descartes of the first two *Meditations*; that is, Descartes the pure epistemologist. This sort of focus reflects the prevalence in past Anglo-American Cartesian scholarship of treatments of epistemological issues from the *Meditations* such as skepticism concerning the senses (see chapter 2), the *cogito* (see chapter 3), and the problem of the circle (see chapter 8). The subtitle of the *Meditations* (in the second edition published in 1642) also highlights demonstrations of "the existence of God and the distinction of the soul from the body," and the particular metaphysical arguments there for the existence of God (see chapter 7) and for mind–body dualism (see chapters 4 and 11) are familiar fare for philosophy scholars and students alike.

More recently, however, commentators have criticized the preoccupation with abstract features of Descartes' epistemology and metaphysics, and have drawn attention to his own concern to provide a method for scientific inquiry and to establish metaphysical foundations for his own form of mechanistic science. Here the proposal is to read the *Meditations* in light of both Descartes' account of the method for scientific investigation in his *Discourse on Method* and his discussion of the details of his mechanistic science in the *Essays* accompanying the *Discourse* and in his *Principles of Philosophy*.

I have nothing against this proposal. Indeed, I concur in Margaret Wilson's judgment that "the increased interest in the whole range of Descartes' writings – including, particularly, the "scientific" ones – is one of the greatest improvements in Cartesian scholarship in recent decades" (Wilson 1999b: 17). I would also note that recent Anglo-American scholarship is in this respect just beginning to catch up with the early modern reaction to Descartes, which emphasized the *Discourse* and *Principles* at least as much as, and sometimes more than, the *Meditations*. For instance, the *Discourse* is most important for the discussion among later Cartesians and anti-Cartesians of the doctrine of the *bête machine*, according to which non-human animals are mere mechanisms devoid of any sensory thought or feeling (see, for instance, Pardies 1672, and the background discussion in Gouhier 1978: 147–53). Descartes argued for this doctrine most explicitly in that text, where he claimed in Part Five that the fact that animals lack language provides sufficient reason to think that their operations do not differ in kind from the operations of a watch (*Discourse on Method*, AT iv, 55–60; cf. AT vii, 229). Moreover, the point of departure for most early modern discussions of Cartesianism in academic circles was the *Principles* rather than the *Meditations* (see the articles on the influence of the *Principles* in Armogathe and Belgioioso 1996). Here it is telling that Spinoza introduced one of his pupils to Descartes' system by providing a summary *more geometrico* of portions of the *Principles* (a summary which became Spinoza's first published text in 1663).

But though the *Meditations* was not as dominant in the early modern period as past scholarship and current teaching may seem to indicate, the treatment there of various epistemological and metaphysical issues did have a distinctive impact on the seventeenth-century reception of Descartes. My intent here is to highlight the particular issues from the *Meditations* that both defenders and critics stressed in the half-century or so following Descartes' death. An appreciation of the historical importance of these issues will hopefully contribute to a balanced assessment of the significance of the *Meditations* (cf. the discussion of Descartes' early modern reception in Lennon 1993).

First, however, we need to have a better sense of what distinguishes this work from the *Discourse* and *Principles*. It must be admitted initially that several familiar elements of the *Meditations* (1641) are both anticipated in the *Discourse* (1637) and repeated in the *Principles* (1644). Thus, Part IV of the *Discourse* and Part I of the *Principles* both mention the so-called "method of doubt" (to be distinguished from the four-part method sketched in Part III of the *Discourse*), the certainty of the *cogito*, and the so-called truth rule, according to which all clear and distinct perceptions are true. Even so, Descartes wrote in 1638, in a somewhat misogynist vein, that he merely mentioned without explaining in detail "the arguments [*raisons*] of the skeptics" in the *Discourse* since the details "did not seem proper for inclusion in a book where I wished even women could understand something while the most intelligent would also find enough material to occupy their attention" (AT i, 560). Though Descartes did say more about the "arguments of the skeptics" in the *Principles*, his comments there leave out the more detailed consideration of the problems of the "evil genius," the possible deceptiveness of God, and the possible circularity of the justification of the truth rule that is found in the *Meditations* and the accompanying *Objections and Replies* (on the relation of the latter to the former, see chapter 1).

The *Discourse* anticipated and the *Principles* repeated the famous *cogito* argument in Meditation II. Indeed, the label is drawn from these other works, which use, as the *Meditations* does not, the Latin *cogito ergo sum* (in the *Principles*) or the French *je pense donc je suis* (in the *Discourse*). What the *Meditations* contributes, however, is an especially subtle version of the *cogito* argument that is more clearly linked than the versions in the *Discourse* and the *Principles* to the truth rule. In particular, the claim in Meditation II that "this proposition, *I am, I exist*, is necessarily true whenever it is put forward by me or conceived in my mind" indicates more clearly than *cogito ergo sum* that the argument is tied to the (clear and distinct) perception of the truth of a proposition and that the certainty of the perception is indexed to the time at which that proposition is perceived. The point about the temporally indexed nature of the certainty is important in light of Descartes' claim in the *Second Replies* that his doubt covers only "knowledge of those conclusions which can be recalled when we are no longer attending to the arguments by means of which we deduced them" (AT vii, 140; cf. 245–6).

Finally, there is the theistic and dualistic metaphysics of the *Meditations*. Once again, the basic features of this metaphysics are present in the *Discourse* and *Principles*. But whereas such features play only a supporting role in these texts, they are front and center in the *Meditations*. This helps to explain the fact that when early modern supporters and critics considered Descartes' arguments for the existence of God and mind–body distinctness, they tended to focus on the versions of these arguments in the *Meditations*. As I indicate below, moreover, the account of the nature of ideas that is crucial for these arguments (cf. chapter 6) was a prominent issue among the later Cartesians.

In contrast to the *Discourse*, which was first published in French and includes disparaging remarks concerning traditional education, the *Meditations* and *Principles* were both Latin texts clearly intended for an academic audience. This is especially evident in the case of the *Principles*, which was written in textbook style. But even in the case of the *Meditations*, Descartes attempted (without success) to enlist the help of the Paris Theology Faculty in promoting his work in the schools. Moreover, he reported to a correspondent that he was heartened by the fact that his Jesuit friend, Denis Mesland, saw fit to adapt the *Meditations* "to the style that is commonly used for teaching" (AT iv, 122).

The project of making the *Meditations* suitable for the schools continued after the death of Descartes in the work of the German-born and Dutch-educated Cartesian Johannes Clauberg (1622–65) (on Clauberg, see Verbeek 1999a). In 1648, Clauberg had helped Frans Burman (1628–79) compose the notes of Burman's interview of Descartes at his home in Egmond; these notes have come down to us as the *Conversation with Burman*. Clauberg later facilitated the importation of Dutch Cartesianism into the German universities, having been appointed to teaching posts in Herborn and Duisburg. It was while in Duisburg, in 1658, that Clauberg published his *Paraphrasis*, a commentary on Descartes' *Meditations*. In following the order of the *Meditations*, Clauberg included a discussion of the issue of methodological doubt so prevalent at the beginning of this text. This issue was particularly sensitive for Dutch critics of Cartesianism (for this point, see Verbeek 1992). Already during his lifetime, Descartes had been condemned in both Utrecht and Leiden for proposing in the *Meditations* a sort of doubt that undermines both a traditional Aristotelian scholasticism that starts with trust in the senses and an orthodox Calvinism that starts with faith in the authority of scripture and the testimony of the Holy Spirit. In his *Defensio cartesiana* (1652) and *Dubitatio cartesiana* (1655), Clauberg sought to defend Descartes against these charges by emphasizing the limited therapeutic role of doubt in removing unfounded philosophical prejudices. These texts stress that doubt is not to be extended to religious or practical matters. Even so, the suggestion there that philosophy can be cleanly separated from theology and practical life was widely criticized by opponents of Cartesianism, and even was at some odds with Clauberg's own attempt to portray doubt as something that helps to renew the health of a diseased soul (see Verbeek 1999b: 118f).

There was a very different treatment of Descartes' methodological doubt in the work of one of the most famous and controversial figures of the period, Baruch Spinoza (1632–77). In the introduction to his summary of Descartes' *Principles*, Spinoza noted the famous objection that given the claim in the *Meditations* that we cannot be certain of anything prior to knowledge of God, Descartes is caught in a circle. For he cannot be certain of a proof of the existence of God without being certain of the premises of that proof, but also cannot be certain of the premises prior to demonstrating God's existence (cf. chapter 8). Spinoza mentioned Descartes' response that doubt does not extend to those clear and distinct perceptions to which we attend, but noted that "this answer does not satisfy some people." The alternative answer he proposed on Descartes' behalf was that doubt depends on an inadequate conception of God, and that this doubt can be removed once we form a clear and distinct conception of him (Spinoza 1985: 236). But since the hyperbolic doubt in the *Meditations* seems to call into question even our clear and distinct conceptions, it is not clear that we can trust such conceptions. In his mature writings, however, Spinoza attempted to sidestep the problem of circularity by rejecting the gap between the clarity and distinctness (or what he also called the adequacy) of conceptions and their truth. In the *Ethics*, this result is said to follow from the fact that our adequate ideas are just God's ideas insofar as he constitutes the essence of our mind. Since God's ideas must be true in the sense of agreeing with their objects, our adequate ideas must also be true in this sense (Spinoza 1985: 472). Thus, Spinoza emphasized that anyone who has an adequate idea of a thing cannot doubt the truth of that thing (Spinoza 1985: 479).

This line of reasoning indicates a fundamental metaphysical disagreement between Spinoza and Descartes. Whereas more orthodox Cartesians such as Clauberg emphasized the theological orthodoxy of the move in the *Meditations* from the existence of the self as a finite *res cogitans* to the existence of an infinite and transcendent God, Spinoza took the decidedly different path of arguing that God is the only substance, and that all finite objects, including our own minds, are modes of that substance. Given this argument, there is no room for Descartes' starting-point of a skeptical self disengaged from external reality. Instead, we have in Spinoza a finite mind that thinks God's thoughts insofar as that mind is simply a particular expression of God as thinking substance. Spinoza did allow that we have ideas that are false in the sense that our mind lacks other ideas in God that are required for complete understanding (Spinoza 1985: 472f). However, what he took to be impossible was the skeptical suggestion in Meditation III that God could make us go wrong even with respect to ideas that we understand completely (AT vii, 36). For Spinoza, this is just the unintelligible possibility that God makes his own adequate ideas to be false.

Whereas Spinoza objected to Descartes' use of hyperbolic doubt, other critics objected that Descartes and his followers did not take such doubt seriously enough. A case in point is provided by the French skeptic, Simon Foucher (1644–96). Foucher's main response to Cartesianism is in a 1675 *Critique* of the first volume (of two total volumes) of the *Search after Truth* of the French Oratorian, Nicolas Malebranche (1638–1715). In this text, Foucher took issue with various "suppositions" and "assertions" from the *Search* that purportedly are contrary to Malebranche's own method for finding the truth. Foucher raised his objections from the perspective of a moderate Academic (as opposed to a more extreme Pyrrhonian) skeptic; indeed, his *Critique* is written in the form of a "Letter by an Academician." One skeptical argument that is particularly prominent in this text is directed against the Cartesian view in Malebranche that we perceive bodies by means of ideas. Foucher urged that since Malebranche followed Descartes in thinking that these ideas are modes of mind, and since both adhered to the view that mind is a substance distinct in nature from body, no ideas can resemble bodies, and thus no ideas can represent their true nature (Foucher 1969: 44–50; for discussion of this argument, see Watson 1966). Foucher also took skeptical consequences to follow from Malebranche's purported endorsement of Descartes' doctrine that necessary and eternal truths derive from God's free will. For Foucher, this doctrine leaves open the possibility that God could change these truths at any moment (Foucher 1969: 30).

In a 1675 response to Foucher, added to the second volume of the *Search*, Malebranche countered with the caustic observation that "when one Critiques a book, it seems to me that it is necessary at least to have read it" (Malebranche 1958–84: ii, 249). He emphasized in particular that Foucher had failed to notice that he had devoted a section of his first volume to a refutation of the view that the ideas that represent bodies are modes of our mind. This is the section where Malebranche defended his thesis of "the vision in God," according to which we perceive bodies by means of ideas in God's intellect that serve to represent them. Malebranche also protested to Foucher that he never had endorsed Descartes' doctrine of the creation of the eternal truths. Indeed, he emphasized in later writings that this doctrine is in fact incompatible with the thesis of the vision in God insofar as the latter requires that necessary and eternal truths are grounded in uncreated ideas in God's intellect rather than in the divine will (see Malebranche 1980: 617f). For Malebranche, the sort of voluntarism present in Descartes' created truths doctrine is unacceptable insofar as it supports the view of God as an arbitrary tyrant whose action is not guided by rational and moral norms.

Malebranche's thesis of the vision in God also turned out to be incompatible with the more traditional Cartesian account of ideas in the work of his main Cartesian critic, Antoine Arnauld. Arnauld drew from the *Meditations* the view that the "objective reality" of our perception of an external object is simply the internal "form" of that perception that serves to relate it to that object (Arnauld 1990: 21, modeled on Descartes' remarks in AT vii, 101ff). Malebranche offered a somewhat weak response to Arnauld's claim that Descartes identified ideas with our perceptions. However, his main objection was that such an identification leads to skepticism insofar as it deprives us of any means of determining that our ideas correspond to the external world. Malebranche insisted that his own view that these ideas are archetypes for God's creation of the objects they represent eliminates this sort of skepticism since, so conceived, the ideas must correspond to their objects (cf. Jolley 1990: 65f).

There is some analogue here of Spinoza's response to skepticism. Though Malebranche insisted on the transcendence of God and thus rejected the Spinozistic conclusion that our minds are modes of God, he nonetheless shared with Spinoza the view that Descartes' radical skepticism is unthinkable given that our knowledge is rooted in God's own ideas. This turn away from Descartes is admittedly not evident in the *Search*, which includes a discussion of method that endorses the view of the *Meditations* that the search for truth must begin with a confrontation of the supposition that God is a deceiver (see Malebranche 1980: 480f). In later writings, however, Malebranche started with the argument that the ideas involved in our perception of necessary and eternal truths must be necessary and eternal features of God's own mind.

Another sort of response to skepticism emerged out of the Foucher–Malebranche exchange. One of Malebranche's friends, the French Benedictine Robert Desgabets (1610–78), took it upon himself to defend Cartesianism against Foucher's attack even before Malebranche had a chance to respond. In a 1675 *Critique of the Critique*, Desgabets attempted to support Malebranche by arguing that it follows from the fact that we have an idea of the external world that such a world exists, and that the immutability of necessary truths is consistent with the fact that they derive from God's free will (Desgabets 1675: 115–22 and 72–4, respectively).

Malebranche was not pleased with the discussion in Desgabets' *Critique* since it falsely implied that he identified ideas with our thoughts and that he accepted Descartes' doctrine of the creation of eternal truths. Moreover, Desgabets' remarks were too terse to render his own position fully intelligible. However, he provided a more complete sketch of his distinctive brand of Cartesianism in an unpublished "Supplement" to Descartes' *Meditations* (included in Desgabets 1983–5). In this commentary, Desgabets took Descartes to task for two principal "faults" connected to the use of methodological doubt at the beginning of the *Meditations*. The first fault is in failing to see that our idea of extended substance must correspond to an object that exists external to our mind. Since Desgabets identified this substance with the essence of extension, and since he held that we cannot think of an object that has no essence, he concluded that we can think of extended substance only if it exists. In Desgabets' view, then, the doubt of the existence of extended substance in Meditation I is much too strong insofar as it allows for the unintelligibility of our thoughts about the material world (see Schmaltz 2002: ch. 3).

Descartes' second fault was in claiming in Meditation II that it follows from the *cogito* that our knowledge of mind does not depend on body. Desgabets' argument begins with the Aristotelian premise that time is the measure of motion. Since the thoughts involved in the *cogito* are temporal, they must be measured in some way by motion. But they could be measured in this way only if they are united to motion. Thus, the *cogito* itself requires the union of our thoughts with motion, a union which itself requires the existence of bodies in motion. Here there is a concern to refute what Immanuel Kant (1724–1804) later called Descartes' "problematic idealism," that is, the view that we can have knowledge of inner experience that does not require the existence of outer objects. Kant's famous "Refutation of Idealism" involved the claim that our knowledge of determinate temporal relations among our inner states presupposes the existence of spatial objects. In contrast, Desgabets' less familiar refutation depends on the claim that by its very nature the temporality of our thought requires a connection to motion (see Schmaltz 2002: ch. 4).

It must be said, however, that these issues concerning methodical doubt and the implications of the *cogito* were not always the most prominent in discussions of Cartesianism in the decades following Descartes' death in 1650. Indeed, the focus in Catholic countries was more on the implications of Cartesian physics for theological doctrines, and in particular the doctrine of the Eucharist. In his *Fourth Objections* to the *Meditations*, Arnauld had anticipated these later disputes by questioning Descartes about the consistency of his denial of sensible qualities in bodies distinct from modes of extension with the Catholic teaching that the "species" of the Eucharistic elements remain after the conversion of the substance of the elements into Christ's body and blood (AT vii, 216–18). In later correspondence, Arnauld also asked Descartes for an explanation of how the Cartesian identification of a body with its extension is consistent with the Catholic doctrine that Christ's body is present in the Eucharist without its local extension. These somewhat abstruse issues played a role in the placement of an edition of Descartes' writings on the *Index* in 1663 (see Armogathe and Carraud 2001). They also were prominent in a 1671 decree against the teaching of anti-Aristotelian philosophy in France that was subsequently used to harass Cartesians in French universities (see Schmaltz 2002: ch. 1).

However, attention shifted to more familiar issues from the *Meditations* with the publication in 1689 of a *Censure of Cartesian Philosophy* by the French cleric and scholar, Pierre-Daniel Huet (1630–1721). Like Foucher, Huet was a skeptic, and like Foucher again, he was brought to a critical view of Cartesianism through a reading of Malebranche. In Huet's case, it was Malebranche's disdain for humanistic learning that prompted a negative reaction to Cartesianism (as shown in Lennon 2003). In the *Censure*, however, Huet attacked Descartes directly. He included a critical discussion of issues in Descartes' natural philosophy such as the identification of matter with extension, the void, the origin of the world, and the cause of gravity. However, the first two of the eight chapters of the *Censure*, which constitute nearly a third of the total text, concern Descartes' views on methodical doubt, the *cogito* argument, and the criterion of truth. Huet offered a barrage of skeptical points to counter these views, including the claim that neither the natural light nor clear and distinct perception provides a reliable criterion of truth, that the transition in the *cogito* argument from *I think* to *I exist* is subject to doubt, and that Descartes' suggestion that God can do the impossible makes any complete escape from doubt impossible.

Huet's *Censure* drew an international response from the Cartesians. However, Huet singled out one in this group as "the Prince of the Cartesians" (for Huet, a term of abuse), namely, the French Cartesian Pierre-Sylvain Regis (or Régis) (1632–1707). As in the case of Huet's *Censure*, a good portion of Regis's *Response* to that text focused on epistemological issues. Regis countered Huet's objection to the *cogito* argument by holding that the connection between thought and existence is known not through discursive argument but rather "by a simple intro-spection of the mind" (Regis 1691: 50). Moreover, Regis insisted that Descartes simply identified the light of nature with clear and distinct perception, and that he correctly claimed that neither can deceive when properly used. On his reading, Descartes' "merely hyperbolic" doubt never brings reason itself into question. Regis claimed that not even Descartes' suggestion that God is the cause of eternal truths can render dubitable our intellectual apprehension of those truths.

The historical significance of Huet's *Censure* is revealed not only by the reaction it received from Regis and other Cartesians, but also by a 1691 Formulary imposed on the philosophy faculty at the University of Paris that condemned various prop-ositions, including several drawn from Descartes. In contrast to the earlier focus on the implications of Cartesian physics for Eucharistic theology, the initial propos-itions of this Formulary emphasize the need for radical doubt in the search for truth, the dependence of our knowledge of God on clear and distinct perception, and the possibility that God is a deceiver. The fact that Huet had highlighted all of these issues supports the hypothesis that his work is responsible for the shift to the emphasis in the 1691 Formulary on Cartesian epistemology.

The Formulary also includes propositions drawn from Jansenist theology. This theology derives from the posthumously published *Augustinus* (1640) of Cornelius Jansenius (1585–1638). In this text, Jansenius called for a return to the emphasis in Augustine on the importance of the workings of grace in the salvation of the elect, and a turn away from the tenet of the Catholic theology of the Jesuits that our will is free to accept or reject the divine offer of grace. The Jesuits were influ-ential in the French court, however, and it was due to pressure from the French government that Jansenius' work was condemned in a series of papal bulls during the 1650s. This official rejection of Jansenism is reflected in the condemnation in the 1691 Formulary of a proposition that takes freedom to consist merely in freedom from constraint, and not freedom from necessity. Though Cartesianism is not directly implicated here, French critics commonly charged that Cartesian philosophy is allied with Jansenist theology against the interests of both church and state (for more on the context of the 1691 Formulary, see Schmaltz 2004).

This theologico-political line of attack against Cartesianism in Catholic France contrasts in an interesting way with an earlier attack against this movement in the Calvinist United Provinces, which resulted in a 1676 condemnation of Dutch Cartesians in Leiden. I have mentioned the objections that Dutch critics offered to the method of doubt during Descartes' own lifetime. This context serves to explain the fact that the 1676 Leiden Condemnation mentioned the same sort of Cartesian appeal to hyperbolic doubt found in the 1691 Paris Formulary. But whereas the latter linked Cartesianism to the Jansenist denial of undetermined human freedom, the former took Cartesians to task for holding that the human will is "absolutely free and undetermined." What was behind the charge in the Leiden Condemnation was the suspicion that Descartes' insistence in Meditation IV that the will is wholly unbounded leads to the theological view, heretical among Dutch orthodox Calvinists, that we can obtain salvation through our own efforts. It is interesting that some Dutch Cartesians responded to this line of objection by claiming that Meditation IV requires only freedom from constraint and not freedom from determination: the very position condemned in the Paris Formulary!

There were further criticisms of Cartesianism in the work of the German philosopher, Gottfried Wilhelm Leibniz (1646–1716). Leibniz had previously had a friendly correspondence with Malebranche's critic, Foucher, and, after learning of the *Censure*, he proposed to Huet that he add Leibniz's own objections to Cartesianism in a future edition of this text. Whereas Huet tended to emphasize the inadequacies of the epistemology of the *Meditations*, however, Leibniz's most famous objections concern the natural philosophy of the *Principles*, and in particular Descartes' account there of the laws of motion. Yet he also took issue, in a 1679 letter, with Descartes' treatment of two issues mentioned in the subtitle of the *Meditations*, namely, the existence of God and the immortality of the soul. With respect to the first issue, Leibniz charged in this letter that Descartes' God "is something approaching the God of Spinoza" insofar as God has neither will nor understanding (Leibniz 1989: 242). We have seen that Spinoza spoke of God's adequate ideas, but Leibniz had in mind Spinoza's claim in the *Ethics* that no ideas pertain to God as substance, since all ideas are modes that follow necessarily from God's nature as a thinking thing (Spinoza 1985: 434f). This Spinozistic conclusion may seem to be far from anything in Descartes. In comments in his *Replies to Objections* to the *Meditations*, however, Descartes did emphasize that since God is the indifferent cause of truth and goodness, divine action is not directed toward any pre-determined ends (see AT vii, 431–2, 435ff). For Leibniz, this consequence of the doctrine of the creation of the eternal truths detracted as much from God's moral goodness as the purported implication in Spinoza that effects follow with "blind necessity" from God. As Malebranche had insisted earlier, so Leibniz claimed that in order to be praiseworthy, God's action must be directed by considerations of moral goodness determined by his intellect.

With regard to the issue of immortality of the soul, Leibniz held in his 1679 letter that what Descartes had to say about this "is useless and could not console us in any way" (Leibniz 1989: 243). Descartes himself admitted that he had shown in the *Meditations* only that the destruction of the body does not entail the annihilation of the soul, and not that God cannot destroy the soul by his "absolute power" (AT vii, 154). This explains why the promise in the subtitle of the first (1641) edition of the *Meditations* of a demonstration "of the immortality of the soul" was changed in the second (1642) edition to a promise of a demonstration of "the distinction of the human soul from the body." However, Lebiniz objected that even if Descartes had established that the substance of the soul cannot perish, he would not have provided all that is required for the sort of immortality that is of moral concern to us. This is so since "immortality without memory is completely useless to morality, for it upsets all reward and punishment" (Leibniz 1989: 243). The emphasis here on the need for memory explains Leibniz's later reaction to the theory of personal identity in the work of John Locke (1632–1704). Locke had added a section on personal identity to the second (1694) edition of his *Essay Concerning Human Understanding*, in which he argued that personal identity consists in sameness of consciousness. In his *New Essays* on Locke's text (largely completed by 1704, but not published until 1765), Leibniz responded that though the appearance of identity through consciousness is necessary for personal identity, it is not sufficient. What is further required is a "real, physical identity" that involves the continued existence of the substance of the soul that has consciousness (Leibniz 1981: 236). In this way, Leibniz attempted to combine the stress in Descartes on the persistence of substance with the emphasis in Locke on the continuation of consciousness for a more adequate account of our immortality (for more on the development of Leibniz's views on this issue, see Wilson 1999c).

The fact that metaphysical issues raised in the *Meditations* were important for Descartes' reception elsewhere on the Continent is indicated by the report of Giambattista Vico (1668–1744) that in 1696 in Naples "one had begun to cultivate the *Méditations métaphysiques*," and that in order to claim that someone was a great philosopher, one had to say that that person "understands René's *Méditations*." The metaphysics of the *Meditations* did indeed play an important role in discussions of Cartesianism in Italy during the first few decades of the 1700s. In particular, it provided material for the dispute between two Neapolitan figures, Paolo Mattia Doria (1661–1746) and Francesco Maria Spinelli (1658–1752). Doria started as a Cartesian, but came to hold that the Cartesian system leads ultimately to the Spinozistic conclusion that God and creatures constitute one unified being. Doria's conclusion – interestingly similar to a line that F. H. Jacobi (1743–1819) later took against Kant (see Beiser 1987: ch. 2) – was that the only way to defeat Spinozism is to reject reason and to embrace religious faith. Spinelli responded on behalf of the Cartesians by emphasizing that the *Meditations* starts not with Spinoza's all-encompassing infinite substance, but rather with a finite substantial thinking thing that realizes its limitations by way of doubt. Thus Descartes was led to the distinction of the self from a perfect God, just as he was led toward the end of the *Meditations* to distinguish our finite mind from body (on the Doria–Spinelli debate, see Belgioioso 1999: chs 3–4).

The importance of the metaphysics of the *Meditations* for the reception of Descartes is illustrated by one last event in Paris. In a stunning reversal of the antipathy for Cartesianism reflected in its 1691 Formulary, the University of Paris adopted a set of statutes in 1720 that incorporated Descartes' writings into the curriculum (see Jourdain 1862–6: ii, 173). The primary author of the statutes was Edmond Pourchot (1651–1734), a member of the Paris philosophy faculty who was a target of the earlier campaign against Cartesianism (see Schmaltz 2004). Pourchot had been one of the first to introduce the physics of Descartes' *Principles* to university students at Paris. However, his statutes emphasized the value not of Descartes' physics but rather of a metaphysics in the *Meditations* that has served "to illustrate the wondrous doctrine of Plato" and "to move it closer to Christian doctrines." We see here the culmination of an earlier campaign by various French Cartesians to defend Descartes by associating him with the Christianized form of Platonism in Augustine. But the metaphysics of the *Meditations* won the day in eighteenth-century France at just the time that Cartesian physics was beginning to be replaced on the Continent by the physics of Newton's *Principia mathematica*.

SIX METAPHYSICAL *MEDITATIONS*; Wherein it is Proved That there is a GOD. And that Mans MIND is really distinct from his BODY. Written Originally in Latin By RENATUS DES-CARTES. [. . .]

All Faithfully Translated into ENGLISH [. . .] By WILLIAM MOLYNEUX. London [. . .] 1680.

MEDITAT. I.
Of Things Doubtful.

Some years past I perceived how many *Falsities* I admitted off as *Truths* in my Younger years, and how *Dubious* those things were which I raised from thence; and therefore I thought it requisite (if I had a designe to establish any thing that should prove *firme* and *permanent* in sciences) that once in my life I should clearly cast aside all my former opinions, and begin a new from some *First principles*. But this seemed a great Task, and I still expected that maturity of years, then which none could be more apt to receive Learning; upon which account I waited so long, that at last I should deservedly be blamed had I spent that time in *Deliberation* which remain'd only for *Action*.

This day therefore I conveniently released my mind from all cares, I procured to my self a Time Quiet, and free from all Business, I retired my self Alone; and now at length will I freely and seriously apply my self to the General overthrow of all my former Opinions.

To the Accomplishment of Which, it will not be necessary for me to prove them all *false* (for that perhaps I shall never atcheive) But because my reason perswades me, that I must withdraw my assent no less from those opinions which seem *not so very certain* and *undoubted*, then I should from those that are *Apparently* false, it will be sufficient if I reject all those wherein I find any *Occasion* of doubt.

Neither to effect this is it necessary, that they all should be run over particularly (which would be an endles trouble) but because the *Foundation* being once undermin'd, whatever is built thereon will of its own accord come to the ground, I shall therefore immediately assault the very *principle*, on which whatever I have believed was *grounded*. Viz.

Whatever I have hitherto admitted as most true, that I received either from, or by my Senses; but these I have often found to deceive me, and 'tis prudence never certainly to trust those that have (tho but once) deceived us.

1 *Doubt*. But tho sometimes the *senses* deceive us being exercised about *remote* or *small* objects, yet there are many other things of which we cannot doubt tho we know them only by the senses? as that at present I am in this place, that I am sitting by a fire, that I have a Winter gown on me, that I feel this Paper with my hands; But how can it be denied that these hands or this body is mine; Unless I should compare my self to those mad men, whose brains are disturbed by such a disorderly melancholick vapour, that makes them continually profess themselves to be Kings, tho they are very poor, or fancy themselves cloathed in Purple Robes, tho they are naked, or that their heads are made of Clay as a bottle, or of glass, &c. But these are mad men, and I should be as mad as they in following their example by fancying these things as they do.

1 *Solution*. This truly would seem very clear to those that never *sleep*, and suffer the same things (and sometimes more unlikely) in their repose, then these mad men do whilst they are awake; for how often am I perswaded in a Dream of these usual occurrences, that I am in this place, that I have a Gown on me, that I am sitting by a fire, &c. Tho all the while I am lying naked between the Sheets.

But now I am certain that I am awake and look upon this Paper, neither is this head which I shake asleep, I knowingly and willingly stretch out this hand, and am sensible that things so distinct could not happen to one that sleeps. As if I could not remember my self to have been deceived formerly in my sleep by the like thoughts; which while I consider more attentively *I* am so far convinced of the difficulty of distinguishing sleep from waking that *I* am amazed, and this very amazement almost perswades me that *I* am asleep.

2 *Doubt*. Wherefore let us suppose our selves *asleep*, and that these things are not *true*, viz. that we open our eyes, move our heads, stretch our hands, and perhaps that we have no such things as hands or a body. Yet we must confess, that what we see in a Dream is (as it were) *a painted Picture*, which cannot be devised

but after the *likeness* of some *real* thing; and that therefore these Generals at least, *viz.* eyes, head, hands, and the whole body are things *really existent* and not *imaginary*; For Painters themselves, (even then when they design Mermaids and Satyrs in the most unusual shapes) do not give them natures altogether new, but only add the divers Parts of different Animals together; And if by chance they invent any thing so new that nothing was ever seen like it, so that 'tis wholy ficti-tious and false, yet the colours at least of which, they make it must be *true Colours*; so upon the same account, tho these General things as eyes, head, hands &c. may be imaginary; yet nevertheless we must of necessity confess the more *simple* and *universal* things to be *True*, of which (as of true Colours) these *Images* of things (whether *true* or *false*) which are in our minds are made; such as are the nature of a body in General, and its Extension, also the shape of things extended, with the quantity or bigness of them, their number also, and place wherein they are, the time in which they continue, and the like, and therefore from hence we make no bad conclusion, that *Physick*, both *Natural*, and *Medicinal*, *Astronomy*, and all other *sciences*, which depend on the consideration of *compound things*, are *Doubtful*. But that *Arithmetick*, *Geometry*, and the like (which treat only of the most *simple*, and *General* things not regarding whether they really are or not) have in them something *certain* and *undoubted*; for whether *I* sleep or wake, *two* and *three* added make five; a *square* has no more sides then *four*, *&c.* neither seems it possible that such *plain truths* can be doubted off.

2 *Solution*. But all this While there is rooted in my mind a certain old opinion of the *being* of an *Omnipotent God*, by whom *I* am *created* in the state *I* am in; and how know *I* but he caused that there should be no Earth, no Heaven, no Body, no Figure, no Magnitude, no Place, and yet that all these things should seem to me to be as now they are? And as *I* very often judge others to Erre about those things which they think they *Thoroughly understand*, so why may not *I* be *deceived*, whenever *I* add *two* and *three*, or count the sides of a *Square*, or whatever other easy Matter can be thought of?

3 *Doubt*. But perhaps *God wills not* that *I* should be *deceived*, for he is said to be *Infinitely Good*.

3 *Solution*. Yet if it were *Repugnant* to his *Goodness* to create me so that *I* should be *always deceived*, it seems also *unagreable* to his *Goodness* to permit me to be deceived *at any time*; Which last no one will affirme: Some there are truely who had rather deny *Gods Omnipotence*, then beleive all things *uncertain*; but these at present we may not contradict. And we will suppose all this of *God* to be *false*; yet whether they will suppose me to become what *I* am by *Fate*, by *Chance*, by a *continued chain* of *causes*, or any other way, because to *erre* is an *Imperfection*, by how much the less *power* they will Assigne to the *Autho*r of my *Being*, so much the more *Probable* it will be, that *I* am so *Imperfect* as to be *always deceived*.

To which arguments *I* know not what to answer but am forced to confess, that there is nothing of all those things which *I* formerly received as *Truths*, whereof at present *I* may not *doubt*; and this doubt shall not be grounded on inadvertency or Levity, but upon strong and premeditating reasons; and therefore *I* must hereafter (if *I* designe to discover any truths) withdraw my assent from them no less then from *apparent falshood*.

But 'tis not sufficient to think only *Transiently* on these things, but I must take care to *remember* them; for dayly my old opinions returne upon me, and mu[c]h against my Will almost possesse my Beleife tyed to them, as it were by a continued *use* and *Right* of *Familiarity*; neither shall I ever cease to *assent* and *trust* in them, whilst I suppose them as in themselves they really are, that is to say, *something doubtful* (as now I have proved) yet notwithstanding *highly Probable*, which it is much more Reasonable to beleive then disbeleive.

Wherefore I conceive I should not do amiss, if (with my mind bent clearly to the contrary side) I should deceive my self, and suppose them for a While altogether *false* and *Imaginary*; till at length the Weights of prejudice being equal in each scale, no ill custome may any more Draw my Judgement from the *true Conception* of things, for I know from hence will follow no dangerous Error, and I can't too immoderately pamper my own Incredulity, seeing What I am about, concernes not *Practice* but *Speculation*.

To Which end I will suppose, not an *Infinitely perfect God*, the *Fountain* of *truth*, but that some *Evil Spirit* which is very *Powerful* and *crafty* has used all his endeavours to *deceive* me; *I* will conceive, the Heavens, Air, Eearth, Colours, Figures, Sounds, and all outward things are nothing else but the delusions of Dreams, by which he has laid snares to catch my easy beleif; I will consider my self as not having hands, Eyes, Flesh, Blood, or Sences, but that *I* falsely think that *I* have all these; *I* will continue firmly in this Meditation; and tho it lyes not in my power to *discover any truth*, yet this is in my power, not to *assent* to *Falsities*, and with a strong resolution take care that the *Mighty deceiver* (tho never so *powerful* or *cunning*) impose not any thing on my beleife.

But this is a laborious intention, and a certain sloth reduces me to the usual course of life, and like a Prisoner who in his sleep perhaps enjoy'd an imaginary liberty, and when he begins to suppose that he is asleep is afraid to waken, but is willing to be deceived by the *Pleasant delusion*; so *I* willingly fall into my old opinions, and am afraid to be Roused, least a toilsome waking succeeding a pleasant rest *I* may hereafter live not in the *light*, but in the confused *darkness* of the *doubts* now raised.

MEDITAT. II.
Of the nature of Mans mind, *and that 'tis easier proved to be then our* body.

By yesterdays Meditation *I* am cast into so great *Doubts*, that *I* shall never forget them, and yet *I* know not how to answer them, but being plunged on a suddain into a deep Gulf, *I* am so amazed that I can neither touch the bottome, nor swim at the top.

Nevertheless, *I* will endeavour once more, and try the way *I* set on yesterday, by removing from me whatever is in the *least doubtful*, as if I had certainly discover'd it to be *altogether false*, and will proceed till *I* find out some *certainty*, or if nothing else, yet at least this *certainty, That there is nothing sure.*

Archimedes required but a *point* which was *firm*, and *immoveable*, that he might move the *whole Earth*, so in the present undertaking Great things may be expected, if *I* can discover but the *least thing* that is *true* and *indisputable*.

Wherefore *I* suppose all things *I* see are *false*, and believe that nothing of those things are really existent, which my deceitful memory represents to me; 'tis evident *I* have no senses, that a Body, Figure, Extension, Motion, Place, &c. are meer Fictions; what thing therefore is there that is *true*? perhaps only *this, That there is nothing certain.*

Doubts and Solutions. But how know *I* that there is nothing *distinct* from all these things (which *I* have now reckon'd) of which *I* have no reason to *doubt*? *Is* there no *God* (or whatever other name *I* may call him) who has put these thoughts into me? Yet why should *I* think this? When *I* my self perhaps am the *Author* of them. Upon which Account, therefore must not *I* be something? 'tis but just now that *I* denied that *I* had any *senses*, or any *Body*. Hold a while – Am *I* so tied to a *Body* and *senses* that *I* cannot *exist* without them? But I have perswaded my self that there is nothing in the World, no Heaven, no Earth, no Souls, no Bodies; and then why not, that *I my self am not*? Yet surely if *I* could perswade my self any thing, *I was*.

But there is *I* know not what sort of Deceivour very *powerful* and very *crafty*, who always strives to *deceive* Me; without Doubt therefore *I am*, if he can *deceive me*; And let him *Deceive* me as much as he can, yet he can never make me *not to Be*, whilst *I think that I am.* Wherefore I may lay this down as a *Principle, that whenever this sentence I am, I exist, is spoken or thought of by Me, 'tis necessarily True.*

But *I* do not yet fully understand *who I am* that now necessarily *exist*, and *I* must hereafter take care, least *I* foolishly *mistake* some other thing *for my self*, and by that means be *deceived* in that thought, which *I* defend as the most *certain* and *evident* of all.

Wherefore *I* will again Recollect, what *I* believed *my self to be* heretofore, before *I* had set upon these Meditations, from which *Notion I* will withdraw whatever may be *Disproved* by the *Foremention'd Reasons*, that in the End, *That* only may Remain which is *True* and *indisputable*.

What therefore have *I* heretofore thought my self? *A Man.* But what is a *man*? shall *I* answer, a *Rational Animal*? By no means; because afterwards it may be asked, what an *Animal* is? and what *Rational* is? And so from one *question I* may fall into greater *Difficulties;* neither at present have I so much time as to spend it about such Niceties.

But I shall rather here Consider, what heretofore represented it self to my thoughts *freely*, and *naturally*, whenever I set my self to understand *What I my self was.*

And the first thing I find Representing it self is, that I have *Face, Hands, Arms,* and this whole *frame* of *parts* which is seen in my *Body*, and which I call my *Body*.

The next thing represented to me was, that I was *nourish'd*, could *walk*, had *senses*, and could *Think*; which functions *I* attributed to my *Soul*. Yet what this *soul* of mine was, *I* did not fully conceive; or else supposed it a small thing like *wind*, or *fire*, or *aire*, infused through my *stronger parts*.

As to my *Body* truly *I* doubted not, but that *I* rightly understood its *Nature*, which (if *I* should endeavour to describe as *I* conceive it) *I* should thus Explain, *viz.* By a *Body* I mean whatever is *capable* of *Shape*, or can be *contained* in a *place*, and so fill's a space that it excludes all other *Bodys* out of the same, that which may be *touch'd*, *seen*, *heard*, *tasted*, or *smelt*, and that which is *capable* of *various Motions* and *Modifications*, not from it *self*, but from any *other thing moving* it, for *I* judged it *against* (or rather *above*) the *nature* of a *Body* to *move it self*, or *perceive*, or *think*, But rather admired that *I* should find these *Operations* in certain *Bodys*.

Doubts and Solutions. But How now (since *I* suppose a certain *powerful* and (if it be lawful to call him so) *evil deluder*, who useth all his endeavours to deceive me in all things) can *I* affirm that I have any of those things, which I have now said belong to the *nature* of a *Body*? Hold – Let me Consider –, Let me think –, Let me reflect – I can find no Answer, and I am weary with repeating the same things over-again in vain.

But Which of these *Faculties* did I attribute to my *Soul*, my *Nutritive*, or *Motive faculty*? yet now seeing I have no *Body*, these also are *mere delusions*. Was it my *sensitive faculty*? But this also cannot be perform'd without a *Body*, and I have seem'd to *perceive* many things in my *sleep*, of which I afterwards understood my self *not* to be *sensible*. Was it my *Cogitative Faculty*? Here I have discovered it, 'tis my *Thought*, this alone cannot be separated from Me, I *am, I exist – tis true*, but for what time *Am I*? Why I *am* as long as *I think*; For it May be that When I cease from *thinking*, I may cease from being. Now I admit of nothing but what is necessarily true: In short therefore I *am* only a *thinking thing*, that is to say, a *mind*, or a *soul*, or *understanding*, or *Reason*, words which formerly *I* understood not; I am a *Real thing*, and *Really Existent*, But what sort of thing? I have just now said it, *A thinking thing*.

But am I nothing besides? I will consider – I am not that *structure* of *parts*, which is called a Mans *Body*, neither am I any sort of *thin Air* infused into those Parts, nor a *Wind*, nor *Fire*, nor *Vapour*, nor *Breath*, nor whatever I my self can feign, for all these things I have supposed *not to Be*. Yet my Position stands firm; *Nevertheless I am something*. Yet perhaps it so falls out that these very things which I suppose not to exist (because to me *unknown*) are in reallity nothing *different* from that very *Self*, which I *know*. I cannot tell, I dispute it not now, I can only give my opinion of those things whereof I have some knowledge. I am sure that I exist, I ask who I am whom I thus know, certainly, the knowledge, of *Me* (precisely taken) depends not on those things, whose existence I am yet ignorant off; and therefore not on any other things that I can *feign* by my *imagination*.

And this very Word (*feign*) puts me in mind of my *error*, for I should *feign* in deed, if I should *imagine* my self any thing; for to *imagine* is nothing else but to think upon the *shape* or *image* of a *corporeal* thing; but now I certainly know that *I am*, and I know also that 'tis possible that all these *images*, and generally whatever belongs to the *Nature* of a *Body* are nothing but *deluding Dreams*. Which things Consider'd I should be no less Foolish in saying, *I will imagine that I may more thoroughly understand what I am*, then if I should say, *at Present I am awake and perceive something true, but because it appears not evidently enough, I shall endeavour to sleep, that in a Dream I may perceive it more evidently and truely.*

Wherefore I know that nothing that I can comprehend by my *imagination*, can belong to the *Notion* I have of *my self*, and that I must carefully withdraw my mind from those things that it may more *distinctly* perceive its *own Nature*.

Let me ask therefore *What I am, A Thinking Thing*, but What is That? That is a thing, *doubting, understanding, affirming, denying, willing, nilling, imagining* also, and *sensitive*. These truely are not a few *Properties*, if they all belong to Me. And Why should they Not belong to me? For am not I the very same who at present *doubt* almost of All things; yet *understand* something, which thing onely I *affirm* to be true, I *deny* all other things, I am *willing* to know more, I *would not* be deceived, I *imagine* many things *unwillingly*, and *consider* many things as coming to me by my *senses*. Which of all these faculties is it, which is not as *true* as that I *Exist*, tho I should *sleep*, or my *Creatour* should as much as in him lay, strive to *deceive* Me? which of them is it that is *distinct* from my *thought*? which of them is it that can be *separated* from *me*? For that I am the same that *doubt, understand*, and *will* is so *evident*, that I know not how to explain it more *manifestly*, and that I also am the same that *imagine*, for tho perhaps (as I have supposed) no thing that can be *imagined* is *true*, yet the *imaginative Power* it self is *really* existent, and makes up a part of my *Thought*; and last of all that I am the same that am *sensitive*, or *perceive corporeal* things as by my *senses*, yet that I now *see* light, *hear* a noise, *feel* heat, these things are false, for I suppose my self *asleep*, but I *know* that I *see, hear*, and am *heated*, that cannot be *false*; and this it is that in me is *properly* called *Sense*, and this strictly taken is the same with *thought*.

By these Considerations I begin a little better to *understand My self* what I am; But yet it *seems*, and I cannot but *think* that *Corporeal Things* (whose *Images* are formed in my *thought*, and which by my *senses*, I perceive) are much more *distinctly known*, then that *confused Notion* of *My Self* which *imagination* cannot afford me. And yet 'tis strange that things *doubtful, unknown, distinct from Me*, should be *apprehended* more *clearly* by *Me*, then a Thing that is *True*, then a thing that is *known*, or then *I my self*; But the Reason is, that my Mind loves to wander, and suffer not it self to be bounded within the strict limits of *Truth*.

Let it therefore Wander, and once more let me give it the Free Reins, that hereafter being conveniently curbed, it may suffer it self to be more easily Govern'd.

Let me consider those things, which of all Things I formerly conceived most *evident*, that is to say, *Bodies* which we touch, which we see, not bodies in General (for those *General* Conceptions are usually *Confused*) but some one *Body* in particular.

Let us chuse for example this piece of *Bees-wax*, it was lately taken from the *Comb*, it has not yet lost all the *tast* of the *Honey*, it retains something of the *smell* of the *Flowers* from whence 'twas gather'd, its *colour*, *shape*, and *bigness* are manifest, 'tis *hard*, 'tis *cold*, 'tis *easily felt*, and if you will knock it with your finger, 'twill *make a noise:* In fine, it hath all things requisite to the most perfect notion of a *Body*.

But behold whilst I am speaking, 'tis put to the Fire, its *tast* is purged away, the *smell* is vanish'd, the *colour* is changed, the *shape* is alter'd, its *bulk* is increased, its become *soft*, 'tis *hot*, it can scarce be *felt*, and now (though you strike it) it makes no *noise*. Does it yet continue the same Wax? surely it does, this all confess, no one denies it, no one doubts it. What therefore was there in it that was so evidently known? surely none of those things which I *perceived* by my *senses*; for what I *smelt*, *tasted*, have *seen*, *felt*, or *heard*, are all *vanish'd*, and yet the *Wax remains*. Perhaps 'twas this only that I now think on, *viz.* that the *Wax* it self was not that *tast of Honey*, that *smell of Flowers*, that *whiteness*, that *shape*, or that *sound*, but it was a *Body* which awhile before appear'd to me *so* and *so modified*, but now *otherwise*. But what is it strictly that I thus imagine? let me consider: And having rejected whatever belongs not to the Wax, let me see what will remain, *viz.* this only, a thing *extended*, *flexible*, and *mutable*. But what is this *flexible*, and *mutable*? is it that I *imagine* that this Wax from being *round* may be made *square*, or from being *square* can be made *triangular*? No, this is not it; for I conceive it capable of *innumerable* such *changes*, and yet I cannot by my *imagination* run over these *Innumerables*; Wherefore this notion of its *mutability* proceeds not from my *imagination*. What then is *extended*? is not its *Extension* also *unknown*? For when it *melts* 'tis *greater*, when it *boils* 'tis *greater*, and yet *greater* when the heat is increased; and I should not rightly judge of the Wax, did I not think it capable of more various *Extensions* than I can *imagine*. It remains therefore for me only to confess, that I cannot *imagine* what this Wax is, but that I *perceive* with my *Mind* what it is. I speak of this *particular* Wax, for of Wax in *general* the *notion* is more *clear*.

But what Wax is this that I only conceive by my mind? 'Tis the same which I see, which I touch, which I imagine, and in fine, the same which at first I judged it to be. But this is to be noted, that the *perception* thereof is not the *sight*, the *touch*, or the *imagination* thereof; neither was it ever so, though at first it seem'd so. But the *perception* thereof is the *inspection* or *beholding* of the Mind only, which may be either *imperfect* and *confused*, as formerly it was; or *clear* and *distinct*, as now it is; the *more* or the *less* I consider the Composition of the Wax.

In the interim, I cannot but admire how prone my mind is to erre; for though I re[s]olve these things with my self *silently*, and *without speaking*, yet am I intangled in *meer words*, and am almost deceived by the usual way of *expression*; for we commonly say, *that we see the Wax it self if it be present*, and not, *that we judge it present by its colour or shape*; from whence I should immediately thus conclude, therefore the Wax is known by the *sight* of the *eye*, and not by the *inspection* of the *mind* only. Thus I should have concluded, had not I by chance look'd out of my window, and seen men passing by in the Street; which men I as usually say that I *see*, as I do now, that I *see* this Wax; and yet I see nothing but their Hair and Garments, which perhaps may cover only *artificial Machines* and *movements*, but I judge them to be men; so that what I thought I only *saw* with my eyes, I comprehend by my *Judicative Faculty*, which is *my Soul*. But it becomes not one, who desires to be wiser than the Vulgar, to draw matter of *doubt* from those ways of *expression*, which the Vulgar have invented.

Wherefore let us proceed and consider, whether I perceived more *perfectly* and *evidently* what the Wax was, when I first look'd on't, and believed that I knew it by my outward *senses*, or at least by my *common sense* (as they call it) that is to say, *by my imagination*; or whether at present I *better understand* it, after I have more diligently enquired both *what it is*, and how it may be *known*. Surely it would be a foolish thing to make it matter of doubt to know which of these parts are true; What was there in my first *perception* that was *distinct?* What was there that seem'd not incident to every other Animal? But now when I distinguish the Wax from its outward adherents, and consider it as if it were naked, with it's coverings pull'd off, then I cannot but really perceive it with my mind, though yet perhaps my judgment may erre.

But what shall I now say as to my *mind*, or my *self?* (for as yet I admit nothing as belonging to me but a *mind*.) Why (shall I say?) should not I, who seem to perceive this Wax so *distinctly*, know my *self* not only more *truly* and more *certainly*, but more *distinctly* and *evidently?* For if I judge that *this Wax exists*, because I *see* this Wax; surely it will be much more *evident*, that *I my self exist*, because *I see this Wax*; for it may be that this that I see is not really Wax, also it may be that I have no eyes wherewith to see any thing; but it cannot be, when I *see*, or (which is the same thing) when *I think that I see*, that I who *think* should not *exist*. The same thing will follow if I *judge that this Wax exists*, because I *touch*, or *imagine* it, &c. And what has been said of Wax, may be apply'd to all other outward things.

Moreover, if the *notion* of Wax seems more *distinct* after it is made known to me, not only by my *sight* or *touch*, but by more and other causes; How much the more *distinctly* must I confess my *self known* unto my *self*, seeing that all sort of reasoning which furthers me in the *perception* of *Wax*, or any other *Body*, does also encrease the proofs of the *nature* of my *Mind*. But there are so many more things in the very *Mind* it self, by which the *notion* of it may be made more *distinct*, that those things which drawn from *Body* conduce to its knowledge are scarce to be *mention'd*.

And now behold of my own accord am I come to the place I would be in; for seeing I have now discover'd that *Bodies themselves* are not *properly perceived* by our *senses* or *imagination*, but only by our *understanding*, and are not therefore *perceived*, because they are *felt* or *seen*, but because they are *understood*; it plainly appears to me, that nothing can possibly be *perceived* by *me easier*, or more *evidently*, than my *Mind*.

But because I cannot so soon shake off the Acquaintance of my former Opinion, I am willing to stop here, that this my new knowledge may be better fixt in my memory the longer I meditate thereon.

MEDITAT. III.
Of GOD, and that there is a God.

Now will I shut my eyes, I will stop my ears, and withdraw all my senses, I will blot out the Images of *corporeal* things clearly from my mind, or (because that can scarce be accomplish'd) I will give no heed to them, as being *vain* and *false*, and by discoursing with my self, and prying more rightly into my own Nature, will endeavour to make my self by degrees more known and familiar to my self.

I am a *Thinking Thing*, that is to say, *doubting, affirming, denying, understanding* few things, *ignorant* of many things, *willing, nilling, imagining* also, and *sensitive*. For (as before I have noted) though perhaps whatever I *imagine*, or am sensible of, as without me, *Is not*; yet that *manner* of thinking which I call *sense* and *imagination* (as they are only certain *Modes* of *Thinking*) I am certain are in Me. So that in these few Words I have mention'd whatever I *know*, or at least Whatever as yet I *perceive* my self to *know*.

Now will I look about me more carefully to see Whether there Be not some other Thing in Me, of Which I have not yet taken Notice. I am sure That I am a *Thinking Thing*, and therefore Do not I know what is Required to make me *certain* of any Thing? I Answer, that in this My *first knowledge* 'tis Nothing but a *clear*, and *distinct perception* of What I affirm, Which would not be sufficient to make me *certain* of the *Truth* of a Thing, if it were *Possible* that any thing that I so *clearly* and *distinctly* Perceive should be *false*. Wherefore I may lay this Down as a *Principle*. *Whatever I Clearly and Distinctly perceive is certainly True*.

But I have formerly Admitted of many Things as very *Certain* and *manifest*. Which I afterwards found to be *doubtful* Therefore What sort of Things were they? *Viz*. Heaven, Earth, Stars, and all other things which I perceived by my

Senses. But What did I perceive of These *Clearly?* *Viz.* That I had the *Ideas* or *Thoughts* of these things in my mind, and at Present I cannot deny that I have these *Ideas* in Mee. But there was some other thing Which I affirm'd, and Which (by Reason of the common Way of Belief) I thought that I *Clearly* Perceived; Which nevertheless, I did not really Perceive; And that was, that there were Certain Things *Without Me* from whence these *Ideas Proceeded*, and to which they were exactly like. And this it was, Wherein I was either *Deceived*, or if by Chance I Judged *truly*, yet it Proceeded not from the strength of my *Perception*.

But When I was exercised about any single and easie Proposition in Arithmetick or Geometry, as that two and three added make five, Did not I Perceive them *Clearly* enough to make me affirm them True? Truly concerning these I had no other Reason afterwards to *Doubt*, but That I thought Perhaps there may be a *God* who might have so created me, that I should be *Deceived* even in those things which seem'd most *Clear* to me. And as often as this Pre-conceived opinion of *Gods great Power* comes into my Mind, I cannot but Confess that he may easily cause me to *Err* even in those things which I Think I perceive most *Evidently* with my Mind; yet as often as I Consider the Things themselves, which I Judge my self to perceive so *Clearly*, I am so fully Perswaded by them, that I easily Break out into these Expressions, Let Who can Deceive Me, yet he shall never Cause me *Not to Be* whilst *I think that I Am*, or that it shall ever be True, *that I never was*, Whilst at Present 'tis True *that I am*, or Perhaps, that Two and Three added make More or Less then Five; for in These things I Perceive a Manifest Repugnancy; And truely seeing I have no reason to Think any *God* a *Deceiver*, Nor as yet fully know Whether there Be *any God*, or *Not*, 'Tis but a slight and (as I may say) Metaphysical Reason of Doubt, which depends only on that opinion of which I am not yet Perswaded.

Wherefore That this Hindrance may be taken away, When I have time I ought to Enquire, Whether there *Be a God*, And if there be One, Whether he can be a *Deceiver*, For whilst I am *Ignorant* of this, I cannot possibly be fully *Certain* of any Other thing.

But now Method seems to Require Me to Rank all My Thoughts under certain Heads, and to search in Which of them *Truth* or *Falshood* properly Consists. Some of them are (as it were) the *Images* of Things, and to these alone the Name of an *Idea* properly belongs, as When I think upon a Man, A Chimera or Monster, Heaven, an Angel, or *God*. But there are others of them, that have *superadded Forms* to them, as when I Will, when I Fear, when I Affirm, when I Deny. I know I have alwayes (when ever I think) some certain Thing as the *subject* or *object* of my Thought, but in this last sort of thoughts there is something *more* which I Think upon then Barely the likeness of the Thing. And of these Thoughts some are called *Wills* and *Affections*, and Others of them *Judgments*.

Now as touching *Ideas*, if they be Consider'd alone as they are in themselves, without *Respect* to any other Things, they cannot Properly be *false*; for Whether I *Imagine* a Goat or a Chimera, 'tis as *Certain* that I *Imagine* one as t'other. Also in the *Will* and *Affections* I need not Fear any *Falshood*, For tho I should *Wish* for *evil Things*, or *Things* that are Not, it is not therefore *Not true* that I Wish for them.

Wherefore there onely Remains my *Judgments* of Things, in which I must take Care that I be not *deceived*. Now the Chief and most usual *Error* that I discover in them is, That I *Judge* Those *Ideas* that are *within* me to be *Conformable* and like to certain things that are *without* Me; for truely if I Consider those Ideas as certain *Modes* of my *Thought*, without Respect to any other Thing, they will scarce afford me an Occasion of *Erring*.

Of these *Ideas* some are *Innate*, some *Adventitious*, and some Others seem to me as Created by my self; For that I understand what *A Thing* Is, What is *Truth*, What a *Thought*, seems to Proceed meerly from my own *Nature*. But that I now *hear* a Noise, *see* the Sun, or *feel* heat, *I* have alwayes *Judged* to Proceed from Things *External*. But Lastly, Mermaids, Griffins, and such like Monsters, are *made meerly* by *My self*. And yet *I* may well think all of them either *Adventitious*, or all of them *Innate*, or all of them *made by my self*, for I have not as yet discover'd their true *Original*.

But *I* ought cheifly to search after those of them which *I* count *Adventitious*, and which I consider as coming from *outward objects*, that I may know what reason I have to think them *like* the things themselves, which they *represent*. Viz. *Nature so teaches Me*; and also I know that they *depend* not on my *Will*, and therefore *not on me*; for they are often present with me against my inclinations, or (as they say) in spite of my teeth, as now whether *I will* or *no* I feel heat, and therefore I think that the *sense* or *Idea* of heat is propagated to me by a *thing* really *distinct* from *my self*, and that is by the *heat* of the *Fire* at which I sit; And nothing is more obvious then for me to judge that That thing should transmit its own *Likeness* into me, rather then that any other thing should be transmitted by it. Which sort of arguments whether firme enough or not I shall now Trie.

When I here say, that *nature so teaches me*, I understand only, that I am as it were *willingly forced* to beleive it, and not that tis *discover'd* to me to be *true* by any *natural light*; for these two differ very much. For whatever is discover'd to me by the *Light* of nature (as that it necessarily Follows *that I am*, because *I think*) cannot possibly be *doubted*; Because I am endowed with no other *Faculty*, in which I may put so great confidence, as I can in the *Light* of nature; or *which* can possibly tell me, that those things are *false*, which *natural light* teaches me to be *true*; and as to my *natural Inclinations*, I have heretofore often judged my self led by them to the election of the *worst part*, when I was in the choosing *one* of two Goods; and therefore I see no reason why I should ever *trust* them in any other thing.

And then, tho these *Ideas depend not* on my *will*, it does not therefore follow that they *necessarily proceed* from *things external*. For as, Altho those *Inclinations* (which I but now mention'd) are in me, yet they seem *distinct* and *different* from my *will*; so perhaps there may be in me some other *faculty* (to me *unknown*) which may prove the *Efficient cause* of these *Ideas*, as hitherto I have observed them to be formed in me whilst I *dream*, without the help of any *External Object*.

And last of all, tho they should *proceed* from things which are *different* from me, it does not therefore follow that they must be *like* those things. For often times I have found the *thing* and the *Idea differing* much. As for example, I find in my self two divers *Ideas* of the Sun, *one* as *received* by my *senses* (and which cheifly I reckon among those I call adventitious) by which it appears to me very *smal, another* as taken from the arguments of Astronomers (that is to say, *consequentially collected*, or some other ways made by me from certain *natural notions*) by which 'tis rendred something bigger then the Globe of the Earth. Certainly both of these cannot be *like* that sun which is *without me*, and my reason perswades me, that that *Idea* is most *unlike* the Sun, which seems to *proceed Immediately* from it self.

All which things sufficiently prove, that I have hitherto (not from a *true judgement*, but from a *blind impulse*) beleived that there are certain things *different* from my self, and which have sent their *Ideas* or *Images* into me by the Organs of my *senses*, or some other way.

But I have yet an other Way of inquiring, whether any of those Things (whose *Ideas* I have *within* Me) are Really Existent *without* Me; And that is Thus: As those *Ideas* are only *Modes* of *Thinking*, I acknowledge no *Inequality* between them, and they all proceed from me in the *same Manner*. But as *one* Represents *one thing*, an *other*, an *other Thing*, 'tis Evident there is a *Great difference* between them. For without doubt, Those of them which Represent *Substances* are something *More*, or (as I may say) have *More* of *Objective Reallity* in them, then those that Represent only *Modes* or *Accidents*; and again, *That* by Which I understand a *Mighty God, Eternal, Infinite, Omniscient, Omnipotent Creatour* of all things besides himself, has certainly in it *more Objective Reallity*, then *Those Ideas* by which *Finite Substances* are Exhibited.

But Now, it is evident by the *Light* of *Nature* that there must be *as much* at least in the *Total efficient Cause*, as there is in the *Effect* of *that Cause*; For from Whence can the *effect* have its *Reallity*, but from the *Cause*? and how can the *Cause* give it that *Reallity*, unless *it self have* it?

And from hence it follows, that neither a *Thing* can be made out of *Nothing*, Neither a Thing which is *more Perfect* (that is, Which has in it self *more Reallity*) *proceed* from That Which is *Less Perfect*.

And this is *Clearly* True, not only in those *Effects* whose *Actual* or *Formal Reallity* is Consider'd, But in Those *Ideas* also, Whose *Objective Reallity* is only Respected; That is to say, for Example of Illustration, it is not only impossible that a stone, Which *was not*, should now begin *to Be*, unless it were produced by *something*, in Which, Whatever goes to the Making a Stone, is either *Formally* or *Virtually*; neither can *heat* be Produced in any Thing, which before was *not hot*, but by a Thing which is at least of as equal a *degree* of *Perfection* as *heat* is; But also 'tis Impossible that I should have an *Idea* of Heat, or of a *Stone*, unless it were put into me by some *Cause*, in which there is at least as much *Reallity*, as I Conceive there is in Heat or a Stone. For tho that *Cause* transfers none of its own

Actual or *Formal Reality* into my *Idea*, I must not from thence conclude that 'tis *less real*; but I may think that the *nature* of the *Idea* it self is such, that of it self it requires no other *formal reality*, but what it has from my *thought*, of which 'tis a *mode*. But that this *Idea* has *this* or *that objective reallity*, rather then any *other*, proceeds clearly from some *cause*, in which there ought to be at least as much *formal reallity*, as there is of *objective reallity* in the *Idea* it self. For if we suppose any thing in the *Idea*, which was not in its *cause*, it must of necessity have this from *nothing*; but (tho it be a most *Imperfect manner of existing*, by which the thing is *objectively* in the *Intellect* by an *Idea*, yet) it is not *altogether nothing*, and therefore cannot proceed from *nothing*.

Neither ought I to doubt, seeing the *reallity* which I perceive in my *Ideas* is only an *objective reallity*, that therefore it must of necessity follow, that the same *reallity* should be in the *causes* of these *Ideas formally*. But I may conclude, that 'tis sufficient that this *reallity* be in the very *causes* only *objectively*. For as that *objective manner* of *being* appertains to the very *nature* of an *Idea*, so that *formal manner* of *being* appertains to the very *nature* of a *cause* of *Ideas*, at least to the *first* and *chiefest causes* of them; For tho perhaps one *Idea* may receive its birth from an other, yet we cannot proceed in *Infinitum*, but at last we must arrive at some *first Idea*, whose *cause* is (as it were) an *Original copy*, in which all the *objective reallity* of the *Idea* is *formally contain'd*. So that I plainly discover by the *light* of *nature*, that the *Ideas*, which are in me, are (as it were) *Pictures*, which may easily *come short* of the *perfection* of those things from whence they are taken, but cannot *contain* any thing *greater* or *more perfect* then them: And the *longer* and *more diligently* I pry into these things, so much the more *clearly* and *distinctly* do I discover them to be *true*.

But what shall I conclude from hence? Thus, that if the *objective reallity* of any of my *Ideas* be *such*, that it cannot be in me either *formarlly* or *eminently*, and that therefore I cannot be the *cause* of *that Idea*, from hence it necessarily Follows, that *I alone* do not only *exist*, but that some other thing, which is the *cause* of that *Idea*, does *exist also*.

But if I can find no *such Idea* in me, I have no argument to perswade me of the *existence* of any thing besides my self for I have diligently enquired, and hitherto I could discover no other *perswasive*.

Some of these *Ideas* there are (besides that which represents *my self* to *my self*, of which in this place I cannot doubt) which represent to me, one of them a *God*, others of them *Corporeal* and *Inanimate* things, some of them *Angels*, others *Animals*, and lastly some of them which exhibite to me *men like my self*.

As touching those that represent *Men* or *Angels* or *Animals*, I easily understand that they may be *made up* of those *Ideas* which I have of *my self*, of *Corporeal* things, and of *God*, tho there were neither *man* (but my self) nor *Angel*, nor *Animal* in being.

And as to the *Ideas* of *Corporeal* things, I find nothing in them of that *perfection*, but it may proceed from my self; for if I look into them more narrowly, and examine them more particularly, as yesterday (*in the second Medit.*) I did the *Idea* of Wax, I find there are but few things which I perceive *clearly* and *distinctly* in them, viz. *Magnitude* or *extension* in *Longitude*, *Latitude*, and *Profundity*, the *Figure* or *shape* which arises from the *termination* of that *Extension*, the *Position* or *place* which divers *Figured Bodies* have in *respect* of each other, their *motion* or *change of place*; to which may be added, their *substance*, *continuance*, and *number*; as to the other, such as are, *Light*, *Colours*, *Sounds*, *Smels*, *Tasts*, *Heat*, and *Cold*, with the other *tactile qualities*, I have but very *obscure* and *confused thoughts* of them, so that I know not, whether they are *true* or *false*, that is to say, whether the *Ideas* I have of them are the *Ideas* of *things* which *really are*, or *are not*. For altho *falshood formally* and *properly* so called, consists only in the *judgement* (as before I have observed) yet there is an other sort of *material falshood* in *Ideas*, when they represent a *thing* as *really existent*, tho it does *not exist*; so, for example, the *Ideas* I have of *heat* and *cold* are so *obscure* and *confused*, that I cannot collect from them, whether *cold* be a *privation* of *heat*, or *heat* a *privation* of *cold*, or whether either of them be a *real quality*, or whether neither of them be *real*. And since every *Idea* must be *like* the thing it represents, if it be *true* that *cold* is nothing but the *privation* of *heat*, that I*dea* which represents it to me as a thing *real* and *positive* may deservedly be apply'd to other Ideas.

And now I see no necessity why I should assigne any other *Author* of these *Ideas* but *my self*; for if they are *false*, that is, represent things that *are not*, I know by the *light* of *nature* that they proceed from *nothing*; that is to say, I harbour them upon no other account, but because my *nature* is *deficient* in something, and *imperfect*. But if they are *true*, yet seeing I discover so little *reality* in them, that that very *reality* scarce *seems* to *be realy*, I see no reason why I my self should not be the *Author* of them.

But also some of those very *Ideas* of *Corporeal* things which are *clear* and *distinct*, I may seem to have borrow'd from the *Idea* I have of *my self*, viz. *Substance*, *duration*, *number*, and the like; For when I conceive a *stone* to be a *substance* (that is, *a thing apt of it self to exist*) and also that I *my self* am a *substance*, tho I conceive *my self* a *thinking substance* and *not extended*, and the *stone* an *extended substance* and *not thinking*, by which there is a great *diversity* between both the *conceptions*, yet they *agree* in this, that they are *both substances*. So when I conceive my self as *now* in being, and also remember, that *heretofore* I *have been*; and since I have *divers* thoughts, which I can *number* or *count*; from hence it is that I come by the notions of *duration* and *number*; which afterwards I apply to other things.

As to those other things, of which the *Idea* of a *body* is made up, as *extension*, *figure*, *place* and *motion*, they are not *formally* in me, seeing I am only a *thinking thing*; yet seeing they are only certain *modes* of *substance*, and I my self also am a *substance*, they may seem to be in me *eminently*.

Wherefore there only Remains the *Idea* of a *God*, wherein I must consider whether there be not something included, which cannot possibly have its *original* from me. By the word *God*, I mean a certain *Infinite Substance*, *Independent*,

Omniscient, *Almighty*, by whom both *I my self*, and every thing else that *is* (if any thing do *Actualy exist*) was created. All which *Attributes* are of such an *high nature*, that the more attentively I consider them, the less I conceive my self possible to be the *Author* of these notions.

From what therefore has been said I must conclude that there is a *God*; for tho the *Idea* of *substance* may arise in me, because that I my self am a *substance*, yet I could not have the *Idea* of an *Infinite substance* (seing I my self am *finite*) unless it proceeded from a *substance* which is *really Infinite*. Neither ought I to think that I have no *true Idea* of *Infinity*, or that I perceive it only by the *negation* of what is *finite*, as I conceive *rest* and *darkness* by the *negation* or *absence* of *motion* or *light*. But on the contrary I plainly understand, that there is *more reality* in an *Infinite substance*, then in a *Finite*; and that therefore the *perception* of an *Infinite* (as *God*) is *antecedent* to the *notion* I have of a *finite* (as *my self*) For how should I know that I *doubt* or *desire*, that is to say, that I *want* something, and that I am *not altogether perfect*, unless I had the *Idea* of a *being more perfect* then *my self*, by *comparing* my self to which I may discover my own *Imperfections*.

Neither can it be said that this *Idea* of *God* is *false Materialiter*, and that therefore it *proceeds* from *nothing*, as before I observed of the *Ideas* of *heat* and *cold*, *&c*. For on the contrary, seeing this *notion* is most *clear* and *distinct*, and contains in it self more *objective reality* then any other I*dea*, none can be more *true* in it self, nor in which *less suspition* of *falshood* can be found. This *Idea* (I say) of a *being infinitely perfect* is most *true*, for tho it may be supposed that such a *being* does *not exist*, yet it cannot be supposed that the I*dea* of such a *being* exhibites to me nothing *real*, as before I have said of the *Idea* of *cold*. This *Idea* also is most *clear* and *distinct*, for whatever I perceive *clearly* and *distinctly* to be *real*, and *true*, and *perfect*, is wholy *contain'd* in this *Idea* of *God*.

Neither can it be objected, that I cannot *comprehend* an *Infinite*, or that there are innumerable other things in *God*, which I can neither *conceive*, nor in the least *think upon*; for it is of the *very nature* of an *Infinite* not to be *apprehendable* by *me* who am *finite*. And 'tis sufficient to me to prove this my *Idea* of *God* to be the most *true*, the most *clear*, and the most *distinct Idea* of all those *Ideas* I have, upon this *account*, that I understand that *God* is *not to be understood*, and that I judge that whatever I *clearly* perceive and know I*mplys* any *perfection*, as also perhaps other innumerable *perfections*, which I am ignorant of, are in *God* either *formally* or *eminently*.

Doubt. But perhaps *I am* something *more* then I take my self to *be*, and perhaps all these *perfections* which I attribute to God, are *potentially* in me, tho at present they do not shew themselves, and break into action. For I am now fully experienced that my *Knowledge* may be *encreased*, and I see nothing that hinders why it may not *encrease* by degrees in *Infinitum*, nor why by my *knowledge* so *encreased* I may not attain to the other *perfections* of *God*; nor lastly, why the *power* or *aptitude* of *having* these perfections may not be sufficient to produce the *Idea* of them in *me*.

Solution. But none of these will do; for first, tho it be true that my *Knowledge* is capable of being *increased*, and that many things are in me *potentially*, which *actually* are not, yet none of these go to the making of an *Idea* of *God*, in which I conceive nothing *potentially*, for tis a certain argument of *imperfection* that a thing *may be encreased Gradually*. Moreover, tho my knowledge may be *more* and *more encreased*, yet I know that it can never be *actually Infinite*, for it can never arrive to that *height of perfection*, which admits not of an *higher degree*. But I conceive God to be *actually* so *Infinite*, that nothing can be *added* to his *perfections*. And lastly, I perceive that the *objective being* of an *Idea* cannot be *produced* only by the *potential being* of a *thing* (which in proper speech is *nothing*) but requires an *actual* or *formal being* to its *production*.

Of all which forementioned things there is nothing that is not *evident* by the *light* of *reason* to any one that will diligently consider them. Yet because that (when I am careless, and the *Images* of *sensible* things *blind* my *understanding*) I do not so easily call to mind the reasons, why the *Idea* of a *being more perfect* then *my self* should of necessity proceed from a *being* which is *really more perfect*; It will be requisite to enquire further, whether *I*, who have this *Idea*, can possibly *be*, unless *such* a *being* did *exist*. To which end let me aske, *from whence* should I *be*? From *my self*? or from my *Parents*? or from any other thing *less perfect* then *God*? for nothing can be thought or supposed *more perfect*, or *equally perfect* with *God*.

But first, If *I* were from my self, I should neither *doubt*, nor *desire*, nor *want* any thing, for I should have given my self all those *perfections*, of which I have any *Idea*, and consequently I my self should be *God*; and I cannot think that those things I *want*, are to be acquired with *greater difficulty* then those things I *have*; but on the contrary, tis manifest, that it were much more *difficult* that *I* (that is, *a substance* that *thinks*) should *arise* out of *nothing*, then that I should *acquire* the *knowledge* of many things whereof I am *Ignorant*, which is only the *accident* of that *substance*. And certainly if I had that *greater thing* (viz *being*) from my self, I should not have *denyed* my self (not only those things which may be easier acquired, but also) All those things, which I perceived are contain'd in the *Idea* of a *God*; and the reason is, for that no other things *seem* to me to be *more difficultly* done, and certainly if they were *Really more difficult*, they would *seem* more *difficult* to me (if whatever *I have*, I *have* from my self) for in those things I should find my *Power* put to a stop.

Neither can I Evade the force of these Arguments by supposing my self to *have alwaies Been, what now I am*, and that therefore I need not seek for an *Author* of my *Being*. For the *Durance* or *Continuation* of my life may be *divided* into *Innumerable Parts*, each of which does not at all *depend* on the *Other Parts*; Therefore it will not follow, that because *a while ago, I was*, I must of necessity *now Be*. I say, this will not follow, Unless, I suppose some *Cause* to *Create me* (as it were) *anew* for *this* Moment (that is, *Conserve me*) For 'tis evident to one that Considers the Nature of *Duration*, that the same *Power* and *Action* is requisite to the *Conservation* of a Thing each *Moment* of its *Being*, as there is to the *Creation* of that Thing *anew*, if it did *not exist*. So that 'tis one of those *Principles* which are *Evident* by the *Light* of *Nature*: that the *Act* of *Conservation* differs only *Ratione* (as the Philosophers term it) from the *Act of Creation*.

Wherefore I ought to ask my self this Question, whether *I*, who *now* Am; have any *Power* to *Cause* my self to *Be hereafter*? (for had I any such *power*, I should certainly *know* of it, seeing I am nothing but a *Thinking Thing*, or at least at present I onely treat of that part of me, which is a *Thing* that *Thinks*) to which, I answer, that I can discover no such *Power* in Me; And consequently, I evidently know that *I depend* on some *Other being distinct* from *my self*.

But what if *I* say that perhaps this *Being* is not *God*, but that *I* am produced either by my *Parents*, or some other *Causes less perfect* then *God*? In answer to which let me consider (as *I* have said before that 'tis *manifest* that whatever is in the *effect*, *so much* at least ought to be in the *cause*; and therefore seeing I am a thing that *thinks*, and have in me an *Idea* of God, it will confessedly follow, that whatever sort of *cause* I assign of my *own Being*, it also must be a *Thinking Thing*, and must have an *Idea* of all those *Perfections*, which I attribute to *God*; Of which *Cause* it may again be Asked, whether it be *from it self*, or from any other *Cause*? If *from it self*, 'tis evident (from what has been said) that it must be *God*; For seeing it has the *Power* of *Existing of it self*, without doubt it has also the *power* of *actually Possessing* all those *Perfections* whereof it has an *Idea* in it self, that is, all those *Perfections* which I conceive in *God*. But if it Be from an *other Cause*, it may again be asked of that *Cause* whether it be *of it self*, or from an *other*; Till at length We arrive at the *Last Cause* of All, Which will Be *God*. For 'tis evident, that this *Enquiry* will not admit of *Progressus in Infinitum*, especially when at Present I treat not only of that Cause which at *first made* Me; But chiefly of that which *conserves* me in this *Instant* time.

Neither can it be supposed that many *partial Causes* have *concurred* to the making Me, and that I received the *Idea* of one of *Gods perfections* from *One* of them, and from an *other* of them the *Idea* of an *other*; and that therefore all these Perfections are to be found *scattered* in the World, but not all of them *Joyn'd* in any one which may Be *God*. For on the contrary, *Unity*, *Simplicity*, or the *inseparability* of All Gods Attributes is one of the *chief Perfections* which I conceive in Him; and certainly the *Idea* of the *Unity* of the *Divine Perfections* could not be *created* in me by any other *cause*, then by *That*, from whence I have received the *Ideas* of his other *perfections*; For 'tis Impossible to make me conceive these *perfections*, *conjunct* and *inseparable*, unless he should also make me know what *perfections* these *are*.

Lastly as touching my *having* my *Being* from my *Parents*. Tho whatever Thoughts I have heretofore harbour'd of Them were *True*, yet certainly they *contribute* nothing to my *conservation*, neither proceed I from them as *I am a Thing* that *Thinks*, for they have onely *predisposed* that *material Thing*, wherein *I*, that is, *my mind* (*which* only at present I take for *my self*) *Inhabits*. Wherefore I cannot *now* Question that I am sprung from them. But I must of necessity conclude that because *I am*, and because I have an *Idea* of a *Being most perfect*, that is, of *God*, it evidently follows that *there is a God*.

Now it only remains for me to examine, how I have received this *Idea* of *God*. For I have neither received it by means of *my Senses*, neither comes it to me *without* my *Forethought*, as the *Ideas* of *sensible* things use to do, when such things *Work* on the *Organs* of my *Sense*, or at least *seem* so to work; Neither is this *Idea* framed by *my self*, for I can neither *detract from*, nor *add* any thing *thereto*. Wherefore I have only to conclude that it is *Innate*, even as the *Idea* of me *my self* is *Natural* to my self.

And truly 'tis not to be Admired that *God* in Creating me should *Imprint* this *Idea* in me, that it may there remain as a *stamp impressed* by the *Workman God* on *me* his *Work*, neither is it requisite that this *stamp* should be a Thing *different* from the *Work* it self, but 'tis very Credible (from hence only that *God Created* me) that I am made as it were according to his *likeness* and *Image*, and that the same *likeness*, in which the *Idea* of a God is contain'd, is *perceived* by Me with the *same faculty*, with which I *perceive my Self*; That is to say, whilst I *reflect* upon my self. *I* do not only *perceive* that I am an *Imperfect* thing, having my *dependance* upon some other thing, and that I am a Thing that Desires *more* and *better* things *Indefinitely*; But also at the same time I understand, that *He* on whom I *depend* contains in him all those *wish'd for things* (not only *Indefinitely* and *Potentially*, but) *Really*, *Infinitely*; and that therefore he is *God*. The whole stress of which Argument lies thus, because I know it Impossible for Me to Be of the same Nature I am, *Viz*. Having the *Idea* of a *God* in me, unless really there were a *God*, a *God* (I say) that very *same God*, whose *Idea I* have in my *Mind* (that is, Having all those *perfections*, which I cannot *comprehend* but can as it were *think upon them*) and who is not *subject* to any *Defects*.

By which 'tis evident that *God* is no *Deceiver*; for 'tis manifest by the *Light* of *Nature*, that all *fraud* and *deceit* depends on some *defect*. But before I prosecute this any farther, or pry into other *Truthes* which may be deduced from this, I am willing here to stop, and dwell upon the Contemplation of this *God*, to Consider with my self His *Divine Attributes*, to behold, admire, and adore the Loveliness of this *Immense light*, as much as possibly I am able to accomplish with my *dark* Understanding. For as by *Faith* we *believe* that the greatest *happiness* of the *next* Life consists alone in the *Contemplation* of the *Divine Majesty*, so we *find* by *Experience* that now we receive from thence the greatest *pleasure*, whereof we are capable in *this Life*; Tho it be much more *Imperfect* then that in the *Next*.

MEDITAT. IV.
Of Truth and Falshood.

Of late it has been so common with me to withdraw *my Mind* from my *sences*, and I have so throughly consider'd how few things there are appertaining to *Bodies* that are *truly* perceived, and that there are more Things touching *Mans mind*, and yet more concerning *God*, which are *well known*; that now without any difficulty *I* can turn my Thoughts from things *sensible*, to those which are only *Intelligible*, and *Abstracted* from *Matter*. And truely *I* have a much more *distinct Idea* of a *Mans mind* (as it is a *Thinking Thing*, having no *Corporeal Dimensions* of *Length*, *Breadth*, and *Thickness*, nor having any other *Corporeal Quality*) then the *Idea* of any *Corporeal Thing* can be. And when I reflect upon my self, and consider how that I *doubt*, that is, am an *imperfect dependent Being*, I from hen[ce] Collect such a *clear* and *distinct Idea* of an *Independent perfect Being*, which is *God*, and from hence only that *I have such an Idea*, that is, because *I* that have this *Idea* do *myself Exist*; I do so *clearly* conclude that *God also Exists*, and that on him my *Being depends* each Minute; That I am Confident nothing can be known more *Evidently* and *Certainly* by *Humane Understanding*.

And now *I* seem to perceive a *Method* by which, (from this Contemplation of the *true God*, in whom the Treasures of *Knowledge* and *Wisdome* are Hidden) *I* may attain the *Knowledg* of other Things.

And first, *I* know 'tis impossible that this *God* should *deceive* me; For in all *cheating* and *deceipt* there is something of *imperfection*; and tho to be *able* to *deceive* may seem to be an Argument of *ingenuity* and *power*, yet without doubt to *have* the *Will* of *deceiving* is a sign of *Malice* and *Weakness*, and therefore is not *Incident* to *God*.

I have also found in my self a *Judicative faculty*, which certainly (as all other things I possess) I have received from *God*; and seeing he will not *deceive* me, he has surely given me such a *Judgement*, that I can *never Err*, whilst I make a *Right Use* of it. Of which truth I can make no doubt, unless it seems, that From hence it will follow, That therefore *I can never Err*; for if whatever I have, I have from *God*, and if he gave me no *Faculty* of *Erring*, I may seem not to be *able to Err*. And truly so it is whilst I think upon *God*, and wholly convert my self to the *consideration* of him, I find no occasion of *Error* or *Deceit*; but yet when I return to the *Contemplation* of *my self*, I find my self liable to *Innumerable Errors*. Enquiring into the *cause* of which, I find in my self an *Idea*, not only a *real* and *positive one* of a *God*, that is, of a *Being infinitely perfect*, but also (as I may so speak) a *Negative Idea* of *Nothing*; that is to say, I am so constituted between God and Nothing or between a perfect *Being* and *No-Being*, that as I am *Created* by the *Highest Being*, I have nothing in Me by which I may be *deceived* or drawn into *Error*; but as I pertake in a manner of *Nothing*, or of a *No-being*, that is, as I my self am *not* the *Highest Being*, and as I *want* many *perfections*, 'tis no Wonder that I should be *Deceived*.

By which I understand that *Error* (as it is *Error*) is not any *real Being* dependant on *God*, but it is only a *Defect*; And that therefore to make me *Err* there is not requisite a *faculty* of *Erring* given me by *God*, but only it so happens that I *Err* meerly because the *Judicative faculty*, which he has given me, is not *Infinite*.

But yet this Account is not fully *satisfactory*; for *Error* is not only a meer *Negation*, but 'tis a *Privation*, or a *want* of a certain *Knowledge*, which *ought* (as it were) to be in me. And when I consider the *Nature* of *God*, it seems impossible that he should give me any *faculty* which is not *perfect* in its *kind*, or which should *want* any of its *due perfections*; for if by how much the more *skilful* the *Workman* is, by so much the *Perfecter Works* proceed from him. What can be made by the *Great Maker* of all things which is not *fully perfect*? For I cannot Doubt but *God* may *Create* me so that I may *never* be *deceived*, neither can I doubt but that he *Wills* whatever is *Best*; Is it therefore *better* for me to be *deceived*, or not to be *deceived*?

These things when I Consider more heedfully, it comes into my Mind, First, that 'tis no cause of Admiration that *God* should do Things whereof I can give no account, nor must I therefore doubt his *Being*, because there are many things done by him, and I not comprehend *Why* or *How* they are done; for seeing I now know that my *Nature* is very *Weak* and *Finite*, and that the *Nature* of *God* is *Immense, Incomprehensible, Infinite*; from hence I must fully, understand, that he can do numberless things, the *Causes* whereof lie *hidden* to Me. Upon which account only I esteem all those Causes which are Drawn from the *End* (viz. *Final Causes*) as of no use in *Natural Philosophy*, for I cannot without Rashness Think my self *able* to Discover *Gods* Designes.

I perceive this also, that whenever we endeavour to know whether the *Works* of *God* are *Perfect*, we must not Respect any *one kind* of Creature *singly*, but the *Whole Universe* of *Beings*; for perhaps what (if considered *alone*) may Deservedly seem *Imperfect*, yet (as it is a *part* of the *World*) is most *perfect*; and tho since I have *doubted* of all things, I have discover'd nothing *certainly* to *Exist*, but *my self*, and *God*, yet since I have Consider'd the *Omnipotency* of *God*, I cannot deny, but that many other things *are made* (or at least, *may be made*) by him, so that I my self *may be* a *part* of this *Universe*.

Furthermore, coming nigher to my self, and enquiring what these *Errors* of mine, are (which are the Only Arguments of my *Imperfection*) I find them to *depend* on *two concurring Causes*, on my *faculty* of *Knowing*, and on my *faculty* of *Choosing* or *Freedome* of my *Will*, that is to say, from my *Understanding*, and my *Will together*. For by my *Understanding alone* I only perceive *Ideas*, whereon I make *Judgments*, wherein (*precisely* so taken) there can be no *Error*, *properly* so called; for tho perhaps there may be numberless things, whose *Ideas* I have *not* in Me, yet I am not *properly* to be said *Deprived* of them, but only *negatively wanting* them; and I cannot prove that *God ought* to have given me a *greater faculty* of *Knowing*. And tho I understand him to be a *skilful Workman*, yet I cannot Think, that he *ought* to have put all those *perfections* in *each* Work of his *singly*, with which he might have *endowed some* of them.

Neither can I complain that *God* has not given me a *Will*, or *Freedom of Choise*, *large* and *perfect* enough; for I have experienced that 'tis *Circumscribed* by *no Bounds*.

And 'tis worth our taking notice, that I have no other thing in me so *perfect* and so *Great*, but I Understand that there may be *Perfecter* and *Greater*, for if (for Example) I consider the *Faculty* of *Understanding*, I presently perceive that in me 'tis very *small* and *Finite*, and also at the same time I form to my self an *Idea* of an other *Understanding* not only *much Greater*, but the *Greatest* and *Infinite*, which I perceive to belong to God. In the same manner if [I] enquire into *memory* or *imagination*, or any other faculties, I find them in my self *Weak* and *Circumscribed*, but in *God* I Understand them to be *Infinite*, there is therefore only my *Will* or *Freedome* of *Choice*, which I find to be *so Great*, that I cannot frame to my self an *Idea* of *One Greater*, so that 'tis by this *chiefly* by which I understand my self to *Bear* the *likeness* and *Image* of God. For tho the *Will* in God be without comparison *Greater* then Mine, both as to the *Knowledge* and *Power* which are *Joyn'd* therewith, which make it more *strong* and *Effective*, and also as to the *Object* thereof, for *God* can apply himself to *more* things then I can. Yet being taken *Formally* and *Precisely* Gods Will seems *no greater* then Mine. For the *Freedome* of *Will* consists only in this, that we can *Do*, or *not Do* such a Thing (that is, *affirm* or *deny*, *prosecute* or *avoid*) or rather in this Only, that we are *so carried* to a Thing which is *proposed* by Our *Intellect* to *Affirm* or *Deny*, *Prosecute* or *Shun*, that we are *sensible*, that we are *not Determin'd* to the *Choice* or *Aversion* thereof, by any *outward Force*.

Neither is it Requisite to make one *Free* that he should have an *Inclination* to both sides. For on the contrary, by how much the more *strongly* I am inclined to *one* side (whether it be that I *evidently perceive* therein Good or Evil, or Whether it be that *God has so disposed* my *Inward Thoughts*) By so much the *more Free* am I in my *Choice*.

Neither truly do *Gods Grace* or *Natural Knowledge* take away from my *Liberty*, but rather *encrease* and *strengthen* it. For that *indifference* which I find in my self, when no Reason inclines me *more* to *one side*, then to *the other*, is the *meanest* sort of *Liberty*, and is so far from being a sign of *perfection*, that it only argues a *defect* or *negation* of *Knowledge*; for if I should always *Clearly see* what were *True* and *Good* I should never *deliberate* in my *Judgement* or *Choice*, and Consequently, tho I were *perfectly Free*, yet I should never be *Indifferent*.

From all which, I perceive that neither the *Power* of *Willing precisely* so taken, which I have from *God*, is the *Cause* of my *Errors*, it being most *full* and *perfect* in its kind; Neither also the *Power* of *Understanding*, for whatever I *Understand* (since 'tis from God that I *Understand* it) I understand *aright*, nor can I be therein *Deceived*.

From *Whence* therefore proceed all my *Errors*? To which, I answer, that they proceed from *hence* only, that seeing the *Will* expatiates it self *farther* then the *Understanding*, I keep it not within the *same bounds* with my *Understanding*, but often extend it to those things which I *Understand not*, to which things it being *Indifferent*, it easily Declines from what is *True* and *Good*; and consequently

I am *Deceived* and *Commit sin*. Thus, for example, when lately I set my self to enquire, Whether any thing doth *Exist*, and found that from my setting *my self* to Examine such a thing, it evidently follows that I *my self Exist*, I could not but *Judge*, what I so *clearly Understood*, to be *true*, not that I was *forced* thereto by any *outward impulse*, but because a *strong Propension* in my *Will* did follow this *Great Light* in my *Understanding*, so that I believed it so much the more *freely* and *willingly*, by how much the less *indifferent* I was thereto. But now I understand, not only, that *I Exist* as I am a *Thing* that *Thinks*, but I also meet with a certain *Idea* of a *Corporeal Nature*, and it so happens that I *doubt*, whether that *Thinking Nature* that is in me be *Different* from that *Corporeal Nature*, or Whether they are *both the same*; but in this *I* suppose that *I* have found no Argument to *incline* me *either ways*, and therefore *I* am *Indifferent* to *affirm* or *deny either*, or to *Judge nothing* of *either*; But this *indifferency* extends it self not only to those things of which I am *clearly ignorant*, but generally to all those things which are *not* so very *evidently known* to me at the Time when my *Will Deliberates* of them; for tho never so probable *Guesses incline* me to *one* side, yet the Knowing that they are only *Conjectures*, and not indubitable *reasons*, is enough to Draw my *Assent* to the *Contrary* Part. Which Lately *I* have sufficiently experienced, when *I* supposed all those things (which formerly *I* assented to as most *True*) as very *False*, for this *Reason* only that *I* found my self *able* to doubt of them in some manner.

If I abstain from *passing* my *Judgment*, when I do *not clearly* and *distinctly* enough perceive what is *Truth*, 'tis evident that I do *well*, and that I am *not deceived*: But if I *affirm* or *deny*, then 'tis that I *abuse* the *freedome* of my *will*, and if I turn my self to that part which is *false*, I am *deceived*; but if I *embrace* the *contrary* Part, 'tis but *by chance* that I light on the *Truth*, yet I shall not therefore be Blameless, for 'tis Manifest by the *light* of *Nature* that the *Perception* of the *Understanding ought* to preceed the *Determination* of the *Will*. And 'tis in this *abuse* of *Free-Will* that That *Privation* consists, which Constitutes *Error*; I say there is a *Privation* in the *Action* as it proceeds from Me, but not in the *Faculty* which I have received from *God*, nor in the *Action* as it *depends* on *him*.

Neither have I any Reason to Complain that God has not given me a *larger Intellective Faculty*, or more *Natural Light*, for 'tis a necessary Incident to a *finite Understanding* that it should not Understand *All* things, and 'tis Incident to a *Created Understanding* to be *Finite*: and I have more Reason to thank him for what he has *bestowed* upon me (tho he *owed* me nothing) then to think my self *Robbed* by him of those things which he *never gave me*.

Nor have I Reason to Complain that he has given me a *Will* larger then my *Understanding*: for seeing the *Will* Consists in *one* thing only, and as it were in an *Indivisible* (viz. *to Will*, or *not to Will*) it seems contrary to its nature that it should be *less* then 'tis; And certainly by how much the *Greater* it is, so much the more *Thankful* I ought to be to *him*, that Gave it me.

Neither can I Complain that God *concurrs* with me in the Production of those *Voluntary Actions* or *Judgements* in which I am *deceived*: for those *Acts* as they *depend* on *God* are altogether *True* and *Good*; and I am in some measure *more perfect* in that I can *so Act*, then if I could *not*: for that *Privation*, in which the *Ratio Formalis* of *Falshood* and *Sin* consists, wants not the *Concourse* of *God*; For it is *not A Thing*, and having respect to him as its *Cause*, ought not to be called *Privation*, but *Negation*; for certainly 'tis no *Imperfection* in *God*, that he has given me a *freedome* of *Assenting* or *not Assenting* to some things, the *clear* and *distinct* Knowledge whereof he has not *Imparted* to my *Understanding*; but certainly 'tis an *Imperfection* in me, that I *abuse* this *liberty*, and *pass* my *Judgement* on those things which I do *not Rightly* Understand.

Yet I see that 'tis Possible with *God* to effect that (tho I should remain *Free*, and of a *Finite Knowledge*) I should *never Err*, that is, if he had endowed my *Understanding* with a *clear* and *distinct* Knowledge of all things whereof I should ever have an *Occasion* of *deliberating*; or if he had only so firmly fix'd in my Mind, that I should never forget, this, *That I must never Judge of a Thing which I do not clearly and distinctly Understand*; Either of which things had *God* done, I easily perceive that *I* (as consider'd in my self) should be *more perfect* then now I am, yet nevertheless I cannot deny but that there *may be a greater perfection* in the *whole Universe* of Things, for that some of its parts are Obnoxius to *Errors*, and some not, then if they were all *alike*. And I have no Reason to Complain, that it has pleased God, that I should *Act* on the *Stage* of this *World* a *Part* not the *chief* and *most perfect* of all; Or that I should not be able to abstain from *Error* in the *first way* above specifi'd, which depends upon the *Evident Knowledge* of those things whereof *I deliberate*; Yet that I may abstain from *Error* by the *other means* abovemention'd, which depends only on this, *That I Judge not of any Thing, the truth whereof is not Evident*. For tho I have experienced in my self this *Infirmity*, that I cannot *always* be intent upon *one* and the *same* Knowledge, yet *I* may by a *continued* and *often repeated* Meditation bring this to pass, that as often as *I* have use of this Rule *I* may Remember it, by which means I may Get (as it were) an *habit* of *not erring*.

In which thing seeing the *greatest* and *chief perfection* of *Man* consists, *I* repute my self to have gain'd much by this days *Meditation*, for that therein *I* have discover'd the *Cause* of *Error, and Falshood*; which certainly can be no other then what *I* have now Declared; for whenever in Passing my Judgement, *I* bridle my *Will* so that it extend it self *only* to those things which I *clearly* and *distinctly* perceive, it is impossible that I can *Err*. For doubtless All *clear* and *distinct* Perception is *something*, and therefore cannot *proceed* from *Nothing*, but must necessarily have *God* for its *Author* (*God*, I say, Who is *infinitely Perfect*, and who *cannot Deceive*) and therefore it Must be *True*.

Nor have I this Day learnt only what I must *beware off* that I be not *deceived*, but also what I must *Do* to Discover *Truth*, for *That* I shall certainly find, if I fully Apply my self to those things *only*, which I *perfectly* understand; and if I distinguish between those and what I apprehend but *confusedly* and *obscurely*, Both which hereafter I shall endeavour.

MEDITAT. V.
Of the Essence *of Things* Material.
And herein Again of God.
And that he does Exist.

There are yet remaining many Things concerning *Gods Attributes*, and many things concerning the *nature* of *my self* or of my *Mind*, which ought to be searched into: but these perhaps I shall set upon at some other Opportunity. And at Present nothing seems to me more requisite (seeing I have discover'd what I must *avoid*, and what I must *Do* for the *Attaining* of *Truth*) then that I imploy my Endeavours to free my self from those doubts into which I have lately fallen, and that I try whether I can have any certainty of Material Things.

But before I enquire whether there be any such things *Really Existent without* Me, I ought to consider the *Ideas* of those things, as they are in my Thoughts and try which of them are *Distinct*, which *confused*.

In which search I find that I *distinctly imagine Quantity*, that which Philosophers commonly call *continued*, that is to say, the *Extension* of that *Quantity* or thing *continued* into *Length*, *Breadth*, and *Thickness*, I can *count* in it divers Parts, to which parts I can assign *Bigness*, *Figure*, *Position*, and *Local Motion*, to which *Local Motion* I can assign *Duration*. Neither are only these *Generals* plainly discover'd and known by Me, but also by attentive Consideration, I perceive Innumerable *particulars* concerning the *Shapes*, *Number*, and *Motion* of These Bodies; The *Truth* whereof is so *evident*, and *agreeable* to my *Nature*, that when I first discover'd them, I seemed not so much to have *Learnt* any thing that is *new*, as to have only *remembred* what I have known *before*, or only to have thought on those things which were in me *before*, tho this be the first time that I have examin'd them so *diligently*.

One thing there is worthy my Consideration, which is, that I find in my self innumerable *Ideas* of certain things, which tho perhaps they *exist no where without* Me, yet they cannot Be said to be *Nothing*, and tho they are *Thought* upon by me at my *will* and *pleasure*, yet they are not *made* by *Me*, but have their own *True* and *Immutable Natures*. As when, for example, I *Imagine* a *Triangle*, tho perhaps such a *Figure Exists no where* out of my *Thoughts*, nor ever *Will Exist*, yet the *Nature* thereof is *determinate*, and its *Essence* or Form is *Immutable* and *Eternal*, which is neither *made* by me, nor *depends* on my mind as appears for that many *properties* may be *demonstrated* of this Triangle, *viz.* That its three Angles are equal to two right ones, that to its Greatest Angle the Greatest side is subtended, and such like, which I now *clearly* know whether *I will or not*, tho before *I* never thought on them, when I *imagine* a Triangle, and consequently they could not be invented by Me. And 'tis nothing to the purpose for me to say, that perhaps this *Idea* of a Triangle came to me by the Organs of *sense*, because I have some-times seen bodies of a *Triangular Shape*; for I can think of Innumerable other *Figures*, which I cannot suspect to have come in through my *senses*, and yet I can *Demonstrate* various *properties* of them, as well as of a *Triangle*, which certainly are all *true*, seeing I know them *clearly*, and therefore they are *something*, and not a meer *Nothing*, for 'tis Evident that *what is true is something*.

And now I have sufficiently Demonstrated, that *what I clearly perceive, is True*; And tho I had *not demonstrated* it, yet such is the *Nature* of my *Mind*, that I could not but give my *Assent* to what I *so* perceive, at least, as long as I *so* perceive it; and I remember (heretofore when I most of all relied on *sensible Objects*) that I held those *Truths* for the most *certain* which I *evidently* perceived, such as are concerning *Figures, Numbers*, with other parts of *Arithmetick*, and *Geometry*, as also whatever relates to *pure* and *abstracted Mathematicks*.

Now therefore, if from this alone, *That I can frame the Idea of a Thing in my Mind*, it follows, *That whatever I clearly and distinctly perceive belonging to a thing*, does *Really* belong to it; Cannot I from hence draw an Argument to Prove the *Existence* of a *God*? Certainly I find the *Idea* of a *God*, or *infinitely perfect Being*, as *naturally* in me, as the *Idea* of any *Figure*, or *Number*; and I as *clearly* and *dis-tinctly* understand that it appertains to his *Nature Always to Be*, as I know that what I can *demonstrate* of a *Mathematical Figure* or *Number* belongs to the *Nature* of that *Figure* or *Number*: so that, tho all things which I have *Meditated* upon these three or four days were not *true*, yet I may well be as *certain* of the *Existence* of a *God*, as I have hitherto been of *Mathematical Truths*.

Doubt. Yet this Argument at first sight appears not so *evident*, but look rather like a *sophism*; for seeing I am used in all other things to *Distinguish Existence* from *Essence*, I can easily perswade my self that the *Existence* of God may be *distinguish'd* from his *Essence*, so that I may *Imagine God* not to *Exist*.

Solution. But considering it more strictly, 'tis manifest, that the *Existence* of God can no more be *seperated* from his *Essence*, then the *Equality* of the *Three Angles* to *two right ones* can be *seperated* from the *Essence* of a *Triangle*, or then the *Idea* of a *Mountain* can be *without* the *Idea* of a *valley*; so that 'tis no less a *Repugnancy* to think of a *God* (that is, *A Being infinitely perfect*) who want *Existence* (that is, who wants a *Perfection*) then to think of a *Mountain*, to which there is *no Valley adjoyning*.

Doubt. But what if I cannot imagine *God* but as *Existing*, or a *Mountain without a Vally*? yet supposing me to think of a *Mountain with a Vally*, it does not from thence follow, that there *Is a Mountain* in the World; so supposing me to think of a *God* as *Existing*, yet does it not follow that *God Really Exists*. For my *Thought imposes* no *necessity* on Things, and as I may imagine a *Winged Horse*, tho no *Horse* has *Wings*, so I may imagine an *existing God*, tho no *God exists*.

Solution. 'Tis true the *Sophism* seems to lie in this, yet tho I cannot conceive a *Mountain* but with a *Vally*, it does not from hence follow, that a *Mountain* or *Vally* do *Exist*, but this will follow, that whether a *Mountain* or a *Vally do* or *do not Exist*, yet they cannot be *seperated*: so from hence that I cannot think of *God* but as *Existing*, it follows that *Existence* is *Inseperable* from *God*, and therefore that he *Really Exists*; Not because my *Thought* does all this, or *Imposes* any *necessity* on any Thing, but contrarily, because the *necessity* of the thing it self (*viz.* of *Gods Existence*) *Determines* me to *think* (thus; for 'tis not in my Power to think a *God* without *Existence* (that is, *A Being absolutely perfect* without the *Cheif Perfection*) as it is in my Power to imagine a Horse either *with* or *without Wings*.

Doubt. And here it cannot be said, that I am forced to suppose *God Existing*, after I have supposed him *endowed* with all *Perfections*, seeing *Existence* is one of them; but that my *First Position* (*viz.* His *Absolute Perfection*) is not *necessary*. Thus, for example, 'tis not *necessary* for me to think all *Quadrilateral Figures* inscribed in a *Circle*; But supposing that I think *so*, I am then *necessitated* to Confess a *Rhombe Inscribed* therein, and yet this is evidently *False*.

Solution. For tho I am not forced at any time to think of a *God*; yet as often as I cast my Thoughts on a *First* and *Cheif Being*, and as it were bring forth out of the Treasury of my Mind an *Idea* thereof, I must of necessity attribute thereto all Manner of *Perfections*, tho I do not at that time *count* them over, or *Remark* each single One; which *necessity* is sufficient to make me hereafter (when I come to consider *Existence* to be a *Perfection*) conclude *Rightly, That the First and Chief Being does Exist*. Thus, for example, I am not obliged at any time to imagine a *Triangle*, yet whenever I please to Consider of a *Right-lined Figure* having only *three Angles*, I am then *necessitated* to allow it all those *Requisites* from which I may argue rightly, *That the Three Angles thereof are not Greater then Two Right Ones*, Tho upon the first consideration this came not into my Thought. But when I enquire what Figures may be *inscribed* within a *Circle*, I am not at all *necessitated* to think that all *Quadrilateral Figures* are of that sort; neither can I possibly imagine this, whilst I admit of nothing, but what I *clearly* and *distinctly* Understand: and therefore there is a great Difference between these *False suppositions*, and *True natural Ideas*, the *first* and *Chief*; whereof is that of a *God*; For by many wayes I understand *That* not to be a *Fiction depending* on my *Thought*, but an *Image* of a *True* and *Immutable Nature*; As first, because I can think of no other thing but *God* to Whose *Essence Existence* belongs. Next because I cannot Imagine *Two* or *More Gods*, and supposing that he is *now* only One, I may plainly perceive it *necessary* for *Him* to *Have been from Eternity*, and *will Be to Eternity*; And Lastly because I perceive many Other Things in *God*, Which I cannot *Change*, and from which I cannot *Detract*.

But whatever way of Argumentation I use, it comes All at last to this one Thing, That I am fully perswaded of the *Truth* of those things only, which appear to me *clearly* and *distinctly*. And tho some of those things, which I so perceive, are obvious to *every* Man, and some are only discover'd by Those that search more *nighly*, and enquire more *carefully*, yet when such *truths* are discover'd, they are esteem'd no less *certain* than the Others. For Example, Tho it do not so easily appear, that in a Rightangled Triangle, the square of the Base is equal to the squares of the sides, as it appears, that the Base is subtended under its Largest Angle, yet the *first Proposition is no less certainly* believed when once 'tis perceived, then this *Last*.

Thus in Reference to *God*; certainly, unless I am overrun with *Prejudice*, or have my thoughts begirt on all sides with *sensible Objects*, I should acknowledge nothing *before* or *easier* then him; For what is more *self-evident* then that there is a *Chief Being*, or then that a *God* (to whose *essence alone Existence* appertains) does *Exist*? And tho serious Consideration is required to perceive thus much, yet *Now*, I am not only equally *certain* of it, as of what seems most *certain*, but I perceive also that the *Truth* of other Things so *depends* on it, that without it nothing can ever be *perfectly known*.

For tho my *nature* be *such*, that during the time of my *Clear* and *Distinct* Perception, I cannot but believe it *true*; yet my *Nature* is *such* also, that I cannot fix the *Intention* of my *Mind* upon one and the same thing alwayes, so as to perceive it *clearly*, and the Remembrance of what *Judgement* I have formerly made is often stirred up, when I cease attending to those reasons for which I passed such a Judgment, other Reasons may then be produced, which (if I did not *know God*) may easily *move* me in my *Opinion*; and by this means I shall never attain to the *true* and *certain Knowledge* of any Thing, but *Wandring* and *Unstable opinions*. So, for example, when I consider the Nature of a Triangle, it plainly appears to me (as understanding the Principles of Geometry) that its three Angles are equal to two right ones; And this I must of necessity think *True* as long as I attend to the *Demonstration* thereof; but as soon as ever I withdraw my Mind from the *Consideration* of its *Proof* (altho I remember that I have once *Clearly* perceived it) yet perhaps I may *doubt* of Its *Truth*, being as yet *Ignorant* of a *God*; For I may perswade my self, that I am so framed by *Nature*, as to be *deceived* in those things which I imagine my self to perceive most *evidently*. Especially when I recollect, that heretofore I have often accounted many things *True* and *Certain*, which afterward upon other Reasons I have Judged as False. But when I perceive that there is a *God*; because at the same time I also Understand that all things *Depend* on Him, and that he is not a *Deceiver*; and when from hence I Collect that all those Things which I *clearly* and *distinctly* perceive are *necessarily True*; tho I have no further Respects to those Reasons which induced me to believe it *True*, yet if I do but remember, that I have *once clearly* and *distinctly* perceived it, no Argument can be brought on the contrary, that shall make me *doubt*, but that I have *true* and *certain* Knowledge thereof; and not onely of that, but of all other *Truths* also which I remember that I have *once Demonstrated*, such as are *Geometrical Propositions* and the like.

What now can be *Objected* against me? shall I say, that I am so made by *Nature*, as to be often *deceived*? No; For I now Know that I cannot be *deceived* in those Things, which I *clearly* Understand. Shall I say, that at other times I have esteem'd many Things *True* and *Certain*, which afterwards I found to be *falsities*? No; for I perceived none of those things *clearly* and *distinctly*, but being Ignorant of this *Rule* of *Truth*, I took them up for Reasons, which Reasons I afterward found to be *Weak*. What then can be said? Shall, I say, (as lately I objected) that Perhaps I am *asleep*, and that what I now think of is no more *True*, then the *Dreams* of People *asleep*? But this it self *moves* not my Opinion; for certainly tho I were *asleep*, if any thing appear'd *evident* to my Understanding, 'twould be *True*.

And Thus I Plainly see, that the *Certainty* and *Truth* of all *Science* Depends on the *Knowledge* of the *True God*, so that before I had *Known Him*, I did *Know nothing*; But now many things both of *God* himself, and of other *Intellectual Things*, as also of *Corporeal nature*, which is the *Object* of *Mathematicks*, may be *Plainly Known* and *Certain* to me.

MEDITAT. VI.
Of Corporeal Beings, *and Their* Existence: *As Also of the Real Difference, Between* Mind *and* Body.

It now remains that I examine whether any *Corporeal Beings* do *Exist*; And already I know that (as they are the *Object* of *Pure Mathematicks*) they *May* (at least) *Exist*, for I *clearly* and *distinctly* perceive them; and doubtless *God* is *able* to *make*, whatever I am *able* to *perceive*, and I never Judged any thing to be *beyond* his *Power*, but what was *Repugnant* to a *distinct perception*. Moreover, such *Material Beings seem* to *Exist* from the *faculty* of *Imagination*, which I find my self make use of, when I am conversant about them: for if I attentively Consider what *Imagination* is, 'twill appear to be only *a certain Application of our Cognoscitive or knowing Faculty to a Body or Object that is before it*; and if it be *before it*, It must *Exist*.

But that this may be made more *Plain*, I must first examine the *difference* between *Imagination*, and *pure Intellection*, or *Understanding*. So, for example, when I *Imagine* a Triangle, I do not only *Understand* that it is a *figure compre-hended* by *three Lines*, but I also *behold* with the *eye* of my *mind* those *three lines* as it were *before Me*, and this is that which I call *imagination*. But if I convert my Thoughts to a *Chiliogone*, or *Figure consisting* of a *Thousand Angles*, I know as well that this Is a *figure comprehended* by a *Thousand sides*, as I know that a *Triangle* is a *Figure Consisting of three sides*; but I do not in the same Manner *Imagine*, or *behold* as *present* those *thousand sides*, as I do the *three sides* of a *Triangle*. And tho at the time when I so think of a *Chiliogone*, I may *confusedly* represent to my self some *Figure* (because whenever I Think of a *Corporeal Object*, I am used to *Imagine* some *Shape* or other) yet 'tis evident that this *Representation* is not a *Chiliogone*, because 'tis in nothing *different* from what I should Represent to my self if I thought of a *Milion-angled figure*, or any other Figure of *More sides*; Neither does such a *Confused Representation* help me in the least to know those *Properties*, by which a *Chiliogone* differs from other *Polygones* or *Manyangled Figures*. But if a Question be put concerning a *Pentagone*, I know I may *Understand its Shape*, as I *Understand* the *Shape*, of a *Chiliogone*, without the help of *Imagination*, but I can also *imagine* it, by applying the *Eye* of my *Mind* to its *Fives sides*, and to the *Area* or *space* contained by Them; And herein I manifestly perceive that there is required *a peculiar sort* of *Operation* in the *Mind* to *imagine* a Thing, which I require not to *Understand* a Thing; which *New Operation* of the *Mind* plainly shews the *difference* between *imagination* and *pure Intellection*.

Besides this, I Consider that this *Power* of *Imagination* which is in me (as it differs from the *Power* of *Understanding*) does not appertain to the *Essence* of *Me*, that is, of *my mind*, for tho I *wanted* it, yet certainly I should be the *same He*, *that* now *I am*: from whence it seems to follow, that it depends on something *different* from *my self*; and I easily perceive that if any *Body* whatever did *Exist*, to which my *Mind* were so *conjoyn'd*, that it may Apply it self when it pleased to *Consider*, or (as it were) *Look* into *this Body*; From hence, I say, I perceive *It may so be*, that by this very *Body* I may *Imagine Corporeal Beings*: So that this *Manner* of *Thinking* differs from *pure Intellection* only in this, that the *Mind*, when it *Understands*, does as it were turn *it self*, to *it self*, or *Reflect* on it self, and *beholds* some or other of those *Ideas* which are in it self; But when it *Imagines*, it *Converts* it self upon *Body*, and therein *beholds* something Conformable to that *Idea*, which it hath *understood*, or *perceived* by *Sense*.

But 'tis to be remembred, that I said, I easily conceive Imagination *May be* so performed, supposing *Body* to *Exist*. And because no so convenient manner of Explaining it offers it self, from thence I *probably* guess, that *Body* does *Exist*. But this I only say *probably*, for tho I should accurately search into all the Arguments drawn from the *distinct Idea* of *Body*, which I find in my *Imagination*, yet I find none of them, from whence I may *necessarily* conclude, *that Body does Exist*.

But I have been accustomed to *Imagine* many other things besides that *Corporeal Nature* which is the *Object* of *pure Mathematicks*; such as are, *Colours, Sounds, Tasts, Pain*, &c. but none of these so *distinctly*. And because I perceive these better by *Sense*, from Which by the Help of the *Memory* they come to the *Imagination*, that I may with the Greater advantage treat of them, I ought at the same time to Consider *Sence*, and to try whether from what I perceive by that way of *Thought*, which I call *Sense*, I can deduce any certain Argument for the *Existence* of *Corporeal Beings*.

And first I will here reflect with my self, what those things were, which being perceived by *Sence* I have heretofore thought *True*, and the *Reasons* why I *so thought*: I will then enquire into the *Reasons* for which I afterwards *doubted* those things. And last of all I will consider what I *ought* to *think* of those Things at *Present*.

/*The Reasons why I Trusted my Senses.*/ First therefore I have always thought that I have had an *Head, Hands, Feet*, and other *Members*, of which *This Body* (which I have look'd upon as a *Part* of *Me*, or Perhaps as my *Whole self*) Consists; And I have also thought that this *Body* of *Mine* is Conversant or engaged among many *Other Bodies*, by which it is Liable to be *affected* with what is *advantagious* or *hurtful*; What was *Advantagious* I judged by a certain *sense* of *Pleasure*, what was *Hurtful* by a *sense* of *Pain*. Furthermore, besides *Pleasure* and *Pain*, I perceived in my self *Hunger, Thirst*, and other such like *Appetites*, as also certain *Corporeal Propensions* to *Mirth, Sadness, Anger*, and other like *Passions*.

As to What hapned to me from *Bodies without*, Besides the *Extension, Figure*, and *Motion* of those *Bodies*, I also perceived in them *Hardness, Heat*, and other *tactile Qualities*, as also *Light, Colours, Smells, Tasts, Sounds*, &c. and by the *Variation* of these I *distinguish'd* the *Heaven, Earth*, and *Seas*, and all other *Bodies* from each other.

Neither was it wholly without Reason (upon the account of these *Ideas* of *Qualities*, which offer'd themselves to my Thoughts, and which alone I *properly* and *Immediately perceived*) that I thought my self to Perceive some Things *Different* from my *Thought, viz.* The *Bodies* or *Objects* from whence these *Ideas* might *Proceed*; for I often found these *Ideas* come upon me without my *Consent* or *Will*; so that I can neither perceive an *Object* (*tho I had a mind to it*) unless it were *before* the Organs of my *Sense*; Neither can I *Hinder* my self from perceiving it, when it is *Present*.

And seeing that those *Ideas* which I take in by sense are much more *Lively, Apparent* and in their kind more *distinct*, than any of those which *I knowingly* and *Willingly* frame by Meditation, or stir up in my *Memory*; it seems to me that they cannot proceed from *my self*. There remains therefore no other way for them to come upon me, but from some other Things *Without* Me. Of Which Things seeing *I* have no other Knowledge but from these *Ideas*, I cannot Think but that these *Ideas* are *like* the Things.

Moreover, Because *I* remember that *I* first made use of my *senses* before my *Reason*; and because *I* did perceive that those *Ideas* which *I* my self did frame were not so *Manifest* as those which *I* received by my *senses*, but very often *made up of their parts*, *I* was easily perswaded to think that *I* had no *Idea* in my *Understanding*, which I had not *First* in my *sense*.

Neither was it without Reason that *I* Judged, *That Body* (which by a *peculiar right I* call my *Own*) to be *more nighly* appertaining to *Me* then any *other Body*. For from It, as from other *Bodies*, *I* can never be *seperated*, *I* was *sensible* of all

Appetites and *Affections in It* and *for It*, and lastly *I* perceived *pleasure* and *Pain* in its Parts, and not in any other Without it. But why from the *sense* of *Pain* a certain *Grief*, and from the *sense* of *pleasure* a certain *Joy* of the Mind should arise, or Why that *Gnawing* of the *stomach*, Which *I* call *Hunger*, should put me in mind of *Eating*, or the *driness* of my *Throat* of *Drinking*, *I* can give no other Reason but *that I am taught so by Nature*. For to my thinking there is no *Affinity* or *Likeness* between that *Gnawing* of the *Stomach*, and the desire of *Eating*, or between the *sense* of *Pain*, and the *sorrowful thought* from thence arising. But in this as in all other *judgments* that I made of *sensible objects*, I seem'd to be taught by *Nature*, for I first perswaded my self that things were *so* or *so*, before ever I enquired into a Reason that may prove it.

  /*The Reasons why I doubt my senses.*/ But afterwards I discover'd many experiments, wherein my *senses* so grosly deceived me, that I would never trust them again; for Towers which seem'd *Round* a far off, nigh at hand appear'd *square*, and *large Statues* on their tops seem'd *small* to those that stood on the ground; and in numberless other things, I perceived the *judgements* of my *outward senses* were *deceived*: and not of my *outward* only, but of my *inward senses* also; for what is more *intimate* or *inward* than *Pain*? And yet I have heard from those, whose Arm or Leg was cut off, that they have felt *pain* in that part which they *wanted*, and therefore I am not *absolutely certain* that any part of me is affected with *pain*, tho I *feel pain* therein. *[Medit 1.]* To these I have lately added two very *general Reasons* of *doubt*; The first was, that while I was *awake*, I could not believe my self to perceive any thing, which I could not think my self sometimes to perceive, tho I were *a sleep*; And seeing I cannot believe, that what I seem to perceive in my *sleep* proceeds from *outward Objects*, what greater Reason have I to think so of what I perceive whilst I am *awake*? The other Cause of Doubt was, that seeing I know not the *Author* of my *Being* (or at least I then *supposed* my self not to know him) what reason is there but that I may be so ordered by *Nature* as to be *deceived* even in those things which appear'd to me most *true*. And as to the *Reasons*, which induced me to give *credit* to *sensible* Things, 'twas easie to return an answer thereto, for finding by experience, that I was impelled by *Nature* to many Things, which *Reason* disswaded me from, I thought I should not far trust what I was taught by *Nature*. And tho the perceptions of my *senses* depended not on my *Will*, I thought I should not therefore conclude, that they proceeded from *Objects different* from my self; for perhaps there may be some other *Faculty* in me (tho as yet *unknown* to me) which might frame those *perceptions*.

  How far the senses are now to be trusted. But now that I begin better to know *my self* and the Author of my *Original*, I do not think, that all things, which I seem to have from my *senses* are *rashly* to be *admitted*, neither are all things so *had*, to be *doubted*. And first because I know that whatever I *clearly* and *distinctly* perceive, *may be* so made by *God* as I perceive them; the *Power* of *understanding clearly* and *distinctly* one Thing *without* the other is sufficient to make Me *certain* that One Thing is *different* from the Other; because it *may* at least be placed apart by *God*, and that it may be esteem'd *different*, it matters not by what *Power* it *may* be so *sever'd*. And therefore from the knowledge I have, that *I my self exist*, and because at the same time I understand that nothing else appertains to my *Nature* or *Essence*, but that I am a *thinking Being*, I rightly conclude, that my *Essence* consists in this alone, that I am a *thinking Thing*. And tho *perhaps* (or, as I shall shew presently, 'tis *certain*) I have a *Body* which is very *nighly* conjoyned to me, yet because on this side I have a clear and *distinct Idea* of my self, as I am only a *thinking Thing, not extended*; and on the other side because I have a *distinct Idea* of my *Body*, as it is onely an *extended* thing, *not thinking*, 'tis from hence *certain*, that I *am really distinct from my Body*, and that I can *exist without* it.

Moreover I find in my self some *Faculties* endow'd with *certain* peculiar waies of *thinking*, such as the *Faculty* of *Imagination*, the *Faculty* of *Perception* or *sense*; without which *I* can conceive my *whole self clearly* and *distinctly*, but (changing the phrase) *I* cannot *conceive* those *Faculties* without *conceiving My self*, that is, an *understanding substance* in which they are; for none of them in their *formal Conception* includes *understanding*; from whence *I* perceive they are as *different* from *me*, as the *modus* or *manner* of a Thing is *different* from the *Thing it self*.

I acknowledge also, that *I* have several other *Faculties*, such as *changing* of *place, putting on various shapes*, &c. Which can no more be understood without a *substance* in which they are, then the foremention'd *Faculties*, and consequently they can no more be understood to *Exist* without that *substance*: But yet 'tis Manifest, that this sort of *Faculties*, to the End they may exist, ought to be in a *Corporeal, Extended*, and not in an *Understanding substance*, because *Extension*, and not *Intellection* or *Understanding* is included in the *Clear* and *Distinct conception* of them.

But there is also in me a certain *Passive Faculty* of *sense*, or of *Receiving* and *Knowing* the *Ideas* of *sensible Things*; of which *Faculty* I can make no use, unless there were in my self, or in something else, a certain *Active Faculty* of *Producing* and *Effecting* those *Ideas*. But this cannot be in my self, for it Presupposes no *Understanding*, and those *Ideas* are Produced in me, tho I help not, and often against my *Will*. There remains therefore no Place for this *Active Faculty*, but that it should be in some *substance different* from me. In which because all the *Reallity*, which is contain'd *Objectively* in the *Ideas* Produced by that *Faculty*, ought to be contain'd *Formally* or *Eminently* (as I have Formerly taken notice) this *substance* must be either *a Body* (in which what is in the *Ideas Objectively* is contain'd *Formally*) or it Must Be *God*, or some *Creature* more *excellent* then a *Body* (In which what is in the *Ideas Objectively* is contain'd *Eminently*) But seeing that *God* is not a *Deceivour*, 'tis altogether Manifest, that *he* does not Place these *Ideas* in me either *Immediately* from himself, or *Mediately* from any other Creature, wherein their *Objective Reallity* is not contain'd *Formally*, but only *Eminently*. And seeing *God* has given me no *Faculty* to discern Whether these Ideas proceed from *Corporeal* or *Incorporeal Beings*, but rather a *strong Inclination* to believe that they are sent from *Corporeal Beings*, there is no Reason Why God should not be counted a *Deceiver*, if these *Ideas* came from any Where, but from *Corporeal Things*. Therefore we must conclude that there are *Corporeal Beings*. Which perhaps are not all the same as I comprehend them by my *sense* (for Perception by sense is in many Things very *Obscure* and *Confused*) but those things at least, which I *clearly* and *distinctly* Understand, that is to say, all those thing which are comprehended under the *Object* of *Pure Mathematicks*; those things I say at least are *True*.

As to What Remains, They are either some *Particulars*, as that the Sun is of such a *Bigness* or *Shape*, *&c.* or they are Things less *Clearly* Understood, as *Light*, *Sound*, *Pain*, &c. And tho these and such like Things may be very *Doubtful* and *Uncertain*, yet because *God* is not a *Deceiver*, and because that (Therefore) none of my Opinions can be *false* unless God has Given me some *Faculty* or other to *Correct* my *Error*, hence 'tis that I am incouraged with the Hopes of attaining *Truth* even in these very Things.

And certainly it cannot be doubted but whatever *I* am taught by *Nature* has something therein of *Truth*. By *Nature* in General I understand either *God* himself, or the *Coordination* of Creatures Made by God. By my *Own Nature* in *Particular* I understand the *Complexion* or *Association* of all those things which are given me by God.

Now there is nothing that this *my Nature* teaches me more *expresly* then that I have a *Body*, Which is not *Well* when I *feel* Pain, that this *Body* wants *Meat* or *Drink* When I am *Hungry* or *Dry*, *&c.* And therefore I ought not to Doubt but that these things are *True*. And by this *sense* of *Pain, Hunger, Thirst*, &c. My *Nature* tells me that *I* am not in my *Body*, as a *Mariner* is in his *Ship*, but that I am most *nighly conjoyn'd* thereto, and as it were *Blended therewith*; so that *I* with *It* make up *one* thing; For Otherwise, when the *Body* were hurt, *I*, who am only a *Thinking Thing*, should not therefore *feel* Pain, but should only *perceive* the Hurt with the *Eye* of my *Understanding* (as a *Mariner perceives* by his *sight* whatever is broken in his Ship) and when the *Body* wants either Meat or Drink, I should only *Understand* this want, but should not have the *Confused sense* of *Hunger* or *Thirst*; I call them *Confused*, for certainly the *Sense* of *Thirst, Hunger, Pain*, &c. are only *Confused Modes* or *Manners* of *Thought* arising from the *Union* and (as it were) *mixture* of the *Mind* and *Body*.

I am taught also by *Nature*, that there are many other *Bodies Without* and *About* my *Body*, some whereof are to be *desired*, others are to be *Avoided*. And because that I Perceive very Different *Colours, Sounds, Smells, Tasts, Heat, Hardness,* and the Like, from thence I Rightly conclude that there are *Correspondent Differences* in *Bodies*, from which these *different perceptions* of *sense* proceed, tho perhaps not *Alike*. And because that some of these *perceptions* are *Pleasant*, others *Unpleasant*, 'tis evidently *certain*, that my *Body*, or rather my *Whole self* (as *I* am compounded of a *Mind* and *Body*) am liable to be *Affected* by these *Bodies* which encompass me about.

There are many Other Things Also which *Nature* seems to teach Me, but *Really* I am not taught by It, but have gotten them by an *ill use* of Passing my Judgement *Inconsiderately*, and from hence it is that these things happen often to be *false*; as that all *space* is *Empty*, in which I find *nothing* that *works* upon my *Senses*; That in a *hot Body* there is something *like* the *Idea* of *Heat* which is in me; That in a *White* or *Green* Body there is the same *Whiteness* or *Greenness* which I *perceive*; And the same *Taste* in a *bitter* or *sweet* Thing, *&c.* That *Stars, Castles,* and Other *Remote* Bodies are of the same *Bigness* and *Shape*, as they are *Represented* to my *senses*: and such like. But that I may not admit of any Thing in this very matter, which I cannot *Distinctly* perceive, it behoves me here to determine more *Accurately* What I mean when I say, *That I am taught a Thing by Nature*.

Here I take *Nature* more *strictly*, then for the *Complication* of all those Things which are Given me by *God*; For in this *Complication* there are many things contain'd which relate to the *Mind alone*, as, That I perceive What is *done* cannot be *not Done*, and all Other things which are known by the *Light* of *Nature*, but of these I speak not at present. There are also many Other Things which belong *only* to the *Body*, as, That it *tends Downwards* and such like, of these also I treat not at Present. But I speak of those Things only which *God* hath bestowed upon me as I am *Compounded* of a *Mind* and *Body together*, and not *differently Consider'd*. 'Tis *Nature* therefore thus taken that teaches me to *avoid troublesome Objects*, and *seek* after *pleasing Ones*; but it appears not that this *Nature* teaches us to conclude any thing of these Perceptions of our *senses*, before that we make by our *Understanding* a diligent examination of *outward Objects*; for to Enquire into the *Truth* of Things belongs not to the *Whole Compositum* of a Man as he Consists of *Mind* and *Body*, but to the *Mind alone*.

So that tho a *star affect* my eye no *more* then a *small spark* of Fire, yet there is in my Eye no *Real* or *Positive Inclination* to *believe* One no bigger then the Other, but thus I have been used to Judge from my Childhood without any Reason: and tho coming nigh the Fire I feel Heat, and Coming too nigh I feel Pain, yet there is no Reason to perswade me, That in the Fire there is any thing *like* either that Heat or that Pain, but only that there is something therein, Whatever it be, that excites in us those *sensations* of Heat or Pain: and so tho in some space there may be nothing that Works on my *senses*, it does not from thence follow, that there is no *Body* there; for I see that in these and many other things I am used to overturn the Order of Nature, because I use these *perceptions* of *sense* (which properly are given me by Nature to make known to the mind what is *advantagious* or *hurtful* to the *Compositum*, wherof the *mind* is part, and *so far* only they are *Clear* and *Distinct* enough) as *certain Rules* immediately to discover the *Essence* of *External Bodies*, of Which they make known nothing but very *Obscurely* and *Confusedly*.

Medit. 4. I have formerly shewn how my *Judgment* happens to be *false* not-withstanding *Gods Goodness*. But now there arises a new *Difficulty* concerning those very things which *Nature* tells me I am to *prosecute* or *avoid*, and concerning my *Internal senses*, Wherein I find many *Errors*, as when a Man being deceived by the Pleasant *Taste* of some sort of Meat, devours therein some hidden Poyson. But in this very Instance it cannot be said, that the Man is impelled by Nature to desire the P*oyson*, for of that he is wholly Ignorant; but he is said to Desire the *Meat* only as being of a grateful *Taste*; and from hence nothing can be concluded but, That *Mans-Nature* is not *All-knowing*, which is no Wonder seeing Man is a *Finite Being*, and therefore nothing but *Finite Perfections* belong to him.

But We often err even in those things to Which we are *Impelled* by *Nature*, as when sick men desire that *Meat* or *Drink*, which will certainly prove Hurtful to them. To this it may perhaps be reply'd, That they *Err* in this because their *Nature* is *Corrupt*. But this Answers not the Difficulty, For a sick man is no less *Gods Creature* then a Man in Health, and therefore 'tis as Absurd to Imagine a *Deceitful Nature* imposed by *God* on the One as on the Other; And as a Clock that is made up of Wheels and Weights does no less strictly observe the *Laws* of its *Nature*, when it is *ill* contrived, and tells the hours *falsly*, as when it answers the Desire of the Artificer in all performances; so if I consider the body of a Man as a meer *Machine* or M*ovement*, made up and compounded of *Bones, Nerves, Muscles, Veins, Blood*, and *Skin*; so that, tho there were no *mind* in It, yet It would perform all those Motions which now are in it (those only excepted which Proceed from the *Will*, and consequently from the M*ind*) I do easily acknowledge, that it would be as *natural* for him (if for example sake he were sick of a *Dropsie*) to suffer that *Driness* of his *Throat* which uses to bring into his mind the *sense* of *Thirst*, & that thereby his Nerves and other Parts would be so disposed as to take Drink, by Which his disease would be encreased; As (supposing him to be troubled with no such Distemper) by the like Driness of Throat he would be disposed to Drink, when 'tis Requisite. And tho, if I respect the Intended use of a Clock I may say that it *Errs* from its *Nature*, when it tells the Hours *wrong*, and so considering the M*ovement* of a M*ans Body* as contrived for such M*otions* as are used to be performed thereby, I may think That also to *Err* from its *Nature*, if its *Throat* is *Dry*, when it has no want of Drink for its *Preservation*. Yet I Plainly discover, that this last *Acceptation* of *Nature* differs much from that whereof we have been speaking all this While, for this is only a *Denomination extrinsick* to the Things whereof 'tis spoken, and *depending* on my *Thought*, while it *Compares* a *sick* man, and a *disorderly* Clock with the *Idea* of an *healthy* man and a *Rectified* Clock. But by *Nature* in its former *Acceptation* I Understand something that is *Really* in the *Things* themselves, which therefore has something of *Truth* in it.

But tho Respecting only a *Body sick* of a Dropsie it be an *Extrinsick Denomination* to say, that its *Nature* is *Corrupt*, because it has a *Dry Throat*, and stands in *no need* of Drink; yet respecting the *Whole Compound* or *Mind joyn'd* to such a *Body*, 'tis not a *meer Denomination*, but a *real Error* of *Nature* for it to *thirst* when *drink* is *hurtful* to it. It remains therefore here to be inquired, how the *Goodness* of *God* suffers *Nature so taken* to be *deceivable*.

First therefore I understand that a *chief difference* between my *Mind* and *Body* consists in this, That my *Body* is of its *Nature divisible*, but my *Mind indivisible*; for while I consider my *Mind* or *my self*, as I am only a *thinking Thing*, I can distinguish *no parts* in Me, but I perceive my self to be but *one entire* Thing; and tho the *whole Mind* seems to be *united* to the *whole Body*, yet a Foot, an Arm, or any other part of the Body being cut off, I do not therefore conceive any *part* of my *Mind* taken away; Neither can its *Faculties* of *desiring, perceiving, understanding*, &c. be called its *Parts*, for tis one and the *same, mind*, that *desires*, that *perceive*s, that *understands*; Contrarily, I cannot think of any *Corporeal* or *extended Being*, which I cannot easily *divide* into *Parts* by my thought, and by this I understand it to be *divisible*. And this alone (if I had known it from no other Argument) is sufficient to inform me, that my *mind* is *really distinct* from my *Body*.

Nextly I find, that my *mind* is not *immediately affected* by all parts of my *body*, but only by the *Brain*, and perhaps only by one small part of it, That, to wit, wherein the *common sense* is said to reside; Which part, as often as it is disposed in the *same manner*, will represent to the *mind* the *same thing*, tho at the same time the other parts of the *body* may be *differently* order'd. And this is proved by numberless Experiments, which need not here be related.

Moreover I discover that the *nature* of my *body* is such, that no part of it can be *moved* by an other *remote* part thereof, but it may also be *moved* in the *same manner* by some of the *interjacent* parts, tho the more *remote* part lay still and acted not; As for example in the Rope,

A—B—C—D

If its end D. were drawn, the end A. would be moved no otherwise, than if one of the intermediate parts B. or C. were drawn, and the end D. rest quiet. So when I feel *pain* in my *Foot*, the consideration of Physicks instructs me, that this is performed by the help of *Nerves* dispersed through the Foot, which from thence being *continued* like Ropes to the very Brain, whilst they are *drawn* in the Foot, they also *draw* the inward parts of the Brain to which they reach, and therein excite a certain *motion*, which is ordain'd by *Nature* to affect the *mind* with a *sense* of *Pain*, as being in the *Foot*. But because these Nerves must pass through the *Skin*, the *Thighs*, the *Loins*, the *Back*, the *Neck*, before they can reach the *Brain* from the *Foot*, it may so happen, that tho *that part* of them, which is in the Foot were not touch'd, but only some of their *intermediate parts*, yet the same *motion*, would be caused in the *Brain*, as when the *Foot* it self is *ill affected*, from whence 'twil necessarily follow, that the *mind* should *perceive* the same *Pain*. And thus may we think of any other *Sense*.

I understand lastly, that seeing each single motion perform'd in that part of the *Brain*, which *immediately affects* the *mind*, excites therein only one sort of sense, nothing could be contrived more conveniently in this case, than that, of all those

Senses which it can cause, it should cause that which *cheifly*, and most *frequently* conduces to the *conservation* of an *healthful Man*; And experience witnesses, that to this very *end* all our *senses* are given us by *Nature*; and therefore nothing can be found therein, which does not abundantly testifie the *Power* and *Goodness* of *God*. Thus for Example, when the Nerves of the Feet are violently and more than ordinarily moved, that motion of them being propagated through the *Medulla Spinalis* of the Back to the inward parts of the Brain, there it signifies to the mind, that something or other is to be felt, and what is this but Pain, as it were in the Foot, by which the Mind is excited to use its indeavours for removing the Cause, as being hurtful to the Foot. But the *Nature* of *Man* might have been so *order'd* by *God*, that That same motion in the Brain should represent to the mind any other thing, *viz.* either it self as 'tis in the Brain, or it self as it is in the Foot, or in any of the other forementioned intermediate parts, or lastly any other thing whatsoever; but none of these would have so much conduced to the *Conservation* of the *Body*. In the like manner when we want drink, from thence arises a certain *dryness* in the *Throat*, which moves the Nerves thereof, and by their means the inward parts of the Brain, and this motion *affects* the *mind* with the *sense* of *thirst*; because that in this case nothing is more requisite for us to know, then that we *want drink* for the *Preservation* of our *Health*. So of the Rest.

From all which 'tis manifest, that (notwithstanding the *infinite Goodness* of God) 'tis impossible but the *Nature* of *Man* as he consists of a *mind* and *body* should be *deceivable*. For if any cause should excite (not in the Foot but) in the Brain it self, or in any other part through which the Nerves are continued from the Foot to the Brain, that *self same* motion, which uses to arise from the Foot being troubled, the *Pain* would be felt *as in the Foot*, and the *sense* would be *naturally* deceived; for 'tis consonant to Reason (seeing that That same motion of the Brain always represents to the mind that same sense, and it oftner proceeds from a cause *hurtful* to the *Foot*, than from any other) I say 'tis reasonable, that it should make known to the *mind* the Pain of the *Foot*, rather than of any other *part*. And so if a *dryness* of *Throat* arises (not as 'tis used from the *necessity* of *drink* for the *conservation* of the *Body*, but) from an *unusual Cause*, as it happens in a *Dropsie*, 'tis far better that it should *then deceive us*; then that it should *always deceive* us when the *Body* is in *Health*, and so of the Rest.

And this consideration helps me very much, not only to *understand* the *Errors* to which my *Nature* is subject, but also to *correct* and *avoid* them. For seeing I know that all my *Senses* do oftener inform me *falsly* than *truely* in those things which conduce to the *Bodies advantage*; and seeing I can use (almost alwayes) more of them than one to *Examine* the same thing, as also I can use *memory*, which joyns present and past things together, and my *understanding* also, which hath already discovered to me all the *causes* of my *Errors*, I ought no longer to fear, that what my *Senses* daily represent to me should be false. But especially those *extravagant Doubts* of my First Meditation are to be turn'd off as ridiculous; and perticularly the *chief* of them, *viz.* That of not *distinguishing Sleep* from *Waking*, for now I plainly discover a great *difference*, between them, for my *Dreams* are never *conjoyned* by my *memory* with the other *actions* of *my life*, as whatever happens to me *awake* is; and certainly if (while I were awake) any person should suddenly appear to me, and presently disappear (as in *Dreams*) so that I could not tell from *whence* he came or *where* he went, I should rather esteem it a *Spectre* or *Apparition feign'd* in my Brain, then a *true Man*; but when such things occur, as I distinctly know *from whence*, *where*, and *when* they come, and I *conjoyn* the *perception* of them by my *memory* with the other *Accidents* of my *life*, I am *certain* they are represented to me *waking* and not *asleep*, neither ought I in the least to doubt of their *Truth*, if after I have called up all my *senses*, *memory*, and *understanding* to their *Examination* I find nothing in any of them, that clashes with other truths; For *God* not being a *Deceiver*, it follows, that In such things I am not *deceived*. But because the *urgency* of *Action* in the common *occurrences* of *Affairs* will not alwayes allow time for such an *accurate examination*, I must confess that *Mans life* is *subject* to many *Errors* about *perticulars*, so that the *infirmity* of our *Nature* must be *acknowledged* by Us.

FINIS.

References

Alanen, Lilli (1994) "Sensory Ideas, Objective Reality and Material Falsity." In J. Cottingham (ed.), *Reason, Will and Sensation: Studies in Descartes's Metaphysics*, pp. 229–50. Oxford: Clarendon Press.

Almog, Joseph (2002) *What Am I? Descartes and the Mind–Body Problem*. Oxford: Oxford University Press.

Annas, Julia and Barnes, Jonathan (1985) *The Modes of Scepticism*. Cambridge: Cambridge University Press.

Anscombe, G. E. M. (1981) "The First Person." In G. E. M. Anscombe, *Metaphysics and the Philosophy of Mind*, pp. 21–36. Oxford: Blackwell.

Aquinas, Thomas (1948) *In Aristotelis librum de anima commentarium*, ed. Angeli M. Pirotta. Turin: Marietti.

——(1951) *Aristotle's De Anima: In the Version of William of Moerbeke and the Commentary of St Thomas Aquinas*, trans. Kenelm Foster and Silvester Humphries. London: Routledge and Kegan Paul.

——(1964) *Summa theologiae*. New York: McGraw-Hill.

Ariew, Roger (1995) "Pierre Bourdin and the *Seventh Objections*." In Ariew and Grene (eds) (1995), pp. 208–26.

——and Grene, Marjorie (eds) (1995) *Descartes and his Contemporaries: Meditations, Objections, and Replies*. Chicago: University of Chicago Press.

Aristotle (1968) *De Anima*, ed. D. W. Hamlyn. Oxford: Clarendon Press.

——(1984) *The Complete Works of Aristotle*, 2 vols, ed. Jonathan Barnes. Princeton, NJ: Princeton University Press.

Armogathe, Jean-Robert (1977) *Theologia cartesiana: L'explication physique de l'Eucharistie chez Descartes et dom Desgabets*. The Hague: M. Nijhoff.

——(1994) "L'approbation des *Meditationes* par la faculté de théologie de Paris (1641)," *Bulletin Cartésien XXI, Archives de Philosophie* 57: 1–3.

——and Belgioioso, Guilia (eds) (1996) *Descartes: Principia Philosophiae (1644–1994)*. Naples: Vivarium.

——and Carraud, Vincent (2001) "La première condamnation des Oeuvres de Descartes, d'apres des documents inédits aux Archives du Saint-Office," *Nouvelles de la République des lettres*: 103–37.

Arnauld, Antoine (1990) *On True and False Ideas: New Objections to Descartes's Meditations and Descartes's Replies*, trans. E. J. Kremer. Lewiston: The Edwin Mellon Press.

Baillet, Adrien (1692) *La vie de M. Des Cartes*. Paris; reprinted Paris: La Table Ronde, 1946.

Beiser, Frederick C. (1987) *The Fate of Reason: German Philosophy from Kant to Fichte*. Cambridge, MA: Harvard University Press.

Belaval, Yvon (1960) *Leibniz critique de Descartes*. Gallimard: Paris.

Belgioioso, Guilia (1999) *La variata imagine di Descartes: gli itinerari della metafisica tra Parigi e Napoli (1690–1733)*. Lecce: Milella.

Bennett, Jonathan (1990) "Why is Belief Involuntary?" *Analysis* 50: 87–107.

Beyssade, Jean-Marie (1992) "Descartes on Material Falsity." In P. Cummins and G. Zoeller (eds), *Minds, Ideas, and Objects: Essays on the Theory of Representation in Modern Philosophy*, North American Kant Society Studies in Philosophy, vol. 2. Atascadero, CA: Ridgeview Press.

——(1994) "Méditer, objecter, répondre." In Jean-Marie Beyssade and Jean-Luc Marion (eds), *Descartes: Objecter et répondre*, pp. 21–38. Paris: Presses Universitaires de France.

Boyle, Robert (1999–2000) *The Works of Robert Boyle*, 14 vols, ed. M. Hunter and E. B. Davis. London: Pickering and Chatto.

Broughton, Janet (2002) *Descartes's Method of Doubt*. Princeton, NJ: Princeton University Press.

Burnyeat, Myles (1982) "Idealism and Greek Philosophy: What Descartes Saw and Berkeley Missed." In Godfrey Vesey (ed.), *Idealism Past and Present*, pp. 19–50. Cambridge: Cambridge University Press.

Chappell, Vere (1986) "The Theory of Ideas." In A. Rorty (ed.), *Essays on Descartes's Meditations*, pp. 177–98. Berkeley, CA: University of California Press.

——(1994a) "Descartes's Compatibilism." In J. Cottingham (ed.), *Reason, Will and Sensation: Studies in Descartes's Metaphysics*, pp. 177–90. Oxford: Clarendon Press.

——(1994b) "L'homme cartésien." In Jean-Marie Beyssade and Jean-Luc Marion (eds), *Descartes: Objecter et répondre*, pp. 403–26. Paris: Presses Universitaires de France.

Clauberg, Johannes (1968) *Johannes Clauberg: Opera Omnia Philosophica*, 2 vols. Hildesheim: G. Olms (first published 1691).

Cook, Monte (1975) "The Alleged Ambiguity of 'Idea' in Descartes's Philosophy," *Southwestern Journal of Philosophy* 6: 87–103.

——(1987) "Descartes's Alleged Representationalism," *History of Philosophy Quarterly* 4: 179–95.

Costa, M. J. (1983) "What Cartesian Ideas Are Not," *Journal of the History of Philosophy* 21: 537–50.

Cottingham, J. (1985) "Cartesian Trialism," *Mind* 94: 218–30; reprinted in George Moyal (ed.), *René Descartes: Critical Assessments*, pp. 236–48. London: Routledge, 1991.

——(1986) *Descartes*. Oxford: Blackwell.

——(1988) "The Intellect, the Will, and the Passions: Spinoza's Critique of Descartes," *Journal of the History of Philosophy* 26: 239–57.

——(1998) *Philosophy and the Good Life*. Cambridge: Cambridge University Press.

Cronin, Timothy J. (1966) *Objective Being in Descartes and Suarez: Analecta Gregoriana*, vol. 154. Rome: Gregorian University Press.

Curley, Edwin (1975) "Descartes, Spinoza and the Ethics of Belief." In Maurice Mandelbaum and Eugene Freeman (eds), *Spinoza: Essays in Interpretation*, pp. 159–89. LaSalle, IL: Open Court.

——(1978) *Descartes against the Sceptics*. Cambridge, MA: Harvard University Press.

Danto, Arthur (1978) "The Representational Character of Ideas and the Problem of the External World." In M. Hooker (ed.), *Descartes: Critical and Interpretive Essays*, pp. 287–98. Baltimore, MD: The Johns Hopkins University Press.

Della Rocca, Michael (2003) "The Power of an Idea: Spinoza's Critique of Pure Will," *Nous* 37: 200–31.

——(forthcoming) "Descartes, the Cartesian Circle, and Epistemology without God," *Philosophy and Phenomenological Research*.

Desgabets, Robert (1675) *Critique de la Critique de la Recherche de la vérité*. Paris: Du Puis.

——(1983–5) *Dom Robert Desgabets: Oeuvres philosophiques inédites*, ed. J. Beaude, 7 vols. Amsterdam: Quadratures.

Devillairs, Laurence (2004) *Descartes et la connaissance de dieu*. Paris: Vrin.

Doney, Willis (ed.) (1987) *Eternal Truth and the Cartesian Circle*. New York: Garland.

Dubois, Jean, Lagane, René, and Lerond, Alain (1992) *Dictionnaire du français classique*. Paris: Larousse.

Eustachius a Sancto Paulo (1609) *Summa philosophiae quadripartita*; extracts translated in R. Ariew, J. Cottingham, and T. Sorell (eds), *Descartes' Meditations: Background Source Materials*. Cambridge: Cambridge University Press, 1998.

Feyerabend, Paul (1978) "Aristotle Not a Dead Dog." In *Science in a Free Society*, pp. 53–85. London: New Left Books.

Foucault, Michel (1972) *Histoire de la folie à l'âge classique*. Paris: Gallimard.

Foucher, Simon (1969) *Critique de la Recherche de la vérité*, ed. R. A. Watson. New York: Johnson (first published 1675).

Frankfurt, Harry (1970) *Demons, Dreamers, and Madmen: The Defense of Reason in Descartes' 'Meditations'*. Indianapolis: Bobbs-Merrill.

Garber, Daniel (1992) *Descartes' Metaphysical Physics*. Chicago: University of Chicago Press.

Gassendi, Pierre (1644) *Disquisitio Metaphysica, seu Dubitationes et Instantiae, adversus Renati Cartesii Metaphysicam et Responsa*. Amsterdam.

Gaukroger, Stephen (1995) *Descartes: An Intellectual Biography*. Oxford: Oxford University Press.

——(2002) *Descartes' System of Natural Philosophy*. Cambridge: Cambridge University Press.

Gewirth, Alan (1941) "The Cartesian Circle," *Philosophical Review* 50: 368–95.

——(1967) "Clearness and Distinctness in Descartes." In W. Doney (ed.), *Descartes: A Collection of Critical Essays*, pp. 250–77. Notre Dame, IN: University of Notre Dame Press.

Gilson, Étienne (1912) *Index Scolastico-Cartésien*. Paris: J. Vrin.

——(1976) *René Descartes: Discours de la méthode, texte et commentaire*. Paris: J. Vrin.

Gouhier, Henri (1978) *Cartésianisme et augustinisme au xviie siècle*. Paris: J. Vrin.

Gregory, Tullio (1974) "Dio ingannatore e genio maligno," *Giornale critico della filosofia italiana* 53: 477–516.

Gueroult, Martial (1968) *Descartes selon l'ordre des raisons*. Paris: Aubier.

——(1984) *Descartes' Philosophy Interpreted According to the Order of Reasons*, 2 vols, trans. Roger Ariew. Minneapolis, MN: University of Minnesota Press.

Hatfield, Gary (1979) "Force (God) in Descartes' Physics," *Studies in History and Philosophy of Science* 10: 113–40; reprinted in George Moyal (ed.), *René Descartes: Critical Assessments*, pp. 123–52. London: Routledge, 1991.

——(1986) "The Senses and the Fleshless Eye: The *Meditations* as Cognitive Exercises." In A. Rorty (ed.), *Articles on Descartes' Meditations*, pp. 45–79. Berkeley, CA: University of California Press.

——(1992) "Reason, Nature, and God in Descartes." In S. Voss (ed.), *Essays on the Philosophy and Science of René Descartes*, pp. 259–87. New York: Oxford University Press, 1993.

——(1998) "The Cognitive Faculties." In M. Ayers and D. Garber (eds), *Cambridge History of Seventeenth Century Philosophy*, pp. 953–1002. Cambridge: Cambridge University Press.

——(2003) *Descartes and the Meditations*. London: Routledge.

Hintikka, Jaako (1962) "*Cogito, ergo sum*: Inference or Performative?," *The Philosophical Review* 71: 3–32.

Huet, Pierre-Daniel (1971) *Censura philosophiae cartesianae*. Hildesheim: G. Olms (first published 1690).

Jolley, Nicholas (1990) *The Light of the Soul: Theories of Ideas in Leibniz, Malebranche and Descartes*. Oxford: Clarendon Press.

Jourdain, Charles (1862–6) *Histoire de l'université de Paris au xviiᵉ et au xviiiᵉ siècle*, 2 vols. Paris: Hatchette.

Kant, Immanuel (2004) *Prolegomena to Any Future Metaphysics, with Selections from the Critique of Pure Reason*, rev. edn, ed. Gary Hatfield. Cambridge: Cambridge University Press.

Kenny, Anthony (1967) "Descartes on Ideas." In W. Doney, (ed.), *Descartes: A Collection of Critical Essays*, pp. 227–49. Notre Dame, IN: University of Notre Dame Press.

——(1968) *Descartes*. New York: Random House.

——(1972) "Descartes on the Will." In R. J. Butler (ed.), *Cartesian Studies*, pp. 1–31. Oxford: Blackwell.

——(1999) "Descartes the Dualist," *Ratio* 12: 114–27.

Larmore, Charles (1998) "Scepticism." In Daniel Garber and Michael Ayers (eds), *The Cambridge History of Seventeenth-century Philosophy*, vol. 2, pp. 1145–92. Cambridge: Cambridge University Press.

——(2000) "La structure dialogique de la Première Méditation," *Philosophie* 65: 55–72.

——(2004) "Un scepticisme sans tranquillité: Montaigne et ses modèles antiques." In V. Carraud and J-L. Marion (eds), *Montaigne: scepticisme, métaphysique, théologie*, pp. 15–31. Paris: Presses Universitaires de France.

Leibniz, G. W. (1976) *Philosophical Papers and Writings*, ed. and trans. Leroy Loemker. Dordrecht: Reidel.

——(1981) *New Essays on Human Understanding*, ed. and trans. P. Remnant and J. Bennett. Cambridge: Cambridge University Press (first published 1765).

——(1989) *Philosophical Essays*, ed. and trans. Roger Ariew and Daniel Garber. Indianapolis, IN: Hackett.

Lennon, Thomas M. (1993) *The Battle of the Gods and Giants: The Legacies of Descartes and Gassendi, 1655–1715*. Princeton, NJ: Princeton University Press.

——(2003) "Huet, Malebranche and the Birth of Skepticism." In Gianni Paganini (ed.), *The Return of Scepticism*, pp. 149–65. Dordrecht: Kluwer.

Locke, John (1985) *An Essay Concerning Human Understanding*, ed. Peter Nidditch. Oxford: Oxford University Press.

Loeb, Louis (1990) "The Priority of Reason in Descartes," *Philosophical Review* 99: 3–43.

——(1992) "The Cartesian Circle." In J. Cottingham (ed.), *The Cambridge Companion to Descartes*, pp. 200–35. Cambridge: Cambridge University Press.

McDowell, John (1986) "Singular Thought and the Extent of Inner Space." In Philip Pettit and John McDowell (eds), *Subject, Thought, and Context*, pp. 137–68. Oxford: Clarendon Press.

——(1994) *Mind and World*. Cambridge, MA: Harvard University Press.

McRae, R. (1965) "'Idea' as a Philosophical Term in the Seventeenth Century," *Journal of the History of Ideas* 26: 175–84.

Malcolm, Norman (1977) "Descartes' Proof that He is Essentially a Non-material Thing." In *Thought and Knowledge: Essays by Norman Malcolm*, pp. 58–84. New York: Cornell University Press.

Malebranche, Nicolas (1958–84) *Oeuvres complètes de Malebranche*, ed. R. Robinet, 20 vols. Paris: Vrin.

——(1980) *The Search after Truth* and *Elucidations of the Search after Truth*, trans. T. M. Lennon and P. J. Olscamp. Columbus: Ohio State University Press.

Marion, Jean-Luc (1981) *Sur la théologie blanche de Descartes: Analogie, création des vérités éternelles et fondement*. Paris: Presses Universitaires de France.

——(1986) "The Essential Incoherence of Descartes' Definition of Divinity." In Amelie Rorty (ed.), *Essays on Descartes's Meditations*, pp. 297–338. Berkeley, CA: University of California Press.

——(1995) "The Place of the *Objections* in the Development of Cartesian Metaphysics." In Roger Ariew and Marjorie Grene (eds), *Descartes and his Contemporaries: Meditations, Objections, and Replies*, pp. 10–11. Chicago: University of Chicago Press.

Markie, Peter (1994) "Descartes's Concepts of Substance." In John Cottingham (ed.), *Reason, Will, and Sensation: Essays in Descartes's Metaphysics*, pp. 63–87. Oxford: Oxford University Press.

Montaigne, Michel de (1965) *The Complete Essays of Montaigne*, trans. Donald M. Frame. Stanford: Stanford University Press.

——(1999) *Les Essais*, 3rd edn, 3 vols, ed. M. Villey. Paris: Presses Universitaires de France.

Moyal, George (ed.) (1991) *René Descartes: Critical Assessments*. London: Routledge.

Murdoch, Dugald (1999) "The Cartesian Circle," *Philosophical Review* 108: 221–44.

Newman, Lex (1999) "The Fourth Meditation," *Philosophy and Phenomenological Research* 59: 559–91.

Nolan, Lawrence (1998) "Descartes's Theory of Universals," *Philosophical Studies* 89: 161–80.

——(2001) "Descartes' Ontological Argument," *Stanford Encyclopedia of Philosophy* (dynamic internet edition: http://plato.stanford.edu/entries/descartes-ontological/).

——(forthcoming) "The Ontological Argument as an Exercise in Cartesian Therapy," *Canadian Journal of Philosophy*.

Normore, Calvin (1986) "Meaning and Objective Being: Descartes and his Sources." In A. Rorty (ed.), *Essays on Descartes's Meditations*. Berkeley, CA: University of California Press.

Pardies, Gaston (1672) *Discours de la connaissance des bêtes*, ed. L. C. Rosenfield. New York: Johnson Reprint, 1972.

Plato (1997) *Complete Works*, ed. John Cooper. Indianapolis, IN: Hackett.

Popkin, Richard (1964) *The History of Skepticism from Erasmus to Descartes*. New York: Humanities Press (a revised and expanded version is *The History of Scepticism from Savonarola to Bayle*. Oxford: Oxford University Press, 2003).

Radner, Daisie (1988) "Thought and Consciousness in Descartes," *Journal of the History of Philosophy* 26: 439–52.

Ragland, C. P. (forthcoming) "Descartes on Divine Providence and Human Freedom," *Archiv für Geschichte der Philosophie*.

Regis, Pierre-Sylvain (1691) *Réponse au livre . . . Censura Philosophiae Cartesianae*. Paris: Cusson.

Risse, Wilhelm (1963) "Zur Vorgeschichte der cartesischen Methodenlehre," *Archiv für Geschichte der Philosophie* 45: 17–32.

Rorty, Richard (1980) *Philosophy and the Mirror of Nature*. Princeton, NJ: Princeton University Press.

Rozemond, Marleen (1998) *Descartes's Dualism*. Cambridge, MA: Harvard University Press.

Ryle, Gilbert (1960) *The Concept of Mind*. New York: Barnes and Noble.

Schiffer, Stephen (1976) "Descartes on his Essence," *Philosophical Review* 85: 21–43.

Schmaltz, Tad (1992) "Descartes and Malebranche on Mind and Mind–Body Union," *The Philosophical Review* 101: 281–325.

——(2002) *Radical Cartesianism: The French Reception of Descartes*. Cambridge: Cambridge University Press.

——(2004) "A Tale of Two Condemnations: Two Cartesian Condemnations in Seventeenth-century France." In G. Belgioioso (ed.), *Studi Cartesiani II: Atti del Seminario "Descartes et ses adversaries," Parigi, 12–13 dicembre 2000*, pp. 203–21. Lecce: Conte.

Secada, Jorge (2000a) "Berkeley y el idealismo." In Javier Echeverría (ed.), *Del renacimiento a la ilustración II*, pp. 197–233. Madrid: Editorial Trotta.

——(2000b) "Descartes, Berkeley y los orígenes del idealismo." In Miguel Giusti (ed.), *La filosofía del siglo xx: balance y perspectives*, pp. 241–67. Lima: Fondo Editorial de la Pontificia Universidad Católica del Perú.

——(2000c) *Cartesian Metaphysics*. Cambridge: Cambridge University Press.

——(2003) "Learning to Understand Descartes," *The Philosophical Quarterly* 53: 437–45.

Sepper, Dennis L. (2002) "The Texture of Thought: Why Descartes' *Meditationes* is Meditational, and Why it Matters." In S. Gaukroger, J. Schuster, and J. Sutton (eds), *Descartes' Natural Philosophy*, pp. 736–50. London: Routledge.

Shoemaker, Sidney (1983) "On an Argument for Dualism." In Carl Ginet and Sidney Shoemaker (eds), *Knowledge and Mind*, pp. 233–58. Oxford: Oxford University Press.

Slowik, Edward (2002) *Cartesian Spacetime: Descartes' Physics and the Relational Theory of Space and Motion*. Dordrecht: Kluwer.

Spinoza, Baruch (1985) *The Collected Works of Spinoza*, vol. I., ed. and trans. E. M. Curley. Princeton, NJ: Princeton University Press.

Suárez, Francisco (1856) *De Anima* in *Opera omnia*, 26 vols, vol. III. Paris: Vivès.

——(1960–6) *Disputaciones Metafísicas*, 7 vols. Madrid: Gredos.

Van Cleve, James (1979) "Foundationalism, Epistemic Principles, and the Cartesian Circle," *Philosophical Review* 88, 55–91; reprinted in Willis Doney (ed.), *Eternal Truth and the Cartesian Circle*, pp. 258–81. New York: Garland, 1987.

Verbeek, Theo (1992) *Descartes and the Dutch: Early Reactions to Cartesian Philosophy, 1637–1650*. Carbondale, IL: Southern Illinois University Press.

——(ed.) (1999a) *Johannes Clauberg (1622–1665) and the Cartesian Philosophy in the Seventeenth Century*. Dordrecht: Kluwer.

——(1999b) "Clauberg et les *Principes* de Descartes." In Verbeek (ed.) (1999a), pp. 113–22.

Watson, Richard (1966) *The Downfall of Cartesianism, 1673–1712: A Study of Epistemological Issues in Late Seventeenth Century Cartesianism*. The Hague: M. Nijhoff.

William of Ockham (1982) *Reportatio*, in *Opera Theologica*, vol. VII, ed. Francis E. Kelley and Girard I. Etzkorn. St Bonaventure, NY: St. Bonaventure University.

Williams, Bernard (1973) "Deciding to Believe." In *Problems of the Self*, pp. 136–51. Cambridge: Cambridge University Press.

——(1978) *Descartes: The Project of Pure Enquiry*. Harmondsworth: Penguin.

Williams, Michael (1986) "Descartes and the Metaphysics of Doubt." In A. O. Rorty (ed.), *Essays on Descartes' Meditations*, pp. 117–39. Berkeley, CA: University of California Press.

Wilson, Margaret D. (1978) *Descartes*. London: Routledge.

——(1993) "Descartes on the Perception of Primary Qualities." In S. Voss (ed.), *Essays on the Philosophy and Science of René Descartes*, pp. 162–76. Oxford: Oxford University Press.

——(1999a) *Ideas and Mechanism: Essays on Early Modern Philosophy*. Princeton, NJ: Princeton University Press.

——(1999b) "Descartes on Sense and 'Resemblance'." In Wilson (1999a), pp. 10–25.

——(1999c) "Leibniz: Self-consciousness and Immortality in the Paris Notes and After." In Wilson (1999a), pp. 373–87.

Wittgenstein, Ludwig (1963) *Tractatus Logico-philosophicus*, trans. D. F. Pears and B. F. McGuinness. London: Routledge and Kegan Paul.

Yolton, John (1975) "Ideas and Knowledge in Seventeenth-century Philosophy," *Journal of the History of Philosophy* 13: 145–66.

Index